Harry Harris

WORLD CUP DIARY

EVERY GAME, EVERY GOAL, EVERY FACT!

© **Know The Score Books**   www.knowthescorebooks.com

Know The Score Books Publications

MATCH OF MY LIFE
Twelve Stars Relive Their Favourite Games

Relive a dozen of the greatest games in history through the eyes of twelve legends who were on the pitch creating history

FULHAM
ISBN: 1905449518
£16.99   Available Now
includes Sean Davis, Simon Morgan, Gordon Davies

ENGLAND WORLD CUP
ISBN: 1905449526
£16.99   Available Now
includes Tony Adams, David Platt, Sir Bobby Robson

LEEDS
ISBN: 1905449542
£16.99   Pub: September 2006
includes Peter Lorimer, Allan Clarke, Dominic Matteo

EUROPEAN CUP FINALS
ISBN: 1905449577
£16.99   Available Now
includes Jamie Carragher, Alec Stepney, Paolo Rossi

WEST HAM
ISBN: 1905449615
£16.99   Pub: November 2006
includes Marlon Harewood, Tony Cottee, Billy Bonds

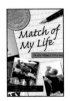
FA CUP FINALS 1953-1969
ISBN: 1905449534
£16.99   Pub: October 2006
includes Bert Trautmann, Dave Mackay, Peter McParland

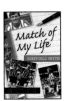
SHEFFIELD UNITED
ISBN: 1905449623
£16.99   Pub: October 2006
includes Tony Currie, Keith Edwards, Tony Agana

LIVERPOOL
ISBN: 190544950X
£16.99   Available Now
includes Jamie Carragher, John Barnes, Tommy Smith

SUNDERLAND
ISBN: 1905449607
£16.99   Pub: October 2006
includes Niall Quinn, Marco Gabbiadini, Gary Rowell

MANCHESTER UNITED
ISBN: 1905449593
£16.99   Pub: September 2006
includes Dwight Yorke, Steve Bruce, Denis Irwin

STOKE CITY
ISBN: 1905449550
£16.99   Pub: September 2006
includes Mike Sheron, Mark Stein, Denis Smith

SPURS
ISBN: 1905449585
£16.99   Pub: October 2006
includes Ossie Ardiles, Clive Allen, Cliff Jones

WOLVES
ISBN: 1905449569
£16.99   Available Now
includes Steve Bull, Bert Williams, John Richards

THE ASHES
ISBN: 1905449631
£16.99 Pub: November 2006
includes Ashley Giles, David Gower,
Merv Hughes

CULT HEROES

Examining the reasons why the twenty biggest cult heroes in a club's history won the hearts of their fans, revealing many new stories and behind-the-scenes anecdotes

CHELSEA
by Leo Moynihan
ISBN: 1905449003
£16.99 Available Now
includes Gianfranco Zola, John Terry,
Peter Osgood

NEWCASTLE
by Dylan Younger
ISBN: 1905449038
£16.99 Pub: October 2006
includes Alan Shearer, Paul Gascoigne,
Jackie Milburn

SOUTHAMPTON
by Jeremy Wilson
ISBN: 1905449011
£16.99 Pub: September 2006
includes Matt Le Tissier, Mick Channon,
Terry Paine

WEST BROM
by Simon Wright
ISBN: 190544902X
£16.99 Pub: September 2006
includes Jeff Astle, Cyrille Regis,
Bob Taylor

OTHER TITLES

TACKLES LIKE A FERRET
by Paul Parker
ISBN: 190544947X
£18.99 Available Now
The autobiography of England, Manchester United, QPR and Fulham's springheeled defender

BURKSEY:
The Autobiography of a Football God
by Peter Morfoot
ISBN: 1905449496
£9.99 Available Now
'Burksey does for football what Spinal Tap did for rock bands' Non-League Paper

HOLD THE BACK PAGE:
Football's Tabloid Tales
by Harry Harris
ISBN: 1905449917
£16.99 Pub: September 2006
The true stories behind the headlines, the bungs, the court cases and the scandals of Harry's thirty years investigating football's shady underbelly

LINES AND LENGTHS
by Paul Smith
ISBN: 1905449453
£16.99 Pub: November 2006
The incredible story of cricket's first rock 'n' roll star

www.knowthescorebooks.com

To pre-order or order any of these books, postage free, please send a cheque made out to Know The Score Books to:

Know The Score Books Ltd, 118 Alcester Road, Studley, Warwickshire, B80 7NT
Tel: 01527 454482   Fax: 01527 452183
Email: info@knowthescorebooks.com

The right of Harry Harris to be identified as the author of this work has been asserted by them in accordance with sections 77 and 78 of the Copyright, Designs and Patents Act, 1988.

Know The Score Books Limited
118 Alcester Road
Studley
Warwickshire
B80 7NT
United Kingdom
www.knowthescorebooks.com

A CIP catalogue record is available for this book from the British Library
ISBN 1-905449-90-9

Jacket and book design by Lisa David

Printed and bound in Great Britain
By Cromwell Press, Trowbridge, Wiltshire

Acknowledgements

I would like to thank Simon Lowe of Know the Score Books for developing the concept for this book, and organising the fastest turn around of any World Cup book by having it published within a week of the Final. To the wonderful skills of designer Lisa David, the research skills of Jim Baldwin and to Gary Double for introducing me to Simon and for his PR expertise.

Harry Harris
July 2006

Photographs Courtesy of EMPICS, Leonie Schwarz

Introduction

The 2006 World Cup in Germany was a breathtaking and controversial orgy of football.

The tournament was blessed with wonderful goals by Joe Cole, Ronaldo, Bastian Schweinsteiger, Fernando Torres, Alessandro del Piero and team Argentina. But equally stained by Ronaldo's controversial antics, the red cards for Rooney and Zidane and the media's baiting of the England manager. The heady mix will ensure the tournament will live long in the memory as one of the classics amongst the 18 World Cups to date.

In this book award-winning journalist Harry Harris charts the story of the 2006 World Cup right back through the past two years of qualifying to the glorious finals themselves.

Amidst this jamboree of football Harry focuses on England's quest for the World Cup and, in particular, the role of captain David Beckham throughout the 2006 campaign and analyses where exactly Sven-Göran Eriksson, in his last tournament as coach, went wrong and adds some pointers for England's future.

Along the way Harry also charts the pre-tournament shenanigans, the media scrum which surrounded the finals and the behind-the-scenes stories which only he, as Britain's foremost football writer, can uncover, just as he did with the FA's decision to appoint 'Big Phil' Scolari to the England job back in April before that incredible about-turn, which left Steve McClaren with the job.

We've packed in every statistic, goal and fascinating fact that we could possibly think of during the finals, plus a whole lot more and hope that this book brings vividly to life the incredible events of the summer of 2006.

Enjoy the trip.

Simon Lowe
Editor-in-Chief
Know The Score Books Ltd

Contents

section four – second round

section five – quarter-finals

section six – final stages

section seven – statistics

Harry Harris

As Chief football writer for the Express Group Newspapers, Harry Harris is the foremost football journalist in the UK. He has written numerous books including Ruud Gullit: Portrait of a Genius, Chelski: the Abramovich Revolution and Wayne Rooney: the story of football's Wonderkid. His breaking of the news that the FA had offered the post of England coach in succession to Sven-Göran Eriksson to Portugal coach 'Big Phil' Scolari in April 2006 set the news agenda for the entire country for weeks. It was merely one of a long line of Harris exclusives including revealing that Terry Venables was receiving irregular payments from Spurs, Paul Merson's drinking and gambling habits, Roy Keane's exit from the Irish squad at the 2002 World Cup and the Glazer takeover of Manchester United. Always controversial and amusing, this was Harry's sixth World Cup, having first covered England at the 1986 tournament for the Daily Mirror.

Dedication

To the memory of Bobby Moore, and my mum Sara, who took me to Wembley to watch the Boys of '66 win the World Cup; I was privileged enough to have been at the old Wembley to see the Final, indeed to have had a 'season ticket' to see all of England's games in 1966.

WORLD CUP DIARY

EVERY GAME, EVERY GOAL, EVERY FACT!

KNOW!
THE SCORE

section
one

preamble

Great Expectations

> ## "We can beat anyone and we don't need to be afraid."
> ### Sven-Göran Eriksson

England captain David Beckham believed England could live up to fans' great expectations in Germany

In the lead up to the 2006 World Cup in Germany Sven-Göran Eriksson's so-called 'Golden Generation' was widely regarded as the best England team since the XI which lifted the World Cup in 1966 and their captain, David Beckham, was feeling comfortable with fans expecting him to lead the country to World Cup glory.

As he looked ahead to the tournament, Beckham observed, "I never complain about expectations being too high. Our fans follow us all over the world and demand we produce. They want results and that's fine."

Expectations are often handicaps for England teams. At the start of the 2005/06 season England were washouts. Following shock results against Denmark and Northern Ireland, expectations took a dive. Then they pulled themselves together to qualify, and then, in their next friendly, produced two late goals to win against much-fancied Argentina; needless to say expectations soared sky high.

There are never any grey areas with England, it's all black or white. Heroes if they win, villains if they lose. World-beaters after a good result, has-beens after bad. But Beckham didn't object to such high expectations, as he believed the fans had an important role to play in Germany, "Their enthusiasm and their passion mean that they can be

Michael Owen was the second senior England player after Ashley Cole to damage a metatarsal during the season leading up to the 2006 World Cup

as good as an extra player to us out there. That is how important the supporters are. To win the World Cup you need all the help you can get and you can never under-estimate the role they play."

After falling short at the quarter-final stages of the previous two major tournaments, Beckham argued with a steely determination, "We can't keep making excuses in competitions because with the talent we have in our country we have to have the aim of going as far as we can. If we're not good enough, we're not good enough, but we know we have got the players."

England's Golden Boy Wonder, Wayne Rooney, could barely contain his excitement as he looked forward to his first World Cup "We want to win every game without underestimating anyone. Don't get me wrong, it will be a difficult tournament, but we can win it. I do not think we need to fear anyone. There is a mixture of youth and experience in the team. We have a lot of match-winners in there, which can only help, and the spirit is certainly the best it has been since I have been involved in the squad. I cannot wait for the World Cup to come around. Hopefully from now until the end of the season I can keep myself fit, free from injury and go to the World Cup fresh."

Propitious words from Rooney as 2006 would see a number of injury hurdles placed in England's way.

The Curse of the Metatarsal

England's carefully laid plans for the tournament started to go badly awry as early as the domestic Christmas

holiday matches when Michael Owen broke the fifth metatarsal of his right foot in a challenge with Spurs and England goalkeeper Paul Robinson at White Hart Lane on New Year's Eve. Initially Owen's metatarsal break seemed merely a minor problem as he had plenty of time to return to full fitness and it would mean he was not weary after a hard season at Newcastle; at least the England skipper thought so. David Beckham suggested that the striker's injury and the early finish to the domestic season negotiated by Eriksson with the Premiership, offered something of a pre-tournament break, "The England team will be fresher than going into previous World Cups," he said, touching the wooden table when I interviewed him at Real Madrid's training ground. "We've gone into tournaments before with players carrying injuries and others missing. Hopefully we can avoid that and have everyone fit – that will give us a great chance."

But as the weeks dragged on with no Owen in the Newcastle line-up everyone from fans to Press to players began to get jumpy. Then, when news broke that he'd had to undergo a second operation on an increasingly problematic injury, everyone feared the worst.

Without Owen, where would England's goals come from? Eriksson's paucity of back-up strikers was cruelly exposed as he gave Peter Crouch and Charlton's Darren Bent run-outs against Uruguay in the one friendly international scheduled between Christmas and the end of the domestic season. Crouch may have scored that

ENGLAND'S METATARSAL VICTIMS SINCE 2002

DAVID BECKHAM
(Apr 2002) Broke second metatarsal in left foot. Played at World Cup three months later, but clearly unfit. Healing time: 9 wks

GARY NEVILLE
(Apr 02) Broke fifth metatarsal in left foot and missed the 2002 World Cup. Healing time: 21 wks

DANNY MURPHY
(May 02) Drafted into the 2002 World Cup squad, but crocked second metatarsal in left foot in training. Healing time: 11 wks

WAYNE ROONEY
(Jun 04) Broke fifth metatarsal in right foot in Euro quarter-final clash with Portugal. Healing time: 14 wks

STEVEN GERRARD
(Sept 04) Broke fifth metatarsal in left foot in 2-1 defeat at Manchester United. Healing time: 10 wks

SCOTT PARKER
(Dec 04) Fractured the second metatarsal in his right foot while playing for Chelsea against Norwich. Healing time: 22 wks

ASHLEY COLE
(Oct 05) Broke fifth metatarsal in right foot in training before World Cup qualifiers against Austria and Poland. Healing time: 15 wks

MICHAEL OWEN
(Dec 05) Damaged fifth metatarsal in right foot when colliding with England team-mate Paul Robinson. Healing time: 17 wks

LEDLEY KING
(Apr 06) Injured fourth metatarsal in his left foot playing against Everton. Healing time: Still KO'd and missed World Cup 2006

WAYNE ROONEY
(Apr 06) Broke fourth metatarsal in right foot playing for Manchester United versus Chelsea. Healing time: 7 wks

> **"To see any player get injured and miss the World Cup... that would be horrible. Horrible."**
> **Wayne Rooney**

night, but he had yet to convince anyone of his international class versus his nuisance value at 6 feet 7 inches. At least England still had Wayne Rooney.

While Owen and fellow injury victim left-back Ashley Cole, who broke a metatarsal in his right foot in October 2005, seemed to have plenty of time to recover, as the weeks rolled by Eriksson and the nation clenched their buttocks each Premiership matchday in the hope that all of England's major players would come through unscathed. Having gone through the torment of 2002 when talismanic skipper Beckham had received his own metatarsal injury at the hands, or at least feet, of an Argentinean defender and lost the inspirational midfield talents of Steven Gerrard to an injury on the last Premiership afternoon, plus experienced right-back Gary Neville, the nation could barely believe it when England's top performers once again began to drop like flies.

The Crisis Deepens

Cole's understudy in the left-back position, Chelsea's Wayne Bridge, was stretchered off during England's friendly victory over Uruguay at Anfield. Thankfully Bridge's injury would not prove as bad as originally feared and he was back playing for his loan club, Fulham, within a few weeks.

Another defender, Sol Campbell, suffered a number of relatively minor injuries, including a twisted ankle at Charlton and a broken nose at Portsmouth in his first game back, but more worryingly Campbell underwent a crisis of confidence which kept him out of much of the second half of Arsenal's season. Campbell's form and injury led to him becoming very much a reserve behind Eriksson's preferred centre-back pairing of Ferdinand and Terry. Having been a regular since 1998, Campbell's world was collapsing in on him. Out of favour for England and out of contention with Arsenal as

Sven's plans began to fall apart as England's finest began to fall like flies with injury after injury

their youthful central defensive partnership of Senderos and Toure set a new record of 10 clean sheets in the Champions League as Arsenal reached the final for the first time, Campbell's wounds were as much mental as physical. Could he recover in time to become the colossus he had been in Japan 2002 when he had been voted into FIFA's team of the tournament alongside Ferdinand? His goal in the Champions League final and Wenger's faith in him above the younger record-breakers for that game went some way to making amends.

Rio Ferdinand himself had missed an entire international tournament

because of his lackadaisical attitude rather than injury. His ban for failing to appear for a drugs test had seen him miss Euro 2004 in Portugal.

It had all looked so different earlier in the season when Ferdinand had been the player to suffer a lapse in confidence and found himself dropped in favour of Campbell for the qualifying match against Austria at Old Trafford. Ferdinand admitted, though he was disappointed at the time, his reaction turned things around. "At times like that you've got to show your character to come through situations where it's a bit negative. It's been well documented that I was not happy. I think if I wasn't unhappy it would be a problem; I'd have to look at myself in the mirror and ask 'am I in the right sport?' You've got to hit back in the right way by putting in good performances and hopefully I've done that." As it happened Campbell picked up an injury in that match and Ferdinand was back, holding his place for the final qualifier against Poland and then Campbell's world imploded.

And then there was Wayne Rooney – the man-boy widely expected to be the player who came of age in the global sense in Germany and produce performances which could carry England to World Cup glory in much the same way that Pelé had become an instantly recognisable figure outside of Brazil after his exploits as a 17 year-old in Sweden.

Having won the Young Player title in England in successive years, Rooney now wanted to become the world's best young player in the World Cup finals. He had the appetite for more individual plaudits in Germany, where, for the first time, there would be an award for the Best Young Player, an official FIFA trophy sponsored by Gillette.

The World Cup seemed made for Rooney. The world was beginning to fear him, which is always as good a weapon as anything in top level football. Lothar Matthäus, captain of Germany's 1990 World Champions, was convinced that Rooney would be "the real star of Germany 2006". Matthäus was joined in his eulogy of Rooney by German national coach Jürgen Klinsmann, who himself netted 47 goals in 108 internationals – 16 in six major championships over a glittering decade, so knows a goalscorer when he spots one. He too feared Rooney. "A World Cup lives by its stars. Rooney

> "You cannot replace Rooney. I don't think there's another player like him in the country – or in Europe."
> Sir Bobby Robson

It looked innocuous at first, but Wayne Rooney's metatarsal break appeared far too serious to allow the Boy Wonder to play in Germany. Sven would have to devise a Plan B to cope with his loss, while the rest of the country fretted about Wayne's rehabilitation on an hourly basis

> ## "Only the winner should touch it, everybody else should leave it alone."
> ### Wayne Rooney

Wayne Rooney refused to handle the World Cup when it visited London, but within weeks his own participation in the tournament had been thrown into doubt causing national turmoil

will become one of those stars. Ronaldo only became World Player of the Year after he scored eight goals in World Cup 2002. The World Cup is the stage for the big guys, for the exceptional players, and I think we will have a couple this summer."

Bringing to Book

As befits the most talented footballer of his age, Rooney was never out of the headlines – with Sir Alex Ferguson likening him to George Best, Paul Gascoigne, and Beckham, in the way that he has become a media target – although the headlines were mostly harmless until the Sunday Mirror's front page screamed that Rooney had blown £700,000 with a bookie, who also happened to be Owen's business partner, and was now refusing to make good the debt, which caused a ripple effect of uncertainty within the England camp. There were suggestions Rooney was furious with Owen for letting him get sucked so heavily into the betting scene, but a spokesmen for Rooney's management company flatly denied the claims.

Eriksson acted quickly to clear up the idea that Rooney and Owen were at loggerheads and Rooney was forced to formally dismiss talk of a rift with his England strike partner. Several of Rooney's England team-mates were also reported to have embarked on heavy gambling stints, although none had accrued losses to such an extreme figure. Eriksson's mission – through informal chats – was to ensure no issues had arisen between any of the players as a consequence. All this just five weeks before England's World Cup squad travelled to southern Portugal for a pre-tournament training camp.

On his first public appearance following those allegations, Rooney resisted the temptation to lift the actual trophy aloft when it arrived in London. The two-day visit – the first time this World Cup had been in this country – was part of FIFA's tour of 31 cities in 29 countries and Rooney was paraded alongside it. "It's bigger than I thought it was," he observed of the 14.5 inch, 13.61lb 18-carat trophy. "It's the biggest tournament in the world and hopefully I'll pick it up in July. Then is the time to pick it up. Only the winners should touch it, everybody else should just leave it alone."

Superstition? Or the fact that a dozen security staff were watching the trophy's every move ensured Rooney kept his hands in his pocket. Emmanuel Maradas, the man appointed to accompany the World Cup on the tour, admitted: "The trophy is very carefully looked after and gets its own seat on the plane – in business class."

Rooney also revealed that he had dreamed about being involved in the World Cup ever since his first awareness of the tournament back in 1998. The 20-year-old said: "I was 12 and watching the England-Argentina game at my Nan's. It was disappointing that we went out on penalties, but afterwards I went out into the street and pretended to be Michael Owen." Now Rooney lines up alongside Owen, his hero: "At the age of 12 I was just a young lad and I wanted to become a professional footballer, but I didn't think it would come too soon."

Ironically, at the launch of his new Nike football boot in late April, Rooney talked about his injury at Euro 2004, when he'd hobbled off the pitch early in the quarter-final with Portugal with a broken foot, arguably taking England's hopes with him. "As soon as I stood up I knew straight away that I'd done something bad. I knew I had to go off, and it was only later on, when I went for the X-ray that it was confirmed I had a broken foot..."

How did that feel? "It was devastating. It was horrible. You just want to keep yourself fit. To see any player get injured and miss the World Cup... that would be horrible. Horrible."

A Nation Obsessed

Little did Rooney know that he would be the player caught up in an injury furore as those hopes for him to make his mark on the World stage in a major fashion seemed in tatters when, on 29th April, just eight weeks before England's opening game of the finals, Rooney suffered his own metatarsal break in a challenge with Portugal full-back Paulo Ferreira during Chelsea's title-clinching 3-0 victory over Manchester United at Stamford Bridge.

It was a totally innocuous challenge, but you could see the concern in the faces of Chelsea's England players Frank Lampard and Joe Cole as Rooney was carried off, even though they were celebrating a second successive Premiership win for their team. Rooney was that crucial to England's hopes of World Cup glory.

Such was the devastation felt by Eriksson that it produced the first public obscenity from the supposedly reserved super-cool Swede in five years. When asked what went through his mind in the immediate aftermath of Rooney's injury, Eriksson replied: "Shit."

That was nothing to what the nation collectively muttered under its breath.

Meanwhile a juggernaut of media speculation began rolling with endless column inches, hours of radio and TV time dedicated to Rooney-watch and whole hour-long TV programmes dedicated to examining the stresses on the young man's body and mind.

Over-hyped? You bet

Throughout all this Rooney maintained a sunny outwards disposition. Sleeping in a reduced-oxygen, or hypoxic, environment is known to stimulate the production of red blood cells, which delivers oxygen to the muscles and so Rooney, as Beckham

Nike were quick to claim that their Rooney endorsed Total 90 Supremacy boots had not contributed to their star's injury

New Boots For Old

The man who developed Rooney's new boot insisted it had nothing to do with the injury which threatened to wreck the England striker's World Cup dream. Rooney was wearing Nike's 'Total 90 Supremacy' boot for the first time at Stamford Bridge when he suffered that broken metatarsal. The finger was again being pointed at the new-style boots, which some people speculated were the major reason behind such a recent spate of metatarsal injuries. Nike pointed out that of the series of England stars to be affected in recent years – including Beckham, Gary Neville and Gerrard – Rooney was the only one contracted to them. And, at the high-profile launch of the 'Total 90 Supremacy' boot, which weighs in at a mere 10.5 ounces and features air technology specifically to cushion and protect the foot, boot developer Cedric Collet insisted there was no added risk to the safety of a player by the use of lighter micro-fibres in the boot's construction rather than old-style leather. "Nothing occurred in any of our tests to indicate the player would be at any risk," said Collet. "The boot incorporates three different types of protection for his foot. I think these injuries are more linked to the speed the game is played at now."

Should Rooney go to Germany if he could not play in the group stage of the tournament was the burning question which the nation faced almost hourly on every news source

had four years earlier, spent the few short weeks prior to the tournament desperately recuperating by sleeping in an Oxygen tent, often accompanied by his girlfriend, Colleen. At least the nation was desperate, while Rooney was recuperating – for with the Boy Wonder's fitness England's World Cup hopes seemed to lie.

Just a month before that injury, Rooney had signed the biggest sporting book deal in British history, a five year, 12 book contract with Harper Collins, but for any rights to be sold overseas, the Manchester United striker had to prove himself at the highest level, and that is in the World Cup. Their gamble on Britain's biggest sporting book deal now looked decidedly unwise.

Former England boss Sir Bobby Robson had no doubt Rooney's absence would be a crushing blow, "The news about Wayne is depressingly sad. Without him we've gone from possible World Cup winners to outsiders. You cannot replace Rooney. I don't think there's another player like him in the country – or in Europe. People who win World Cups are top individuals. Who won the World Cup for Argentina in 1986? It was Diego Maradona. What you need is your top players for the quarters, semis and final. That's when Rooney becomes crucial. If you can get him back for the quarter-finals then you take a chance and take him."

The race to get Rooney fit for the latter stages of the tournament was on.

To Go, Or Not To Go?

Sir Alex Ferguson and Sven-Göran Eriksson were soon at loggerheads over Rooney's ability to return to fitness in time to take part in the finals. United's club doctor, Dr Mike Stone, left his post, apparently dismissed after annoying Ferguson by making public positive news about Rooney's progress, although the official version of events was somewhat different. Scan followed scan with

Eriksson still insisting he would take him to Germany even if Rooney could only recover to play in the final. Why? "To win the final," he contended. "If we think he can make part of the World Cup, he will be in and why shouldn't he?"

There were those that argued that Rooney would be taking up one place in the squad that could be filled by a fully fit player, who may be of far more use then a crocked Wayne. But it was clearly a risk Eriksson was willing to take – others disagreed however, although their own agendas were barely hidden below the surface.

Sir Alex Ferguson was hardly in favour of risking a half-fit Rooney in the finals. Fergie said, "I don't want any complications with Wayne's broken foot – especially with a bandwagon gathering pace to get him to the World Cup come hell or high water. For the sake of the boy himself and the rest of the England team, we at United will do everything possible to get him fit in time. But I am not going along with this half-baked idea of Wayne going to Germany 80% fit and then find him being pressured into playing before he is ready. That was the experience of David Beckham in the last World Cup, and it was a disaster – because he wasn't right."

Eriksson's reply? "Miracles happen in life now and then."

The Curse Continues

But worryingly Rooney wasn't the only England star to leave Stamford Bridge on crutches that April day. Chelsea's inspirational skipper John Terry, the man tipped by many to eventually take over the England captaincy from David Beckham, hobbled away from the game on a sprained ankle, although his manager was adamant there was no threat to the defender missing out on Germany, "I know he was hurt, but it's not the kind of injury that is a problem for the future. He will be ready physically to join the national team on the first day. I think

mentally he can forget Chelsea now for a couple of months and start to concentrate on England." At least Terry had the sweet smell of success in his nostrils having captained Chelsea to back-to-back Premiership titles, the first club to achieve that feat aside from Manchester United in the Premiership era.

Meanwhile over at White Hart Lane, Spurs' Ledley King, who had forced his way into Sven's starting line-up in the latter qualifying matches, was hobbling out of the fray after also breaking a metatarsal in the game against Everton.

And even worse news was to arrive at Eriksson's door before he could lay his worried head to the pillow that night. Making his first appearance in a Premiership game in four months at Birmingham as a second half substitute, Michael Owen had suffered a setback in his rehabilitation. Suddenly in just one day, England's squad appeared decimated.

A visibly upset Owen stepped tentatively out of St Andrew's and admitted: "My foot does not feel right. I felt something go after 10 minutes. But it's not the kind of pain I experienced when I needed a second operation a few weeks ago." Owen contacted surgeon John Hodgkinson, who performed both operations on the foot after the accidental clash with Paul Robinson. In January, doctors had predicted he would be fit to resume training within about three months. But Owen had needed a second operation when surgeons opted to insert a larger screw in the broken bone to help strengthen it and accelerate his recovery. It clearly was still not right.

With the whole country on Owen and Rooney watch, many fans could be forgiven for missing the good news on the injury front which was that Ashley Cole, England's outstanding left-back, returned to the Arsenal first team for the first time since October. Cole had already made one abortive comeback for Arsenal reserves and so his first steps back into action were

> "I am not going along with this half-baked idea of Wayne going to Germany 80% fit and then find him being pressured into playing before he is ready."
> Sir Alex Ferguson

> "My foot does not feel right. I will have to go and see the surgeon. Until then I don't know how serious it is."
> Michael Owen

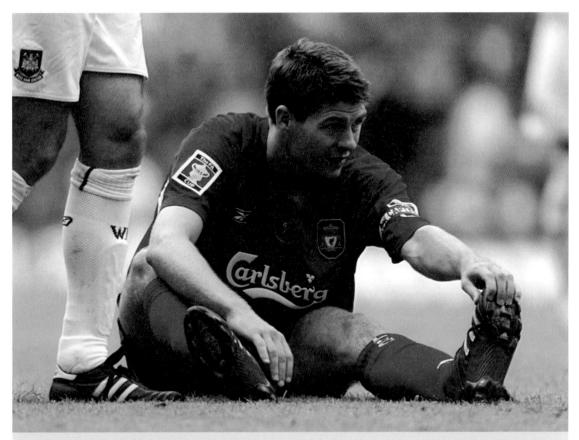

Down and out? No, thankfully. Liverpool captain Gerrard raised himself from a Motson-induced injury to crack home the late equaliser in the FA Cup Final which allowed his team to triumph on penalties

tentative, but at least there was some encouragement for England supporters.

There was also encouragement on the deadline front as FIFA confirmed that England could wait until June 9 to replace any injured player in their squad, rather than having to name a squad of fully fit players on the 15th May deadline. So the England boss had until the day before their opening game against Paraguay to evaluate Rooney's progress, and possibly even Owen's.

Filling the Void

With Rooney's scans confirming he would probably not play until 1 July, the debate raged as to how Eriksson would set his team up to play the three group games which it now seemed that Rooney would miss.

Joe Cole offered to fill the void, "I would be honoured to step into Wayne's shoes. I would play anywhere the manager wants me to play. If he wants me to play that role for England then I will, it is no problem. I am a different sort of player to Wayne. He is his own man and a great player, but I would give it a go and do my best for the team. I have played in most positions before and when you play for England you cannot pick and choose."

Another option would be to push Steven Gerrard forward and thus relieve what many observers felt was an uncomfortable situation with both Gerrard and Frank Lampard playing in too similar a style to be effective in central midfield. Gerrard himself had been forced to sit out the 2002 World Cup through injury and would not

wish it on anyone, let alone the nation's brightest star. "It would be a disaster for England if we had to go to the World Cup finals without Wayne. He is idolised around the country and is our main man. I think it is impossible to have a successful World Cup without Wayne. He's our key man. If he doesn't make it, then it obviously is an opportunity for people like Peter Crouch, Jermain Defoe and Darren Bent, but we'd much prefer to have a fit Rooney. Hopefully, Wayne won't go through what I went through in 2002. It was a terrible experience and a nightmare watching it back home on the telly."

Gerrard starred in the final big domestic match of the season, the FA Cup Final at the Millennium Stadium, which he almost single-handedly won for Liverpool. But even the talismanic

Liverpool captain was not immune to providing the nation with an injury scare when John Motson, commentating on the Cup Final for the BBC, seized eagerly upon the opportunity to scare the country witless as Gerrard went down towards the end of normal time in a riveting game suffering from cramp. "Could this be an injury scare to keep Gerrard out of the World Cup Finals?" muttered Motty. The nation's hearts sank into its collective boots.

That Gerrard soldiered on to crack home one of the greatest FA Cup Final goals of all time soon gave the lie to Motson's scaremongering as the commentator admitted himself after watching Gerrard's bullet of an equaliser fly into Shaka Hislop's net from fully 35 yards. Would that a similar effort should defeat the same keeper when the pair met wearing the shirts of England and Trinidad & Tobago on 15th June, but that would depend on how Eriksson chose to use the Liverpool skipper, who had shown enough goalscoring potential throughout a season which had begun back in July due to Liverpool's elongated qualification process for the Champions League to lay claim to play as support to a lone striker in Rooney's absence.

Sven's Men

So when Eriksson named his squad for Germany all eyes were on pointers as to how he would cope with having a tentative Owen, who lacked match practice, and the loss of Rooney for the early games in the tournament – or longer. What nobody expected was exactly how he chose to provide sufficient back-up for his two frontline strikers.

Conventional wisdom had it that Jermain Defoe would travel as cover for Owen, while Rooney, being such a one off could not be directly replaced, but at least the likes of Cole or Gerrard could step into the breach. Peter Crouch was a certainty as he provided Eriksson's main Plan B as exemplified by the stirring victory against Argentina when he came off the bench to assist

England's late 3-2 win and then Darren Bent would also probably go as a fifth striker to add cover and because, as the highest scoring Englishman in the Premiership in 2005/06, he had probably earned it.

The seismic shock which greeted Eriksson's chosen 23 could have been felt in Berlin itself. Only four strikers – two of them injury doubts and one of

them a teenager who had yet to play Premiership football. Theo Walcott, the Southampton prodigy for whom Arsenal had paid a sum of around £12 million in the January transfer window, had made just 23 first class appearances, scored 5 goals and all of those in the Championship. He had never even played for Arsenal in the Premiership, although he had scored

Eriksson watches the most controversial player ever to have been selected for a World Cup squad, Theo Walcott, in his first training session – incredibly the first time that Sven had seen Walcott in action

"The biggest selection story in the history of England's World Cup"

Pro-Walcott

Harry Redknapp believed Eriksson's decision "could be a tactical master-stroke". "I was a little surprised to see him included but the lad is a real talent," said Redknapp. "He has so much ability and his pace is frightening. He is quicker than anyone else I have seen. Seriously, the boy glides over the park. If he walked across a puddle, he wouldn't make a splash. He can run with the ball at tremendous speed and that can really hurt defences. Give him a bit of space and he will kill you. Yes, Theo is inexperienced, but he is a great player to chuck on from the bench. He may still be a kid but he won't be daunted by mixing with the likes of Beckham and Gerrard. He is a confident lad. This could be a tactical master-stroke from Sven."

five goals in 11 England U17 matches. Even more astonishingly, Eriksson had never seen Walcott play in the flesh. He had acted purely on the advice of his assistant Tord Grip and Arsenal manager Arsène Wenger.

It was clearly one in the eye for those pundits who had long criticised Eriksson for his caution in both selection and playing tactics. Everyone could understand why Eriksson would gamble on the fitness of a player who has scored 33 goals in 74 internationals in Owen. There was debate about risking Rooney, but everyone understood why Eriksson wanted to take him if at all possible. But Walcott?

The Mail's Brian Woolnough called it, "The biggest selection story in the history of England's World Cup." Eriksson admitted he only decided on the morning of the squad announcement to include Walcott, "I thought a lot about it during the last month," he said. "It is a gamble, of course it is a gamble, I can't deny that, but it is a nice one. He is a great talent. I have 23 players, why not take one gambling? I am excited to see him. He's a big talent and pace in football today is worth a lot. I spoke to Arsène Wenger and he's excited as well, very much so. For me it's a good squad, an interesting squad. There are some new players, some young players and it is an attacking squad with a lot of pace which is necessary in a World Cup."

Walcott's inclusion sparked Theo Fever as the nation scrambled for facts, information and trivia about its newest footballing Wonder Kid, partly quartising the pain of Rooney's losing battle with his metatarsal. It also polarised opinions amongst every commentator in the country.

Anti-Walcott

Former England manager Graham Taylor was quick to criticise Wenger's role in Walcott's inclusion. Taylor, speaking at an event for Pukka Pies, the sponsor of the official England Supporters Band, said: "It is the biggest decision that perhaps any international manager has taken on the eve of a big tournament. He has listened to Wenger, who has persuaded him that Walcott is worth taking. So having not given the job to Wenger, Wenger has now picked our team."

But Walcott's inclusion deflected attention from the emerging talent of Spurs' flying right winger Aaron Lennon, who had enjoyed an excellent first season in the Premiership since joining Tottenham from Leeds the previous summer with his explosive skills, pace and developing maturity. With Eriksson valuing pace highly and Lennon impressing in late season games which the manager did actually witness, the chances were that this 19-year-old would feature heavily in Germany. Being a right-winger, however, did mean that he would have to dislodge David Beckham from the team. Meanwhile on the other flank, the inclusion of the squad's only left-footed attacker, Stuart Downing, rounded off a turbulent season, which was largely marred by injury.

But what about those who were left out in favour of the shock inclusion? Jermain Defoe only made the stand by list, along with Andy Johnson, while Charlton's Darren Bent was cast aside having started against Uruguay. Suffering the disappointment of being left behind were the likes of Shaun Wright-

World Cup Teenagers

All the cynics worried about the youthful suitability of Theo Walcott (who would become the second youngest player in the history of the competition if he played in Germany) to be in England's World Cup squad clearly did not know much about football history. Prior to the 1958 World Cup finals, the youngest ever player Pelé undertook a psychological evaluation, scoring 68 points from a possible 123. Psychologist João Carvalhaes concluded that he was 'infantile and without fighting spirit' and therefore not suitable to represent his country on a global stage. The prodigy immediately went on to become the youngest-ever player to win the tournament, scoring twice in the 5-2 win against Sweden in the final.

Phillips, Phil Neville and Ledley King. Wright-Phillips was left out after a disappointing season which saw his first-team opportunities limited after joining Chelsea from Manchester City. King failed to recover from that metatarsal injury, while Defoe spent much of the last third of the season on the bench for Tottenham. At least he could sit tight and wait for the result of the Rooney situation. While it wasn't quite the end for Neville either.

Beckham's World Cup Obsession

In the run up to the World Cup England Captain David Beckham admitted that he suffered from obsessive compulsive disorder, speaking of his addiction to rearranging hotel rooms and lining up cans of soft drinks to make "everything perfect". In a TV interview screened in April 2006, Beckham said he has tried to break his cycle of repetitive behaviour, but cannot stop. OCD, as it

"We've got three fridges. In the drinks one, everything is symmetrical. If there's three cans, he'll throw one away because it has to be an even number"
Victoria Beckham

Even numbers of drinks, shirts hanging according to colour or brand new personalised trainers, David Beckham's public admission of low level OCD reflected his compulsive nature. Matched by his desire to follow his hero Bobby Moore in lifting the World Cup

*David Beckham's ills with Argentinean players began back at France 98
with that red card for kicking out at Diego Simeone*

is known, affects one in 60 people in Britain, ranging from mild traits to a debilitating dependency on rituals of cleanliness, symmetry or other issues. In the interview on ITV1, he said: "I've got this obsessive compulsive disorder where I have to have everything in a straight line or everything has to be in pairs. I'll put my Pepsi cans in the fridge and if there's one too many then I'll put it in another cupboard somewhere. I'll go into a hotel room and before I can relax, I have to move all the leaflets and all the books and put them in a drawer. Everything has to be perfect." Asked if he wanted to stop his obsessive behaviour, he said, "I would like to. I've tried and can't stop."

Beckham admitted he was also addicted to having tattoos, partly because he enjoys the pain. The England captain said that his wife, Victoria, calls him a "weirdo" because of his condition. Newspapers have delighted in stories of Beckham's eccentric behaviour, with reports that he wears white clothes to match his furniture, buys 30 pairs of identical Calvin Klein underpants every fortnight, will only wear brand new trainers and insists on lining up his shirts according to colour.

Mrs Beckham, who had revealed her husband's inner secrets before, told one interviewer: "If you open our fridge, it's all co-ordinated down either side. We've got three fridges – food in one, salad in another and drinks in the third. In the drinks one, everything is symmetrical. If there's

three cans, he'll throw one away because it has to be an even number."

That obsession in particular allegedly annoyed his England room-mate of many years, Gary Neville, so much that he asked to change. Beckham said that his team-mates at Real Madrid were unaware of his condition, but that players at his former club, Manchester United, would deliberately rearrange his clothes in hotel rooms or move magazines around to make them "wonky" to infuriate him.

Beckham is not the first footballer to admit to suffering from OCD, which is estimated to affect more than two million people at some point in their lives. The former England star Paul Gascoigne said that he was obsessed with cleanliness and needed help for the condition. Other famous sufferers include the actor Billy Bob Thornton, who has spoken of having to repeat words and count up to particular numbers, and the singer Natalie Appleton, who is obsessed with cleanliness and broke down in tears when she had to touch a tree on the reality show I'm A Celebrity Get Me Out of Here. A spokesman for the charity OCD UK said: "There is still a lot of stigma about the condition and even GPs are not very good at picking up on it. Young men in particular are often reluctant to come forward and ask for treatment, so to have someone like David Beckham come out and talk about it is very good."

In my own, personal experience I have found footballers to be obsessive by nature. Writing Paul Merson's autobiography was like delving into the dark corners of the mind. The former Arsenal and England forward was obsessive about becoming a footballer, and you do need to be 'dedicated' if not actually obsessive, but then he became obsessive with gambling, drink and finally drugs before he sought help.

Beckham, though, is also obsessive about wanting to win the World Cup, knowing 2006 might well be his last chance – as it could be for several of the older players within the Golden Generation. And his obsession did not stop with winning. Beckham is a closet statto as he revealed exclusively to me. Prior to the World Cup warm up game in Geneva, he was surfing the internet to find out exactly where he stood in the all-time list of England captains. He currently lies fourth, but has his sights on pushing into the top three. The World Cup-winning captain of 1966, Bobby Moore, skippered England 90 times, the same number as Billy Wright, and next comes Bryan Robson on 65. Beckham said, "I had my computer in my room and was actually on i-tunes at the time. Somebody had mentioned about me being fourth-highest captain and I wondered what the other players were on, and whether I could catch them. I

saw Bryan Robson and thought that was possible, then I saw the other two and thought 'We'll see!' It would be nice to catch them because the three players in front of me are players I have always looked up to. You dream of being mentioned in the same sentence as these players."

Beckham inadvertently knighted the legendary Moore as he added: "To be even mentioned in the same breath as Sir Bobby Moore is an amazing honour. If that is in the history books, then I would be more than happy."

Don't Cry For Me Argentina

Beckham has had a rough ride as an England player, starting with his infamous dismissal against Argentina at France 98. Despite appearances Beckham doesn't dislike all Argentinean footballers. Former Real Madrid team-mate Esteban Cambiasso, Beckham said, was "a great person". Diego Maradona is his idol. And he was matey enough with Juan Sebastian Veron when the two of them were at Manchester United together. "I really don't know why they don't like me," Beckham. "It's weird I have had so many problems with them." But it got to the point, according to Simeone, the man who induced Beckham to kick him to earn red in France, where the Real Madrid star has even learned to swear in an Argentine dialect just to improve his method of insulting Simeone when they meet in Primera Liga games!

Nearly four years later, in April 2002, it was another Argentinean, Deportivo La Coruna's Aldo Duscher, who broke Beckham's foot with a tackle and sent a nation into a panic about the captain's metatarsal. Medical bulletins about the state of Beckham's injury dominated the news for the next six weeks, just as the nation suffered with Rooney prior to Germany 2006.

Beckham's next red card after that dismissal against Argentina was against Mexican side Necaxa in the World Club Championship in Brazil in January 2000. The referee was Horacio

Elizonda.... from Argentina. The first time he was sent off for Real Madrid, it was for a foul on Valencia's Argentinean international Pablo Aimar. Then there was a nasty injury sustained at the hands of Murcia's Argentinean Jose Luis Acciari.

"My first season at Real Madrid," Beckham said, "every tackle, every booking, every problem, turned out to be connected with an Argentinean player, which was bizarre."

For all Beckham's status as one of the world's top players, he has never lit up a major tournament. Following his sending off in France and England's dismal performance at Euro 2000, at the 2002 World Cup Beckham was not properly fit, and in Euro 2004 he missed two penalties. He said: "There has been the odd couple of games where I have been close to being my best in tournaments. But there have been a lot of people out there who have documented I haven't done as well in the World Cup as I could have done. I always want to put people right. Let's hope I can do that in this World Cup."

With England potentially facing a quarter-final tie against Argentina in Germany, Beckham's nemesis could be facing him once again, giving him the opportunity to lay that ghost to rest and prove his class at the highest level. Could he take it?

> "To be even mentioned in the same breath as Sir Bobby Moore is an amazing honour."
> David Beckham

England's Road to Glory?

"I believe this team can go a long way – but you get nothing if you don't work hard"   David Beckham

Beckham can't believe he's seeing red again, this time for losing his head and clattering Austria's Andreas Ibertsberger twice in as many minutes

Ten games, 26 players, 10,000 miles and countless headlines. That's what England's qualification campaign for the 2006 World Cup boiled down to. But there was plenty more to the story of how England reached Germany.

On the day England qualified for the 2006 World Cup, David Beckham's sending-off against Austria robbed him of the chance to chalk up his half-century of appearances as England captain against Poland at Old Trafford in England's last World Cup qualifier. Beckham hates missing games, always a big incentive, then, not to get sent off! At the time of that red card, which made him the first England player in history to be dismissed twice, he called the day

"one of the worst of my life", referring to concerns over the health of his three-year-old son, Romeo, taken into hospital during the week suffering from convulsions, which possibly led to his overt frustration and pointed to flaws in his character when it comes to top level matches, which have been a concern ever since he lashed out at Diego Simeone of Argentina in France 98 to earn that first red card as an England player.

Against Austria Beckham was irresponsible to chase after opponent Andreas Ibertsberger, who admittedly provoked him, less than a minute after his first booking – even if the contact with his opponent seemed to be minimal on both occasions. Beckham's act of petulance left England to play the final half-hour with ten men in a match that they could not afford to draw. If they had failed to hold on to their lead, he would unquestionably have been to blame, his guilt doubled by suspension for what would have been a crucial final match against Poland, but, in the end, recriminations were not needed. England held on for a slender victory.

It was ironic that Beckham had lacked self-control against Austria after lecturing Wayne Rooney on the subject during England's embarrassing 0-1 defeat in Belfast a month earlier. Rooney insisted his high-profile bust-up with Beckham was now long forgotten. "David has been a great friend to me. He is a great captain and a terrific player. We speak to each other off the pitch. He is so up for the World Cup Finals, probably more than anyone else, because he takes so much more stick. It has been very unfair, especially if you look at his performances for England, which have been great. I was very frustrated when so much was made of our argument during the Northern Ireland game. Arguments happen on and off the pitch, but they happen because you try and help one

another and because you care. I would be more concerned if they didn't happen. Then there would be something wrong. We spoke in the dressing room afterwards and everything was sorted out."

Perversely, red-carded Beckham left the Old Trafford pitch to a standing ovation and so the backlash from the media, which criticised his uncontrolled temper, was tempered by understanding from the fans, who perceived a certain amount of harshness from the referee. The captain mustered a smile and said "we'll see" when asked if he feared that the reaction to this red card might be as extreme as his first. Although one man urged the media at Old Trafford to "bury him", this time the tide of public and media opinion, was with him.

But all the recriminations were halted in their tracks by England's result and one from Prague later that night, where Holland's 2-0 win over the Czech Republic confirmed England would at least finish as one of the best runners-up and thus had secured a place in Germany.

> "Arguments happen on and off the pitch, but they happen because you try and help one another and because you care."
> Wayne Rooney

England coach Sven-Göran Eriksson recalled, "We got the result of the Holland game when we were sitting and eating. The players, staff and myself were delighted. There has been a lot of discussion about whether England were going or not — especially after the Northern Ireland game. Our critics started to say maybe not. I've said for two years that we would

> "England are one of the four or five teams that can win the World Cup"
> Sven-Göran Eriksson

England's frustrating night's work in Belfast was epitomised by the spat between Rooney and Beckham following the young star's loss of cool

"As the hype increases, expectancy levels reach fever pitch"

Sven ignores David James as he leaves the pitch after being responsible for Austria's unlikely comeback from two goals down. This would prove to be James' last competitive start as England goalkeeper

qualify and have a very good World Cup. I will go on saying it. But to win it we must play better than we have done this season."

England's captain agreed, "Everyone knows we can play a lot better. We have great individuals, but this team is not about individuals," Beckham said. "I believe this team can go a long way – but you get nothing if you don't work hard. Now we have to get down to some more hard work and playing a lot better. People have said the players are against each other in this squad – that some players are more involved in picking the team than others. But the players have always stuck together and people don't realise just what great character we've got in this team and how much we care."

Qualification merely served to heap the pressure of expectation further onto the shoulders of all within the England set up, rather than relieve any of that which had built up through England's turgid progress through a very simple group.

BBC pundits and ex-England captains Alan Shearer and Gary Lineker had accused Sven's players of lacking passion after the narrow win over Austria. To them Eriksson blasted: "Those names who were talking about the game, I don't agree with them at all. Shearer has his opinion, but I don't

share it with him. There were far more positives than negatives from this game. I think the passion was there. We also worked very well as a team after David Beckham was sent off. I can't agree with them. England are one of the four or five teams that can win the World Cup."

As ever with a World Cup, as the hype increases, expectancy levels reach fever pitch, and the England captain guarded against complacency when England drew the comparatively straightforward Paraguay, Sweden and Trinidad and Tobago in Group B. Beckham said: "It is still a difficult group to play in. We cannot afford to take it lightly and if we do that we will find ourselves in trouble." Never a truer word spoken, as England's stuttering qualification performances, vows of silence and on-pitch arguments had proved.

England's World Cup 2006 Qualifiers

SEPTEMBER 4, 2004
Austria 2   England 2
(Vienna; Att: 48,500)

While Soho Square was still reeling from one of its most bitter internal power-struggles, Sven-Göran Eriksson's side contrived to increase the pressure on their manager by squandering a two-goal lead.

DID YOU KNOW?
This was the first time England had conceded a two-goal lead since the 3-2 defeat by Portugal at Euro 2000. Gary Neville, Beckham and Owen were all survivors.

The blame fell upon goalkeeper David James, who has not played in a competitive international since, after Andreas Ivanschitz's shot went straight through him for the equaliser after England had lead 2-0. That was not the only aspect of the game that seemed to go wrong – Ashley Cole and Wayne Bridge's partnership down the left no longer looked viable.

There was confusion when substitutions were made, with Bridge coming off instead of the injured Steven Gerrard, and suddenly Eriksson was under pressure again. Most of all the game signalled the return of the theory that there were favoured players in Eriksson's side selected regardless of form.

But Eriksson hit back at the critics, "I think the worst thing I could do at this moment is to panic, changing five players for Wednesday's game in Poland, taking out Owen, Beckham or whoever else. I will not panic. I will stick to more or less the same formation."

Everything had looked to be going to plan as Gerrard looped in a belter midway through the second half, after lax defending left Lampard with an open goal from Beckham's direction-switching free-kick for the opener. England should have coasted home against easy-pickings opponents even when substitute Roland Kollmann cracked a free-kick over the wall and beyond the slow-moving James. But then the keeper made the mother of all cock-ups to let Ivanschitz's weak deflected shot squirm under his body and roll over the line.

England: **James; G Neville, Terry, King, A Cole; Beckham, Gerrard (Carragher 82), Lampard, Bridge (J Cole 84); Smith (Defoe 76), Owen**
Subs not used: **Robinson, Dyer, Wright-Phillips, Vassell**
Goals: **Lampard (24) 0-1; Gerrard (65) 0-2; Kollmann (71) 1-2; Ivanschitz (72) 2-2**
Booked: **Beckham**
Man of the match: **Lampard**

SEPTEMBER 8, 2004
Poland 1 England 2
(Katowice; Att: 38,000)

Having lulled us into a false sense of insecurity, ruthless Eriksson dropped David James and Alan Smith. In came Spurs duo Paul Robinson and Jermain Defoe. Defoe marked his first England start with a sweet turn and finish to put England ahead.

The ghosts of Katowice, where Alf Ramsey experienced the beginning of the end in 1973, threatened to haunt them when Zurawski gave Robinson no chance. Ashley Cole's low cross and an Glowacki own goal, which Owen tried to claim, ensured reputations were redeemed.

England extended their unbeaten run against the Poles to 13 games and 31 years. Defoe looked, for one half at least, like a natural England striker. Given the ball, he swivelled in the area and beat Liverpool's Jerzy Dudek from close range.

The match was noted for the vow of silence the players kept after what they perceived as unjustifiably harsh treatment following the defeat to Austria, particularly of the dropped James. They just waved at reporters who faced a media black-out from the squad and responded by calling the footballers 'childish', amongst other less pleasant things. Eriksson commented, "I can understand it [the media black-out after criticism of David James]. There should be a limit to the criticism of individual players. They don't agree with it and are trying to defend the group."

England: **Robinson; G Neville (Carragher 30), Terry, King, A Cole; Beckham (Hargreaves 89), Lampard, Gerrard, Bridge; Defoe (Dyer 87), Owen**
Subs not used: **James, Wright-Phillips, Smith, Vassell**
Goals: **Defoe (36) 0-1; Zurawski (47) 1-1; Glowacki og (57) 1-2**
Booked: **Owen**
Man of the match: **Defoe**

OCTOBER 9, 2004
England 2 Wales 0
(Old Trafford; Att: 65,224)

Back with a bang for Beckham as he hogged the headlines for the right and wrong reasons.

Owen again tried and failed to claim a goal, this time Lampard's early strike, and with Wales weak and

David Beckham celebrates his curling long range goal which set the seal on a solid 2-0 victory over Wales

woeful in the absence of the suspended Robbie Savage, England were always in command with the fit-again Wayne Rooney a constant menace.

In England's first home game against the Welsh in 21 years, Beckham sealed the victory with a beauty of a curler into the top corner, but then lost his head with two stupid challenges on Ben Thatcher. Getting booked and suspended was bad enough. Boasting that he "had the brains" to do it provoked FIFA president Sepp Blatter into attacking him and brought widespread derision.

The game saw the return of Rooney, possibly in the role he should always play for England – behind the two strikers. The teenager was playing for England for the first time since breaking that metatarsal at Euro 2004.

With Gerrard injured, Eriksson played Tottenham striker Defoe in a 4-3-3 formation, with Nicky Butt as a holding midfielder. England looked solid and Lampard scored after four minutes.

But soon after he sealed victory with a brilliant, swooping shot from the left side of the box, Beckham cracked a rib in a challenge with Thatcher – and sought retribution, picking up a booking which ruled him out of the visit to Azerbaijan.

England: **Robinson; G Neville, Campbell, Ferdinand, A Cole; Beckham (Hargreaves 85), Butt, Lampard; Defoe (Smith 70), Owen, Rooney (King 87)**
Subs not used: **James, Terry, J Cole, Wright-Phillips**
Goals: **Lampard (4) 1-0; Beckham (76) 2-0**
Booked: **Beckham**
Man of the match: **Rooney**

OCTOBER 13, 2004
Azerbaijan 0 England 1
(Baku; Att: 15,000)

On the eve of the game Beckham called a reporter to tell him that he had not been foolish in picking up the Thatcher booking in the game against Wales – he had done it on purpose. Beckham claimed that, knowing the rib injury would rule him out of the Azerbaijan game anyway, he "took a yellow" to clear his suspension. Beckham sustained enormous media criticism for the decision to admit to his motives for deliberately getting booked.

But he picked a good game to miss – torrential rain, a howling gale and a terrible pitch making any sort of normal football impossible.

Jermaine Jenas, in his only competitive start for England to date, was handed Beckham's No.7 shirt as well as his slot on the right as Eriksson stuck with the front trio of Rooney, Defoe and stand-in skipper Owen.

It was Owen who claimed the vital goal, rising in the box to trickle home a header from Ashley Cole's cross to leave England in pole position.

England: **Robinson; G Neville, Ferdinand, Campbell, A Cole; Butt, Jenas (Wright-Phillips 72), Lampard; Rooney (J Cole 85), Owen, Defoe (Smith 55)**
Subs not used: **King, James, Terry, Hargreaves**
Goal: **Owen (22) 0-1**
Booked: **Butt, Cole, Rooney**
Man of the match: **Owen**

MARCH 26, 2005
England 4 Northern Ireland 0
(Old Trafford; Att: 65,239)

Two disastrous performances in friendlies – against Spain and the Netherlands – preceded Eriksson's 50th match in charge. After Rooney had to be substituted at the Bernabeu stadium the previous November to save him from being sent off, the teenager was the saviour for Eriksson once again at Old Trafford.

After a first half stalemate, the victory was comfortable in the end once Joe Cole broke the deadlock straight after half-time. Owen stole the second off Lampard's toe and a fabulous Rooney run ended in a Chris Baird own goal. Rooney was untamable. Lampard claimed another deflected strike and with England in total command it could have been more.

There was no hint as to what lay in wait for England at Windsor Park six months ahead.

England: **Robinson; G Neville, Ferdinand, Terry, A Cole; Beckham (Dyer 72), Lampard, Gerrard (Hargreaves 72), J Cole; Rooney (Defoe 81), Owen**
Subs not used: **James, Carragher, King, Heskey**
Goals: **J Cole (47) 1-0; Owen (52) 2-0; Baird og (53) 3-0; Lampard (62) 4-0**
Man of the match: **Rooney**

MARCH 30, 2005
England 2 Azerbaijan 0
(St. James' Park; Att: 49,046)

England were unchanged for the first time in the campaign.

After four against the Irish, the expectations were enormous against a side smashed for eight by the Poles four days earlier, but instead England stuttered. Owen had a night to forget, missing a hatful of chances and picking up a booking that ruled him out of the game in Cardiff.

Michael Owen's handball against Azerbaijan was spotted by the referee and the yellow card earned him a suspension from England's game in Cardiff

It was not until six minutes into the second period that Gerrard's volley bounced its way over the line to ease the tensions. Then Beckham, timing his run from half-way to perfection, killed Azerbaijan off with the second. Beckham's goal was a source of relief for the England captain, who took a long ball from Lampard on his chest just after the hour to run on goal and score.

The most memorable moment came in the post-match press conference when the Azerbaijan coach – Brazil's 1970 World Cup-winning captain Carlos Alberto – ranted at Owen after reading that Owen had promised to score five against his team. Alberto was so outraged he described England's current highest goalscorer as a "midget".

England: **Robinson; G Neville, Ferdinand (King 78), Terry, A Cole; Beckham (Defoe 84), Gerrard, Lampard, J Cole; Rooney (Dyer 78), Owen**
Subs not used: **Carragher, James, Jenas, Heskey**
Goals: **Gerrard (51) 1-0; Beckham (62) 2-0**
Booked: **Beckham, Owen**
Man of the match: **Rooney**

SEPTEMBER 3, 2005
Wales 0 England 1
(Millennium Stadium; Att: 70,715)

A sixth straight competitive win represented the best run since 1985 under Bobby Robson as England partially erased the memory of their 4-1 battering in the friendly in Denmark two weeks earlier.

Eriksson's 4-5-1 formation was implemented in order to accommodate Joe Cole and Wright-Phillips as well as Beckham, Lampard and Gerrard, who had all been consulted by Eriksson on what line-up they should play. The players did not want Defoe in the side – he had been ineffective in a dreadful 4-1 friendly defeat to Denmark in Copenhagen the previous month.

Beckham played as the "quarterback" in a 4-5-1 formation that left lone striker Rooney isolated and struggled to bring Lampard and Gerrard into the game.

Only Robinson's Banks-like save from John Hartson's first-half header kept England on terms at the break. Even Cole's deflected opener at the start of the second half did not bring the confidence back.

Rooney was denied by the outstanding Welsh keeper Danny Coyne,

but the longer the game went on, the more pressure England were under, leaving John Toshack to predict they might well end up behind the Poles in the final analysis as the seeds of England's demise against Northern Ireland were sown.

There was mild criticism of Lampard from Eriksson – uncharacteristic for him – but most of all the England coach was desperate to deny the suggestions that he was giving in to player-power in the selection of his team.

England: **Robinson; Young, Carragher, Ferdinand, A Cole; Beckham, Lampard, Gerrard (Richardson 84), Wright-Phillips (Defoe 68), J Cole (Hargreaves 77); Rooney**
Subs not used: **Upson, Kirkland, P Neville, D Bent**
Goal: **J Cole (54) 0-1**
Man of the match: **Beckham**

SEPTEMBER 7, 2005
Northern Ireland 1 England 0
(Windsor Park; Att: 14,069)

The darkest day of Eriksson's reign, his first defeat in 22 qualifiers and England's first loss in Belfast since 1927. It was the ultimate indignity for Eriksson and his shell-shocked team as they slumped to arguably the worst World Cup defeat since the 1-0 humiliation by the USA in 1950.

Rooney was a liability, booked and so close to being sent off. His temperament was again under scrutiny. Beckham's first-half free-kick hit the bar with Maik Taylor a spectator, but Ireland's sheer spirit found Eriksson's side complacent. Even so, they would probably have got away with a point had not Rio Ferdinand's concentration dropped to play David Healy onside for the goal that made him an overnight hero in Belfast. Eriksson admitted: "It was a disaster".

Eriksson said, 'If anyone doubts I am in charge of this team they are badly wrong. My relationship with David Beckham is very good. That is important, he is the captain. But if people think he has other favours they are absolutely wrong.'

England: **Robinson; Young, Ferdinand, Carragher, A Cole; Wright-Phillips (J Cole 53), Lampard (Hargreaves 80), Beckham, Gerrard (Defoe 75), Rooney; Owen**
Subs not used: **Upson, Kirkland, P Neville, D Bent**
Goal: **Healy (73) 1-0**
Booked: **Rooney**
Man of the Match: **Robinson**

DID YOU KNOW?
Before kick-off Northern Ireland were below Rwanda in the FIFA World rankings.

David Healy lashes into England's net to cause the biggest upset since the 1950 World Cup humiliation by the USA. Eriksson's darkest hour as England manager followed a 4-1 defeat by Denmark as the season got off to a poor start

OCTOBER 8, 2005
England 1 Austria 0
(Old Trafford; Att: 64,822)

Beckham's decision to hand the spot-kick duties to Lampard was vindicated when the Chelsea midfielder drilled home after Owen was held in the box. The striker was denied another cast-iron penalty soon after. But England failed to turn their advantage into goals and when Beckham became the first England captain to be sent off after three rash challenges in as many minutes it became a backs-to-the-wall exercise.

The 10 men held on in a nervy finish, although there were no celebrations – until the news came in from Wenceslas Square. With Rooney, Ashley Cole and Gary Neville to come back there was no reason for pessimism. Tournament form tends to bear little relation to struggles in qualifying.

Rooney said: "We've qualified and we are delighted with that. We want to win against Poland and finish top of the group. That's our priority. I think we could be playing better. We haven't had the best of starts to the season with England."

England: **Robinson, Young, Terry, Campbell (Ferdinand 65), Carragher, Beckham, Gerrard, Lampard, J Cole (King 62), Crouch, Owen (Richardson 80)**
Subs not used: **Kirkland, Wright-Phillips, D Bent, Defoe**
Goal: **Lampard (pen 24) 1-0**
Booked: **Beckham, J Cole**
Sent Off: **Beckham (second yellow)**
Man of the Match: **Lampard**

OCTOBER 12, 2005
England 2 Poland 1
(Old Trafford; Att: 65,467)

Lampard sent England to the finals at the top of Group Six when he struck a superb volley ten minutes from time to give a vastly-improved, Rooney-inspired England the victory they deserved. "We've answered a few questions," said the Chelsea midfielder. "We wanted to play with a lot of pace and we did."

Owen opened the scoring to equal Lineker's England record of 22 competitive goals, changing the entire mood surrounding Eriksson and his team with an instinctive flick.

Ledley King proved that England are a better side when playing with a holding midfielder, the Spurs captain bringing the anchor that gave Lampard the freedom to roam forward which brought his deserved late winner. Like King, replacing the injured Gerrard, Wright-Phillips stepped into the absent Beckham's boots. At the heart of everything, Rooney dazzled.

Crouch came on for Wright-Phillips – his arrival met by a chorus of jeers which were followed by guilty applause soon afterwards as the giant striker collected the ball in his own six-yard box, played it out intelligently and when the ball reached the other end of the pitch Lampard thundered a volley home to win the game. Crouch's rehabilitation in England fans' eyes had begun.

Eriksson urged the supporters who barracked Crouch to lay off the 6ft 7in striker, "I understand the crowd as he [Shaun Wright-Phillips] gave flair and beat people, but I think it was the right decision as Shaun got a bad knock. I'm sorry if anyone thinks Peter Crouch is a not a good footballer. He had played just one and a half internationals before this game. He has something which other players don't and he's good on the floor as well. It is very harsh to judge him yet."

England: Robinson, Young, Ferdinand, Terry, Carragher, Wright-Phillips (Crouch 67), King, Lampard, Cole (Smith 87), Rooney, Owen (Jenas 84)
Subs Not Used: **P Neville, Kirkland, D Bent, Defoe**
Goals: **Owen (44) 1-0, Frankowski (45) 1-1, Lampard (81) 2-1**
Man of the Match: **Rooney**

Throughout qualifying Eriksson was criticised for lacking the courage to axe his leading players, even when they had clearly lost form. He shouldered the blame for the low-key performances that threatened England's qualification, "There's not just one reason we struggled, but probably two or three. One was my fault because I insisted on playing important players even if they weren't in 100 per cent form. And it wasn't just one player – there were maybe three or four." Although not naming them, he was referring to the cornerstones of

his England side: David Beckham, Rio Ferdinand, Frank Lampard and Steven Gerrard.

Eriksson dropped just one of those players in the run-in to qualification – Ferdinand. But he insisted there was more logic than blind loyalty behind his policy, "I did it because I believe in this squad and I believe they will play in the World Cup. I knew they could play much, much better – and they have. I had to think long and hard about the situation, more so because it was at the start of this season. As a team we hadn't warmed up for the new season, we hadn't found our rhythm or our match sharpness. And during the summer I think we lost a little bit of our spirit to work together, run for each other. Even if some of them – very, very important players – are not in form, I think I should persist with them if they are not injured. We can discuss if that is right or not until we die – but every time you take out important players they lose confidence. And to get players in form – important players – you have to play them. For the last World Cup we had, say, two, three or four key players. Now we have ten and that's why I'm always telling you that

we are going to have a very good World Cup – even though I can't guarantee you we'll win. I will never win over all my critics. You can say what you like, but this is the best squad and the best team we have ever had."

England's Warm-Up Friendlies

NOVEMBER 12, 2005
Argentina 2 England 3
(Geneva; Att: 29,000)

Michael Owen scored twice in the final three minutes to make a statement of intent ahead of Germany. Eriksson had sent on much-maligned striker Peter Crouch and the Liverpool star's aerial presence terrified the Argentineans. Owen said, "Even when Argentina scored the supporters stuck behind us, the atmosphere was great. Before the game we thought we could win it and when you lose a goal then it is a setback. But the important thing was that we showed we have got the character to come back from something like that. It could have gone either way today and that just shows there is not too much difference between the top teams in the world."

Frank Lampard lashes in a dazzling volley against Poland to win the qualifying group for England

"You can say what you like, but this is the best squad and the best team we have ever had."
Sven-Göran Eriksson

There were post-match allegations, later refuted by Hernan Crespo, that the Argentinean players arrived by coach singing songs that branded the England players 'whores' and 'poofs'. But Beckham remarked, "We don't mind them singing before the game as long as they're not singing after it. We'll take that every time we come up against them."

Argentina's behaviour was condemned by the United Nations, who had organised the match in Switzerland to promote sportsmanship. England refused to rise to the bait, as Beckham said, "The same sort of thing happened on their coach after they beat us at the 1998 World Cup. But whatever happens outside the game doesn't really interest our players. We're just going to enjoy this performance and result. We have shown the togetherness you need to be a big team and I hope we've sent a message to the rest of the world that this England team never knows when it is beaten."

Wayne Rooney, who tormented the Argentina defence throughout, scored England's opener to level the scores after Crespo had put Argentina ahead. Argentina went in front again in the second half through Walter Samuel's header, but there was no stopping Owen at the end after Crouch came on to distract the Argentine defence.

Both Gary Neville and Ashley Cole were missed. Most of the danger came down England's left-hand side. Hardly surprising as left-back Wayne Bridge had barely kicked a ball in eight months. Sure enough, Rodriguez breezed past the Chelsea defender and sent over a cross that brushed Rio Ferdinand's leg before providing Crespo with a tap-in. Eriksson realised the folly of his selection and sent on Paul Konchesky for the second half.

Ledley King was another not entirely at ease. Having looked imperious against Poland, he was made to look the squarest of pegs by the outstanding Riquelme. King gave away the free-kick that led to Argentina restoring their lead and Eriksson had to re-think King as the No1 holding player, leading

to his club colleague Michael Carrick coming seriously into the equation.

One interesting aspect of the game was the versatility of Steven Gerrard, who started in left midfield, then briefly moved into a central role with Lampard when King made way for Joe Cole. He ended up at right-back when Young came off from there supplied the pinpoint cross for Owen to head the first of his last-gasp goals. Gerrard said: "It was a great victory. We had belief we could beat them and it was a great game to play in. On this evidence, we can mix it with anyone."

But midfield colleague Frank Lampard had his sights set on the World Champions, "If you look at the players in our squad we believe we can compete against the best, and Argentina are definitely one of those sides. But Brazil are the ultimate benchmark."

Michael Owen celebrates his winning goal against Argentina while keeper Roberto Abbondanzieri cannot believe the turnaround in the last three minutes

England: Robinson; Young (Crouch 81), Ferdinand, Terry, Bridge (Konchesky 45); King (J Cole 59), Beckham, Lampard, Gerrard; Owen, Rooney
Subs not used: James, Campbell, Wright-Phillips, Defoe, Carrick
Goals: Crespo (35) 1-0, Rooney (39) 1-1, Samuel (54) 2-1; Owen (87) 2-2; Owen (90) 2-3
Booked: Young, Lampard, J Cole
Man of the Match: Rooney

DID YOU KNOW?
The dazzling victory over Argentina inspired a betting bonanza on England winning in Germany. Fans bet more than £500m on an England victory, making Eriksson's team joint third favourites.

MARCH 1, 2006
England 2 Uruguay 1
(Anfield; Att: 40,013)

Peter Crouch and Joe Cole scored the goals as England came from behind once again to record a victory that had the Kop chanting "Easy, easy". Yet, it had been hard until Crouch came off the bench. With 15 minutes remaining, Crouch equalised Omar Pouso's stunning opener to spare England's blushes.

England returned to basics, good wing-play picking out a target man. Cole's skill took him past Diego Lugano on the left, opening up a crossing opportunity with his favoured right foot. The ball dropped into the box where Crouch headed home. Then Cole, the man of the match, latched on to a cross from Shaun Wright-Phillips to make it a late turnaround.

Starved of decent service, Charlton striker Darren Bent endured a frustrating, lonely night. Wayne Bridge provided much concern after being caught accidentally by the sliding Paul Robinson as they both tried to stop the marauding Gonazalo Vargas. He was carried off, but a scan revealed only sprained ligaments to Bridge's right ankle. Bridge, newly arrived at Craven Cottage on loan from Chelsea, had been trying to rebuild his career after a left ankle break. With Ashley Cole lasting only four minutes of a reserve outing for Arsenal on Monday, England's left-back options looked sparse. Jamie Carragher, the Kop's darling, ran on to replace the stricken Bridge and immediately showed his versatility.

Only John Terry of Eriksson's first-choice defenders impressed. Rio Ferdinand's concentration was awry once again, the centre-back gifting possession to Diego Forlan, ex-United. At least Ferdinand recovered well to block Forlan's shot.

Gary Neville was greeted with a flurry of boos from the Scouse sections of England's support, following his recent taunting of Liverpool fans, but these cat-calls were swiftly drowned out. The Kop even chorused "One Gary Neville", probably a first.

England: Robinson; G Neville, Ferdinand, Terry (King 45), Bridge (Carragher 31); Beckham (Wright-Phillips 63), Gerrard (Jenas 45), Carrick, J Cole; Rooney (Crouch 63), D Bent (Defoe 82)
Subs not used: Young, James, Brown, Richardson, Green
Goals: Pouso (26) 0-1, Crouch (75) 1-1, J Cole (90) 2-1
Booked: Beckham, Carragher

> **DID YOU KNOW?**
> *Against Uruguay Peter Crouch wore No.12 on his back and No.21 on his front.*

MAY 25, 2006
England B 1 Belarus 2
(Madejski Stadium; Att: 22,032)

Theo Walcott's much-anticipated England bow came as a replacement

Theo Walcott lashes in a stinging half volley gainst Belarus. He won his first full cap and became England's youngest ever footballer five days later against Hungary

for Owen at the Madejski Stadium and ensured Eriksson could see, for the first time in match action, his searing pace. Eriksson felt more than satisfied, "He showed that the pace he has is incredible. Two of the Belarus players had to play rugby to stop him.'" Eriksson was relieved to see several of his senior stars coming through this B international, but also was thrilled by the kids. The 2-1 defeat was immaterial. He said: "Michael Owen has completed a good hour and seems fine. He looked very fit and is feeling no reaction to his injury. Ashley Cole needed to play a full 90 minutes and has done that. The same goes for Sol Campbell and Jamie Carragher while Peter Crouch did a good show out there. It's always disappointing to lose, but tonight the result is not that important. What matters is winning against Paraguay next month."

Aaron Lennon also showed his pace on the right wing, and caused Belarus left-back Sergei Omelyanchuk to foul him persistently finally earning two yellow cards in the space of a minute with just over quarter of an hour remaining. But the bad news was that third choice goalkeeper Robert Green suffered a bad groin injury just four minutes after replacing David James at half-time and was out of the World Cup, being relaced by Liverpool's fourth choice goalkeeper Scott Carson, pointing to England's woeful lack of depth in the goalkeeping department. Manchester United keeper Ben Foster flew back from his holiday in Dubai to join the England squad following the injury to Green.

England: James (Green 45 (Carson 49)); Hargreaves, Campbell, Carragher, A Cole; Lennon, Jenas (J Cole 62), Carrick, Downing (Dawson 79); Owen (Walcott 62), Crouch (Defoe 79)
Subs Not Used: P Neville, Bridge, Johnson
Goals: Jenas (34) 1-0, Kutuzov (49) 1-1, Kornilenko (82) 1-2
Man of the Match: Aaron Lennon

MAY 30, 2006
England 3 Hungary 1
(Old Trafford; Att: 56,323)

Peter Crouch sparked a craze for robotic dancing with his celebration after scoring England's third goal against Hungary

Michael Owen looked tentative in the 3-1 win over Hungary, but Eriksson was pleased overall with England's performance, which underlined Beckham's value. Beckham created goals for Gerrard and Terry and caused numerous problems with his pinpoint crosses. Eriksson said: "What can I say about David Beckham – I have never ever understood the critics about him. The assists he has you cannot find anywhere in all the world. He is not a dribbler like many other players but he doesn't need to dribble, he just strokes the ball in and there it comes."

Eriksson was satisfied with his experiment of playing Carragher in the holding role in midfield for the first half, though the Liverpool player had to switch to right-back in the second after Gary Neville suffered a minor hamstring pull. The formation allowed Gerrard freedom to devote his energies to attack and he responded with a dynamic display.

Substitute Crouch scored England's third after Hungary skipper Pal Dardai had given the visitors hope with a brilliant strike, and Theo Walcott also came off the bench to become England's youngest-ever player at 17 years 75 days. Eriksson added: 'He [Walcott] gets confidence every time he trains with us and plays with us. I think in the World Cup we will see him, not from the beginning maybe, but maybe coming off the bench. And with the pace he showed once again, I think he will be very useful.'

The game was most significant for two goal celebrations. Terry's goal was his first for England and his 'baby-cradling' celebrations – in the style made famous by Bebeto in the 1994 World Cup – marked the birth of his twins a fortnight earlier. Crouch's clinical piece of finishing after collecting a pass from Joe Cole left the nation obsessed with his dance-routine goal celebration, a copy of his robotic disco dancing at the Beckhams' televised party. Crouch's joy at scoring was in stark contrast to the boos that greeted his introduction as a substitute against Poland in the qualifier on the same ground in October. His rehabilitation was complete and he was now England's cult hero. It was cool to like Crouch.

Lampard had previously proved reliable from the spot, but his first-half spot-kick was saved by a diving Gabor Kiraly. Lampard put in the work in a bid to make sure he does not miss again, "When you take penalties you take them with the idea you might miss one one day – it comes with the territory."

England: **Robinson; G Neville (Hargreaves 45), Ferdinand, Terry (Campbell 76), A Cole; Beckham, Carragher, Lampard, J Cole; Gerrard (Crouch 65); Owen (Walcott 65)**
Goals: **Gerrard (47) 1-0, Terry (51) 1-1, Dardai (55) 2-1, Crouch (84) 3-1**
Booked: **Campbell, Beckham**
Man of the Match: David Beckham

JUNE 3, 2006
England 6 Jamaica 0
(Old Trafford; Att: 70,373)

Beckham recommended Eriksson went out on the Old Trafford pitch and milk the applause after his final game as manager on English soil. Eriksson was planning a quiet exit after the 6-0 thumping of Jamaica, but instead strolled to the centre of the pitch with his arms uncharacteristically aloft to huge applause, "It was a very good farewell for me. I enjoyed it very much. I didn't expect it."

Eriksson was encouraged by the improvement in Owen, who netted for the first time in any game of senior football since 17 December 2005. It was his 36th goal for his country as he completed his first 90 minutes of the year following a lengthy injury absence. Crouch scored a hat-trick, but was reprimanded by Eriksson for his 'joke' penalty miss.

Lampard began the goal bonanza, Jamaica's Jermaine Taylor headed into his own net and fellow defender Omar Daley was no luckier when a Crouch shot struck him and flew in the net, although the Liverpool striker claimed the goal. Owen raced through to score his first goal of the year 2006 before Crouch claimed his second of a sunlit day with a tap-in. He spurned his chance of a hat-trick by hopelessly skying an 82nd minute penalty won by Owen, only to rifle in England's sixth in the dying minutes after a neat Owen pass. The classy finish from the edge of the area made for a perfect send-off for England.

Eriksson's last home game as England manager rewarded him with the best winning margin of his five and a half years at the helm. He was forced to make two precautionary changes to his defence before the break, taking Terry off for Campbell and replacing Ashley Cole with Bridge on the left.

Crouch tried to chip his penalty, embarrassingly putting it over the bar. "My criticism of Crouch is how he took the penalty," said Eriksson. "It was a golden opportunity to practice penalty shootouts and he joked about it. He was sorry afterwards – he apologised, and I think he knew before I started to talk that I was unhappy with him. He can miss penalties, but not taking them that way. Apart from the penalty he was fantastic and it will be difficult not to start him against Paraguay – how can I leave him out after a hat-trick and that performance?"

England: Robinson (James 45); Carragher, Ferdinand, Terry (Campbell 33), A.Cole (Bridge 35); Beckham (Lennon 68), Gerrard (Downing 78), Lampard (Carrick 68), J Cole; Owen, Crouch
Goals: **Lampard (11) 1-0, Taylor (og) (17) 2-0, Crouch (29) 3-0, Owen (32) 4-0, Crouch (66) 5-0, Crouch (89) 6-0**
Man of the Match: **Peter Crouch**

Preparations were complete. Injuries to the likes of West Ham's Nigel Reo-Coker and Charlton's Luke Young meant changes to the standby list with Everton's Phil Neville and Spurs' Michael Dawson recalled, but barring disaster in the training camp they would not be needed.

The Saga Of The Foot

In fact the only story that the nation remotely cared about in the lead up to the tournament was Rooney's foot.

In an early training session at their Buhlerhohe Schlosshotel base near Baden Baden, Rooney was caught on camera in training performing a scissor kick, which stunned even the England coaching staff. He was clearly out to impress everyone that he was ready for the fray.

Wayne Rooney was all smiles when he returned to England's base camp with the good news that he was fit to play a part in the World Cup

The drama came to a head when Rooney flew back to Manchester for the fateful final scan on June 7th.

The nation collectively held it's breath, which was finally allowed out when news emerged thhat Rooney would be returning to Germany to take his place in the squa.

The fuming Sir Alex Ferguson had been put in his place by a combination of Eriksson's insistence that Rooney would be fit and the Boy Wonder himself being so desperate to play.

The country spared little thought for the plight of Jermain Defoe whilst celebrating Rooney's return to fitness, but it seemed to most impartial observers that it was just as big a gamble to send the Spurs striker home as it was to keep Rooney. Would Eriksson's gamble prove England's undoing?

All Change Please

> "The FA can confirm that Sven-Göran Eriksson will leave his post as England head coach after the World Cup in Germany."
> www.thefa.com

Sven-Göran Eriksson leaves Soho Square after announcing that he will vacate the post of England manager after the 2006 World Cup in Germany

The announcement on Monday 23rd January 2006 that Sven-Göran Eriksson would step down after the World Cup finals in Germany, two years before his contract was due to expire, followed a momentous day of intense negotiation between the Swede and FA chief executive Brian Barwick. It followed successive weekends of damaging revelations in the News of the World, who duped Eriksson and his advisers into believing an undercover reporter was a rich Arab sheik who wanted to give the Swede a new job, eliciting numerous misguarded slips of the tongue from him.

A statement on www.thefa.com said: "The FA can confirm that Sven-Göran Eriksson will leave his post as England head coach after the World Cup in Germany." Barwick said: "This is for the benefit of everyone connected with English football, especially the fans. There has been so much speculation surrounding this matter in recent weeks and months, it was important to resolve it now. This is the right outcome and I would like to thank Sven and his advisors for their tremendous co-operation. As I have said before, our main objective is giving Sven and the England team the best chance of achieving success at the World Cup." A compensation deal was hammered out with the Swede being paid off with a third of the £9m he would have earned from two years' salary.

> "If our rivals think that Sven leaving will unsettle our squad, or blunt our desire and commitment to win, they can think again."
>
> John Terry

Brian Barwick, the FA's Chief Executive, lead the shambolic hunt for England's new head coach

> The FA's hunt for Eriksson's replacement began to descend into farce

The process of finding a successor began immediately and Barwick announced that a man would be in place before the tournament, so he could assess the team during the finals for the forthcoming Euro 2008 qualifiers. Howard Wilkinson, the former FA technical director, who as England caretaker-manager was Eriksson's immediate predecessor, laid down the first gauntlet to the FA saying, "My point of view as chairman of the League Managers' Association is we would hope that English contenders for the position have got more than a head start."

Those contenders were soon lined up as Bolton Wanderers manager Sam Allardyce, Charlton boss Alan Curbishley, Manchester City's Stuart Pearce, who continually suggested that such speculation was ridiculous considering he had only been in that job about a year, and Middlesbrough manager and Sven's number two in the national set up, Steve McClaren.

But then there were the non-Englishmen, the out-of-work Martin O'Neill and PSV Eindhoven and Australia coach Guus Hiddink, who had performed miracles in guiding South Korea to the 2002 World Cup

semi-finals. Three Englishmen and two 'foreigners', although it soon became clear that the five-man selection committee, set up by Barwick, had different ideas about the criteria for the new boss to the likes of Wilkinson. Suddenly 'English' became 'British' and O'Neill, a Northern Irishman, was included. Then it was understood that the FA were hunting for 'the best man for the job' and Hiddink came firmly into the frame. But Hiddink let it be known through his agent that he would not countenance going through an interview and shortlist process as the FA desired. He believed his CV gave him credence to be appointed directly. The FA prevaricated and instead Hiddink announced his decision to join the Russian FA straight after the World Cup.

As well as the hunt for Eriksson's successor, the other major issue was how the Swede's departure would affect the England team's chances in Germany. Former England defender Terry Butcher insisted they would not be affected as the situation mirrored the experiences of Sir Bobby Robson and Terry Venables, who led England to the semi-finals of the 1990 World Cup and Euro 96 respectively, in the

knowledge they would not be in the job following the tournament. Butcher said precipitously, "All these people getting carried away with the fact that it will harm our chances – absolute tosh. The only thing that will harm our chances is if Wayne Rooney gets injured." Instead the Motherwell boss believed the news of Eriksson's departure could in fact unite the squad as it did in his experience ahead of Italia 90. "It made everybody stick together. It really had us focussed as we wanted to do well for the gaffer in his last tournament. There were a lot of players there who were playing in their last World Cup. In this squad there is only really probably Sol Campbell, Gary Neville and David Beckham that could be playing in their last World Cup. The others have still got plenty of tournaments to go for after this, but they will want to make it a special one for Sven-Göran Eriksson. I think it can only have a positive effect."

John Terry was determined England's World Cup bid would not be disrupted, "If our rivals think that Sven leaving will unsettle our squad, or blunt our desire and commitment to win, they can think again. We are

Sven had suffered years of being hounded by the English press and Scolari cited this as one of the major reasons why he was becoming the first man in over 40 years to turn down the England job

all in it together. Sven is the manager and will be until the tournament is over, so nothing has changed as far as the World Cup is concerned in my eyes. He picks the team, but once you cross the touchline it's the players who carry the hopes of the whole country. It's up to us. We understand and accept that. We play for the fans and the dream to see England crowned world champions for the second time.'

Eriksson himself was looking forward to the relief provided by the light at the end of his tunnel: "Now there's been an agreement we have to look at the World Cup and concentrate on that. At the moment this is the most important thing because we have a chance to win it. Let us not spoil that."

But the FA's hunt for Eriksson's replacement began to descend into farce as two rounds of interviews did not result in any unanimity amongst the selection committee. At this juncture Arsenal Vice-Chairman David Dein stepped in, not necessarily to ensure that his own manager Arsène Wenger was not headhunted as has been widely assumed, but to steer the committee

towards another foreign manager and sidestep the media who were focussed on those big five players, McClaren, Curbishley, Pearce, Allardyce and O'Neill, in the race to become England boss.

Meanwhile David Beckham believed Eriksson was the "obvious choice" to take over at Real following coach Wanderlei Luxemburgo's dismissal. The Swede was 2/1 favourite to get the job, according to Ladbrokes, and if Eriksson wanted a character reference, he need look no further than Beckham to provide one. "Sven is one of the best managers around and his name was bound to come into the equation. I think he would work well."

But when Real President Martin revealed his own personal wish list, Eriksson was not among the names on it: Jose Mourinho, Arsene Wenger, Rafael Benitez, Fabio Capello, Carlos Ancelotti and Marcelo Lippi were those put forward as possible candidates by Martin.

A measure of the special bond between captain and coach came when Beckham became one of the first people that Eriksson told that he would be leaving the post after the

World Cup. "I felt I had to speak to my captain," said the Swede, who said Beckham had said "I'm sorry" in reply.

Beckham added, "I think Sven is a great manager. The togetherness he brings to the team and the confidence he gives the players is a great attribute. It's important that we concentrate on winning something because for three seasons we haven't and for a big club like Real Madrid you need to be winning trophies."

And it was to a man who had won plenty of trophies that the FA selection committee had indeed turned their thoughts. Portugal coach Luis Felipe 'Big Phil' Scolari had won the previous World Cup in Japan and Korea as manager of Brazil, and taken Portugal to the final of Euro 2004, on both occasions defeating England at the quarter-final stage. Undoubtedly Scolari had superb credentials for the job.

But he wasn't English.

The clamour for a native had been going on for years during Eriksson's reign, led by journalists such as the Daily Mail's Jeff Powell. Appointing Scolari was never going to appease these Little Englanders. And when I revealed the story of the FA's determination to appoint Scolari in the Express, having learned it from an impeccable source, the furore it created was astonishing.

Big Mac, Not Big Phil

Steve McClaren viewed himself as a potential England manager from the moment he began working as Eriksson's assistant five years ago. At the time he had yet to branch out as a Premiership manager. "As soon as I started working with England, this job was one of the possibilities I thought of for the future, otherwise what was the point of working with England? I enjoy working with [England] players. It's like a club when you join up – the spirit and the camaraderie is fantastic."

But was McClaren the right man for the job? Not according to his long-serving former England defender Gareth Southgate. Southgate claimed in The Sunday Times that the Boro dressing room deserved as much credit

as McClaren for the improvement in Middlesbrough's form since the 4-0 home defeat by Aston Villa on 4 February, which saw one Boro supporter race onto the pitch throw his season ticket into McClaren's face. His criticism was contained in a general statement about all the four English contenders for the post, who he considered too inexperienced. "If you had them four years on you would have the ideal scenario," he said. "They would all have had much more experience and would probably have worked at bigger clubs." His remarks seemed to have scuppered McClaren's chances. A senior player rubbishing his own manager's credentials always has an impact.

But did the FA view McClaren as an England manager in waiting anyway? It seemed not, as when the five-man FA selection panel had first met, McClaren did not receive a single vote to be nominated as Sven-Göran Eriksson's successor. Instead, the vote went to Big Phil Scolari, who then, infamously, became the first manager

> "If they want an answer now then it has to be "No". It is over."
> 'Big Phil' Scolari

in modern times to directly turn down the chance to become England boss when offered the job. Back in 1962 Jimmy Adamson, then current Footballer of the Year and number two to England coach Walter Winterbottom at the 1962 World Cup, turned down the England job when approached, and Ipswich manager Alf Ramsey was actually the FA's second choice. No-one since has ever said "No" when formally offered the England post.

Mind you some great managers have never been asked, Brian Clough and Jack Charlton among those considered too risky, too much of a loose cannon. Yet, in this latest farce the FA went for the loosest cannon of them all – Scolari.

The Brazilian had been offered £2.5million a year, but shocked the FA with his very public U-turn, blaming media intrusion for pulling out. "I don't want anything more to do with this England matter because in the space of two days my life was invaded, my privacy was disrupted," Scolari said. "This is not part of my life and it never will be. I am not the coach and will not be coach." There

'Big Phil' Scolari announces to the world that he is rejecting the FA's advances

Steve McClaren, the new England manager, arrives for his first press conference carrying a folder marked 'Euro 2008 fixtures'

> **"This is the biggest honour that any coach can have and is obviously the highlight of my career."**
> Steve McClaren

was also speculation that he had become the victim of death threats from Portugal fans angry at his apparent defection prior to the World Cup Finals.

Possibly to ensure that problem was knocked directly on the head, Scolari revealed the FA wanted an immediate commitment, but he insisted he would not be able to give them an answer until his contract with Portugal finished on July 31. Scolari said: "They keep pushing me for an answer, to say yes or no. But if they want an answer now then it has to be "No". I am fully committed to Portugal and that is where my loyalties must remain until July 31 and I will not think or talk about anything else until after then. That, it seems, is not good enough for the FA, so it is over."

It was back to the drawing board for the FA selection panel, although it didn't take much to plump for a compromise candidate. The one thing which had united the members of the committee was that each one of them

had made Steve McClaren their second choice. So when the Brazilian turned the job down, McClaren was the only serious alternative – and he had the added attraction of actually wanting the job. When Barwick called to offer him the post, the Boro manager was left to contend with the realisation that he had secured the job by default. Yet there were also positives. His appointment offered continuity, given that he has worked with the players as a member of Eriksson's coaching staff over the past five years. The Swede insisted there would be "no problem at all" with McClaren working with the national squad at this summer's World Cup finals, something which had concerned him as he had publicly called for the new man "not to interfere" during the finals. "I have always said Steve's an extremely good coach and he has always done an extremely good job for us," said Eriksson. "When I took this job I told them I don't want to have people around me just saying 'yes'. I want opinions so we can discuss, and he has an opinion."

The LMA were naturally delighted. "We are not xenophobic," said John Barnwell, the chief executive of the League Managers' Association, "but this augurs well for the future. Another foreign manager would have been damaging. I was talking to Gordon Taylor and he told me about a top, top player who has just finished playing and this player was saying: "What's the point of me taking my A-licence and trying to get a top job if we have more years under a foreign coach?" This appointment by the FA will give a lot of credibility back to English coaching. I'm not concerned about those who say that foreign coaches have improved our perform-ance in other sports like cricket, or rugby, because not many countries play those sports, but football is global. International football is your country pitting your best against the best of another country, and that includes coaches and managers. If they are not good enough, prepare them better."

Gareth Southgate made a qualified U-turn, "I think good managers listen to the opinion of senior players and the coaching staff around them," he said when discussing McClaren's quali-ties. But he denied making specific criticisms of the manager as not being "ready" for England. "Steve has been the person with the best experience and CV in terms of English coaches. Now the appointment has been made, when he takes over in August it is for everybody to get behind him, and hopefully he'll make a success of it. We have all given opinions before the appointment, voiced our feelings, but now he's been given it I firmly believe that he has to be given the chance to do the job. I'm a very proud Englishman and I want him to do well. I was speaking about all of the candidates at the time and I was saying that in an ideal scenario, four years down the line, everyone would be looking at

"Let's go and win the World Cup"
Sven-Göran Eriksson

Steve McClaren smiles for the cameras after being appointed as Erkisson's successor

STEVE McCLAREN

BORN

3 May 1961, York

PLAYING CAREER

Hull City, Derby County, Lincoln City, Bristol City, Oxford United

305 games, 18 goals

MANAGERIAL/COACHING CAREER

Domestic

1992-95 Oxford United
(youth, reserve team coach)

1999-2001 Manchester United
(assistant manager)

1995-99 Derby County
(first-team coach)

2001-2006 Middlesbrough
(manager)

Middlesbrough record
P 248   W 97   D 60   L 91

Honours

League Cup 2004

International

2000-present England (coach)

4 May 2006 announced as new England Head Coach from 1 August

them all in a different light. The fact is the job is available now, not in four years, and they have to give it to the best person."

But there had been a spanner in the works prior to McClaren's appointment. Publicist Max Clifford had been advising McClaren and his agent Colin Gordon on how to handle a story which he feared would undermine his candidacy. The outcome was a stage-managed kiss and tell in that Saturday's Sun newspaper, in which McClaren admitted to an affair while separated from his wife. Having seen at first hand the way in which the tabloids delved ruthlessly and relentlessly into Eriksson's private life, McClaren has received media training on how to deal with difficult questions. His teeth have become straighter and, with them, his smile whiter. Said Clifford, "After the Prime Minister it's probably the most media-scrutinised job in Britain. I like the man, he's got a wider view and realises that there's more to the media than the sports media. He's gone on to a bigger stage now and personal PR is all about stage management."

So McClaren had a clean bill of health, the astonishing progress of Middlesbrough to the UEFA Cup Final and the support of the entire selection committee – well, of sorts. He was also clearly the best candidate of those available to the FA. If only their bungling had not seen two of the best football managers in the world head for the hills.

McClaren was finally appointed and unveiled at Soho Square a week after Scolari had sensationally pulled out of the job. "This is the biggest honour that any coach can have and is obviously the highlight of my career," said McClaren, who signed a four-year contract from 1st August, taking him up to the 2010 World Cup in South Africa. "It's a massive challenge and one that I welcome. I have hugely enjoyed my time at Middlesbrough and am very grateful to the club. However, this was an opportunity I couldn't refuse."

The Man No-One Wanted?

So is it applicable to dub McClaren the first England manager in history to be – "The Man No One Wanted?" Let's examine the evidence.

Firstly, he does not carry the 'People's Choice' tag that Clough would have achieved decisively. All opinion polls suggest that the general public will not be inspired by the Boro boss.

Next, the media. In a radio poll, England reporters voted Martin O'Neill by far the media darling, and not one voted for McClaren.

Most tellingly, inside the FA's elite Selection Group, chief executive Brian Barwick voted for O'Neill, Arsenal vice-chairman David Dein hailed the CV of Scolari as by far the most compelling candidate, Dave Richards, the Premier League chairman, campaigned for Sam Allardyce, Noel White simply wanted an Englishman, and consultant Sir Trevor Brooking was the lone voice speaking up for Alan Curbishley.

If McClaren goes on to win the World Cup, in similar fashion to Ramsey, then no-one is going to look back and reflect on a flawed and farcical selection process that ended up with a new England coach delivered by a consensus that the Boro boss was the least offensive choice.

And the England players themselves probably breathed a sigh of relief when McClaren was appointed as he was already well known to them and was far less likely to upset the applecart than a fresh manager. After all, wouldn't David Beckham have more chance of staying on as England captain under McClaren than Scolari? Of course he would.

So the England players' committee endorsed the appointment of McClaren, even though some on the Selection group were adamant that Beckham and the boys should not be consulted.

The FA received a lot of criticism over the way the selection process was handled, with so many individuals having an input, but Barwick said the set-up of the organisation meant it

Eriksson was determined that the shenanigans over the search for his replacement would not interfere with his preparation for the World Cup

was inevitable, "We are the FA and we have to take people with us. I enjoyed having some experience around it. It always looks complicated from the outside, but it is less complicated and convoluted from the inside. People are able to be appointed in discreet ways, but we accept, as the Football Association, it is difficult for people to keep secrets."

The outgoing manager was relieved to be out of the firing line for once. Eriksson believed the timing of the appointment of his successor would have no particular impact on the side's World Cup chances as he vowed to go out on a high, "I know that I have the full support of the players and the FA and it is important to stress to everyone just how committed I am to achieving success this summer. I care passionately about this job and I want everyone to know that. I have always enjoyed the incredible support of the fans and I know how important they will be to us in Germany. This summer is the culmination of everything we have been working towards over the last five years. Let's go and win the World Cup."

section two

preliminaries

World Cup Qualifying

The major surprises came in Africa where Nigeria, Cameroon, South Africa and Egypt, who would later win the African Cup of Nations all failed to qualify; Cameroon for the first time since 1986. The man who missed the vital penalty in the Indomitable Lions' final game against Egypt, Pierre Wome, lived in fear of his life after fans invaded the pitch seeking blood and later besieged his family home. Senegal, conquerors of Champions France in the opening match of the 2002 tournament, also missed out.

In South America Colombia and Chile failed to qualify and resurgent Ecuador and Paraguay joined Brazil and Argentina in the draw, with twice winners Uruguay only making a play-off with Australia after finishing fifth.

In the North America zone, the usual suspects, USA and Mexico qualified easily, but it was Trinidad and Tobago who took all the headlines after securing their first ever finals appearance thanks to Wrexham defender Dennis Lawrence's header in Bahrain won them a play-off. Much like Jamaica in 1998, Trinidad's team had a distinctly British feel with the likes of former Manchester United legend Dwight Yorke, West Ham's Shaka Hislop, Coventry's Stern John and Port Vale's Chris Birchall also in their squad.

Pierre Wome was the architect of Cameroon's first failure to qualify for a World Cup finals since 1986, missing the vital penalty against Egypt which saw his side finish one point behind Ivory Coast

Australia bade farewell to the Oceania zone by only dropping one point in their all too easy qualification – a 2-2 draw in the Solomon Islands. The Socceroos should have more competition now they have graduated to the Asian Zone from the 2008 World Cup qualifying tournament. They eventually earned their first World Cup finals place since the last German hosted tournament in 1974 by defeating Uruguay in a two-legged play-off.

In Europe, several big countries left it late before sealing their place in Germany, while other hit rocky patches that cost them dearly. The European Champions Greece failed to qualify after making a dismal start to their campaign whilst suffering from a hangover after winning Euro 2004. Denmark also failed to qualify thanks to a poor start, although they nearly snatched a play-off place after a barnstorming finish to their campaign. Belgium, Bulgaria, Russia and Romania were perhaps other surprise casualties.

Aside from England's blip in Belfast, France only won two of their five home matches in a group where draws dominated. It wasn't until a Thierry Henry inspired win in Dublin that their place in Germany was assured, and Ireland were condemned to spend the summer watching on TV, along with the rest of the home nations, all of whom had campaigns to forget – save that September night at Windsor Park.

The play-offs saw straightforward wins for Spain and the Czechs, but the tie between Switzerland and Turkey was far from straightforward. A first minute penalty award to the Swiss did not bring referee Mr De Bleeckere too many admirers amongst the partisan crowd and by the time the pulsating game had finished six goals, eight yellow cards and several further penalty decisions later, with Switzerland holding on to win through to Germany on away goals, all sorts of objects rained down on the departing players sparking fisticuffs. Punches and kicks were exchanged amid the uproar, with several injuries the result.

The upshot of the carnage was a FIFA decree that Turkey should play their next six internationals behind closed doors and that three players plus one of their coaching staff should be suspended for stringent periods. On the Swiss side, two players, Huggel and Meyer, would miss matches. Huggel, importantly, was banned for six games, meaning he could not be selected for the World Cup.

CAF (Africa) Tables

First placed country in each group qualifies

GROUP 1 TABLE

		Overall					Home					Away						
	P	W	D	L	F	A	W	D	L	F	A	W	D	L	F	A	GD	Pts
1 Togo	10	7	2	1	20	8	5	0	0	13	2	2	2	1	7	6	12	23
2 Senegal	10	6	3	1	21	8	4	1	0	14	3	2	2	1	7	5	13	21
3 Zambia	10	6	1	3	16	10	4	0	1	6	2	2	1	2	10	8	6	19
4 Congo	10	3	1	6	10	14	2	1	2	8	6	1	0	4	2	8	-4	10
5 Mali	10	2	2	6	11	14	2	2	1	10	6	0	0	5	1	8	-3	8
6 Liberia	10	1	1	8	3	27	1	1	3	1	10	0	0	5	2	17	-24	4

GROUP 2 TABLE

		Overall					Home					Away						
	P	W	D	L	F	A	W	D	L	F	A	W	D	L	F	A	GD	Pts
1 Ghana	10	6	3	1	17	4	4	1	0	9	1	2	2	1	8	3	13	21
2 Congo DR	10	4	4	2	14	10	4	1	0	11	4	0	3	2	3	6	4	16
3 South Africa	10	5	1	4	12	14	3	1	1	8	6	2	0	3	4	8	-2	16
4 Burkina Faso	10	4	1	5	14	13	4	0	1	9	3	0	1	4	5	10	1	13
5 Cape Verde Isl	10	3	1	6	8	15	2	1	2	4	7	1	0	4	4	8	-7	10
6 Uganda	10	2	2	6	6	15	2	2	1	5	4	0	0	5	1	11	-9	8

GROUP 3 TABLE

		Overall					Home					Away						
	P	W	D	L	F	A	W	D	L	F	A	W	D	L	F	A	GD	Pts
1 Ivory Coast	10	7	1	2	20	7	4	0	1	14	3	3	1	1	6	4	13	22
2 Cameroon	10	6	3	1	18	10	4	1	0	8	3	2	2	1	10	7	8	21
3 Egypt	10	5	2	3	26	15	4	0	1	18	7	1	2	2	8	8	11	17
4 Libya	10	3	3	4	8	10	2	3	0	6	2	1	0	4	2	8	-2	12
5 Sudan	10	1	3	6	6	22	1	1	3	3	8	0	2	3	3	14	-16	6
6 Benin	10	1	2	7	9	23	1	2	2	6	9	0	0	5	3	14	-14	5

GROUP 4 TABLE

		Overall					Home					Away						
	P	W	D	L	F	A	W	D	L	F	A	W	D	L	F	A	GD	Pts
1 Angola	10	6	3	1	12	6	5	0	0	8	1	1	3	1	4	5	6	21
2 Nigeria	10	6	3	1	21	7	4	1	0	11	2	2	2	1	10	5	14	21
3 Zimbabwe	10	4	3	3	13	14	3	1	1	7	5	1	2	2	6	9	-1	15
4 Gabon	10	2	4	4	11	13	1	4	0	7	4	1	0	4	4	9	-2	10
5 Algeria	10	1	5	4	8	15	1	2	2	5	10	0	3	2	3	5	-7	8
6 Rwanda	10	1	2	7	6	16	1	2	2	5	6	0	0	5	1	10	-10	5

GROUP 5 TABLE

		Overall					Home					Away						
	P	W	D	L	F	A	W	D	L	F	A	W	D	L	F	A	GD	Pts
1 Tunisia	10	6	3	1	25	9	4	1	0	16	3	2	2	1	9	6	16	21
2 Morocco	10	5	5	0	17	7	4	1	0	12	3	1	4	0	5	4	10	20
3 Guinea	10	5	2	3	15	10	4	1	0	11	3	1	1	3	4	7	5	17
4 Kenya	10	3	1	6	8	17	3	1	1	6	5	0	0	5	2	12	-9	10
5 Botswana	10	3	0	7	10	18	2	0	3	6	7	1	0	4	4	11	-8	9
6 Malawi	10	1	3	6	12	26	1	3	1	8	7	0	0	5	4	19	-14	6

AFC (Asia) Tables

Top two countries in each group qualify. Third placed countries meet for right to face fourth placed team in CONCACAF to play-off to reach the finals

GROUP A TABLE

		Overall					Home					Away						
	P	W	D	L	F	A	W	D	L	F	A	W	D	L	F	A	GD	Pts
1 Saudi Arabia	6	4	2	0	10	1	3	0	0	8	0	1	2	0	2	1	9	14
2 South Korea	6	3	1	2	9	5	2	0	1	4	2	1	1	1	5	3	4	10
3 Uzbekistan	6	1	2	3	7	11	1	2	0	5	4	0	0	3	2	7	-4	5
4 Kuwait	6	1	1	4	4	13	1	1	1	2	5	0	0	3	2	8	-9	4

GROUP B TABLE

		Overall					Home					Away						
	P	W	D	L	F	A	W	D	L	F	A	W	D	L	F	A	GD	Pts
1 Japan	6	5	0	1	9	4	3	0	0	5	2	2	0	1	4	2	5	15
2 Iran	6	4	1	1	7	3	3	0	0	4	1	1	1	1	3	2	4	13
3 Bahrain	6	1	1	4	4	7	0	1	2	2	4	1	0	2	2	3	-3	4
4 Korea DPR	6	1	0	5	5	11	0	0	3	1	6	1	0	2	4	5	-6	3

AFC PLAY-OFFS

3 Sep 2005	Uzbekistan 1 v 0 Bahrain (match void due to technical error by referee)
8 Oct 2005	Uzbekistan 1 v 1 Bahrain
12 Oct 2005	Bahrain 0 v 0 Uzbekistan (Bahrain won on away goals)

CONMEBOL (South America) Table

First four countries qualify as of right and fifth placed country enters a play-off with the top placed team in Oceania

			Overall					Home					Away						
FINAL TABLE																				
		P	W	D	L	F	A	W	D	L	F	A	W	D	L	F	A	GD	Pts
1	Brazil	18	9	7	2	35	17	7	2	0	23	6	2	5	2	12	11	18	34
2	Argentina	18	10	4	4	29	17	7	2	0	19	7	3	2	4	10	10	12	34
3	Ecuador	18	8	4	6	23	19	7	2	0	17	5	1	2	6	6	14	4	28
4	Paraguay	18	8	4	6	23	23	6	2	1	15	6	2	2	5	8	17	0	28
5	Uruguay	18	6	7	5	23	28	6	1	2	15	10	0	6	3	8	18	-5	25
6	Colombia	18	6	6	6	24	16	4	3	2	18	6	2	3	4	6	10	8	24
7	Chile	18	5	7	6	18	22	3	5	1	9	6	2	2	5	9	16	-4	22
8	Venezuela	18	5	3	10	20	28	3	2	4	12	14	2	1	6	8	14	-8	18
9	Peru	18	4	6	8	20	28	3	4	2	14	11	1	2	6	6	17	-8	18
10	Bolivia	18	4	2	12	20	37	4	2	3	13	9	0	0	9	7	28	-17	14

CONCACAF (North America) Table

After two previous rounds, the top three countries qualify as of right and the fourth placed team enter play-off with play-off winner from Asia

			Overall					Home					Away						
THIRD ROUND TABLE																				
		P	W	D	L	F	A	W	D	L	F	A	W	D	L	F	A	GD	Pts
1	United States	10	7	1	2	16	6	4	1	0	8	0	3	0	2	8	6	10	22
2	Mexico	10	7	1	2	22	9	5	0	1	16	5	2	1	1	6	4	13	22
3	Costa Rica	10	5	1	4	15	14	4	0	1	11	5	1	1	3	4	9	1	16
4	Trinidad & Tobago	10	4	1	5	10	15	3	1	1	8	5	1	0	4	2	10	-5	13
5	Guatemala	10	3	2	5	16	18	3	0	1	10	5	0	2	4	6	13	-2	11
6	Panama	10	0	2	8	4	21	0	2	3	2	8	0	0	5	2	13	-17	2

FINAL PLAY-OFF

12 Nov 2005	Trinidad & Tobago 1 v 1 Bahrain
16 Nov 2005	Bahrain 0 v 1 Trinidad & Tobago (Trinidad won 2-1 on aggregate)

OFC (Oceania) Table

First placed team enters play-off with fifth placed team from South America

ROUND 2 TABLE								
	P	W	D	L	F	A	GD	Pts
1 Australia	5	4	1	0	21	3	18	13
2 Solomon Islands	5	3	1	1	9	6	3	10
3 New Zealand	5	3	0	2	17	5	12	9
4 Fiji	5	1	1	3	3	10	-7	4
5 Tahiti	5	1	1	3	2	24	-22	4
6 Vanuatu	5	1	0	4	5	9	-4	3

OFC PLAY-OFFS

12 Nov 2005	Uruguay 1 v 0 Australia
16 Nov 2005	Australia 1 v 0 Uruguay (Australia won 4–2 on penalties)

Controversial scenes in the second leg of Turkey versus Switzerland saw objects shower the Swiss players such as Marco Streller after a 4-2 defeat secured their passage to the finals on away goals and knocked out Turkey

UEFA (Europe) Tables

First place country in each group qualifies, plus two best second placed teams. Remaining six second placed teams play-off over two legs for final three places

GROUP 1 TABLE

		Overall					Home					Away						
		P	W	D	L	F	A	W	D	L	F	A	W	D	L	F	A	GD	Pts
1	Holland	12	10	2	0	27	3	5	1	0	13	1	5	1	0	14	2	24	32
2	Czech Republic	12	9	0	3	35	12	5	0	1	23	8	4	0	2	12	4	23	27
3	Romania	12	8	1	3	20	10	5	0	1	11	4	3	1	2	9	6	10	25
4	Finland	12	5	1	6	21	19	3	0	3	11	10	2	1	3	10	9	2	16
5	Macedonia	12	2	3	7	11	24	1	2	3	6	9	1	1	4	5	15	-13	9
6	Armenia	12	2	1	9	9	25	1	1	4	4	10	1	0	5	5	15	-16	7
7	Andorra	12	1	2	9	4	34	1	1	4	2	15	0	1	5	2	19	-30	5

GROUP 2 TABLE

		Overall					Home					Away						
		P	W	D	L	F	A	W	D	L	F	A	W	D	L	F	A	GD	Pts
1	Ukraine	12	7	4	1	18	7	3	2	1	8	4	4	2	0	10	3	11	25
2	Turkey	12	6	5	1	23	9	2	3	1	9	6	4	2	0	14	3	14	23
3	Denmark	12	6	4	2	24	12	4	2	0	15	4	2	2	2	9	8	12	22
4	Greece	12	6	3	3	15	9	4	1	1	8	3	2	2	2	7	6	6	21
5	Albania	12	4	1	7	11	20	3	0	3	7	9	1	1	4	4	11	-9	13
6	Georgia	12	2	4	6	14	25	1	3	2	8	11	1	1	4	6	14	-11	10
7	Kazakhstan	12	0	1	11	6	29	0	0	6	4	15	0	1	5	2	14	-23	1

GROUP 3 TABLE

		Overall					Home					Away						
		P	W	D	L	F	A	W	D	L	F	A	W	D	L	F	A	GD	Pts
1	Portugal	12	9	3	0	35	5	6	0	0	24	2	3	3	0	11	3	30	30
2	Slovakia	12	6	5	1	24	8	4	2	0	16	3	2	3	1	8	5	16	23
3	Russia	12	6	5	1	23	12	4	2	0	14	2	2	3	1	9	10	11	23
4	Estonia	12	5	2	5	16	17	3	1	2	10	5	2	1	3	6	12	-1	17
5	Latvia	12	4	3	5	18	21	2	3	1	9	6	2	0	4	9	15	-3	15
6	Liechtenstein	12	2	2	8	13	23	1	2	3	8	9	1	0	5	5	14	-10	8
7	Luxembourg	12	0	0	12	5	48	0	0	6	3	23	0	0	6	2	25	-43	0

GROUP 4 TABLE

		Overall					Home					Away						
	P	W	D	L	F	A	W	D	L	F	A	W	D	L	F	A	GD	Pts
1 France	10	5	5	0	14	2	2	3	0	7	0	3	2	0	7	2	12	20
2 Switzerland	10	4	6	0	18	7	2	3	0	10	3	2	3	0	8	4	11	18
3 Israel	10	4	6	0	15	10	2	3	0	8	6	2	3	0	7	4	5	18
4 Ireland	10	4	5	1	12	5	2	2	1	7	3	2	3	0	5	2	7	17
5 Cyprus	10	1	1	8	8	20	0	1	4	4	10	1	0	4	4	10	-12	4
6 Faroe Islands	10	0	1	9	4	27	0	0	5	1	12	0	1	4	3	15	-23	1

GROUP 5 TABLE

		Overall					Home					Away						
	P	W	D	L	F	A	W	D	L	F	A	W	D	L	F	A	GD	Pts
1 Italy	10	7	2	1	17	8	5	0	0	11	5	2	2	1	6	3	9	23
2 Norway	10	5	3	2	12	7	2	2	1	6	3	3	1	1	6	4	5	18
3 Scotland	10	3	4	3	9	7	1	2	2	3	3	2	2	1	6	4	2	13
4 Slovenia	10	3	3	4	10	13	2	1	2	7	7	1	2	2	3	6	-3	12
5 Belarus	10	2	4	4	12	14	1	2	2	6	6	1	2	2	6	8	-2	10
6 Moldova	10	1	2	7	5	16	1	2	2	4	4	0	0	5	1	12	-11	5

GROUP 6 TABLE

		Overall					Home					Away						
	P	W	D	L	F	A	W	D	L	F	A	W	D	L	F	A	GD	Pts
1 England	10	8	1	1	17	5	5	0	0	11	1	3	1	1	6	4	12	25
2 Poland	10	8	0	2	27	9	4	0	1	14	4	4	0	1	13	5	18	24
3 Austria	10	4	3	3	15	12	3	1	1	8	5	1	2	2	7	7	3	15
4 Northern Ireland	10	2	3	5	10	18	2	1	2	8	9	0	2	3	2	9	-8	9
5 Wales	10	2	2	6	10	15	1	1	3	6	8	1	1	3	4	7	-5	8
6 Azerbaijan	10	0	3	7	1	21	0	3	2	1	5	0	0	5	0	16	-20	3

GROUP 7 TABLE

		Overall					Home					Away						
		P	W	D	L	F	A	W	D	L	F	A	W	D	L	F	A	GD	Pts
1	Serbia & Montenegro	10	6	4	0	16	1	3	2	0	8	0	3	2	0	8	1	15	22
2	Spain	10	5	5	0	19	3	3	2	0	10	2	2	3	0	9	1	16	20
3	Bosnia-Herzegovina	10	4	4	2	12	9	2	3	0	6	2	2	1	2	6	7	3	16
4	Belgium	10	3	3	4	16	11	2	1	2	13	6	1	2	2	3	5	5	12
5	Lithuania	10	2	4	4	8	9	1	2	2	5	4	1	2	2	3	5	-1	10
6	San Marino	10	0	0	10	2	40	0	0	5	2	15	0	0	5	0	25	-38	0

GROUP 8 TABLE

		Overall					Home					Away						
		P	W	D	L	F	A	W	D	L	F	A	W	D	L	F	A	GD	Pts
1	Croatia	10	7	3	0	21	5	4	1	0	13	2	3	2	0	8	3	16	24
2	Sweden	10	8	0	2	30	4	4	0	1	15	2	4	0	1	15	2	26	24
3	Bulgaria	10	4	3	3	17	17	3	0	2	10	9	1	3	1	7	8	0	15
4	Hungary	10	4	2	4	13	14	2	2	1	8	4	2	0	3	5	10	-1	14
5	Iceland	10	1	1	8	14	27	1	0	4	9	14	0	1	4	5	13	-13	4
6	Malta	10	0	3	7	4	32	0	3	2	2	11	0	0	5	2	21	-28	3

UEFA PLAY-OFFS

12 Nov 2005	Norway 0 v 1 Czech Republic
16 Nov 2005	Czech Republic 1 v 0 Norway (Czech Republic won 2-0 on aggregate)

12 Nov 2005	Spain 5 v 1 Slovakia
16 Nov 2005	Slovakia 1 v 1 Spain (Spain won 6-2 on aggregate)

12 Nov 2005	Switzerland 2 v 0 Turkey
16 Nov 2005	Turkey 4 v 2 Switzerland (Switzerland won on away goals)

The Contenders

The exciting thing about a book such as this is that, as it is written as the tournament progresses, it will naturally follow the slings and arrows of outrageous fortune which befall the 32 competing nations. I write this in the week leading up to the start of the tournament, with the world's hopes hanging on each of the 23 footballers, plus coaching team selected to represent their country. My wish is simply for a memorable tournament, with fantastic football and, naturally, an England win. But in order to lift the World Cup in Berlin England had to overcome the world's finest. And prior to the tournament beginning this was how the contenders shaped up and how I felt about their chances.

All rankings are from official FIFA rankings and odds are those offered to win the tournament by Bet365, both on 9 June 2006.

GROUP A
No host nation had ever failed to qualify for the Second Round of a World Cup, so the Germans seemed certs to go through. But it was not beyond the realms of possibility that either Ecuador or Costa Rica could do a Scotland on either Germany or Poland, and shock one of the two Group A favourites.

POLAND
Ranking 29   Odds 126/1

Liverpool goalkeeper Jerzy Dudek was the biggest name of four shock omissions made by coach Pawel Janas, who opted to keep his squad on their toes rather than in relaxed mode in the lead up to the tournament. Dudek was left out in favour of Legia Warsaw's 21 year-old keeper Lukasz Fabianski, who had just two friendly caps to his name.

Wolverhampton Wanderers striker Tomasz Frankowski, the team's joint top scorer in qualifying along with Maciej Zurawski, but who had failed miserably in the Championship, left-back Tomasz Rzasa and centre-half and former captain Tomasz Klos were also left out due to rank bad form. Instead, Janas selected Wisla Krakow striker Pawel Brozek, full-back Dariusz Dudka and Cracovia central midfielder Piotr Giza, who had only a handful of friendly caps between them. "We are all somewhat in shock," former Celtic and Poland striker Jackie Dziekanowski told Reuters after the squad was announced. "It is maybe a good thing that Janas is stamping his authority on the team. At the end of the day, the trainer has to take responsibility and he is certainly taking it." A 1-0 defeat by Lithuania in warm-up sounded alarm bells, although a 1-0 win over Croatia boded better.

COSTA RICA
Ranking 26   Odds 751/1

Costa Rica strike legend Paulo Wanchope announced that he would be hanging up his international boots after appearing in the World Cup. The former Derby, Manchester City and West Ham forward had scored 43 times in 69 matches for his country. "Yes, I'll quit. I'm happy with what I've contributed to the squad and it's nice to be able to decide in this way." Coach Alexandre Guimaraes dropped Roy Miller from his initial 24-man selection, which included Alajuelense team-mates Harold Wallace and Michael Rodriguez, who were recovering from knee injuries. Defender Carlos Johnson and striker Bryan Ruiz were on standby in case the defensive duo fail to recover in time.

Striker Winston Parks was also left out of the squad, with goalkeeper Adrian de Lemos and defender Cristian Montero the other significant players to miss out. "This is a list we've been studying in great detail based on the characteristics of our opponents," revealed the canny Guimaraes.

Having lost all three of their warm-up games, including a 4-0 thrashing by Ukraine, the Central Americans looked less likely to cause problems than in previous tournaments.

GERMANY
Ranking 19   Odds 9/1

Jürgen Klinsmann suffered horrendous media coverage in the build up to the Finals, to the point that he was summoned to attend a meeting by Chancellor Angela Merkel. Under his guidance, the national team lurched into crisis, culminating in a humiliating 4-1 friendly defeat by Italy. Public hysteria called for Klinsmann to be sacked. His position was not helped by the fact that he lived in California and sometimes coached the team via e-mail. The row deepened over Klinsmann's choice of goalkeeper. Franz Beckenbauer let it be known that he favoured veteran Oliver Kahn, of Bayern Munich, and had little sympathy for the coach's choice, Jens Lehmann of Arsenal. The nation's mood swung wildly going into the World Cup. A 4-1 victory over a weakened USA side was followed by a 7-0 hammering of Luxembourg and then a desperate 2-2 draw with Japan in which the Germans only just scraped back from two goals down, then a last, morale-boosting 3-0 win over Colombia.

Like his England counterpart, the Germany coach called up an uncapped player with a reputation for pace. The Borussia Dortmund midfielder, David Odonkor, had clocked 100 metres in 10.9 seconds. "We believe that he can help us with his cheekiness, something we're missing," Klinsmann said. Odonkor took the place of injured Bayern Munich winger Sebastian Deisler. Out-of-form Schalke 04 striker Kevin Kuranyi failed to make the cut, while striker Mike Hanke of VfL Wolfsburg won a place despite being suspended for the first two matches because of a sending-off in last year's Confederations Cup. Klinsmann included Jens Nowotny in his squad, despite the defender's near two-year absence from international football.

DID YOU KNOW?
Germany coach Klinsmann had his squad taking apart wrist-watches and putting them back together again as part of their preparation for the tournament. This exercise was designed to improve their focus and concentration.

ECUADOR
Ranking 39   Odds 301/1

Very much an unknown quantity, although any team which finishes third behind Brazil and Argentina in qualifying had to have a good chance of performing well. Aston Villa defender Ulises De la Cruz was named in Ecuador's squad, while coach Luis Fernando Suarez also included former English-based strikers Agustin Delgado and Ivan Kaviedes, who had recent disciplinary problems. Delgado had an unproductive spell at Southampton after signing in a £3.5m deal, while Kaviedes had a brief stay at Crystal Palace. Goalscoring forward Franklin Salas was out with a knee injury and was Ecuador's major absentee.

The Ecuadorians did not show much promise in warm-up games. Having lost to Japan, they drew 1-1 with Colombia and lost 2-1 to Macedonia. Popular opinion held that without the advantage of altitude (Ecudor's capital Quito is 9,200 feet above sea level), they would struggle.

The Way Of The Pfist

Germany had little chance of winning because of their lack of skill, according to Togo's German coach Otto Pfister. "Germany have no chance. I don't think they can even get to the final, or even the semi-final," said Pfister, who took over as Togo coach in February. "I think if they get to the quarter-final they do very well," It's quite simple, you need skill and Germany doesn't have that. Carlos Alberto Parreira of Brazil has another problem, he has to think who is on the bench. Germany don't even know who to put on the pitch."

GROUP B

Following the draw, all the pundits were lining up to suggest how easy this group would be, leaping ahead of themselves and considering the possibility of England meeting hosts Germany in the first knock-out stage, and eventually facing Brazil in the semi-final. Hold on a minute. Didn't anyone recall how England have been notoriously slow starters in the World Cup? Well, I did. All the way back to Mexico 1986 when I stayed in the England camp for weeks in the build up to the opening game against a Portugal side so demoralised by weeks of wranglings over their bonuses, that the squad threatened to go back home. What happened next? You've guessed it; Portugal beat England in the opening game.

So I didn't count on it being the perceived cakewalk through the group. With England in the World Cup there is always a drama, and there would be nothing more mind-blowing then having to face a country England and Sven simply find impossible to beat, Sweden, in the final group game, needing all three points to go through.

ENGLAND
Ranking 10   Odds 8/1

I was fascinated by the prospect of England being unpredictable, because Sven the Swede had no Plan B, and that might just throw his home country into confusion. In the past England have had problems with Sweden because they are Premiership junkies who know our game inside out. This time, it would be harder to know what Peter Crouch is up to, or what Theo Walcott might do when he comes off the bench.

Such was Eriksson's predicament over Rooney that he could even utilise Steven Gerrard as a supporting striker. I believe that Eriksson's failure to give Gerrard a settled role in the side could be more of a factor in England's World Cup chances than Rooney's fitness. And worse news for England was that the defence worried me. Was John Terry as good as everyone thinks?

DID YOU KNOW?
FA sponsors McDonalds ran a competition to find England's mascot should the team reach the final. Unfortunately for them the winner entered via the Glasgow branch and proved to be a half-Scottish, half-Russian boy, who wanted the Ukraine to win and declared, "I don't want England to be in the final. I don't want them to win."

SWEDEN
Ranking 16   Odds 41/1

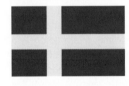

Southampton defender Alexander Ostlund was left out, but remained on standby as coach Lars Lagerback named a squad that included Arsenal's Freddie Ljungberg and Aston Villa captain Olof Mellberg. Juventus's Zlatan Ibrahimovic and Barcelona's Henrik Larsson were among four strikers. IFK Gothenburg defender Karl Svensson got a surprise call, while uncapped Bayer Leverkuson defender Fredrik Stenman was drafted in.

Sweden's warm-up was poor as they had not won in six games and not at all in 2006, including 1-1 draws with Saudi Arabia and Chile and a goalless draw with Jordan. They also succumbed 3-0 in Dublin to Ireland.

DID YOU KNOW?
England had not beaten Sweden for 38 years and 11 games since a 3-1 win in May 1968.

DID YOU KNOW?
Six of the Swedish squad appeared in all of Sweden's 10 qualifying games.

PARAGUAY

Ranking 33   Odds 201/1

Teenage midfielder Jose Montiel, 18, was one of a number of young players selected by Paraguay coach Anibal Ruiz. "This is the future of our football," Ruiz explained. "More than 50 percent of this squad are young enough to play at another three World Cups." Montiel, who as child sold pies in the street to help his family earn some extra income, played at the World Under-17 championships in Peru in 2005 and made his full international debut against Venezuela as a 17 year-old. Other youngsters included were Bayern Munich midfielder Julio dos Santos, his club-mate Roque Santa Cruz, forward Nelson Haedo Valdez and midfielders Edgar Barreto and Cristian Riveros.

At the opposite end of the age scale, Ruiz also included veterans Roberto Acuna and Jose Cardozo, despite their unimpressive form at club level. Acuna, 33, had played only a handful of games this season for Deportivo La Coruna in Spain, while Cardozo, 35, had been released by Argentina's San Lorenzo after a lacklustre year. But Cardozo's World Cup was over before it had begun as injury forced him to drop out and Dante Lopez of Olimpia in Paraguay was drafted in. Acuna had played impressively for his country after making an international comeback in last year's World Cup qualifier at home to Argentina, which Paraguay won 1-0. England would underestimate their opening opponents at their peril.

Sleeping Giants

Paraguay's experienced centre-half Carlos Gamarra was in no doubt as to who he expected to claim the trophy, "Brazil are the absolute favourites," he said. "Germany always seem to be asleep, as nobody expects anything from them, but they suddenly wake up and always get to the final stages."

TRINIDAD & TOBAGO

Ranking 47   Odds 1501/1

Brazilian fans have a reputation as being noisy, colourful and dressing imaginatively, but the supporters of Trinidad & Tobago are equally vibrant. Many years ago I ventured to Trinidad to watch their team fail narrowly to qualify for the World Cup for the first time against the USA. That morning tens of thousands created snake-like queues for miles waiting to gain entry for an afternoon kick off. The music, the colours, the excitement they generated was awesome. On that day, unknown kids called Yorke and Latapy were in tears for just missing out on the World Cup, but now both have come out of retirement to gain their day in the global spotlight.

There were plenty of UK-based players in the Trinidad & Tobago squad, with the most famous, captain Dwight Yorke, of course, well-known to many of England's squad. But a string of defeats in warm-up, including a 2-1 reverse against Wales, suggested the Caribbean side would be out of their depth.

Party Animals

34-year-old former Manchester United and Aston Villa star Dwight Yorke was so excited at playing in the Finals, "not that my life has been that bad before," he said. "But if there was anything missing from it, this is now like putting the icing on the cake. To be leading the Trinidad and Tobago team to the World Cup is the best thing possible that could have happened to me. We've got this reputation for being party animals – and I can't argue that all the lads love a good time. The difference is we now party at the right time."

DID YOU KNOW?
Trinidad's squad was the oldest of the qualifying teams with an average age over 29, with Falkirk's Russell Latapy, nearly 38, the eldest.

GROUP C

Argentina and Holland were the big guns in a fascinating group, but the Dutch were no longer truly formidable World Cup foes, while Argentina had some wonderful attacking midfield players who could illuminate the tournament and their team had the look of potential winners. But could muscular Ivory Coast put cats amongst either of these countries' pigeons?

ARGENTINA
Ranking 9   Odds 9/1

Argentineans never lack confidence. Midfielder Esteban Cambiasso stuck his neck out to predict how his team was going to fare. "It's very difficult to say which teams are going to be in the final, but what I am sure of is that Argentina are going to reach the semi-finals." A prediction all the more amazing in its confidence because when the Argentine squad was announced it lacked many of their biggest names.

Coach Jose Pekerman only named four players who appeared in the 2002 tournament, and left big names such as Walter Samuel, Juan Sebastian Veron and Javier Zanetti at home. Bayern Munich midfielder Martin Demichelis also missed out, while uncapped Independiente goalkeeper Oscar Ustari beat German Lux to a place. Barcelona teenage sensation Lionel Messi was included despite his calf injury, while Boca Juniors striker Rodrigo Palacio was rewarded for his excellent season with a place, as was fellow striker, Julio Cruz, who scored 17 goals for Inter in Serie A.

One big name that did make the squad was Manchester United's Gabriel Heinze, who recovered from a cruciate knee ligament injury against Villarreal in the Champions League in time. With the repercussions still reverberating around Buenos Aires, Pekerman had staked his reputation on his somewhat surprising selection being able to perform. My feeling was he would be repaid and they would at least reach the last four.

DID YOU KNOW?
Argentina had the worst disciplinary record of the teams who qualified for Germany with 43 yellow cards and 4 red cards in their 18 games.

HOLLAND
Ranking 3   Odds 13/1

Holland striker Ruud van Nistelrooy emerged from the uncharacteristically light workload of a frustrating season with Manchester United primed for a big World Cup to spearhead his hunt for a new club. The goal ace was livid at his regular place on the bench during the second half of the Red Devils' season, but I believed this lack of action would ultimately benefit the Oranje in Germany, "I am no longer bothered by little pains or complaints and I am not burned out after a long and tough season," van Nistelrooy told De Telegraaf. "I feel that I am fitter than ever and cannot wait to go to the World Cup."

Holland manager Marco van Basten left Dutch strike starlet Klaas-Jan Huntelaar at home. Huntelaar, who led the Eredivisie scoring charts this season, instead lead the Young Oranje into the Under-21 European Championships.

Middlesbrough midfielder George Boateng also failed to make it. The 31-year-old was included in van Basten's 28-man pre-World Cup squad, but Boateng was one of five players to be culled. Others to miss out were AZ Alkmaar defender Barry Opdam, Hamburg midfielder Nigel de Jong, Romeo Castelen, the Feyenoord forward and Spurs' influential Edgar Davids, although the camp may have been more harmonious because of his omission.

The inclusion of Jan Kromkamp, who played sporadically for Liverpool during the season was a surprise. The Dutch warmed up with a 2-1 win over Mexico. And a bruising 1-1 draw with Australia left Van Basten with four injury worries ahead of Holland's opening game.

IVORY COAST
Ranking 32   Odds 81/1

Ivory Coast's French manager Henri Michel largely kept faith with the squad that won silver at the last African Cup of Nations in Egypt. But Siaka Tiene, the St-Etienne player, was dropped, with striker Abdoul Kader Keita replacing him.

The squad included three British-based players – Chelsea striker Didier Drogba and Arsenal defensive duo Kolo Toure and Emmanuel Eboue. The Ivorians looked powerful and strong in defence which meant they would be in contention in every game and able to give any opponent a fright, and with the likes of Drogba up front, had strikers to score goals in tight games.

Warm-up games boded well. A narrow 3-2 defeat in Spain was followed by 1-1 away draws with Switzerland and Chile.

The Ivorians' final pre-tournament game was won 3-0 against Slovenia with Drogba scoring twice.

DID YOU KNOW?
First choice Ivory Coast goalkeeper Jean-Jacques Tizie was given a potion by a witch doctor to improve his performances during the World Cup, but the concoction left Tizie in hospital after almost going blind and hearing voices. "I almost died," he said. "The doctors said they were very lucky with me."

DID YOU KNOW?
The 2006 World Cup was the only one which the united nation of Serbia & Montenegro will ever compete in as, on 21 May 2006, Montenegro voted to seceed from Serbia to form their own nation state. Not that Serbia will miss them as there was only one Montenegrin in the squad following the knee ligament injury to striker Mirko Vucinic.

SERBIA & MONTENEGRO
Ranking 44   Odds 81/1

Australian-born midfielder Ivan Ergic was the surprise inclusion in the Serbia & Montenegro squad. The uncapped Basel midfielder was brought in as back-up for Zvonimir Vukic, who was suffering from a foot injury. "He is a fine young player, I have followed him a lot," said assistant coach Goran Stevanovic.

Coach Ilija Petkovic also included Manchester United defender Nemanja Vidic and ex-Chelsea striker Mateja Kezman. Former Aston Villa forward Savo Milosevic was included. "The chosen ones have shown superb qualities in the qualifiers," said Petkovic. "We can say this is the best this country can offer." The national team coach kept faith with the youth in his squad by selecting defender Dusan Basta of Red Star Belgrade and striker Mirko Vucinic of Lecce, who also both took part in the Under-21 European Championship prior to the World Cup.

Controversy reigned after Petkovic selected his own son, Dusan, in place of Mirko Vucinic, who went down with a knee injury in those championships. The intense media derision which greeted the choice eventually lead to Dusan walking out of the squad on the 6 June, after the deadline for non-injured players to be allowed to be replaced, so Serbia were left one man short.

Petkovic fantasised that an unfancied team like his would surprise everyone by winning the World Cup. "It would be nice for a change if a team that has never won the World Cup before does it this time. It would be stunning and a joy for football fans around the world. Naturally, I hope we can be that mouse, but it will be a tall order. I have always been optimistic in life and we are going to Germany in high spirits with a positive approach."

The Serbs only played one warm-up game, drawing 1-1 with Uruguay in late May, preferring to concentrate on squad preparation.

GROUP D

The easiest group to call? Or the one which will provide the biggest shock? Iran's comeback from 2-0 down to thrash Bosnia 5-2 in the week before the World Cup suggested all would not be as simple as hot favourites Mexico and Portugal might have thought.

MEXICO
Ranking 4   Odds 51/1

Mexico coach Ricardo La Volpe included 37year-old defender Claudio Suarez, who appeared in the 1994 and 1998 tournaments, after impressing following his return to the national team. Two naturalised players, Brazilian-born Antonio Naelson (also known as Zinho) and Argentine-born Guillermo Franco, were in the squad, as was La Volpe's son-in-law Rafael Garcia.

La Volpe caused controversy when he omitted tricky left-winger and inventor of the bunny-hop move at France 98, Cuauhtemoc Blanco, 33, from his original 26-man squad. The move caused fans to demonstrate outside the Mexican FA and led to La Volpe ranting publicly, "While I am team coach Blanco will not be recalled." The winger had only featured in two of La Volpe's selections during qualifying.

With the exception of its four foreign-based players, the squad had been in a training camp since 2 April as the Mexicans hoped togetherness would add to their chances.

Their intensive warm-up programme included a 1-0 victory over Venezuala, a 2-1 win against DR Congo and two narrow defeats in Europe, 1-0 to France and 2-1 to Holland. Mexico looked in good shape to progress from their group, but unlikely to go any further.

PORTUGAL
Ranking 7   Odds 23/1

Portugal coach Luiz Felipe Scolari, having put all thoughts of taking the England job well out of reach, was counting on veteran attacker and former FIFA World Player of the Year Luis Figo, a member of the nation's 'Golden Generation', who came so close to glory in their own country at Euro 2004. "He's one of our mainstays, not only because of how he plays, but also because of what he represents and the way he worries opponents," said Big Phil. Scolari kept faith with his most experienced players as he stuck with trusted talent like Portugal's all-time leading scorer Pauleta.

Pauleta, of Paris Saint-Germain, was joined up front by Benfica striker Nuno Gomes and St-Etienne's Helder Postiga. Fulham's Luis Boa Morte, who missed Euro 2004 through injury, was included at the expense of Ricardo Quaresma, who'd had an impressive season for FC Porto. Dynamo Moscow's Francisco Costinha and Chelsea loan midfielder Nuno Maniche made the squad despite not featuring regularly for their club sides in recent months.

Portugal had a light warm-up programme including a 4-1 win over the Cape Verde Islands thanks to a Pauleta hat-trick and a 3-0 defeat of Luxembourg.

DID YOU KNOW?
Only twice have Mexico reached the quarter-finals of a World Cup and on both occasions they did so in a tournament being held in their own country.

DID YOU KNOW?
Portugal were playing in their second successive World Cup for the first time.

IRAN

Ranking 23   Odds 751/1

Iran manager Branko Ivankovic said he'd like to separate politics from sport during the World Cup in a bid to stop the Western press turning the event into a political football. The coach wouldn't bar the squad from speaking on any topic, but hoped all lines of press questioning focussed on the games. "We don't have any restrictions, but I would rather people built a clear wall between sport and politics. Of course, it is hard for the players to switch off completely from what is going on in Iran, but we have a young ambitious squad who I am convinced will only be thinking about the football."

The biggest surprise was the selection of Saipa midfielder Masoud Shojaee, tipped for great things by Ivankovic. There were five Europe-based players selected, including Bayern Munich's former Asian Player of the Year Ali Karimi. Also included was veteran striker Ali Daei, who would be playing in his second World Cup after appearing in France eight years ago.

Iran pulled off a couple of impressive warm-up results. They drew 2-2 in Croatia, only concedin a late penalty after leading twice. Then they came from two goals down to hammer Bosnia-Herzegovina 5-2.

ANGOLA

Ranking 57   Odds 751/1

Angola coach Luis Oliveira Goncalves' 23-man squad showed just four changes to the one he had named for the African Cup of Nations. Injuries ruled out midfielder Gilberto and striker Maurito, while goalkeeper Goliath and defender Jacinto were the others to miss out. The replacements included Portugal-based duo of Mateus and Marco Airosa, as well as Hull City's Rui Marques.

Narrow 1-0 defeats in warm-up games by Argentina, Turkey and the USA proved their defensive solidity, but it was goals that the Angolans severely lacked.

Goncalves said, "We are aware that we are one of the most humble teams in the tournament... but we will do everything we can. But for us, it is a victory just to be at the World Cup. We are going to try to play well and represent our country and the African continent with dignity." I hope they did, but I could not see them picking up any more than a token point for their efforts, although I expected a bruising encounter in their first match against former colonial overlords Portugal.

GROUP E

In my opinion this group had more than a touch of Death about it. With Italy, the USA and the Czech Republic amongst the top-ranked nations and Ghana as one of Africa's new breed, every match would contain twists and turns, no quarter asked or given. I fancied one of the European nations would not make it through.

ITALY
Ranking 13   Odds 10/1

The Italian national team went into the World Cup embroiled in the kind of scandal that wrecks World Cup dreams. A nationwide probe into match-fixing, illegal gambling and transfer bungs engulfed national coach Marcello Lippi, Juventus' General Manager, Luciano Moggi, and their sons. The investigation delved into dealings by GEA World, a sports management agency run by Moggi's son Alessandro, which has nearly 200 Italian players and coaches on its books. Lippi, who previously coached at Juventus, denied that he had ever come under pressure from Moggi to select certain players for the national side to enhance their value. Prime Minister Romano Prodi declared the scandal "has symbolised to people the depth of the crisis of ethics and how it has entered every sector of public life".

Lippi believed it was the team's duty to restore the good name of Azzurri football. "We know we have this responsibility. We hope to feed the enthusiasm with good results." After a 1-1 draw with Switzerland the week before the finals, when at least the Italian fans refrained from booing their own team unlike they had during that week's public training sessions, that looked like an uphill struggle. The scandal was set to cost a very good Italy side a chance of at least reaching the semi-finals.

But the scandal touched other nations too, including England's Group B opponents, Sweden. Tax police searched the Turin homes of Swedish striker Zlatan Ibrahimovic and Italy captain Fabio Cannavaro, two of Juventus' best players, who play for their national teams. Juventus goalkeeper Gianluigi Buffon was included, despite his link to the ongoing investigation into gambling, but one of Italy's refereeing representatives,

Massimo De Santis, was withdrawn by his national association as the scandal bit deeper, embroiling him.

AC Milan striker Filippo Inzaghi, the 32 year-old striker, who had not played for the national team since October 2003 due to a series of injuries, was included. However, there was no place for Real Madrid forward Antonio Cassano or Livorno's Cristiano Lucarelli, whose 19 goals in Serie A this season had pushed him into contention.

Udinese forward Vincenzo Iaquinta was given the nod ahead of Lucarelli as back up for target man Luca Toni, who was Europe's top scorer in 2005/06 with 31 goals. Playmaker Francesco Totti was named after returning from a three-month layoff late in the season due to a bad injury which had looked set to destroy his World Cup chances.

Could Lightning Strike Twice?

All doom and gloom in the run up to Germany for the three times winners, then. Mind you, the last time Italy had such a scandal hanging over them entering into a World Cup was in 1982. Then the selection of striker Paolo Rossi, who had only recently returned from a suspension after being found guilty of match-fixing, proved to be crucial to Italy's triumph as the Juventus star scored an unforgettable hat-trick to send Brazil crashing out and then also scored in the semi-final and Final to win the Cup.

DID YOU KNOW?
If the FIFA rankings of the teams in each of the eight World Cup groups were added together then the toughest group was not Group C as many people believed, but in fact Group E where Italy, USA & Czech Republic were all in the top 13.

USA
Ranking 5   Odds 81/1

The United States were one of the success stories of the 2002 World Cup finals, but USA coach Bruce Arena was forced to make a change just a day after announcing his 23-man group for Germany. Los Angeles Galaxy defender Chris Albright was drafted in to replace experienced Columbus Crew defender Frankie Hejduk, 31, who tore knee ligaments, ruling him out of what would have been his third World Cup. Captain Claudio Reyna, going to his fourth World Cup, was one of seven English-based players including Manchester United keeper Tim Howard and two players from Premiership new-boys Reading, Marcus Hahnemann and Bobby Convey.

Arena was convinced he had a better squad than that which took eventual runners-up Germany to the brink in the quarter-finals four years ago. "We're a more experienced team and we have better players," said Arena, "The guys with all the pressure are (Czech coach Karel) Bruckner and (Italy coach Marcello) Lippi," he quipped. "There's no pressure on Mr. Arena." Well, I don't agree. Suddenly the USA had a world ranking far exceeding their true worth and they would be heading for a fall.

Warm-up results were mixed. The USA defeated Latvia and Angola, both 1-0, and Venezuela 2-0, but lost to Morocco 1-0.

CZECH REPUBLIC
Ranking 2   Odds 29/1

One of my favoured teams if all is well in their camp. But like Eriksson, Czech Republic coach Karel Bruckner felt he had to include several injured players in his squad. His biggest concern was influential midfielder Vladimir Smicer, who had torn a tendon and then suffered a blood clot in his thigh. Smicer pulled out and was replaced by Rangers' Libor Sionko. Also injured was Aston Villa striker Milan Baros, who damaged a foot in the 3-0 win over Trinidad & Tobago on 3 June, but Bruckner stuck with Baros allowing him a chance to get fit for the latter stages.

Striker Vratislav Lokvenc was recovering from a serious knee injury, while key defender Zdenek Grygera of Ajax was also struggling. Striker Jan Koller was on course to play after a knee injury which had kept him on the sidelines for months. Announcing his squad on 15 May, Bruckner told reporters, "As late as Friday and Saturday we were having our doctors examine players and we were still weighing various alternatives."

The Czech squad boasted a strong defence and plenty of attacking options. In fact with Chelsea keeper Petr Cech to contend with, the Czech Republic would be amongst the hardest teams to score against in the entire tournament.

Their warm-up games also included a 2-0 win over Saudi Arabia and a 1-0 victory against Costa Rica. They looked very strong indeed.

GHANA
Ranking 48   Odds 301/1

Ghana head coach Ratomir Dujkovic made drastic changes to the team which competed at the 2006 African Cup of Nations, including calling in an uncapped defender and several players who had been absent from the national team for several years. Less than half the players who competed in the continental tournament, in which Ghana failed to advance out of the first round, made the trip to Germany. Of the recognised names, Stephen Appiah captained the squad, while Chelsea's Michael Essien returned after sitting out the African Cup of Nations due to injury.

GROUP F

Brazil would be a joy to watch, as they always are, and be everyone's preferred choice to win the tournament – if it was not to be England. Also Croatia would be as unpredictable as always, but have enough talent in their side to think they can take on even the World Cup holders. The Samba Men looked blessed with an easy route into the knockout stages, but the intriguing question was, who was likely to join them? All three of their group opponents had good reason to be optimistic.

Packed with attacking options, Brazil's opponents know that if they sit back and defend they could be embarrassed. Defensively vulnerable, the only hope is to try to attack them. We would be seeing a few high scoring games.

BRAZIL
Ranking 1   Odds 7/2

Brazil coach Carlos Alberto Parreira confidently named his starting XI for the opening match in early May. Of course most of the Brazilian starting XI are world names, but of the fringe players, Sao Paulo captain Rogerio Ceni, who scored more than 50 goals from free-kicks and penalties in his career, won a place as a third-choice goalkeeper when Marcos, the previous selection, failed to regain fitness. Injury kept out central defender Roque Junior, who started the 2002 World Cup Final, while Germany-based Gilberto won a spot as reserve to Roberto Carlos at left-back.

But there was a chink in Brazil's seemingly impregnable armour. Their strikers were bang out of form. Adriano and his international strike partner Ronaldo, had both experienced troubled seasons. Adriano admitted, "I am unhappy, and Ronaldo is like me. He is not in his best form at Real Madrid. We want to recover to play at our best in the World Cup." The world waited to see if the Brazilians would once more make hay while the sun shone in this summer of international football, or if miserable club form would see the heavy favourites struggle.

Their only warm-up game saw a comfortable 4-0 victory over New Zealand in Geneva with Ronaldo and Adriano, two of the much vaunted 'Fab Four' of Adriano, Kaka, Ronaldo and Ronaldinho, finding the net.

CROATIA
Ranking 23   Odds 67/1

Croatia avoided any last-minute surprises, opting instead to instil security and faith into their squad. Coach Zlatko Kranjcar said: "I had revealed I would pick the players who carried the burden of qualifying, so I've had a pretty clear picture of who to choose. I can feel a great team spirit and I think we're capable of doing it."

But qualification from a tough group would stretch a Croatian squad shorn of the stars who propelled them to a third place finish in their inaugural World Cup in 1998. Without the likes of Davor Suker, it was difficult to see where goals were going to come from against Japan and Australia.

The team struggled in warm-up games drawing 2-2 with Iran only thanks to a late penalty and then lost 1-0 to Poland and 2-1 to Spain.

DID YOU KNOW?
Due to political circumstances in the Kingdom of Yugoslavia shortly before World War II, Croatian sports teams were allowed to compete under Croatian flag, so the first full Croatian international could be considered a 4-0 victory over Switzerland played in Zagreb on 4 April 1940.

AUSTRALIA
Ranking 42   Odds 126/1

Harry Kewell missed Australia's friendly with Greece in Melbourne after limping out of Liverpool's FA Cup win with a groin injury, while Everton's Tim Cahill was also crocked and received treatment in Australia for a knee injury, which forced him to miss the game against Greece. But both players were fit enough for coach Guus Hiddink to keep in his squad.

The pair were two of a handful of Premiership-based players to have been picked by the Dutch coach. Middlesbrough's Mark Schwarzer and Mark Viduka, who was named as captain, Blackburn's Lucas Neill and Brett Emerton, along with Newcastle's Craig Moore and Cahill of Everton were also selected. Former Rangers star Tony Vidmar was sadly forced to retire after being diagnosed with a serious heart complaint. It was galling for Vidmar who had experienced three failures at the play-off stage of qualification in the past, before scoring one of the vital penalties which saw Australia through against Uruguay to reach their first finals for 32 years.

Warm-up went well with a 1-1 draw in Holland proving the Aussie's durability and determination. Luke Wilkshire earned a red card for his tackle on Giovanni van Bronckhorst. Tim Cahill tapped in the equaliser after Viduka's penalty was saved. In their final game the Australians defeated Liechtenstein 3-1 thanks to two late goals.

For me, Australia could be the surprise package. They had goalscorers aplenty in their team and a wealth of experience, although not on the international stage. It wouldn't surprise me if they made the Second Round.

JAPAN
Ranking 18   Odds 301/1

It took him four years to get tough, but Japan coach Zico's bold selection of five strikers represented a final throw of the dice. The Brazilian axed Tatsuhiko Kubo and Takayuki Suzuki and included Seiichiro Maki and Keiji Tamada in a bid to end Japan's woeful form in front of goal. With Kubo worryingly prone to injury and the Serbian-based Suzuki no longer an automatic choice, Zico's decision made sense even if Maki himself was shocked. 'I watched it on TV and was stunned,' Maki confessed. "But I'm not going to Germany on vacation. I want to do my bit and help us win our matches."

Maki's inclusion provided a welcome shake-up to a Japan team, who finished last in May's three-team Kirin Cup behind Scotland, against whom Japan played out a goalless draw, and Bulgaria, to whom they lost 2-1.

The 2-2 draw with Germany the week before the tournament began gave Zico's men much more hope. But simply advancing from Group F would be seen as a major accomplishment for Japan, who reached the last 16 on home soil under Frenchman Philippe Troussier four years ago on a wave of emotion and national sentiment and thanks to being seeded in their group. Things would be different this time around.

GROUP G

In one of the most open groups in the competition, France seemed odds on to qualify as winners, but who would follow them? Could Switzerland overcome their injury problems and South Korea the lack of their incredible and fervent support? And how on earth would Togo fare?

FRANCE
Ranking 8   Odds 12/1

France, with their ageing midfield, looked to a world class striker in the prime form of his life to carry them to glory. Thierry Henry had just become the first player to receive the Football Writers' Association Footballer of the Year award three times, had played in the Champions League Final and finished as the Premiership's top goalscorer once again. Most importantly for his peace of mind, he had made the momentous decision to remain at Arsenal for the rest of his career. He seemed settled and ready to explode into life after the rigours of another tumultuous Premiership season. The high-profile failure of France in 2002, when Henry earned himself a red card against Uruguay, made Germany all the more important for Thierry to make a global impact. He was my tip to be the Golden Boot winner.

All was not harmonious in the French camp, however, as Lyon keeper Gregory Coupet was beside himself with frustration after France boss Raymond Domenech announced Fabien Barthez as his World Cup No.1. "It is not hell, but it is a big swindle," Coupet told Canal+. "I will have to keep my head up and be ready psychologically in order to help the team during the World Cup." The fans clearly wanted Coupet, as they chanted his name during the tight 1-0 warm-up win over Mexico.

The warm-up game s cost one English-based striker his place in the squad. Liverpool's Djibril Cissé broke his leg early in France's 3-1 win against China. The French won that game with two very late goals, but looked better in defeating Denmark 2-0, although they had earlier struggled to see off Mexico in a match marking Zinedine Zidane's 100th cap.

Could the French hold it together? My tip was for them to come unstuck against Italy in the quarter-final.

SWITZERLAND
Ranking 35   Odds 126/1

Switzerland coach Koebi Kuhn was another man banking on several players who struggled with injury during the season, including top scorer Alexander Frei, fellow striker Marco Streller and Hamburg midfielder Raphael Wicky. And Kuhn was forced to recall former first team regular Hakan Yakin from holiday having left him out of his initial squad. The 29 year-old playmaker had missed much of the 2005/06 season with a groin injury, but the hamstring injury to starlet striker Johan Vonlanthen saw Yakin return to the fold. Vonlanthen disputed the decision to replace him, claiming that he had time to recover, but Kuhn did not want to take the risk.

There were also call-ups for Arsenal's 19 year-old defender Johan Djourou and FC Zurich midfielder Blerim Dzemaili, who both made their international debut in a 3-1 friendly win over Scotland in March. Regular Swiss goalkeeper Pascal Zuberbühler was handed the number one shirt despite coming under criticism from the national media.

The Swiss looked solid as ever in their warm-up games with 1-1 draws against Italy and the Ivory Coast boding well. Their final game saw a 4-1 defeat of China with both Alexander Frei and Marco Streller scoring twice. They were unbeaten since the 4-2 defeat in November by Turkey which saw them qualify on away goals.

But the Swiss' lack of quality in front of goal could well cost them dear and I expected them to struggle to overcome South Korea for second place behind France in Group G.

SOUTH KOREA
Ranking 29   Odds 251/1

English-based duo Park Ji-Sung and Lee Young-Pyo, along with Wolves striker Seol Ki-Hyeon were named in South Korea's squad. Park was one of 10 veterans who helped the Koreans reach the last four in 2002. The most notable absentee was injured striker Lee Dong-Gook. "We've a very balanced squad which can surprise a lot of people in the world," said Dutch-born coach Dick Advocaat. "We showed in the past that we can do something. We still are in a very difficult group with France, Togo and Switzerland, but we are capable of making at least the second round and from that moment everything is possible."

The Koreans looked unsteady in warm-up, particularly when being easily beaten 3-1 by Ghana at Easter Road in their last game. A goalless draw with Norway and a 2-0 win over Bosnia-Herzegovina suggested better things could be possible, though.

Whether the Koreans could reproduce the incredible passion which was generated in their home country and put-paid to Italy and Spain en route to the semis last time around, was open to question, but it would be tight between them and Switzerland.

TOGO
Ranking 61   Odds 751/1

Togo's German coach Otto Pfister was disappointed that Arsenal's Emmanuel Adebayor, scorer of 11 goals for Togo in qualification, did not join the squad until after the Champions League final – even though he took no part because he was cup-tied, having played for Monaco earlier in the competition.

Along with the Ivory Coast, Angola and Ghana, Togo were playing in the World Cup finals for the first time and the West Africans were the first of the 31 visiting teams to arrive in Germany. After a narrow 1-0 win over Liechtenstein in their only warm-up game, the team were given a police motorcycle escort to their training base in Wangen. "My heart is beating for both Togo and Germany – hopefully they'll both make it to the final," effused Wangen mayor Michael Lang.

Controversy overshadowed the Togo squad when players and officials from the national FA failed to agree on payments for the tournament. Pfister walked out four days before their first game and there was talk of former Cameroon coach Winfried Schafer taking over. They entered the tournament in disarray.

DID YOU KNOW?
Togo completed their qualifying games with an unbeaten run of 9 matches (7 wins) after losing 2 of their opening three games. Arsenal's Emmanuel Adebayor was Togo's top scorer in qualification with 11 goals in 11 matches.

Henry's Secret World Cup Trauma

Thierry Henry was ready to make up for his secret World Cup disappointment. As a 20 year-old Henry was on the bench when France won the World Cup in Paris in 1998. The Arsenal skipper was poised to come on as a substitute against Brazil when Marcel Desailly received a red card and Henry was told to sit down again. He'd never told the story before, but recalled the bitter-sweet memories of the 3-0 win whilst chatting to me. Henry said: "I was warming up and I was supposed to come on 10 minutes after the beginning of the second half, but Marcel Desailly got sent off and the plan changed. On the spur of the moment I was disappointed that I didn't come on. But once you know you are going to lift that cup – I was 20 and I played six games – I couldn't be that upset."

GROUP H
The European nations seemed by far the strongest teams in this group and I could not see any other qualifiers than Spain and the Ukraine.

SPAIN
Ranking 5   **Odds 15/1**

Liverpool striker Fernando Morientes, scorer of 26 goals in 43 internationals, was left out of Spain's squad after coach Luis Aragones preferred to bolster his side's defence. Valencia centre-back Carlos Marchena was included despite a mediocre season. In favour was Valencia striker David Villa, scorer of 24 Primera Liga goals, who was the favourite to lead the line with support from either Raul or Atletico Madrid's want-away Fernando Torres. "I've given priority to the players who suit the way we play. We can't put the interests of individual players before those of the team and its stability," a tense Aragones told a news conference. "It isn't always a case of just taking the 11 best players."

Raul and Barcelona midfielder Xavi were both included despite missing much of the season with serious knee ligament injuries. The Real Madrid striker had not scored since returning to action in the middle of February. Another suffering was Chelsea's Asier Del Horno, who failed to recover from an ankle tendon injury.

Spain's warm-up programme made impressive viewing. A comfortable 2-0 win over Egypt was followed by a 2-1 victory against Croatia, although that win was earned by Fernando Torres' last gasp goal.

Aragones had gambled on players he trusted, but could they be the squad to shake off Spain's perennial under-achievers tag and reach the latter stages? I don't think so.

> **DID YOU KNOW?**
> *There were five Premiership players in the Spanish squad; Liverpool team-mates Jose Reina, Xabi Alonso and Luis Garcia, and Arsenal's Jose Antonio Reyes and Cesc Fabregas. Chelsea full-back Asier del Horno would have been in if fit.*

UKRAINE
Ranking 45   **Odds 67/1**

Ukraine had to be taken reasonably seriously as contenders after becoming the first European team to qualify for the World Cup by winning their group ahead of European champions Greece, as well as Turkey and Denmark.

Their captain and AC Milan striker Andriy Shevchenko moved from Milan to Chelsea for a British record £30.5 million on the eve of the World Cup. Shevchenko was his club's top scorer with 19 goals in 28 league appearances, plus another nine Champions League strikes and his nascent nation's hopes rested firmly on his goalscoring shoulders. But Shevchenko had been struggling for form since damaging his knee in early May against Parma, although he seemed fit enough to play a major role in Ukraine's first appearance at a major soccer tournament. He scored in his first game back as Ukraine defeated Luxembourg 3-0 in their last game before the tournament.

Previously a 4-0 hammering of Costa Rica and a goalless draw in Italy signalled Ukraine's potential as dark horses.

> **DID YOU KNOW?**
> *Ukraine Coach Oleg Blokhin is a legend who played for the USSR 109 times and represented them in two World Cups. He was named European Footballer of the Year in 1975, something which Ukraine's current star man Andriy Shevchenko also achieved in 2004.*

> **DID YOU KNOW?**
> *Dominant Ukrainian clubs Dynamo Kiev and Shakhtar Donetsk provided 13 players for their 23-man squad for the finals.*

SAUDI ARABIA
Ranking 34   Odds 1001/1

Veteran striker Sami Al-Jaber was set to appear at his fourth World Cup finals after he was named in coach Marcos Paqueta's squad. Al-Jaber, who also captains the team, was lured out of international retirement at the start of 2005. The 33 year-old had a short spell with Wolverhampton Wanderers and played a major role in the team's qualification. Former Asian Player of the Year Nawaf Al Temyat, another Al Hilal player, had overcome a series of injuries to make a welcome return to the squad. Asian club champions Al Ittihad contributed seven players to the team, including reigning Asian Player of the Year Hamad Al-Montashari, while newly crowned Saudi champions Al Shabab provided just one player, goalkeeper Mohammad Khojah.

Of their seven warm-up games the Saudis lost five, suffering 2-1 defeats by Poland and Belgium and a 2-0 defeat by the Czech Republic. They did manage a 1-0 win over Togo.

In an attempt to concentrate minds away from the distractions of the Western world, Paqueta removed alcohol from the minibars and adult channels from the TVs in the players' rooms at the Saudi Arabian team hotel.

DID YOU KNOW?
The biggest representation from any one club in any one squad was Riyadh's Al Hilal, domestic league and cup winners in 2004-05, who boasted nine players in Saudi Arabia's squad.

DID YOU KNOW?
Only two national squads – Italy and Saudi Arabia – were made up entirely of players from clubs from their own national leagues.

TUNISIA
Ranking 21   Odds 301/1

Tunisia coach Roger Lemerre opted for Francileudo dos Santos and Ziad Jaziri to lead the attack as expected. Dos Santos, a Brazilian-born striker, had scored an impressive 18 goals in 28 internationals. Rangers' Hamed Namouchi had to have intensive treatment on an ankle ligament injury in order to make the finals, but just scraped in.

But Lemerre had to call up Bastia's Chaouki Ben Saada to replace striker Issam Jomaa, who suffered a knee injury. Ben Saada had scored one goal in 12 international appearances and became the sixth French-born player in the Tunisian squad.

Tunisia warmed up with a comprehensive 3-0 win over Belarus, who just five days earlier had beaten England B. They then drew 0-0 with Uruguay in the LG Cup, but lost on penalties to the South Americans.

Harry Says

For me the winners had to come from a group of six countries, England, Italy, Argentina, France, Germany and, of course, perennial favourites and World Cup holders, Brazil. But let's leave the final pre-tournament word to the world's greatest player. Speaking on the eve of the opening game and quite possibly adopting a good deal of kidology, Pelé dismissed Brazil's chances as he believed "favourites always lose. Brazil are favourites and with that tag they can't win. Favourites always lose. In 2002, it happened to France. In 1990, Argentina lost the final match against Germany. In 1982, Brazil were favourites and lost against Italy and Holland are always favourites and always lose. I never wanted to be favourite. We must consider Germany, the hosts, as candidates. Italy are a good team and England have a great squad too."

Stadia
World Cup 2006 Venues

Olympiastadion, Berlin
World Cup capacity: 66,021 seats

The venue for the 1936 Olympics, famed for the spat between Adolf Hitler and American sprint legend Jesse Owens, was renovated to host the World Cup Final at a "not expensive" £165m. The vast bowl of the stadium sits 12 meters lower than its surrounding area. The roof rises 68 meters above pitch level and is made of transparent panels. The western stand remains open, faithful to the original design, to reveal the "Glockenturm", the original 1936 Olympic Bell Tower, to the spectators. Hertha Berlin's modern Olympiastadion boasts 113 VIP suites, a set of restaurants and two vast underground garages.

Rheinenergiestadion, Cologne
World Cup capacity: 40,590 seats

The RheinEnergieStadion was rebuilt stand-by-stand for the World Cup on the site of the two previous Müngersdorfer Stadiums. The compact arena's stands are almost on top of the pitch and are a far-cry from the former incarnation which had a running track. The rebuilding process cost £75m over the course of just two years. The inauguration of the stadium took place in March 2004, when Germany defeated Belgium 3-0. It is the home of the local Bundesliga team, FC Köln, and of the local NFL Europe team, the Cologne Centurions.

Signal Iduna Park, Dortmund
World Cup capacity: 60,285 seats

Formerly known as the Westfalenstadion, its home club, Borussia Dortmund, averaged gates of 77,000 in 2004/05. That was the highest figure in Europe and due in no small part to the huge terraced area in the Sudtribuhne. The 82,500 capacity drops to 67,000 for internationals, which are all-seated. The ground was initially built for the 1974 World Cup and has since had the corners filled in. Its incredible acoustics have seen it rechristened as 'the Opera House' by Dortmund fans.

Commerzbank Arena, Frankfurt
World Cup capacity: 43,324 seats

Work began on upgrading Eintracht Frankfurt's famous Waldstadion in 2002 and lasted three years. The result is the stunning, light and airy Commerzbank Arena featuring a transparent, retractable roof supported by a webbed grid of steel wires. The ground was given a dry-run for the World Cup at the 2005 Confederations Cup when it was chosen as the venue for the final between Brazil and Argentina. The 30 tonne video cube suspended from the roof became the centre of a betting scandal during the World Cup when Paul Robinson hit it with a clearance and Ladbrokes revealed people had been trying to lay bets on that eventuality occurring on the day of the game against Paraguay.

DID YOU KNOW?
The "old" Waldstadion hosted the first NFL Europe game on 23 March 1991 when the London Monarchs defeated Eintracht Galaxy 24-11.

Veltins-Arena, Gelsenkirchen
World Cup capacity: 48,426 seats

The AufSchalke Arena opened in August 2001 and hosted the 2004 Champions League final between Porto and Monaco. The 52,000-capacity ground is at the cutting edge of stadium technology, incorporating electronic admission, a removable pitch and retractable roof. Schalke 04's home was renamed as the Veltins-Arena after the naming rights were sold to the German brewery.

DID YOU KNOW?
The ground incorporates a 5km beer pipeline to keep the beer flowing during football matches, concerts or any other event the venue is used for.

AOL Arena, Hamburg
World Cup capacity: 45,442 seats

West Germany famously lost in Hamburg during the 1974 World Cup finals to their cross-border rivals East Germany. The venue for the 1-0 defeat – the Volksparkstadion – is no more, having been replaced by the AOL Arena. The old ground was raised in four stages and the pitch rotated 90 degrees in a two-year project completed in 2000. For the World Cup the 55,000 capacity for Hamburg SV home games was reduced due to standing restrictions.

DID YOU KNOW?
Kevin Keegan starred for Hamburg SV in the late 1970s winning back to back European Footballer of the Year Awards.

AWD Arena, Hanover
World Cup capacity: 39,297 seats

Formerly known as the Niedersachsenstadion, the AWD Arena has been Hannover 96's home since 1959. The venue was renovated for the World Cup at a cost of £43m. The relic of the old, bowl-shaped ground has been built up on all sides and an overhanging roof has been added. The 50,000 capacity for Bundesliga matches will be reduced to 39,000 during the World Cup. The stadium boasts 66 speakers and a 26,400 watt PA system.

DID YOU KNOW?
The four huge, crane-like concrete floodlights of the old ground were nicknamed "toothbrushes" by the locals.

Fritz-Walter Stadion, Kaiserslautern
World Cup capacity: 41,513 seats

The Fritz-Walter-Stadion was upgraded in preparation for the World Cup, but unlike the other 11 venues it retained some of its original character. Its existing, steeply-banked stands have been added to on several occasions since first opening in 1920. FC Kaiserslautern's home is also known locally as "Betzenberg", due to its location on Betzenberg Mountain.

DID YOU KNOW?
Fritz Walter, after whom the stadium is named, was West Germany's World Cup winning-captain in 1954 and played for Kaiserslautern throughout his career.

Zentralstadion, Leipzig
World Cup capacity: 38,898 seats

Zentralstadion has been dubbed the "stadium within a stadium" as VFB Leipzig's new ground was built within the walls of the city's old 100,000 capacity venue. The original arena, built in 1956, had fallen into disrepair in the 1990s. While facilities have improved beyond recognition, the seating has diminished and it is one of the World Cup's smaller venues, holding just 38,000. It was also the cheapest of the five new tournament stadia, built at £60m.

DID YOU KNOW?
Zentralstadion was the only World Cup stadium to stand in the former East Germany as well as being the sole venue without a team in the top-flight of the Bundesliga. FC Sachsen Leipzig, who were founded in 1990, are currently in the third tier of German football.

Allianz Arena, Munich
World Cup capacity: 59,416 seats

One of five totally new stadia built for the World Cup, the Allianz Arena was the most expensive at £190m. The three-tiered ground north of Munich hosted the opening match. It's spectacular translucent facade, made up of 2,874 panels, is lit up at night in a variety of colours. Both Munich's rival teams – Bayern and TSV Munich 1860 – share the stadium. But it was Englishman Owen Hargreaves who scored the ground's first Bundesliga goal.

DID YOU KNOW?
The decision to move out of the old Olympic Stadium, in which Germany won the 1974 World Cup, won 65.8% of the vote in a referendum which had a 37.5% turn out – the highest ever in a Bavarian referendum.

Franken-Stadion, Nuremburg
World Cup capacity: 36,898 seats

The Franken-Stadion has had a number of facelifts down the years, the most recent costing £38m. The tournament's smallest venue first opened in 1928 and was a marching area for the Hitler Youth in the 1930s. It had an overhaul in 1963 and changed name from the Urban Stadium in another redevelopment between 1987 and 1991. The stadium's latest developments coincided with tenants 1 FC Nürnberg returning to the top-flight.

DID YOU KNOW?
Typically Germanic environmentally-friendly thinking means all rainwater that falls on the Franken-Stadion is recycled for use elsewhere in the stadium.

Gottlieb-Daimler-Stadion, Stuttgart
World Cup capacity: 47,757 seats

Stuttgart's Gottlieb-Daimler-Stadion hosted the third place play-off match. The ground, which used to be called the Neckar-Stadion, hosted Germany's first international match after the Second World War. It also witnessed the country's first international as a reunified country in 1990 and the international retirement of present German coach Jürgen Klinsmann. VfB Stuttgart's 47,000-capacity ground was also the venue for the 1993 athletics World Championships.

DID YOU KNOW?
The ground's two new video screens were the biggest of their kind in Europe with a 115 sq m viewable area.

Match Officials

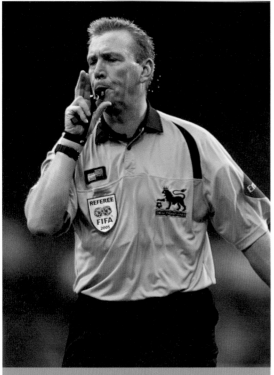

England's representative on the match officials panel, Graham Poll

21 referees, representing 20 different nationalities, emerged from a gruelling series of tests and examinations to be chosen by the FIFA Referees Committee to officiate at the 2006 World Cup.

When making their decision, the committee members evaluated the performances of a shortlist of 44 candidates during FIFA competitions, continental championships and in national leagues over a period of 18 months. The referees' performances at the two FIFA workshops in Frankfurt in the Spring of 2006 were likewise taken into account. At the second workshop, the match officials underwent comprehensive medical checks and a fitness test. In addition, the referees all completed a psychological test and underwent interviews with members of the FIFA Referees Committee.

But the initial referees selected had to wait to see if they would make it to the finals. Because FIFA believed that familiarity between officials is important in producing the best possible performance on the pitch, Germany 2006 was the first World Cup to feature only refereeing trios from the same country, or at least from the same confederation. The selected referees were reliant on their assigned assistants also passing fitness and aptitude tests in Frankfurt from 18 to 21 April. Of the three assistants for each referee at this point in the selection process, at least two had to successfully complete the tests. If they failed to do so, the entire group – including the nominated referee – would be excluded from the list of World Cup officials and replaced by another quartet.

This fate befell Greek referee Kyros Vassaras and his Spanish counterpart Manuel Mejuto Gonzalez. As some of their assistants failed to reach the required standards, Vassaras and Mejuto Gonzalez were taken off the list being replaced by two original members of the support and development group, Italy's Roberto Rosetti and Spain's Luis Medina Cantalejo.

Three other referees Guatemalan referee Carlos Batres had to pull out of the fitness tests during the assistant referees' workshop at the end of March. The official was forced to admit defeat in his attempts to regain full fitness after suffering a cruciate ligament injury in December 2005 that ended his 2006 World Cup ambitions. Batres was replaced in Germany by Mexico's Marco Rodriguez.

On 29 May Jamaica's Peter Prendergast picked up a bad knee injury and he, and his two assistants, Anthony Garwood (Jamaica) and Joseph Taylor (Trinidad and Tobago), were unable to officiate at the World Cup. With it being so late in the preparations, the team were not replaced.

Late in the piece Italy withdrew one of their two referees due to his involvement in the match-fixing scandal engulfing the professional game in the country. Massimo de Santis and his assistants, Alessandro Griselli and Marco Ivaldi all missed out on the finals. This team were also not replaced.

The support and development group – another World Cup first – consisted of five referees and ten assistants who would take part in all training sessions and meetings, and would only step into the fray in the event of another match official being unable to take part for whatever reason, such as injury or illness.

During the course of the final pre-World Cup workshop, the referees were also brought up to speed on the interpretations of the Laws of the Game that were passed by the International Football Association Board (IFAB). The IFAB stressed that the referees and their assistants had to follow these directives at the World Cup and clamp down on time-wasting, reckless play (including elbows and brutal fouls), reckless and dangerous tackles, shirt-pulling and simulation (diving), all with the ultimate objective of protecting the players, and with it, the game in general.

The refereeing trios arrived in Germany on 26 May, using the Hotel Kempinski Gravenbruch in Frankfurt/Neu-Isenburg as their headquarters for the duration of the tournament.

FIFA were determined to stamp out the kind of lunging, dangerous foul that Trinidad & Tobago's Densill Thoebald committed on Steven Gerrard

	Family Name	First Name	Country	Date of Birth
THE 21 TRIOS OF MATCH OFFICIALS FOR THE 2006 WORLD CUP				
Referee	ABD EL FATAH	Essam	Egypt	30.12.1965
Assistants	DANTE	Dramane	Mali	09.12.1961
	NDOYE	Mamadou	Senegal	27.12.1961
Referee	AMARILLA	Carlos	Paraguay	26.10.1970
Assistants	ANDINO	Amelio	Paraguay	24.12.1962
	BERNAL	Manuel	Paraguay	17.06.1963
Referee	ARCHUNDIA	Benito	Mexico	21.03.1966
Assistants	RAMIREZ	José	Mexico	27.11.1962
	VERGARA	Hector	Canada	15.12.1966
Referee	BUSACCA	Massimo	Switzerland	06.02.1969
Assistants	BURAGINA	Francesco	Switzerland	07.01.1966
	ARNET	Matthias	Switzerland	02.06.1968
Referee	CODJIA	Coffi	Benin	09.12.1967
Assistants	NTAGUNGIRA	Celestin	Rwanda	11.05.1966
	ADERODJOU	Aboudou	Benin	13.02.1961
Referee	DE BLEECKERE	Frank	Belgium	01.07.1966
Assistants	HERMANS	Peter	Belgium	27.06.1966
	VROMANS	Walter	Belgium	21.04.1968

	Family Name	First Name	Country	Date of Birth
Referee	ELIZONDO	Horacio	Argentina	04.11.1963
Assistants	GARCIA	Dario	Argentina	29.10.1961
	OTERO	Rodolfo	Argentina	14.12.1962
Referee	IVANOV	Valentin	Russia	04.07.1961
Assistants	GOLUBEV	Nikolay	Russia	09.11.1970
	VOLNIN	Evgueni	Russia	27.06.1962
Referee	KAMIKAWA	Toru	Japan	08.06.1963
Assistants	HIROSHIMA	Yoshikazu	Japan	22.05.1962
	KIM	Dae Young	Korea Republic	15.08.1962
Referee	LARRIONDA	Jorge	Uruguay	09.03.1968
Assistants	RIAL	Walter	Uruguay	09.01.1964
	FANDINO	Pablo	Uruguay	11.10.1966
Referee	MAIDIN	Shamsul	Singapore	16.04.1966
Assistants	PERMPANICH	Prachya	Thailand	13.08.1962
	GHULOUM	Eisa	United Arab Emirates	01.03.1966
Referee	MEDINA CANTALEJO	Luis	Spain	01.03.196
Assistants	GIRALDEZ CARRASCO	Victoriano	Spain	18.09.1964
	MEDINA HERNANDEZ	Pedro	Spain	17.12.1962
Referee	MERK	Markus	Germany	15.03.1962
Assistants	SCHRAER	Christian	Germany	15.03.1962
	SALVER	Jan-Hendrik	Germany	01.03.1969
Referee	MICHEL	Lubos	Slovakia	16.05.1968
Assistants	SLYSKO	Roman	Slovakia	04.08.1973
	BALKO	Martin	Slovakia	08.03.1972
Referee	POLL	Graham	England	29.07.1963
Assistants	SHARP	Philip	England	05.04.1964
	TURNER	Glenn	England	06.11.1964
Referee	POULAT	Eric	France	08.12.1963
Assistants	DAGORNE	Lionel	France	09.07.1961
	TEXIER	Vincent	France	25.11.1962

	Family Name	First Name	Country	Date of Birth
Referee	RODRIGUEZ	Marco	Mexico	10.11.1973
Assistants	CAMARGO	José Luis	Mexico	25.09.1972
	LEAL	Leonel	Costa Rica	21.11.1976
Referee	ROSETTI	Roberto	Italy	18.09.1967
Assistants	COPELLI	Cristiano	Italy	14.06.1967
	STAGNOLI	Alessandro	Italy	02.02.1965
Referee	RUIZ	Oscar	Colombia	01.11.1969
Assistants	TAMAYO	Fernando	Ecuador	17.12.1963
	NAVIA	José	Colombia	05.12.1963
Referee	SHIELD	Mark	Australia	02.09.1973
Assistants	GIBSON	Nathan	Australia	7.08.1972
	WILSON	Ben	Australia	26.06.1975
Referee	SIMON	Carlos	Brazil	03.09.1965
Assistants	TAVARES	Aristeu	Brazil	17.10.1962
	CORONA	Ednilson	Brazil	04.02.1965

THE FIVE REFEREEING TRIOS FOR THE SUPPORT AND DEVELOPMENT GROUP

	Family Name	First Name	Country	Date of Birth
Referee	AL GHAMDI	Khalil	Saudi Arabia	02.09.1970
Assistants	AL KADRI	Hamdi	Syria	12.04.1965
	ARABATI	Fathi	Jordan	05.02.1964
Referee	CHANDIA	Carlos	Chile	14.11.1964
Assistants	JULIO	Cristian	Chile	11.02.1964
	GONZALEZ	Rodrigo	Chile	21.12.1962
Referee	DAMON	Jerome	South Africa	04.04.1972
Assistants	MOLEFE	Enock	South Africa	04.06.1968
	YEBOAH	Justice	Ghana	23.04.1961
Referee	GUEZZAZ	Mohamed	Morocco	01.10.1962
Assistants	DJEZZAR	Brahim	Algeria	23.01.1963
	ENDENG ZOGO	Jean Marie	Cameroon	11.10.1962
Referee	STOTT	Kevin	USA	09.07.1967
Assistants	STRICKLAND	Chris	USA	29.11.1966
	BARKEY	Gregory	USA	20.08.1963

section
three

group stage

Day One
Friday 9 June 2006

Opening Ceremony

A parade of 158 World Cup winners was the highlight of the opening ceremony, which also featured lederhosen clad dancers and 182 drummers from Upper Bavaria

At Last The 2006 World Cup Arrives With A Bang

Hosts Germany got the tournament off to a flying start, beating Costa Rica in a six goal thriller with Thorsten Frings cracking home an early contender for goal of the tournament

Down The Pole

Unfancied Ecuador produce the first shock of the tournament with a 2-0 victory over Poland, whose coach lays the blame for the defeat firmly at the feet of his team

"I don't think I got the tactics wrong, everything depends on the performance and attitude of the players."

Pawel Janas (Poland)

Germany 4 v Costa Rica 2
Group A
Allianz Arena, Munich
Attendance: 64,950
Kick-off: 6pm   Temperature: 26°C

Paulo Wanchope, obscured on right of picture, grabs Costa Rica's second goal, but hosts Germany ran out 4-2 winners in a fabulous opening game

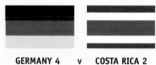

GERMANY 4   v   COSTA RICA 2

Referee: Horacio Marcelo Elizondo

Scorers

6'	Lahm	Wanchope 12', 73'
17', 61'	Klose	
87'	Frings	

Teams

01	Lehmann	Porras 18
03	Friedrich	Marin 03
17	Mertesacker	Umana 04
21	Metzelder	Gonzalez 12
16	Lahm	Martinez 05
07	Schweinsteiger	Fonseca 06
08	Frings	Solis 08
18	Borowski	Centeno 10
19	Schneider	Sequeira 20
20	Podolski	Gomez 11
11	Klose	Wanchope 09

Substitutes

72'	> 05 Kehl < 18 Borowski	02 Drummond > 05 Martinez <	67'
79'	> 10 Neuville < 11 Klose	07 Bolanos > 08 Solis <	78'
90'	> 22 Odonkor < 19 Schneider	14 Azofeifa > 11 Gomez <	90'

Discipline

Fonseca foul	31'

63%	Ball Possession	37%
10	Shots on target	2
11	Shots off target	2
11	Fouls	15
7	Corner Kicks	3
3	Offsides	3

Official FIFA Man of the Match
Miroslav Klose

My bags packed, I'm off to the World Cup.

So far I've received Nationwide giant flags, a flashing electronic T-shirt that my five year-old, Poppy, thinks is classy, my Three Lions Samsung Mobile phone, cans of beer and a Magnum of Man of the Match Carling Champagne for my NTLWorld podcasting shows and I'm heading off to Frankfurt for England's opener.

No World Cup has ever been more heavily sponsored, and I was to be a guest of Samsung Mobile and my old mate there Mark Mitchinson. I'd be finding out how the other half live in the grand-sounding Samsung Partners Festa over this first weekend of the world's biggest ever football jamboree. Well, surely there's enough plugs in those opening lines to keep me going throughout this tournament!

I got the vibe I would not be disappointed, having already sampled the Korean corporation's hospitality in their super executive box not far from Roman Abramovich at the Bridge.

STATE OF PLAY							GROUP A	
	P	W	D	L	F	A	GD	Pts
GERMANY	1	1	0	0	4	2	+2	3
COSTA RICA	1	0	0	1	2	4	-2	0
ECUADOR	0	0	0	0	0	0	0	0
POLAND	0	0	0	0	0	0	0	0

DID YOU KNOW?
Miroslav Klose celebrated his 28th birthday with two goals to take his Finals tally to 7 goals in 8 appearances.

For five World Cups I have been sitting there in the press box, first with biro and note book, then with laptop, and now things will be very different for me. I won't have the pressure of writing match reports as my column as Group Chief Football Writer for Express Newspapers has more to do with analysis and unearthing the big football news stories of the day.

Departure was via the Harrods private lounge and then champagne lunch on the flight before arriving on the outskirts of Frankfurt at the Hahn Airport, as Frankfurt's main airport was naturally bursting to capacity. It took a 90-minute coach ride to the Arabella Sharaton Am Busing Palais hotel.

A team from Grass Roots of Mark Taylor and Mirlinda Shaqiri had been assembled to take care of our every whim, well almost. And on arrival there was a bright red England shirt with my name on the back awaiting me in my hotel room. Mark told me he wanted me to wear it for The Game. How could I refuse?

We settled in just in time to watch hosts Germany open the scoring and then, the possibility of an opening day shock, as Cost Rica equalised through Paulo Wanchope, well known for his spell in English football. The Germans went on to restore their lead in a thrilling enough opening half, and ran out 4-2 winners, although Paulo did collect another fine goal. During the commentary, the German equivalent to John Motson called him Wonchopper!

That night was spent fine dining at the four star Schloss Reinhartshausen, situated in the wine growing region of Rheingau on the banks of the Rhine, where we were entertained by impressionist Jon Culshaw, of Dead Ringers fame, and I was asked by Mark to make a short speech to the Samsung guests, which I did, predicting a 2-0 win for England. With many of the guests having their other halves present, I suggested I would take questions about the Footballers Wives, as well as any on England and the

Ecuador 2 v Poland 0
Group A
Veltins-Arena, Gelsenkirchen
Attendance: 52,000
Kick-off: 9pm   Temperature: 21°C

Dejection amongst Polish fans as their team goes down 2-0 in what many saw as a shock, but any team that finishes third in the South American qualification section, as Ecuador did, are going to be tough to handle

finals. One lady quickly asked "What will Posh be wearing?"

"Not a lot," I suggested.

Between the Pina Coladas on the terrace before the meal, it was a case of dashing into another room to see the replays from Germany's opening game on a large format screen.... Samsung, of course.

Miroslav Klose had bagged a decisive brace, while Torsten Frings' spectacular 35-yard effort set the seal on a successful, if not totally convincing start for the hosts. Philipp Lahm had opened the scoring some six minutes into the tournament with a beautifully-curled effort from the left corner of the box. Klose's pair incuded a second goal midway through the second half, before Wanchope netted his second to ensure a nervy finish.

Wanchope had silenced the very partisan crowd with an equaliser in the 12th minute, when the youthful German backline were exposed by a through ball. Klinsmann was caught on camera with a sarcastic smile and his hand pointing to what he perceived to be an obvious offside. With all the analysis in German it was hard to tell what he was saying when the fabulous graphics showed that Wanchope was actually onside before he fired a low shot past Jens Lehmann to level the scores. Other interesting reactions on the German bench included injured superstar Michael Ballack's zealous celebrations and reserve goalkeeper Oliver Kahn's broad smiles as his fierce rival, Jens Lehmann, conceded those two goals.

There was one other game on the opening day and Agustin Delgado scored one goal and made one as Ecuador got only their second ever World Cup campaign off to a flying start with victory over Poland in Gelsenkirchen. Delgado's 24th-minute flick-on set up the opener for Carlos Tenorio before the former Southampton man sealed victory from point-blank range with 10 minutes to play. Poland's hopes of reaching the second round looked bleak while the Latin Americans will enter uncharted territory if they get into the last 16.

Ecuador coach Luis Fernando Suarez had vowed to play attractive football and his team lived up to that pledge, a stark contrast to their dreadful start to their first World Cup four years ago, when Italy took a 2-0 lead inside 20 minutes of their first match in Japan. Poland, who won the Olympic title on German soil in 1972 and then finished third in the West Germany-hosted World Cup two years later, badly needed someone of the calibre of Grzegorz Lato who was tournament top scorer in 1974 with seven goals and, with 95 caps, is still the most-capped Polish player.

The outnumbered Ecuador fans made their presence felt against the vast contingent of Polish supporters who seemed to occupy all but one corner of the Veltins Arena, the home of Schalke – a German team founded in 1904 by Polish miners. Ecuador skipper Ivan Hurtado was winning his 131st cap, yet was sprightly enough to block a Krzynowek shot. The killer blow came after 80 minutes when Poland waited for an offside flag which – correctly – never came and substitute Ivan Kaviedes squared for Delgado to roll the ball into the net. Jelen and fellow substitute Pawel Brozek both hit the woodwork late on, but Ecuador were full value for their win.

So tomorrow I will sit in Frankfurt's Commerzbank Arena with a glass of bubbly, rather than my mobile and computer. Perhaps, after all those years of toil, it's time I enjoyed a touch of luxury. Only trouble is that I do have a long memory, having watched in '66 as a lad of just 14 and covered my first World Cup for the Daily Mirror in Mexico in 1986, that England have a notorious problem with their opening game and I go to sleep worrying about England's historical slow starts.

However, I have a feeling that even without Wayne Rooney, England will give a good account of themselves against Paraguay. I am confident of raising a glass or two to that on Saturday night.

ECUADOR 2 v POLAND 0

Referee: Toru Kamikawa

Scorers

24'	C Tenorio
80'	Delgado

Teams

12	Mora	Boruc 01
04	De la Cruz	Jop 02
03	Hurtado	Baszczynski 04
17	Espinoza	Bak 06
18	Reasco	Zewlakow 14
08	Mendez	Sobolewski 07
14	Castillo	Krzynowek 08
16	Valencia	Szymkowiak 10
20	E Tenorio	Smolarek 15
11	Delgado	Radomski 16
21	C Tenorio	Zurawski 09

Substitutes

65'	10 Kaviedes / 21 C Tenorio	21 Jelen / 07 Sobolewski	67'
69'	02 Guagua / 03 Hurtado	05 Kosowski / 08 Krzynowek	77'
83'	06 Urrutia / 11 Delgado	23 Brozek / 09 Zurawski	84'

Discipline

31'	Hurtado foul	Smolarek foul	36'
70'	Mendez delaying free-kick		

46%	Ball Possession	54%
9	Shots on target	6
4	Shots off target	5
16	Fouls	8
3	Corner Kicks	11
2	Offsides	3

Official FIFA Man of the Match

Agustin Delgado

STATE OF PLAY							GROUP A
	P	W	D	L	F	A	GD Pts
GERMANY	1	1	0	0	4	2	+3 3
ECUADOR	1	1	0	0	2	0	+2 3
COSTA RICA	1	0	0	1	2	4	-2 0
POLAND	1	0	0	1	0	2	-2 0

Day Two
Saturday 10 June 2006

Sven's Men Make Heavy Work of Win

England get off to a great goalscoring start, but wilt in the Frankfurt heat as Eriksson's selection policy and substitutions are questioned again

Trinidad Jubilant at Battling Point

Despite being down to ten men for 44 minutes, the smallest nation ever to qualify for the World Cup pick up a point against Sweden

Argentina Pushed All the Way by Ivory Coast

In a feast of attacking football Argentina show why they are serious contenders with a 2-1 victory over Ivory Coast secured by Javier Saviola's goal

"I don't regret what I did picking the team and it was vital to get this win."
Sven-Göran Eriksson (England)

England 1 v Paraguay 0
Group B
Commerzbank Arena, Frankfurt
Attendance: 48,000
Kick-off: 3pm   Temperature: 29°C

ENGLAND 1   v   PARAGUAY 0

Referee: Marco Rodriguez

Scorers
3'   Gamarra (og)

Teams

England	Paraguay
01 Robinson	Villar 01
02 Neville	Caniza 21
05 Ferdinand	Gamarra 04
06 Terry	Caceres 05
03 Cole	Toledo 03
07 Beckham	Bonet 06
08 Lampard	Acuna 10
04 Gerrard	Paredes 13
11 Cole	Riveros 16
10 Owen	Valdez 18
21 Crouch	Santa Cruz 09

Substitutes

56' > 20 Downing < 10 Owen	22 Bobadilla > 01 Villar <	8'
82' > 16 Hargreaves < 11 Cole	23 Cuevas > 06 Bonet <	68'
	02 Nunez > 03 Toledo <	82'

Discipline

19'	Gerrard foul		Valdez foul	22'
63'	Crouch dissent			

56%	Ball Possession	44%
6	Shots on target	5
7	Shots off target	11
13	Fouls	11
6	Corner Kicks	1
4	Offsides	3

Official FIFA Man of the Match
Frank Lampard

STATE OF PLAY							GROUP B
	P	W	D	L	F	A	GD Pts
ENGLAND	1	1	0	0	1	0	+1 3
PARAGUAY	1	0	0	1	0	1	-1 0
SWEDEN	0	0	0	0	0	0	0 0
TRIN & TOB	0	0	0	0	0	0	0 0

Paul Robinson saves Carlos Parades' flying effort as England cling on amidst a furore over water replenishment in the oppressive heat to win a vital three points

You always pray there will be no trouble, but there were going to be tens of thousands of England fans in town without tickets for their first game in the World Cup.

Paraguay were accused of selling nearly half of their tickets to touts who were charging fans up to £645 a seat. At least 1,500 of the Paraguayan FA's allocation of 3,300 tickets for the Group B opener 'disappeared' amid claims that they had been passed on to black-market ticket agencies in Britain and Europe. The four travel companies in the Paraguayan capital of Asuncion who were chosen to sell most of the tickets complained they were short-changed. Siboney, one of the four firms, says that, while it received between 200 and 300 tickets for Paraguay's other games, against

DID YOU KNOW?
The game was decided by the 30th own goal in the history of the World Cup. It was the second time England have been beneficiaries of an own goal. They beat Czechoslovakia 2-0 in 1982, courtesy of an effort from Trevor Francis and an own goal from Jozef Barmos.

Fans spent an astonishing £200m in the country's supermarkets stocking up on provisions on the Saturday morning prior to England's World Cup opener against Paraguay. Supporters bought 10 million cases of beer and six million pizzas, while Tesco alone revealed that they sold three million barbecue sets as temperatures soared.

DID YOU KNOW?
The last time that England played a World Cup tie on June 10th was in 1962 when they lost 1-3 to Brazil in the quarter-finals in Chile. Gerry Hitchens scored England's goal.

Sweden and Trinidad & Tobago, it got just 40 for Frankfurt. Despite the shortage in Paraguay, tickets are readily available in Europe – at exorbitant prices.

The FA declined to comment beyond advising fans not to buy black-market tickets. The thought was ever present about the fans' behaviour as I joined the Samsung party on the eight kilometre coach journey from hotel to stadium. SP Kim, President of Samsung Electronics UK, addressed his party at the front of the coach 'praying for a victory for the England team'. That brought warm applause.

I have made thousands of these coach trips to football stadia around the world, normally in the company of other journalists from rival newspapers. This was the first time my companions were from the corporate sector and, without that fierce rivalry that exists within the newspaper industry and all the petty jealousies attached to it, this was a pleasant experience.

FIFA's Elite hospitality package gave us a special room, providing a Lanson champagne reception and wonderful food, wines and beer from Anheuser Busch, plus some good quality Reisling and red. The Samsung executive seats were a mere four rows behind Sven and the England dug out and the searing heat the players experienced was something we also had to endure. I probably lost a pound just sitting there, drenched in sweat, so imagine how tough it was for the players, who each lost around eight pounds.

After the game, when I checked back with the Sunday Express sports editor Scott Wilson, the feedback was that the media planned a panning for the boys in the papers back home. "Not good enough without Rooney" was the theme. I told Scottie that I was the closest to the action of any football writer at the World Cup and could tell him from first hand experience it must have been 100 degrees at ground level. Under those circumstances it was a relatively impressive result in beating a team who would be more used to such conditions and therefore able to cope the more the game wore on, therefore Paraguay had the edge in the second half.

I detected, though, that when Owen was substituted, he looked a touch thoughtful sitting back on the bench. I wondered whether all was well with his recovery programme. He lacked conviction. Owen never likes being taken off, and didn't look at all pleased with himself, the fact that he failed to score, or even looked likely to.

I spotted Jenas being summoned to come on in injury time, but sod's law, the seconds ticked by and the whistle blew before he crossed the line. I thought that might be the closest he would get to playing in the Finals.

When Joe Cole went up front, as Downing came on for Owen, it was clear that any dissension in the camp at sending home Jermain Defoe was correct. Sven's four forwards meant the squad was very light in this department, while they waited for Wayne. Then Hargreaves replaced Joe Cole, but just before that Cole went down injured and Sven had Walcott preparing for the fray. However, after Cole recovered the coach changed his mind and went for Downing instead.

Yet, Eriksson's men then struggled to create clear opportunities and there were several areas of concern as the team fell back and back, but England claimed three points in Frankfurt, and I had seen far worse opening performances from the national team in World Cups.

Gerrard had been named in the starting line after the Liverpool skipper sufficiently recovered from the stiff back and he stiffened up England's midfield and along with some others he had a good first half, but faded in the heat. Yet Gerrard had barely settled into the game when England snatched the lead, with Beckham whipping in a free-kick from the left flank after Joe Cole was fouled by Delio Toledo. The

The Prince's entry to the ground was captured by Samsung party member Sue Prebble

Sweden 0 v Trinidad & Tobago 0

Group B
Signal Iduna Park, Dortmund
Attendance: 62,959
Kick-off: 6pm   Temperature: 16°C

Sweden were devastated after dominating the match but failing to find the back of Shaka Hislop's net. It led to yet another dressing room bust up between Freddie Ljungberg and Olof Mellberg (pictured, no.3)

SWEDEN 0 v TRINIDAD & TOBAGO 0

Referee: Shamsul Maidin

Teams

SWEDEN		TRINIDAD & TOBAGO
23 Shaaban		Hislop 01
06 Linderoth		John 03
03 Mellberg		Sancho 05
04 Lucic		Lawrence 06
05 Edman		Gray 08
09 Ljungberg		Birchall 07
07 Alexandersson		Edwards 11
08 Svensson		Theobald 18
21 Wilhelmsson		Samuel 12
10 Ibrahimovic		John 14
11 Larsson		Yorke 19

Substitutes

62' > 20 Allback < 08 Svensson	13 Glen > 18 Theobald < 53'
78' > 18 Jonson < 21 Wilhelmsson	09 Whitley > 12 Samuel < 66'
79' > 16 Kallstrom < 06 Linderoth	

Discipline

90'	Larsson foul	
		A John foul 16'
		A John foul (second yellow) 46'
		Yorke time wasting 74'

SWEDEN		TRINIDAD & TOBAGO
60%	**Ball Possession**	40%
6	**Shots on target**	1
17	**Shots off target**	5
8	**Fouls**	10
8	**Corner Kicks**	1
2	**Offsides**	1

Official FIFA Man of the Match
Dwight Yorke

STATE OF PLAY							GROUP A
	P	W	D	L	F	A	GD	Pts
ENGLAND	1	1	0	0	1	0	+1	3
SWEDEN	1	0	1	0	0	0	0	1
TRIN & TOB	1	0	1	0	0	0	0	1
PARAGUAY	1	0	0	1	0	1	-1	0

DID YOU KNOW?
Sweden failed to win their opening match at a World Cup for the seventh consecutive time. Their last win in an opener dates back to 1958 when they beat Mexico 3-0.

ball went in off the head of Paraguay skipper Carlos Gamarra. But the initial euphoria quickly subsided as it became a slog in the conditions and, although England saw plenty of the ball, Paraguay remained in the game, with Carlos Paredes getting his shot deflected wide of Paul Robinson's post by one of his own players.

At the final whistle those who hadn't played prepared to warm down and Rooney thrilled the England fans who had stayed behind long enough to witness the training session.

Garth Crooks was performing his round of interviews just by the tunnel entrance with the fans chanting "there's only one Gabby Logan" at him! Garth is much under-rated by the media, but he knows his football and he sensed that all was not right with Owen, who had opted out of the media mixed zone and had been smuggled out of a side door along with a few of the other England stars who preferred to avoid the media scrum.

I rang Garth that evening and he laughed when I told him I preferred him to Gabby!

I had bumped into FA chairman Geoff Thompson and a few journalist pals on the way into the ground, and watched as many fans were warmly greeted by Prince William. Alan Ball, there working for BBC, bumped into the Prince. Ballie said, "Good to meet you your highness." Prince William responded, "Call me William, and my mum told me all about you and the Boys of '66 and how she presented the trophy to Bobby Moore." Ballie was very impressed by the Prince's relaxed style and only a couple of inconspicuous minders. Then in came the wife of the England captain surrounded by a pack of thuggish looking apes.

Back to the hotel in time to catch up with events that would brighten England's day – an unexpected draw between Trinidad & Tobago and Sweden that left England top of the group. Not a bad result, surely. Enough to tip the balance toward optimism. And it was all down to an old friend. Veteran goalkeeper Shaka Hislop, a late replacement for Kelvin Jack, who sustained a head injury just before kick-off, made a series of stunning saves to deny Sweden. Hislop became the oldest player in the tournament so far at the age of 37 years and 108 days.

The fact the World Cup minnows gained a point was remarkable given that Avery John was sent off in the first minute of the second half. But they dug deep to rattle the Swedes and showed they were not prepared to stand on any ceremony with Zlatan Ibrahimovic left reeling after a stiff challenge by Avery John. Trinidad made a rare breakaway in the 34th minute and Carlos Edwards stung former Arsenal goalkeeper Rami Shaaban's fingers with a shot from distance.

However they were again forced onto the back foot four minutes later when Larsson escaped his marker only for his header to clear the bar. Hislop came to Trinidad's rescue when he did well to turn over a thumping drive from Wilhelmsson and proved equal to a stinging shot from Ibrahimovic in the 43rd minute as Trinidad managed to escape the first half on level terms.

John's sending off following a challenge on Wilhelmsson was questionable. He did appear to take both the ball and the man. Yorke then showed his defensive ability by blocking Larsson's close-range effort as Sweden ramped up the pressure – but to no avail. There were wild scenes of celebration as Yorke and his players gained a shock result of such enormous benefit to England.

World Cup fervour had taken a grip back home where more than half of the UK tuned in to watch England's game, around 31 million, one of the biggest ever TV audiences.

Argentina 2 v Ivory Coast 1
Group C
AOL Arena, Hamburg
Attendance: 49,480
Kick-off: 9pm   Temperature: 17°C

Hernan Crespo opens the scoring for Argentina in an entertaining encounter with World Cup debutants Ivory Coast

It was estimated that while 12.8m watched on TV at home, another 18m were in pubs and city centres watching on big screens. In this technological age even more watched on computers or listened on radio. BBC2, ITV1, Channel 4 and Five managed a combined audience of barely one mullion between 2pm and 4pm as an alternative to the football fix.

While there was limited trouble in Frankfurt, live screenings in certain UK city centres risked being shut down because of violent outbreaks. Merseyside police recommended halting the screenings in Liverpool, putting on Wimbledon tennis instead. There were problems at Canary Wharf too, which led to the screen being closed for England's next match against Trinidad & Tobago.

We watched the evening game downstairs in the basement of the Restaurant Vinum where there was a big screen. Shame for the wives and girlfriends as the lads were glued to the rich entertainment as Argentina and the Ivory Coast locked horns. For Mark it was like watching his beloved Chelsea with Drogba and Crespo head to head in the battle of the centre-forwards, and both of them scoring as Argentina took a hard fought win.

After the meal Mark, his lovely wife Lynn, Jim Slater (marketing and CRM Director for phones 4u), his missus Michelle, and myself ended up in the lively street opposite the Opera House listening to a soul singer as fans from all nationalities mixed in the rarefied atmosphere of a World Cup night in Frankfurt.

There must have been 40,000 England fans there, many of them gathered down by the river where there was a giant floating screen that could be viewed from both banks. There was inevitably the odd unruly incident, a stand-off with the police, and a few objects thrown, but nothing that could remotely be described as a riot, so on the whole it was relatively peaceful.

Over the years you become familiar with the sounds of England games, the sirens, police, ambulance, mostly police, and there were a few such sounds that pierced the barmy night air, but no where near as frequent as I have experienced on so many such occasions wrecked by the yobs.

I discovered that there was another party in town that night. Team Rooney gathered in an exclusive Italian restaurant. Around the table were gathered some of the most powerful and influential men in the football career of the kid on whom England's hopes of winning the World Cup hinged. Rooney's agent Paul Stretford hosted the fine dining, champagne and exquisite wine in this lavish, all expenses paid night out. Stretford's guest were Nike, Coke, publishers Harper Collins, EA sports, and also, strangely enough, a key figure behind the scenes at Manchester United. The group celebrated England's opening win over Paraguay, but on the menu was Rooney's metatarsal, and his incredible recovery rate.

When Ronaldo was ushered away from a clinic specialising in psychological disorders to be hassled into playing an abortive role in the World Cup Final in France, the conspiracy theory held that the Brazilian sponsors were responsible for lobbying for his

appearance. Brian Marwood is one of the most genuine football figures in the game, and as head of football for Nike, he was one of the privileged inner circle of Team Rooney.

A former PFA leading light and ex-Arsenal winger Marwood has high principles and he told me in Frankfurt: "There is no influence being brought to bear, how could there be? The decision rests with the medical experts and that's precisely how it should be. Paul Stretford would agree with that, and so would I, and so would everyone around the table. Part of the talk, as it happens, was that five weeks ago none of us thought we would be here talking about Wayne Rooney playing in the tournament. It is a bonus merely to have him here, and when he plays has nothing to do with what any of us might have to say about the matter. All I can tell you is that knowing Wayne the way that I do, is that he is itching to play."

Because Marwood's integrity is unimpeachable, there can be no suspicion of any enforced pressure from the Team Rooney camp.

Sir Alex Ferguson had insisted Rooney would not take any part in the group stages, so he would be completely exasperated to discover just how determined Rooney is to play even just a bit part in the game against Trinidad and Tobago.

Other News

Togo's German coach Otto Pfister resigned over the unresolved dispute over players' payments

ARGENTINA 2   v   IVORY COAST 1

Referee: Frank De Bleeckere

Scorers

24'	Crespo	Drogba	82'
38'	Saviola		

Teams

01	Abbondanzieri	Tizie 01
21	Burdisso	Eboue 21
02	Ayala	K Toure 04
06	Heinze	Meite 12
03	Sorin	Boka 03
18	Maxi	Akale 02
08	Mascherano	Zokora 05
05	Cambiasso	Kalou 08
10	Riquelme	Keita 18
07	Saviola	Y Toure 19
09	Crespo	Drogba 11

Substitutes

64'	> 14 Palacio < 09 Crespo	15 Dindane 08 Kalou	> 56'
76'	> 22 Gonzalez < 07 Saviola	14 B Kone 02 Akale	> 62'
90'	> 16 Aimar < 10 Riquelme	09 A Kone 18 Keita	> 77'

Discipline

41'	Saviola *time wasting*	Eboue *foul*	62'
49'	Heinze *foul*	Drogba *foul*	90'
81'	Gonzalez *foul*		

60%	Ball Possession	40%
4	Shots on target	8
4	Shots off target	9
13	Fouls	14
3	Corner Kicks	6
6	Offsides	0

Official FIFA Man of the Match
Javier Saviola

STATE OF PLAY						GROUP C	
	P	W	D	L	F	A	GD	Pts
ARGENTINA	1	1	0	0	2	1	+1	3
IVORY COAST	1	0	0	1	1	2	-1	0
HOLLAND	0	0	0	0	0	0	0	0
SERB & MON	0	0	0	0	0	0	0	0

Day Three
Sunday 11 June 2006

Bathed In Orange

Leipzig was swathed in celebrating Dutch fans after Arjen Robben's goal gave them victory in a tight game against Serbia & Montenegro

Divine Intervention

Mexican goalkeeper Oswaldo Sanchez thanks his recently deceased father for the inspiration to defeat Iran

Colonial War

Portugal survive a few uncomfortable moments to secure a bruising 1-0 victory against former colony Angola

"The confidence Felipe (Sanchez's father) gave him was like an angel from up above watching him. With that angel watching I'm sure he will be able to make a lot of saves." Ricardo La Volpe (Mexico)

Holland 1 v Serbia & Montenegro 0

Group C
Zentralstadion, Leipzig
Attendance: 37,216
Kick-off: 3pm   Temperature: 27°C

Arjen Robben celebrates the only goal of the game

HOLLAND 1 v SERBIA & MONTENEGRO 0

Referee: Markus Merk

Scorers

18'   Robben

Teams

Holland	Serbia & Montenegro
01 van der Sar	Jevric 01
14 Heitinga	Dragutinovic 03
04 Mathijsen	Gavrancic 06
13 Ooijer	Djordjevic 14
05 van Bronckhorst	Krstajic 20
20 Sneijder	Duljaj 04
18 van Bommel	Stankovic 10
08 Cocu	Djordjevic 11
17 van Persie	Nadj 17
09 van Nistelrooy	Kezman 08
11 Robben	Milosevic 09

Substitutes

	Holland	Serbia & Montenegro	
60'	> 06 Landzaat < 18 van Bommel	07 Koroman > 14 Djordjevic <	43'
69'	> 07 Kuyt < 09 van Nistelrooy	19 Zigic > 09 Milosevic <	46'
86'	> 03 Boulahrouz < 04 Mathijsen	21 Ljoboja > 08 Kezman <	67'

Discipline

	Holland	Serbia & Montenegro	
56'	van Bronckhorst foul	Stankovic foul	34'
85'	Heitinga time wasting	Koroman ungentlemanly conduct	64'
		Dragutinovic foul	81'
		Gavrancic foul	90'

61%	Ball Possession	39%
6	Shots on target	4
6	Shots off target	7
23	Fouls	15
4	Corner Kicks	6
3	Offsides	2

Official FIFA Man of the Match
Arjen Robben

WAGS, otherwise known as Wives And Girlfriends, is the squad of beautiful women who have adorned the newspapers because they are the partners of England's footballers. Posh, Coleen and Alex are household names, but there are plenty more that have yet to be introduced. They were either pictured out shopping or in their bikinis by the hotel swimming pool.

What they didn't expect was that the English press would be billeted in their Baden-Baden hotel, and there was some speculation that the wives made an effort to have the press corps evicted, but the hotel management refused to comply.

The WAGs livened the place up. The bars Garibaldi's and Leo's revised their opening times as Wayne's fiancée Coleen McLoughlin, Alex Curran (Steven Gerrard's partner), Elen Rives

DID YOU KNOW?
Serbia & Montenegro's starting line-up was older than any of Yugoslavia's starting teams at a World Cup.

The clean sheet kept by the Dutch was the 15th in Marco van Basten's 22 matches as coach. It was also the 10th successive clean sheet in competitive matches, extending the European record already held by the Netherlands. Holland's unbeaten streak in competitive matches extended to 13, one match short of their national record set between October 1971 and July 1974. The Dutch also brought an end to Serbia & Montenegro's 13 game undefeated sequence in competitive contests.

STATE OF PLAY							GROUP C
	P	W	D	L	F	A	GD Pts
ARGENTINA	1	1	0	0	2	1	+1 3
HOLLAND	1	1	0	0	1	0	+1 3
IVORY COAST	1	0	0	1	1	2	-1 0
SERB & MON	1	0	0	1	0	1	-1 0

Iran 1 v Mexico 3
Group D
Franken-Stadion, Nuremberg
Attendance: 41,000
Kick-off: 6pm   Temperature: 16°C

Mexico's influential substitute, winger Antonio Zinha celebrates scoring his side's third and clinching goal

(Frank Lampard) and Carly Zucker (Joe Cole), to name but a few, have hit the nightlife.

Wives, families, sisters, brothers, friends and bodyguards combined for a fascinating entourage. The English press were in the same Brenner's Park Hotel to which the players were regular visitors. A peaceful co-existence twixt reporters and footballers may long have been considered impossible, but the chance for both sides to prove they can behave themselves in each other's company could go a long way to mending a lot of fractured relationships.

The hotel's decision to segregate most of the press members in the fifth-floor attic rooms proved unnecessary. The Carraghers and the Joe Coles proved to be a popular group, while the Crouchs were a charming bunch. Within the confines of the hotel, the Owen family and the Robinsons lunched on the terrace without fear of interruption. Beckham did not hit town, choosing to take his wife Victoria and sons to the team hotel when the players were given Sunday off, but it was the captain who defended Eriksson's Family England.

Traditionally, the players' families are invited in the night after a match; last weekend after the Jamaica match the players rested on Saturday night,

warmed down on Sunday morning and were then reunited with their families at lunchtime. "All managers are different and previous England managers haven't done it. This manager likes a relaxed atmosphere around the hotel," Beckham said. "We've seen the wives, kids and girlfriends for a day and a half and that's it. In the past they might not have had that pleasure of seeing the families and kids, but we've always had it with Sven and it's not affected the players and it's not a distraction."

Perhaps not unexpectedly for a 'day off', there was plenty of transfer activity surrounding the England camp. Manchester United made an offer for Michael Carrick and Tottenham announced they had rejected a bid of around £10m and wanted more like £15m. Only a possible deal involving out-of-favour United striker Ruud van Nistelrooy, wanted by Bayern Munich, could persuade the White Hart Lane club to do business. Spurs' Dutch coach Martin Jol is a

IRAN 1   v   MEXICO 3

Referee: Roberto Rosetti

Scorers

36'	Golmohammadi	Bravo	28', 76'
		Zinha	79'

Teams

01 Mirzapour	Sanchez 01
04 Golmohammadi	Salcido 03
05 Rezaei	Mendez 16
13 Kaabi	Osorio 05
20 Nosrati	Pineda 14
02 Mahdavikia	Marquez 04
06 Nekounam	Torrado 06
08 Karimi	Pardo 08
14 Teymourian	Franco 10
09 Hashemian	Borgetti 09
10 Daei	Bravo 19

Substitutes

62'	15 Borhani / 20 Nosrati	23 Perez / 06 Torrado	45'
81'	21 Madanchi / 08 Karimi	07 Zinha / 10 Franco	45'
		17 Fonseca / 09 Borgetti	52'

Discipline

55'	Nekounam *time wasting*	Torrado *foul*	19'
		Salcido *foul*	90'

47%	**Ball Possession**	53%
5	**Shots on target**	5
2	**Shots off target**	2
19	**Fouls**	22
5	**Corner Kicks**	6
2	**Offsides**	1

Official FIFA Man of the Match
Omar Bravo

known admirer of van Nistelrooy, who was involved in an end-of-season bust-up with Sir Alex. Ferguson was also linked with a move for Mahamadou Diarra from French club Lyon, who plays in a similar position to Carrick, while Spurs have been linked with Didier Zokora of St-Etienne as a defensive replacement.

Meanwhile German defender Robert Huth agreed a five-year deal with Middlesbrough to be signed after the World Cup finals. A lack of first team football with champions Chelsea was behind his decision to leave Stamford Bridge. New Boro manager Gareth Southgate held talks with Huth and, ironically, Southgate's switch into the Boro hotseat to replace England manager-to-be Steve McClaren created a centre-half vacancy at the Riverside Stadium. Said Huth, "They approached me after the season and I was very affected by the offer. I had offers from other English clubs, but they all had four or five central defenders, so I decided to go to Middlesbrough where I will see enough playing time. I met with Gareth Southgate and I had a very intensive

conversation with him. It was very interesting. For me the most important thing was to play."

The Chelsea set were also much in evident besides Robert, and Frank, Terry and Joe in the England camp. Arjen Robben, the Chelsea winger was at the heart of an impressive performance by Marco van Basten's young Dutch side against Serbia & Montenegro. Robben scored the only goal of the game in the 18th minute. The blend of youth along with the experience of Phillip Cocu, Mark van Bommel and Ruud van Nistelrooy looked perfectly balanced, while the fluidity of their attack should make them dangerous to any side. The forthcoming meeting with Argentina is already making my mouth water.

Former Aston Villa striker Milosevic should have done better when given time and space to shoot in the penalty area, but his effort was feeble and Edwin van der Sar made an easy save. That proved costly as Robben then beat the offside trap to run on to Robin van Persie's volleyed pass and finish with aplomb as keeper Dragoslav Jevric came out to meet him. The goal sent

STATE OF PLAY — GROUP D

	P	W	D	L	F	A	GD	Pts
MEXICO	1	1	0	0	3	1	+2	3
IRAN	1	0	0	1	1	3	-2	0
ANGOLA	0	0	0	0	0	0	0	0
PORTUGAL	0	0	0	0	0	0	0	0

ANGOLA 0 v **PORTUGAL 1**

Referee: Jorge Larrionda

Scorers

4'   Pauleta

Teams

01	Joao Ricardo	Ricardo	01
03	Jamba	Meira	05
05	Kali	Miguel	13
20	Loco	Nuno Valente	14
21	Delgado	Ricardo Carvalho	16
07	Figueiredo	Petit	08
08	Macanga	Tiago	19
11	Mateus	Figo	07
14	Mendonca	Ronaldo	17
17	Ze Kalanga	Pauleta	09
10	Akwa	Simao	11

Substitutes

59'	09 Mantorras / 10 Akwa	06 Costinha / 17 Ronaldo	60'
70'	13 Edson / 17 Ze Kalanga	18 Maniche / 08 Petit	72'
80'	06 Miloy / 07 Figueirido	10 Viana / 19 Tiago	82'

Discipline

28'	Jamba foul	Ronaldo foul	26'
45'	Loco foul	Nuno Valente foul	79'
52'	Macanga foul		

42%	Ball Possession	58%
2	Shots on target	9
8	Shots off target	10
27	Fouls	20
2	Corner Kicks	5
1	Offsides	0

Official FIFA Man of the Match

Luis Figo

Angola 0 v Portugal 1

Group D
RheinEnergieStadion, Cologne
Attendance: 45,000
Kick-off: 9pm   Temperature: 20°C

The physical battle ended roughly equal between two old foes. Here Angola's Andre Macanga comes off better against Portugal skipper Luis Figo, but Figo's extra guile created Pauleta's goal to win the match

the 25,000 orange-clad fans in Leipzig's Zentralstadion into raptures.

With the half-hour mark approaching, Milosevic had a chance to make amends for his earlier miss, but sliced a first-time shot wide. Then Kezman was off-target with a far-post header from Djordjevic's cross. Robben was running rings round Nenad Djordjevic and once again he tormented the Serbian full-back before sliding in a low shot that missed the far-post by an inch. Serbia coach Ilija Petkovic had seen enough and replaced his unhappy right-back. Ognjen Koroman, lately of Portsmouth, came on and Igor Duljaj moved to right-back to try to stifle Robben.

Savo Milosevic had been hugely disappointing and it was little surprise when he was replaced at the break, with the towering Nikola Zigic taking his place. But Serbia failed to use his height throughout the half.

Robben remained the chief danger, and he – who else – nearly connected with an overhead kick. Holland held on comfortably.

Serbian Koroman gave me one of my favourite moments of the tournament so far. After being fouled just outside the Dutch box, he leapt to his feet waving an imaginary yellow card at the referee in order to get his assailant booked, but only succeeded in rightly receiving one himself.

Bravo, the headline writer's dream, gave Mexico the lead 28 minutes into the game with a close-range effort before Yahya Golmohammadi levelled for the Iranians eight minutes later. But Omar Bravo restored his team's advantage 14 minutes from time after the Iranian defence hit the self-destruct button, and three minutes later Brazil-born midfielder Zinha sealed the win for Mexico with a well-placed header. Mexico's two goals in a little over two minutes killed off an Iran team who had been in the ascendancy early in the game, but sat back as the match went on, offering little threat in the second period.

Mexico goalkeeper Oswaldo Sanchez had flown home in midweek to grieve for his recently deceased father, but returned to Germany to play and the celebrations at the final whistle were all the more powerful.

Angola can feel proud of their first performance on the big stage, especially as they had been thrashed 6-0 and 5-1 in their only previous encounters with their former colonial rulers. But a nervous start turned out to be their undoing. Just 15 seconds were on the clock when Pauleta broke free on the left of the box and slotted past goalkeeper Joao Ricardo. On that occasion the ball just missed the far post, but the PSG striker made no mistake in the fourth minute to net his 47th international strike. It came from an Angolan free-kick that Jamba punted up field, with the defender horrified to see it headed straight into the path of the on-rushing Luis Figo.

The Portugal skipper motored easily past the out-of-position left-back to reach the box and lay the ball back for Pauleta to apply a simple finish past last man Kali, with the

Other News

Theo Walcott added to England's injury woes after being seen out and about with a strapping on his lower left leg after straining a calf during training. Better news for Theo was the naming of a baby Greater Flamingo chick at the Wildfowl & Wetlands Trust at Slimbridge in Gloucestershire after England's baby-faced striker.

The Togo saga continued as former Cameroon coach Winfried Schaefer arrived to meet officials of the Togo FA to discuss taking over, but did not appear at the scheduled press conference to unveil him saying that he wanted to talk more before committing to the job. Meanwhile the players, including Arsenal striker Emmanuel Adebayor, announced that they would play in their opening game against South Korea despite the ongoing crisis.

goalkeeper already having been taken out of the equation.

Cristiano Ronaldo's luck deserted him in the 34th minute when his header from a Figo corner bounced back off the crossbar, but the next chance was Angola's and Ricardo had to dive to his right to tip Andre's 25-yard drive round the post. Ricardo then palmed away a fierce drive from Ronaldo and the unfancied Africans must have been delighted to still be in the game going into the break. Ronaldo was eventually replaced by Costinha. Tiago saw a drive saved, but Loco panicked at the other end when presented with a sight of goal and hacked wildly wide. Everton's Nuno Valente was the last to be booked before Simao headed a late chance wide from a Figo free-kick.

After such a destabilising start, the Africans had done magnificently to make a match of it, especially as their defensive lynchpin, Yamba Asha, was suspended until August due to a doping offence.

DID YOU KNOW?
Eight of the Angolan squad played for Portuguese clubs last season.

Portugal's undefeated run now stretched to 15 matches – their longest unbeaten run in international football. They had also recorded 6 clean sheets in their last 7 World Cup 2006 matches including qualifiers.

DID YOU KNOW?
On the last occasion Portugal & Angola had met the game was abandoned with twenty minutes remaining with the Portuguese 5-1 ahead after Angola's indiscipline saw them receive four red cards.

Portugal goalkeeper Ricardo won his 50th cap, five years after making his debut against the Republic of Ireland, becoming the 18th Portuguese player to reach this milestone.

Day Four
Monday 12 June 2006

Aussie Rules

Australia came from a goal behind with six minutes left to triumph 3-1 thanks to two goal Tim Cahill. It was the Aussies' first goals and first points in their fourth World Cup match

Czech This Out

Karel Bruckner's team got off to a flying start through Jan Koller's close range header, but suffered a potentially huge blow when the giant striker was carried off with a torn hamstring. Tomas Rosicky set the seal on a comfortable win with two classic goals

Italian Style

In a flowing, passionate game, Andrea Pirlo's opening goal allowed Italy to see off the sturdy challenge of Ghana

"I think the referee will thank God for the result – it was a clear foul on the goalie."

Guus Hiddink (Australia)

Australia 3 v Japan 1
Group F
Fritz Walter Stadion, Kaiserslautern
Attendance: 46,000
Kick-off: 3pm   Temperature: 38°C

AUSTRALIA 3 v **JAPAN 1**

Referee: Essam Abdel Fatah

Scorers

84', 89' Cahill	Nakamura	26'
90' Aloisi		

Teams

01 Schwarzer	Kawaguchi 23
02 Neill	Komano 03
03 Moore	Miyamoto 05
05 Culina	Santos 14
20 Wilkshire	Tsuboi 19
07 Emerton	Nakazawa 22
13 Grella	Fukunishi 15
23 Bresciano	Nakata 07
14 Chipperfield	Nakamura 10
10 Kewell	Takahara 09
09 Viduka	Yanagisawa 13

Substitute John Aloisi fires home the clinching third goal deep into injury time to send Australian fans into raptures

Substitutes

52' > 04 Cahill < 23 Bresciano	02 Moniwa > 19 Tsuboi < 54'
60' > 19 Kennedy < 03 Moore	18 Ono > 13 Yanagisawa < 78'
74' > 20 Wilkshire < 15 Aloisi	16 Oguro > 02 Moniwa < 90'

Discipline

32' Grella *foul*	Miyamoto *foul* 30'
57' Moore *foul*	Takahara *delaying restart* 39'
68' Cahill *foul*	Moniwa *foul* 67'
77' Aloisi *foul*	

52%	Ball Possession	48%
14	Shots on target	5
8	Shots off target	6
20	Fouls	10
5	Corner Kicks	3
5	Offsides	3

Official FIFA Man of the Match
Tim Cahill

Australia recorded their first ever victory at the World Cup – 32 years after the nation's only previous appearance at the finals, also on German soil in 1974 – but not without a big scare.

A goalkeeping error from Mark Schwarzer handed Japan a 1-0 half-time lead. Celtic midfielder Shunsuke Nakamura clipped a left-footed cross into the six-yard box from the right and, as Schwarzer came to collect through a gaggle of players from both teams, he mis-read the flight of the ball and was also partially obstructed. Nakamura's fortuitous goal came less than a minute after the Australians should have taken the lead in their most inspired passage of play in the opening 45 minutes.

The manner of that goal added to the frisson of fractious relations between the two sides which had begun following accusations by the President of the Japanese FA, who accused Australia of targeting opponents' ankles with foul tackles and evidenced Luke Wilkshire's

DID YOU KNOW?
Australia was the first team at this tournament to come back to win after being 1-0 down. No other team has scored three goals in the last seven minutes in World Cup history.

DID YOU KNOW?
Japan, who put out their oldest ever starting line-up at a World Cup, have yet to win their opening match of a tournament. In 1998 they were beaten (1-0) by Argentina. Four years later they were held to a 2-2 draw by Belgium.

STATE OF PLAY   GROUP F

	P	W	D	L	F	A	GD	Pts
AUSTRALIA	1	1	0	0	3	1	+2	3
JAPAN	1	0	0	1	1	3	-2	0
BRAZIL	0	0	0	0	0	0	0	0
CROATIA	0	0	0	0	0	0	0	0

sending off in their final warm-up match against Holland.

Socceroos boss Guus Hiddink abandoned his surprise 5-3-1-1 formation, which had left his team exposed down the flanks by Japan's mobile strikers, and kick-started his team into life eight minutes after the restart with the introduction of Cahill for Bresciano and then Joshua Kennedy, Australia's version of Peter Crouch, for Newcastle defender Craig Moore. But as the heat took its toll and the pace of the game dropped, the Japanese looked like they would hold out and had plenty of chances to kill the game off.

When the Australians did break through, Kawaguchi was on hand to deny them, the 31 year-old dropping sharply to his right to brilliantly deny Viduka as the Middlesbrough striker thumped his free-kick low through the defensive wall. Aloisi replaced Wilkshire as Hiddink took his last throw of the dice and the Osasuna forward was to have an impact on the outcome of the game.

But first enter the other substitute, Everton's Tim Cahill, who struck a loose ball home from 12 yards out. As the seconds ticked away Takashi Fukunishi came close to restoring Japan's lead, but his right-foot strike from the edge of the area was just wide. Japan also had a good penalty shout turned down when Cahill appeared to commit a foul in the area. For my money it should have been given.

Cahill, however, gave the Socceroos the lead with a minute left of regular time with a fine effort from outside the box that beat Kawaguchi before hitting the post and crossing the goal line. Aloisi completed the win with a fine finish from inside the penalty area as defenders backed away.

Arsenal's £8million new-boy Tomas Rosicky turned in a scintillating two-goal display as the Czech Republic roared past an outclassed United States with a 3-0 win in their Group E opener. The only downside to a clinical victory for the Czechs was what appeared to be

Czech Republic 3 v USA 0
Group E
Veltins Arena, Gelsenkirchen
Attendance: 52,000
Kick-off: 6pm   Temperature: 28°C

Zdenek Grygera proved a class act rampaging down the flank from his right-back position for the Czechs

a severe hamstring injury suffered by opening goalscorer Jan Koller. With Milan Baros' foot injury predictably ruling him out, there was even more emphasis on the giant Koller as a lone front-man, so the text-book header he powered home just five minutes into the game would have been a crushing disappointment to the US. The goal was created by a magnificent pass out of defence from David Rozenhal to Zdenek Grygera, whose cross invited Koller's brutal finish. It was a reminder of Koller's qualities which the US should not really have needed, but, from that moment on, defensive duo Eddie Pope and Middlesbrough target Oguchi Onyewu got to grips with the giant striker and kept him out of the game until he suffered the injury whilst chasing a through ball, which must threaten his participation in the remainder of the tournament just before the break. It was a particularly sad moment for Koller as he had missed most of the domestic season with a cruciate knee injury.

The one obvious consolation for Bruckner is that his midfield, while ageing, remains lethal. Karel Poborsky may no longer dash about the pitch as he did a decade ago, but he is still a reliable outlet on the right flank, while Pavel Nedved retains the ability to control a game in the fashion which made him European Footballer of the Year in 2004. And then there is Rosicky, at 25 the baby of the three.

It was Rosicky's play-off goal against Norway which got the Czechs to Germany in the first place and now here he looks eager to make his mark. The 30-yard thunderbolt which fizzed past Kasey Keller to double his country's lead nine minutes before the interval was astounding enough. But Rosicky was not finished. Another shot from the midfielder's right boot came crashing back off the crossbar midway through the second period. Then, 14 minutes from time, he raced clear onto one of Nedved's trademark eye-of-the-needle passes and gleefully clipped a third into the corner with a predatory finish on the run.

No-one in the capacity 52,000 crowd could have failed to be impressed and Arsenal manager Arsene Wenger is no doubt glad he got in ahead of the pack to sign Rosicky from Borussia Dortmund before the World Cup began.

The final scoreline was harsh on the USA, who came within an inch of equalising when Claudio Reyna hit a post. But they have still to win a World Cup Finals game of any description in Europe and a repeat of their 2002 quarter-final appearance looks a forlorn hope.

Marcello Lippi said Italy had a little bit extra after goals from Andrea Pirlo and Vincenzo Iaquinta gave them a 2-0 win over World Cup debutants Ghana in their opening Group E match. "I'm delighted with the result.

CZECH REP 3 v USA 0

Referee: Carlos Amarilla

Scorers

5'	Koller
35', 76'	Rosicky

Teams

01	Cech	Keller	18
02	Grygera	Onyewu	22
22	Rozehnal	Mastroeni	04
21	Ujfalusi	Pope	23
06	Jankulovski	Cherundolo	06
08	Poborsky	Reyna	10
04	Galasek	Beasley	17
10	Rosicky	Convey	15
20	Plasil	Lewis	07
11	Nedved	McBride	20
09	Koller	Donovan	21

Substitutes

44'	12 Lokvenc / 09 Koller		05 O'Brien / 06 Cherundolo		45'
82'	19 Polak / 08 Poborsky		09 Johnson / 04 Mastroeni		45'
85'	17 Stajner / 10 Rosicky		16 Wolff / 20 McBride		77'

Discipline

16'	Rozehnal foul	Onyewu foul	04'
58'	Lokvenc foul	Reyna foul	59'
80'	Rosicky foul		
87'	Grygera foul		

52%	Ball Possession	48%
3	Shots on target	4
7	Shots off target	6
13	Fouls	16
2	Corner Kicks	5
0	Offsides	9

Official FIFA Man of the Match
Tomas Rosicky

STATE OF PLAY   GROUP E

	P	W	D	L	F	A	GD	Pts
CZECH REP	1	1	0	0	3	0	+3	3
USA	1	0	0	1	0	3	-3	0
GHANA	0	0	0	0	0	0	0	0
ITALY	0	0	0	0	0	0	0	0

Ghana 0 v Italy 2
Group E
AWD Arena, Hanover
Attendance: 43,000
Kick-off: 9pm   Temperature: 26°C

Italy substitute Vincenzo Iaquinta slots the ball into Ghana's net after latching onto a poor backpass by Sammy Kuffour, who earlier had come close to severely injuring Iaquinta with a scything tackle

Our opponents showed themselves to be as strong as we thought they would be. Under certain aspects they were better than us," said Lippi. "But I think overall we deserved to win. We knew they were physically strong, but over the 90 minutes we had that little bit extra. I was especially pleased with the way we closed them down because when they get in space, that's when they are dangerous.'

Lippi's surprise decision to start with Simone Perrotta ahead of Mauro Camoranesi in midfield paid off. He said playmaker Francesco Totti, returning after a broken ankle, had not suffered a serious injury before he was taken off and added that he never planned to play him for 90 minutes.

"I didn't substitute him because of the tackle – I was going to substitute him anyway," said the Italy coach of his key player, who has only once managed to last a full match since returning from three months on the sidelines. "There were some positive

GHANA 0 v **ITALY 2**

Referee: Carlos Eugenio Simon

Scorers

	Pirlo	40'
	Iaquinta	83'

Teams

22	Kingston	Buffon	01
15	Pantsil	Zaccardo	02
04	Kuffour	Nesta	13
05	Mensah	Cannavaro	05
06	Pappoe	Grosso	03
11	Muntari	Totti	10
08	Essien	Perrotta	20
10	Appiah	Pirlo	21
18	Addo	De Rossi	04
03	Gyan	Toni	09
14	Amoah	Gilardino	11

Substitutes

45'	07 Shilla / 06 Pappoe	16 Camoranesi / 10 Totti	56'
68'	19 Pimpong / 14 Amoah	15 Iaquinta / 11 Gilardino	64'
89'	12 Tachie-Mensah / 03 Gyan	07 Del Piero / 09 Toni	82'

Discipline

41'	Muntari *foul*	De Rossi *foul*	10'
65'	Gyan *foul*	Camoranesi *foul*	62'
		Iaquinta *time wasting*	88'

52%	Ball Possession	48%
8	Shots on target	14
11	Shots off target	5
27	Fouls	20
4	Corner Kicks	12
20	Offsides	8

Official FIFA Man of the Match
Andrea Pirlo

signs from Francesco, I was pleased with what he did."

A newly cropped Totti, who said he had his hair cut four hours before kick-off, was pleased with his display in his first truly major test since his ankle operation. "Initially, I couldn't find the right position. Once we'd scored our first goal, though, they opened up a bit and everything became a little easier."

Substitute Vincenzo Iaquinta, whose late goal added to Andrea Pirlo's 40th minute pearler, was delighted with his first goal for the national side. "It's an incredible feeling to get a goal in a World Cup. I think I justified Lippi's decision to send me on and I'm glad I've been able to repay his faith in me," said the Udinese forward. It was a poetic moment for purists of the game as Iaquinta had been crudely brought down just previously by Sammy Kuffour, only to discover that he had been given offside and a dead cert red card turned into a free-kick to Ghana. For Iaquinta's goal, Kuffour left a pass back to his goalkeeper woefully short and the Italian pounced to put the game beyond doubt.

The game was packed choc full with fast, flowing and committed football, last ditch tackles and bags of goalmouth excitement. It completed a marvellous day of attacking football – all the better for knowing that Brazil enter the fray tomorrow.

STATE OF PLAY — GROUP E

	P	W	D	L	F	A	GD	Pts
CZECH REP	1	1	0	0	3	0	+3	3
ITALY	1	1	0	0	2	0	+2	3
GHANA	1	0	0	1	0	2	-2	0
USA	1	0	0	1	0	3	-3	0

Day Five
Tuesday 13 June 2006

No Go Togo

The turning point for Togo. Jean-Paul Abalo leaves the field after seeing red for conceding the free-kick from which Korea's Lee Chun Su fired home the equaliser

Stalemate

France and Switzerland shared a dull, goalless draw in fierce heat, much to the frustration of Thierry Henry

Joga Bonita?

Brazil's stilted performance raised as many questions as answers, although a 1-0 win thanks to Kaka's goal proved the adage that good teams who play badly still win

"We could have beaten them in the first half. They could have won the match in the second half."

Raymond Domenech (France)

South Korea 2 v Togo 1

Group G
Commerzbank Arena, Frankfurt
Attendance: 48,000
Kick-off: 3pm   Temperature: 30°C

Togo's goalkeeper Kossi Agassa watches the ball bounce into the net after Korea's Lee Chun Soo scored his side's equalising goal to turn the game on its head

SOUTH KOREA 2   v   TOGO 1

Referee: Graham Poll

Scorers

53'	Lee Chun Soo	Mohamed	31'
72'	Ahn Jung Hwan		

Teams

01	Lee Woon Jae	Agassa 16
02	Kim Young Chul	Nibombe 02
04	Choi Jin Chul	Tchangai 05
06	Kim Jin Kyu	Assemoassa 19
12	Lee Young Pyo	Abalo 03
22	Song Chong Gug	Salifou 07
07	Park Ji Sung	Cherif-Toure 10
13	Lee Eul Yong	Romao 15
17	Lee Ho	Senaya 18
14	Lee Chun Soo	Mohamed 17
19	Cho Jae Jin	Adebayor 04

Substitutes

45'	> 09 Ahn Jung Hwan < 06 Kim Jin Kyu	23 Toure > 18 Senaya <	56'
67'	> 05 Kim Nam Il < 13 Lee Eul Yong	13 Forson > 19 Assemoassa <	61'
83'	> 18 Kim Sang Sik < 19 Cho Jae Jin	06 Aziawonou > 07 Salifou <	86'

Discipline

41'	Kim Young Chul foul	Abalo foul	22'
50'	Lee Chun Su foul	Romao foul	23'
		Abalo foul (second yellow)	52'
		Tchangai foul	90'

59%	**Ball Possession**	41%
8	**Shots on target**	4
11	**Shots off target**	7
17	**Fouls**	17
4	**Corner Kicks**	4
2	**Offsides**	4

Official FIFA Man of the Match
Ahn Jung Hwan

The German press stirred it up for Beckham after Victoria and the rest of the family rolled into Frankfurt at the weekend. The mass circulation tabloid Bild abused the whole family including mum Sandra who, the paper charmingly observed, has "a smile like a peasant". They described son Romeo as looking like a girl – "he should have been called Juliet" – while sister Joanne is described as "lardy". "Look at her arms, look at her breasts, look at her bum, very British. She belongs on a beach in Majorca drinking sangria out of buckets and you can count on her to be the first one up on the table topless," the paper said.

Beckham was controlled, but clearly perturbed when discussing the story, "I've come to terms with people criticising me as a footballer at times, but when it comes to my family that's one thing I won't accept and never will.

For some reason one person maybe has found it funny to criticise my mum, my sister and my children. I find it sad that someone drops to that level. But it's just one sad person sitting in a room trying to think of something that will maybe put me off the next game. I'm not going to let it do that."

Beckham had not overlooked Australia's success in scoring three goals against Japan in the last 10 minutes of a match played in conditions as sapping as those faced by England. "It was very impressive to see them do that when it was as hot as it was," he said. So now it would be England's responsibility to demonstrate a similar conviction in dismissing their next opponents. "We're not underestimating Trinidad & Tobago. We've got a stronger team than them, but this is football and things can happen. We've got to go into the game thinking we're playing the best team in the World Cup, because they've got players who can hurt us and capitalise on mistakes or bad play," he said.

STATE OF PLAY						GROUP G	
	P	W	D	L	F	A	GD Pts
SOUTH KOR	1	1	0	0	2	1	+1 3
TOGO	1	0	0	1	1	2	-1 0
FRANCE	0	0	0	0	0	0	0 0
SWITZERLAND	0	0	0	0	0	0	0 0

Given their rare success, for an England team, in taking three points from the opening match of a major tournament, the players were disappointed by the criticism. But Beckham wisely observed, "That's part and parcel of playing for England and of being a footballer these days. Sometimes you find it a little strange, but the expectations are so high that when you don't perform or you don't beat teams like people expect you to, there's going to be criticism and you have to accept it."

A fussy referee had objected throughout the match to Crouch's jumping technique, but a quiet word from the skipper helped avert the threat of a second yellow card. "As captain you have to notice things like that," he said. "I think I just said to Crouchie, 'You don't have to put your arms up to jump' – because, at the

In keeping with their incredible support during the 2002 World Cup, thousands of Korean fans joined together to watch the game against Togo on a big screen outside the Seoul City Hall

France 0 v Switzerland 0
Group G
Gottlieb-Daimler-Stadion, Stuttgart
Attendance: 52,000
Kick-off: 6pm   Temperature: 31°C

Switzerland's goalkeeper Pascal Zuberbühler and defender Philippe Senderos challenge for the ball with France's Patrick Vieira as the game descended into a physical battle

FRANCE 0   v   SWITZERLAND 0

Referee: Valentin Ivanov

Scorers

Teams

France		Switzerland	
16	Barthez	Zuberbühler	01
03	Abidal	Magnin	03
05	Gallas	Senderos	04
15	Thuram	Muller	20
19	Sagnol	P Degen	23
10	Zidane	Cabanas	07
06	Makelele	Vogel	06
04	Vieira	Wicky	08
22	Ribery	Barnetta	16
11	Wiltord	Frei	09
12	Henry	Streller	11

Substitutes

69'	14 Saha / 22 Ribery	10 Gygax / 11 Streller	57'
84'	08 Dhorasoo / 11 Wiltord	02 Djourou / 20 Muller	74'
		05 Margairaz / 08 Wicky	81'

Discipline

64'	Abidal foul	Magnin foul	42'
72'	Zidane foul	Barnetta foul	45'
90'	Sagnol foul	P Degen foul	56'
		Cabanas foul	72'
		Frei handball	90'

France		Switzerland
49%	Ball Possession	51%
6	Shots on target	3
6	Shots off target	3
17	Fouls	18
4	Corner Kicks	1
5	Offsides	0

Official FIFA Man of the Match
Claude Makelele

end of the day, no one's going to out-jump him. There are situations where sometimes I have to calm players down. Sometimes it's me that I have to calm down."

Soccer has long lagged behind more popular sports like Cricket, Rugby Union and Australian Rules football down under, but millions of Aussies stayed up all night to watch and then celebrate their win and media and politicians quickly jumped on the World Cup bandwagon after victory over Japan. Special praise was reserved for Australia's Dutch coach Guus Hiddink, nicknamed 'Aussie Guus', after his tactical gamble in bringing on goalscorers Tim Cahill and John Aloisi was rewarded. "I think Guus is indeed a hero, the greatest Dutchman ever

DID YOU KNOW?
This was Switzerland's first ever clean sheet at a World Cup, having failed to keep one in all of their previous 22 World Cup matches – an all-time World Cup record. The Swiss are unbeaten in five matches in 2006.

DID YOU KNOW?
France's last World Cup goal was the late third scored by Emmanuel Petit in the 1998 World Cup Final. They are now only one match short of equalling the record held by Bolivia, who set the World Cup record by not scoring a goal in five consecutive matches between 1930 and 1994.

STATE OF PLAY							GROUP G
	P	W	D	L	F	A	GD	Pts
SOUTH KOR	1	1	0	0	2	1	+1	3
FRANCE	1	0	1	0	0	0	0	1
SWITZERLAND	1	0	1	0	0	0	0	1
TOGO	1	0	0	1	1	2	-1	0

BRAZIL 1 v CROATIA 0

Referee: Benito Archundia Tellez

Scorers

44' Kaka

Teams

01	Dida	Pletikosa	01
02	Cafu	Simunic	03
03	Lucio	Kovac	04
04	Juan	Tudor	05
06	Roberto Carlos	Simic	07
11	Ze Roberto	Srna	02
05	Emerson	Babic	08
10	Ronaldinho	Kovac	10
08	Kaka	Kranjcar	19
07	Adriano	Prso	09
09	Ronaldo	Klasnic	17

Substitutes

69' > 23 Robinho < 09 Ronaldo	16 J Leko > 10 N Kovac < 40'
	18 Olic > 17 Klasnic < 57'

Discipline

43'	Emerson foul	N Kovac foul	32'
		R Kovac foul	67'
		Tudor foul	90'

52%	Ball Possession	48%
8	Shots on target	4
9	Shots off target	4
18	Fouls	19
5	Corner Kicks	7
3	Offsides	4

Official FIFA Man of the Match

Kaka

STATE OF PLAY							GROUP F
	P	W	D	L	F	A	GD	Pts
AUSTRALIA	1	1	0	0	3	1	+2	3
BRAZIL	1	1	0	0	1	0	+1	3
JAPAN	1	0	0	1	1	3	-2	0
CROATIA	1	0	0	1	0	1	-1	0

Brazil 1 v Croatia 0
Group F
Olympiastadion, Berlin
Attendance: 72,000
Kick-off: 9pm   Temperature: 20°C

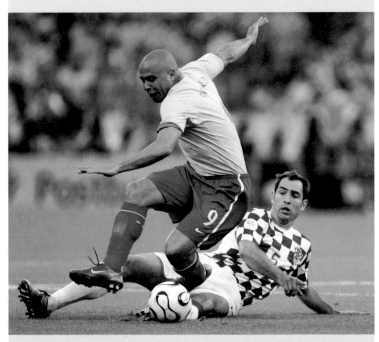

The portly Ronaldo looked a shadow of his dangerous self during Brazil's opening win, being shackled by Croatia's rugged Igor Tudor

created," Labour opposition MP Anthony Albanese told reporters.

The question over injured Czech Republic striker Jan Koller's return to his team's became 'when' rather than 'if'; relief for the side whose perfect start was soured by worries over him. Koller was initially said by coach Karel Bruckner to have sustained a 'serious' injury, but a team spokesman later said it was not as bad as they had thought. "Definitely his start in further matches is not ruled out," team doctor Petr Krejci said on the Czech Republic Football Association's website.

Less fortunate was Serbia & Montenegro defender Nemanja Vidic, who was ruled out for the rest of the World Cup after picking up a knee injury in training. Team spokesman Aleksandar Boskovic said, 'A detailed medical check up established damage to his left knee ligaments and he will be sidelined for several weeks at least.' Vidic, who had been suspended for Serbia & Montenegro's opening 1-0 defeat by the Netherlands, was injured after sliding to collect a loose ball and was carried off the training pitch in a lot of pain.

Action was hard to come by today as France and Switzerland played out a bore draw with Thierry Henry an isolated shadow of his Arsenal self. The service into him was so poor he was moved to comment on Ribery's inaccuracy in the post-match interviews.

Much of the day's football was dull and out of character with the rest of the tournament so far, although some excuse may be found in the fact that it was by far the hottest day yet.

Kaka celebrates his magnificent goal which won the game for Brazil

DID YOU KNOW?
Goalkeeper Stipe Pletikosa made his 50th international appearance for Croatia in this game.

DID YOU KNOW?
Brazil have won their last eight World Cup matches which is a new record, breaking Italy's seven successive victories between 1934 and 1950. Brazil's last defeat dates back to 1998 when they lost the final against France (3-0). They've kept a clean sheet in their last three World Cup matches.

At least there were goals, if little more excitement, in the other Group G match as South Korea came from behind to defeat Togo 2-1. There was a good deal of embarrassment when the anthems were played as the Korean Aegukga was played twice and everyone looked confused with the mascots not knowing what to do when Togo's Salut à toi, pays de nos aieux did finally blare over the tannoy. Another substitute proved the inspiration, with the hero of Korea's victory over Italy in 2002, Ahn Jung Hwan, firing home a cracking winning goal from 25 yards. Togo had led until Jean-Paul Abalo was rightly sent off by the excitable Graham Poll, who produced his second yellow and red cards in the wrong order. But the biggest disappointment came in Berlin where Brazil nudged past a game Croatia only thanks to Kaka's curling 25 yard shot. Judging by the fitness levels of their tubby star centre-forward Ronaldo, who looked overweight and off the pace, it is more than likely he's had far too many late nights. There was speculation that his team-mates had a go at him at half time during their less than impressive 1-0 win. There were reports back in Brazil that other team-mates had complained about his lack of movement on the training field, too. It was best summed up by Robert Kovac, the Croatia defender, who said that marking him had been "very easy". He added, "I don't know what happened to him, he didn't run. He must be tired. He hardly touched the ball."

Tostão, the 1970 World Cup winner, writing in Folha de São Paulo, described Ronaldo as "slow and weird". In the same paper, one of Brazil's most respected football writers, Juca Kfouri, wrote: "Parreira has to drop Ronaldo, to preserve his enormous name. It was torture to see him like an unsteady heavyweight, wandering around the grass, as if what was happening around him had nothing to do with him."

Adriano was also the target of some justifiable flak. "The two looked as if they were having a wander around the garden,"O Globo reported. "How on earth do you challenge for a World Cup like that? The most obvious answer is to improve fitness levels, which is why it was so extraordinary that Ronaldo should have disappeared off into the night after Tuesday's match. The team needs more movement. We hope in the next game Ronaldo can help us to have more offensive motion," Kaká, who scored the winning goal..

Ronaldo was a sad sight, it must be said, as I remember Ronaldo as the slim, rapier fast striker. But at 29 he looked washed up. Little wonder Chelsea were no longer interested in signing him. Who would be? Maybe Celebrity Fit Club!

Other News

One unnamed newspaper reporter, seeking out more information than was provided by England's daily press conference, attempted to hide in the variety of trees and scrub that overlook the training ground in a bid to grab a sneak peek into Sven's plans. Sadly for him, he was spotted by the German security guards and politely requested to leave.

Day Six
Wednesday 14 June 2006

Spanish Eyes Are Smiling

Luis Aragones' Spain team showed unprecedented togetherness in a 4-0 rout of much-fancied Ukraine, started by Xabi Alonso's early header

Sand Storm

Saudi Arabia are denied at the death by a soaring header by Radhi Jaidi in an entertaining second half between the two desert neighbours

The Late Late Show

Germany's dramatic late victory, thanks to Oliver Neuville's goal, sparked national fervour as the hosts all but qualified for the knockout stages

"If we show what we can do I know we can be amongst the top teams at this tournament."

Luis Aragones (Spain)

Spain 4 v Ukraine 0
Group H
Zentralstadion, Leipzig
Attendance: 43,000
Kick-off: 3pm   Temperature: 27°C

The Ukrainian wall leaps to prevent David Villa's free-kick, but no.14, Gusin, only succeeds in deflecting the ball past his own goalkeeper

SPAIN 4   v   **UKRAINE 0**

Referee: Massimo Busacca

Scorers

13'	Alonso
17'	Villa
48'	Villa *(penalty)*
81'	Torres

Teams

01 Casillas	Shovkovskiy 01
03 Pernia	Nesmachniy 02
05 Puyol	Yezerskiy 05
15 Sergio Ramos	Rusol 06
22 Pablo	Vashchuk 17
08 Xavi	Tymoschuk 04
14 Alonso	Gusev 09
16 Senna	Gusin 14
11 Luis Garcia	Rotan 21
21 Villa	Shevchenko 07
09 Torres	Voronin 10

Substitutes

55'	06 Albelda > / 14 Alonso <	08 Shelayev > / 09 Gusev <	45'
55'	07 Raul > / 21 Villa <	16 Vorobey > / 14 Gusin <	45'
77'	18 Fabregas > / 11 Luis Garcia <	11 Rebrov > / 09 Rotan <	64'

Discipline

Rusol *foul*	17'
Vashchuk *denying a goalscoring opportunity*	47'
Yezerskiy *foul*	52'

50%	Ball Possession	50%
15	Shots on target	3
6	Shots off target	3
9	Fouls	12
9	Corner Kicks	1
0	Offsides	8

Official FIFA Man of the Match
Xavi

The day before England's next match I decided to go in search of what was happening with Wayne Rooney inside the England camp after days of will he? won't he? play against Trinidad & Tobago. Now back in my office compiling all the details of this diary, I was still in touch with those behind the scenes inside the England camp and made contact with a couple of my now infamous 'insiders' as the conspiracy theories intensified over Wayne and the court of King Sven.

The arrival of independent Doctor Angus Wallace to assess Rooney's recovery rate appeared to indicate that the England coach intended to play the striker as a late substitute against Trinidad & Tobago. Indeed my information is that Eriksson had told Rooney privately to prepare for twenty minutes' action. With opinion split among the England medical staff, with Leif Sward, the team doctor, declaring Rooney ready to play and Ivan Carminati, the fitness coach, publicly stating on Italian TV that the striker was only "70 per cent", Wallace was summoned at short notice from

STATE OF PLAY							GROUP H
	P	W	D	L	F	A	GD Pts
SPAIN	1	1	0	0	4	0	+4 3
UKRAINE	1	0	0	1	0	4	-4 0
SAUDI ARAB	0	0	0	0	0	0	0 0
TUNISIA	0	0	0	0	0	0	0 0

Saudi Arabia 2 v Tunisia 2
Group H
Allianz Arena, Munich
Attendance: 66,000
Kick-off: 6pm   Temperature: 22°C

Sami Al Jaber, playing in his fourth World Cup, scored a dramatic late goal to put Saudi Arabia ahead just 90 seconds after entering the fray

Nottingham to the team's hotel in Nuremberg as "insurance issues" hovered in the background.

Wallace had examined the scan on Rooney's foot a week earlier and had declared that the striker should not play until after the group stage.

So, I believed the doctor was really there to confirm that Rooney was unfit and give Eriksson no option but to delay his comeback. But my spy inside the team hotel told me that Eriksson, for so long perceived as the ice-man on the bench, had now become such a loose cannon that no-one could be quite sure what he planned to do next. As Eriksson knew he was 'out of here' once England's campaign was over, the Swede in charge of making the decision on whether Rooney played or not, did not seem to care about the consequences he would leave behind in English football.

My mole had been studying Eriksson's demeanour and the mood inside the dressing room and told me: "There are some very, very nervy people around the England camp at the moment and I am told quite categorically that Rooney will not play any part against Trinidad & Tobago. I cannot tell you who has told me, but it is a very good source and I have no reason to disbelieve it. But the unknown quantity is that no-one really knows what is going on in Sven's mind at the moment. If Wayne plays even for a few minutes on Thursday night, it will cause yet another media frenzy. Why risk Wayne now, its going to be a big enough risk later on when it really matters, but it cannot surely matter against Trinidad & Tobago? Whether Brian Barwick can tell an England coach who to pick or not is one issue, and I doubt whether he can, but the FA chief executive must be concerned about the future selection process, not just of Manchester United players, but all players in the Premier League, if the FA take a risk with someone like Rooney and it all goes pear-shaped."

As for the players, there was most definitely a feeling that Rooney had become too much of a distraction, as my informant said: "There has become a fixation about Rooney within the entire camp. So it was hardly a surprise when the BBC news crew was at the training ground and the reporter said 'England need Wayne Rooney,' and Gary Neville passed by saying 'no, we don't.'"

Well, this is the World Cup, and you would expect such paranoia within the England camp, it goes with the territory, and it usually has the effect of motivating the players a touch more than the main motivational factor – actually trying to win the World Cup.

But Rooney wasn't the only one causing huge problems internally. Michael Owen's fury at being substituted against Paraguay after about an hour was confirmed to be by my insider. "Yes, Michael was furious at being taken off, and he has been conspicuous by his absence lately, if you notice he has not been put forward by the FA for any media interviews. He will continue to play in Rooney's absence and the hope is that he has a better hour than he did against Paraguay."

In contrast to one Owen trying to stay out of the way of the press, Owen Hargreaves forced his way to the front of the media queue. A German journalist who has observed Hargreaves in many media interviews had never seen him so angry as he was when he volunteered to speak to the media to tell them that he deserves more respect

from the British public and he is in the squad on merit.

Radhi Jaidi was proud and probably shocked to discover he had created World Cup history, well, of sorts. He emulated Bolton legend Nat Lofthouse by scoring in the World Cup finals. The giant Tunisian defender headed an injury-time equaliser in the 2-2 draw with Saudi Arabia. He became the first Bolton player to score on football's biggest stage since centre-forward Lofthouse, now Bolton's president, netted in a 4-2 quarter-final defeat by Uruguay in Switzerland in 1954. Jaidi, 30, said: "I had no idea that a Bolton player had not scored at the World Cup for so long, that's amazing to know. Everyone in Bolton knows Nat Lofthouse. I've heard what a great player he was and know what a nice man he is. If he was the first Bolton player to score at the World Cup then thank God I am the second because Tunisia would probably be going out if we had lost to Saudi Arabia. I love Bolton and want to present a good image of the club worldwide."

Jaidi admitted his side had to buck up their ideas against Spain and Ukraine in their final two Group H matches if they were to make it to the knockout stages for the first time, "We didn't perform at our best and we've got to improve in the last two games. It will be tough playing against the likes of Raul and Andriy Shevchenko but I play against so

SAUDI ARABIA 2 v TUNISIA 2

Referee: Mark Shield

Scorers

57'	Al Kahtani	Jaziri	23'
84'	Al Jaber	Jaidi	90'

Teams

21	Zaid	Boumnijel	01
02	Dokhi	Haggui	03
03	Tukar	Trabelsi	06
04	Al Montashari	Jaidi	15
13	Sulimani	Jemmali	18
06	Al Ghamdi	Mnari	12
08	Noor	Bouazizi	13
14	Khariri	Chedli	14
16	Aziz	Namouchi	20
18	Al Temyat	Jaziri	05
20	Al Kahtani	Chikhaoui	09

Substitutes

66'	23 Mouath > / 18 Al Temyat <	08 Nafti > / 13 Bouazizi <	54'
75'	07 Ameen > / 08 Noor <	10 Ghodhbane > / 14 Chedli <	69'
82'	09 Al Jaber > / 20 Al Kahtani <	02 Essediri > / 09 Chikhaoui <	82'

Discipline

	Haggui foul	35'
	Bouazizi foul	36'
	Chedli foul	65'
	Chikhaoui foul	79'

55%	Ball Possession	45%
10	Shots on target	2
6	Shots off target	4
12	Fouls	15
4	Corner Kicks	3
1	Offsides	1

Official FIFA Man of the Match
Jaziri

STATE OF PLAY — GROUP H

	P	W	D	L	F	A	GD	Pts
SPAIN	1	1	0	0	4	0	+4	3
SAUDI ARAB	1	0	1	0	2	2	0	1
TUNISIA	1	0	1	0	2	2	0	1
UKRAINE	1	0	0	1	0	4	-4	0

DID YOU KNOW?
This is the fourth time that Germany/ West Germany have won their opening two group matches at a finals; interestingly the previous two occasions prior to this tournament was in 1990, in Italy, and in 1974 when they were again the host nation. On both occasions they won the World Cup.

DID YOU KNOW?
This was the first ever World Cup victory for (West) Germany through an injury-time goal.

The narrow triumph meant that Germany remain unbeaten against Poland, winning 11 and drawing four, and now have a record of 14 wins and one draw in international matches played in Dortmund.

many great strikers in the Premiership that I am looking forward to the challenge. But I'll be happy if Shevchenko is still not fully-fit against us!"

Following their 4-0 thrashing by Spain, Saudi coach Marcos Paqueta labelled Ukraine "a weak team" and believed his side will progress to the last 16. Spain had looked the part in destroying the east Europeans with a blend of passing and swift attacking on the break, which resulted in the first straight red card of the tournament for Vladislav Vashchuk, who tugged Torres back by the shorts as he raced through on goal. Villa's penalty was the first of the World Cup so far and made the score 3-0. The fourth Spanish goal, finished by Torres, was the result of wonderful teamwork.

The World Cup always throws up countless stories, endless headlines, and trivia surrounding tickets and the fans. I loved the fans' guide "Fans shown the blue card on how to behave" relating to the distribution of thousands of cards handed to England fans telling them how to treat their hosts with respect. Produced by the authorities in Nuremberg and designed to avoid our beloved supporters causing offence to the locals, these small blue cards point out that it is acceptable to chant football songs and to "celebrate and have a good time", but they will cross the line if the behaviour becomes violent or rowdy. Well, that truly is the idiot's guide to good behaviour. Of course it did reiterate that Nazi salutes and the wearing of Nazi insigna are against the law. And goosestepping and the wearing of joke Nazi helmets, although lawful, are deeply offensive. Again a

sure-fire recipe to ensure that some of the idiots do exactly that.

Hadn't they noticed in Nuremberg that the British Ambassador, Sir Peter Tory, who was based in Berlin, had already accused English fans of "plain bad manners" because songs such as 'Ten German Bombers' were "rude and plainly offensive"?

Back in Blighty, the Wrexham club shop was doing a roaring trade in Trinidad & Tobago shirts and memorabilia in recognition of the club's much-loved centre-half Dennis Lawrence. Naturally the Welsh, Irish, and notably Scots were backing anyone apart from the English. Again, no change there, really.

On a night when Germany worked up to fever pitch as the team played at the Borussia Dortmund stadium, also known as the Opera House, for its incredible acoustics, England suffered the consequences of a FIFA mandarin's crass decision to use a hotel in the centre of Nuremburg.

Because FIFA decide where teams must stay the night before games, the FA had no option but to reside at Le Meridien Grand Hotel, opposite the main railway station, which had become a gathering point for fans of all nations, and German fans celebrating their last minute defeat of local rivals Poland only served to ratchet up the decibel levels. Groups of German fans outside the windows sang "Beckham, Beckham wake up" to keep the England captain awake for as long as they could.

Neuville and Ballack had both hit the crossbar in a remarkable scramble in the 90th minute and Germany's chance seemed to have gone at the end of a fiercely competitive game. Then up popped substitute Oliver Neuville to score in stoppage time, prodding home another substitute, David Odonkor's, cross. The goal succeeded in heightening the sense of patriotic fervour that had swept the nation since the tournament began six days ago. Jürgen Klinsmann punched the air in delight as the final whistle blew 60 seconds later, while

Other News

While England coach Eriksson announced that Wayne Rooney was fit enough to be considered to take part in the following day's game against Trinidad & Tobago, Argentina's teenage wing sensation, Lionel Messi, suffered a setback in his return from injury due to injuring his left foot in training.

Angola engaged the services of psychologist Laurindo Vieira of the capital Luanda's prestigious Catholic University to help them prepare for Friday's Group D game against Mexico.

Germany 1 v Poland 0

Group A
Signal Iduna Park, Dortmund
Attendance: 65,000
Kick-off: 9pm   Temperature: 20°C

David Odonkor, the 22 year-old from Borussia Dortmund, changed the course of the game with his pace and crossing from the right, setting up Neuville's late, late winner

GERMANY 1   v   POLAND 0

Referee: Luis Medina Cantalejo

Scorers

90'   Neuville

Teams

Germany	Poland
01 Lehmann	Boruc 01
03 Friedrich	Bosacki 19
17 Mertesacker	Baszczynski 04
21 Metzelder	Bak 06
16 Lahm	Zewlakow 14
07 Schweinsteiger	Sobolewski 07
13 Ballack	Krzynowek 08
08 Frings	Smolarek 15
19 Schneider	Radomski 16
20 Podolski	Zurawski 09
11 Klose	Jelen 21

Substitutes

63'	22 Odonkor / 03 Friedrich	18 Lewandowski / 08 Krzynowek	76'
69'	10 Neuville / 20 Podolski	17 Dudka / 14 Zewlakow	83'
76'	18 Borowski / 07 Schwiensteiger	23 Brozek / 21 Jelen	90'

Discipline

57'	Ballack foul	Kryznowek foul	03'
67'	Odonkor foul	Sobolewski foul	28'
69'	Metzelder foul	Sobolewski foul (second yellow)	74'
		Boruc time wasting	90'

49%	Ball Possession	51%
12	Shots on target	3
14	Shots off target	4
22	Fouls	16
10	Corner Kicks	4
6	Offsides	2

Official FIFA Man of the Match
Philipp Lahm

the Westfalenstadion reverberated to the tune of Schwarz und Weiss, the anthem their supporters have adopted for the tournament.

Almost assured of their place in the knockout stages, the victorious players embarked on a lap of honour, as Klinsmann's youngsters ignited the competition with their sheer enthusiasm. Much of the pre-match discussion had centred on Miroslav Klose and his decision to stand under the German flag after moving from his native Poland at the age of eight. Having scored twice in his adopted country's 4-2 win over Costa Rica, he seemed mystified when his allegiance to the cause was questioned by the media, adding that the German national anthem was the only one he knew. But he showed a grasp of how high emotions were running in Poland when he suggested that the opposition would "play like men with a knife between their teeth". The historical reasons for enmity between the two nations run deep and there were fears that neo-nazi groups from both countries would use the game as an excuse to cause trouble in much the same way that right wing groups did in Britain in the 1980s. There was post-match trouble, but it was easily contained by the Police.

STATE OF PLAY							GROUP A
	P	W	D	L	F	A	GD Pts
GERMANY	2	2	0	0	5	2	+3 6
ECUADOR	1	1	0	0	2	0	+2 3
COSTA RICA	1	0	0	1	2	4	-2 0
POLAND	2	0	0	2	0	3	-3 0

Day Seven
Thursday 15 June 2006

Spiderman

Ecuador's Ivan Kaviedes dons a spiderman mask to celebrate his country's first ever qualification for the knockout stages of a tournament thanks to a 3-0 win over Costa Rica

He's Back

Wayne Rooney put the controversy of his injury behind him to replace a disconsolate Michael Owen and inspire England to victory over tenacious Trinidad & Tobago

Oh Freddie Freddie

Sweden also leave it late to notch the winner which sends Paraguay home and puts the Swedes in a great position to qualify for the next round

"You could write a book about that, what happened in the last few weeks with Rooney."

Sven-Göran Eriksson (England)

Costa Rica 0 v Ecuador 3
Group A
AOL Arena, Hamburg
Attendance: 50,000
Kick-off: 3pm   Temperature: 23°C

COSTA RICA 0   v   ECUADOR 3

Referee: Coffi Codjia

Scorers

C Tenorio	08'
Delgado	54'
Kaviedes	90'

Teams

Costa Rica	Ecuador
18 Porras	Mora 12
12 Gonzalez	De la Cruz 04
04 Umana	Reasco 18
15 Wallace	Espinoza 17
03 Marin	Hurtado 03
06 Fonseca	Castillo 14
10 Centeno	Valencia 16
08 Solis	E Tenorio 20
20 Sequeira	Mendez 08
09 Wanchope	C Tenorio 21
11 Gomez	Delgado 11

Substitutes

29' > 19 Saborio < 06 Fonseca		10 Kaviedes > 21 C Tenorio < 45'
56' > 16 Hernandez < 12 Gonzalez		02 Guagua > 17 Espinoza < 68'
84' > 13 Bernard < 10 Centeno		06 Urrutia > 16 Valencia < 73'

Discipline

10'	Marin foul	Castillo foul	44'
28'	Solis foul	De la Cruz foul	54'
		Mora foul	60'

46%	Ball Possession	54%
4	Shots on target	6
9	Shots off target	10
22	Fouls	11
4	Corner Kicks	3
2	Offsides	3

Official FIFA Man of the Match
Agustin Delgado

Ecuador's Agustin Delgado, 'The Tin Man', rifles in at Porras' near post to put Ecuador 2-0 ahead and effectively clinch qualification for the second round

With World Cup fever in full swing it's not surprising Rooney came top with a third of the votes, sporting heroes are evidently popular with the great British public with cricket ace Freddie Flintoff and rugby star Jonny Wilkinson also making the top ten.

Rooney was passed fit earlier this afternoon by independent medical advisors, Angus Wallace and Chris Moran, from the Queen's Medical Centre in Nottingham. Their statement said that they had "Wayne's best interests at heart, as our sole concern is Wayne's well-being – now and in the future. This morning's evaluation involved examining Wayne, watching him train, studying video footage of him in full-contact training over the past two days and discussions with the England medical staff. The injury has healed and we are satisfied that Wayne is as fit as he can be. We have carried out a full risk assessment related to returning him to play at this stage and that assessment has indicated that he is at no more risk than any other player who has recovered from an injury and is returning to competitive sport. It is our professional medical opinion that Wayne Rooney is now available to play in the World Cup."

Rooney would play some part against Trinidad & Tobago. Everything was going to be OK – or at least that was what popular opinion held.

STATE OF PLAY — GROUP A

	P	W	D	L	F	A	GD	Pts
ECUADOR	2	2	0	0	5	0	+5	6
GERMANY	2	2	0	0	5	2	+3	6
POLAND	2	0	0	2	0	3	-3	0
COSTA RICA	2	0	0	2	2	7	-5	0

England 2 v Trinidad & Tobago 0
Group B
Franken-Stadion, Nuremburg
Attendance: 41,000
Kick-off: 6pm   Temperature: 22°C

> "You haven't seen the best of us yet. I know we can play better"
> David Beckham

Peter Crouch soars above Trinidad & Tobago's Brent Sancho, but the goal later caused controversy when German TV pictures showed that the Liverpool striker pulled Sancho's dreadlocks to gain an advantage

While not exactly offering a ringing endorsement of the news, Manchester United nevertheless confirmed that the FA had kept them fully informed of the striker's progress. And they also offered their best wishes to both Rooney and England for the remainder of the tournament.

The Boys of 2006 booked their place in the second round after another less than convincing performance. But hey, six points out of six. Who cares? Beckham set up Crouch's headed opener seven minutes from time. Gerrard added an injury-time rocket past the same goalkeeper he defeated at the same point in the game in the FA Cup Final, but it needed the introduction of Rooney to galvanise matters.

Becks made an honest assessment, "It's very fair to say that you have not seen the best of us yet. We know we can play better and there is much more to come. We never give hope of winning, but they got 11 men behind the ball and made it tough for us. The good thing was we ended the game strongly and got those goals in the second half which we haven't been doing lately."

Eriksson showed a sense of abandoned adventure in bringing on Rooney and Aaron Lennon and moving Beckham to right-back in order to break stubborn Trinidad down. And he confirmed that he was now giving serious consideration to starting Rooney in Tuesday's game against Sweden to give him more time to work up his match sharpness. Would it be Owen who gave way?

Crouch was the hero, scoring his sixth goal in his last five internationals, but the German press called him 'The Goal Post' on their front page, but what was going on with Michael Owen? The out-of-touch Newcastle striker lasted just 58 minutes before being replaced by Rooney and had now played only one full game all year. Yet Owen, who also came off after 55 minutes against Paraguay, insisted: "I wouldn't say I've played the two best games of my career, but I'm

content." Content! His body language didn't say 'content'. He shook Sven's hand, but looked down, not at him. It looked a limp shake too.

But Owen said, "I'm not the kind of player like Wayne Rooney who will always be involved even when we are playing badly. My job is more about getting on the end of crosses." But Trinidad & Tobago coach Leo Beenhakker was far from impressed and said: "England deserved to win, but they lost their patience too quickly. They played the ball over their midfield too much. Their first choice was always the long ball and they will have to play with more patience to go on in this tournament. Against stronger, better teams, England will have to do more."

There was still no sign of Theo, and despite Wayne's return, England looked thin on the ground for strikers. At least Aaron Lennon played brilliantly, having a hand, and head in both goals, and going past his full-back at will.

But, I suppose, better thin, than fat. And talking of fat....Big Ron. The tubby Brazil striker was whisked to hospital in the early hours of Wednesday after being taken ill. The health scare was a dramatic echo of the seizure which hit him before the '98 World Cup final in France. This time doctors simply took an endoscopy (inserting a camera into his throat) and ruled that the striker was OK to return to training.

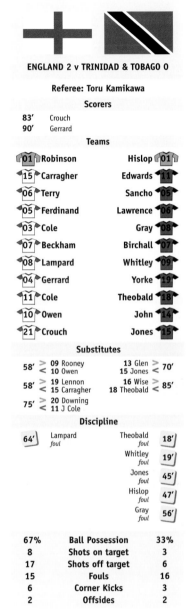

ENGLAND 2 v TRINIDAD & TOBAGO 0

Referee: Toru Kamikawa

Scorers

83'	Crouch
90'	Gerrard

Teams

01	Robinson	Hislop	01
15	Carragher	Edwards	11
06	Terry	Sancho	05
05	Ferdinand	Lawrence	06
03	Cole	Gray	08
07	Beckham	Birchall	07
08	Lampard	Whitley	09
04	Gerrard	Yorke	19
11	Cole	Theobald	18
10	Owen	John	14
21	Crouch	Jones	15

Substitutes

58'	> 09 Rooney < 10 Owen		13 Glen > 15 Jones <	70'
58'	> 19 Lennon < 15 Carragher		16 Wise > 18 Theobald <	85'
75'	> 20 Downing < 11 J Cole			

Discipline

64'	Lampard *foul*	Theobald *foul*	18'
		Whitley *foul*	19'
		Jones *foul*	45'
		Hislop *foul*	47'
		Gray *foul*	56'

67%	Ball Possession	33%
8	Shots on target	3
17	Shots off target	6
15	Fouls	16
6	Corner Kicks	3
2	Offsides	2

Official FIFA Man of the Match
David Beckham

STATE OF PLAY							GROUP B
	P	W	D	L	F	A	GD Pts
ENGLAND	2	2	0	0	3	0	+6 6
SWEDEN	1	0	1	0	0	0	0 1
TRIN & TOB	2	0	1	1	0	2	-2 1
PARAGUAY	1	0	0	1	0	1	-1 0

Other News

Rumours abounded amongst England fans that Rooney had never actually broken his metatarsal. More that he had a chipped flake off the bone, which meant that Eriksson's confidence that his striker would be fit was more understandable.

Ivory Coast players used their day off to spend a staggering £14,000 on computer games, DVDs and CDs in a electrical shop near Cologne. (Sun)

Tesco said sales of Caribbean food and drink had soared north of the border as Scots prepared to cheer on Trinidad & Tobago. Buyer Simon Dunn said: "We've seen huge increases in the sale of rum in Scotland by nearly 15% and the sale of mangoes has increased by a staggering 47% in the past two weeks alone."

DID YOU KNOW?
England have won their last eight matches since losing to Northern Ireland in September 2005. The winning streak equals the best under Eriksson and is two matches short of the all-time England record of 10 successive wins which was set nearly 100 years ago. They have won all nine matches they have played with Peter Crouch on the field.

Aaron Lennon's appearance in the second half made him England's second youngest player at a World Cup, exactly eight years after Michael Owen set the record. Six of England's 10 youngest players at World Cups have been selected by current coach Sven-Goran Eriksson and Walcott was yet to come.

A television set was ordered for the British delegation room at a Brussels summit on the future direction of the European Union so Prime Minister Tony Blair could keep his eye on the match.

Trinidad fans in Port of Spain cannot believe that England have scored so late in the game to deny their boys a famous point

Ronaldo commented, "I don't care if the coach chooses to drop me or is forced to put me on the bench. I'm not a troublemaker and I never have been. I know coach Carlos Alberto Parreira has said he wants me to play against Australia on Sunday, but I'm also aware of the fuss over my performance against Croatia on Tuesday. So if the coach wants to drop me, fine. I will go to the bench obediently. I won't cause problems. I admit that I didn't play well in the last game, but in the Ronaldo

Manual Of Football it is not obligatory for me to play well in every match.

I don't know what was wrong with me on Wednesday because I didn't feel ill after the 1-0 win over Croatia. Perhaps it was the heat because people said it was the hottest day for many years in Germany."

Earlier in the day Ecuador scored their biggest ever World Cup victory which meant both they and Germany had qualified for the knockout stages and both Costa Rica and Poland were

out. The South Americans played a brand of attacking football which combines pace and flank play. They will provide stiff opposition for England if they meet them in Round Two.

England's victory meant they had qualified for the knockout stages, while Sweden's late win thanks to Freddie Ljungberg's header denied them the chance to be confirmed as Group winners, but sent Paraguay home.

In tonight's German highlights show, the broadcasters revealed camera angles which 'clearly showed' that Crouch had pulled defender Brent Sancho's dreadlocks in order to gain an advantage when jumping for England's opening goal. It seems the phoney war, propagating enmity between the two old enemies has begun in the expectation of a possible meeting next week in the last sixteen.

Paraguay 0 v Sweden 1
Group B
Olympiastadion, Berlin
Attendance: 72,000
Kick-off: 9pm   Temperature: 19°C

PARAGUAY 0   v   SWEDEN 1

Referee: Lubos Michel

Scorers
Ljungberg **89'**

Teams

22 Bobadilla	Isaksson	01
04 Gamarra	Lucic	04
02 Nunez	Mellberg	03
05 Caceres	Linderoth	06
21 Caniza	Edman	05
06 Bonet	Ljungberg	09
10 Acuna	Alexandersson	07
13 Paredes	Kallstrom	16
16 Riveros	Wilhelmsson	21
09 Santa Cruz	Ibrahimovic	10
18 Valdez	Larsson	11

Substitutes

62'	19 Dos Santos > / 16 Riveros <	20 Allback > / 10 Ibrahimovic <	45'
63'	20 Lopez > / 09 Santa Cruz <	18 Jonson > / 21 Wilhelmsson <	68'
81'	08 Barreto > / 06 Bonet <	17 Elmander > / 10 Kallstrom <	86'

Discipline

03'	Caniza *foul*	Linderoth *foul*	14'
51'	Acuna *foul*	Lucic *foul*	48'
54'	Nunez *foul*	Allback *foul*	60'
74'	Paredes *foul*		
85'	Barreto *foul*		

48%	**Ball Possession**	52%
4	**Shots on target**	13
13	**Shots off target**	6
15	**Fouls**	18
3	**Corner Kicks**	6
1	**Offsides**	3

Official FIFA Man of the Match
Freddie Ljungberg

Around 50,000 Swedish fans congregated in Berlin to cheer their team to a late victory which gave them a great chance of making it through to the knockout stages

DID YOU KNOW?
Henrik Larsson played his 11th World Cup match, equalling the Swedish record shared by Bosse Larsson and Karl-Oskar Svensson.

STATE OF PLAY							GROUP B	
	P	W	D	L	F	A	GD	Pts
ENGLAND	2	2	0	0	3	0	+6	6
SWEDEN	2	1	1	0	1	0	+1	4
TRIN & TOB	2	0	1	1	0	2	-2	1
PARAGUAY	2	0	0	2	0	2	-2	0

Day Eight
Friday 16 June 2006

Champions Elect?

In a tetchy game Argentina prove their class with a dazzling display of passing and movement, plus some of the best goals of this or any World Cup as Lionel Messi showed

Holland Qualify

The fast, flowing football continued as Holland just managed to keep Ivory Coast at bay to make it through to the knockout stages. Robin van Persie scored the opening goal from a deflected free-kick

Mexican Misery

Mexico failed to breach Angola's defences much to the chagrin of their massed fans watching in Mexico City's main plaza, despite only facing ten men for the final 11 minutes

"The draw is a signal that we have arrived and are building a very good team."

Luis Oliveira Goncalves (Angola)

Argentina 6 v
Serbia & Montenegro 0

Group C
Veltins Arena, Gelsenkirchen
Attendance: 52,000
Kick-off: 3pm   Temperature: 19°C

Diego Maradona celebrates Argentina's fourth goal in their 6-0 annhilation of Serbia & Montenegro. Conspicuous by his presence and regularly featured on the TV coverage, Maradona had already become a talisman for the young team to aspire to

ARGENTINA 6 v SERBIA & MONTENEGRO 0

Referee: Roberto Rosetti

Scorers

6', 41'	Rodriguez
31'	Cambiasso
78'	Crespo
84'	Tevez
88'	Messi

Teams

01	Abbondanzieri	Jevric	01
21	Burdisso	Duljaj	04
02	Ayala	Gavrancic	06
06	Heinze	Krstajic	20
03	Sorin	Dudic	15
18	Rodriguez	Koroman	07
08	Mascherano	Stankovic	10
22	Gonzalez	Nadj	17
10	Riquelme	Djordjevic	11
07	Saviola	Kezman	08
09	Crespo	Milosevic	09

Substitutes

17'	> 05 Cambiasso < 22 Gonzalez	02 Ergic > 17 Nadj <	45'
50'	> 11 Tevez < 22 Saviola	21 Ljuboja > 07 Koroman <	58'
70'	> 19 Messi < 18 Rodriguez	18 Vukic > 09 Milosevic <	74'

Discipline

36'	Crespo *kicking the ball away*	Koroman *foul*	07'
		Nadj *foul*	27'
		Krstajic *foul*	42'
		Kezman *foul*	64'

50%	Ball Possession	50%
10	Shots on target	2
2	Shots off target	3
12	Fouls	19
3	Corner Kicks	4
3	Offsides	0

Official FIFA Man of the Match
Juan Riquelme

Crouch insisted England would raise their game and overcome either Germany or Ecuador in the second round. "Would I prefer Germany or Ecuador? We've just got to win the next game against Sweden. We'd love to have nine points out of nine and I am sure, whoever we get in the next round, we will improve and win that as well. It was great to score in a World Cup and it was a special moment for me. I was still thinking about that first-half miss."

STATE OF PLAY							GROUP C
	P	W	D	L	F	A	GD Pts
ARGENTINA	2	2	0	0	8	1	+7 6
HOLLAND	1	1	0	0	1	0	+1 3
IVORY COAST	1	0	0	1	1	2	-1 0
SERB & MON	2	0	0	2	0	7	-7 0

DID YOU KNOW?
Substitute Lionel Messi became Argentina's youngest player at the World Cup (18 years and 357 days). Messi also became the sixth youngest goalscorer ever in the finals. Pelé is the youngest at 17 years and 239 days. For this game Messi wore boots praising Maradona's "Hand of God" goal in the 1986 World Cup.

DID YOU KNOW?
Roberto Ayala equalled Javier Zanetti's career record of 102 caps for Argentina. Diego Simeone is the Argentine record holder with 106. Captain Savo Milosevic won his 100th cap, becoming the first Serbia and Montenegro player to reach this milestone. He has won 72 caps for Yugoslavia and 28 for Serbia and Montenegro.

DID YOU KNOW?
The 6-1 win over Serbia & Montenegro equalled Argentina's biggest ever World Cup win, against Peru in 1978.

Much of the focus was inevitably on Rooney after he came on for the final 32 minutes. But Crouch was also quick to praise the contribution of Lennon and Downing as substitutes on the two flanks, "There was a lift when Wayne came on – but not just Wayne. I thought Aaron Lennon and Stewart Downing gave us a real lift as well, especially attacking-wise. I think we needed that, fresh legs to come on and run at players."

It seemed that for once Germany were more fearful of meeting England than the other way around as Germany coach Oliver Bierhoff was keen to avoid a clash with England in the second round. "I would prefer to play Sweden rather than England, who remain favourites to win Group B," said Bierhoff, who works alongside head coach Jürgen Klinsmann. "But then again a big win early in the knock-out

states could give us a major confidence booster for the remaining matches."

My next assignment on the World Cup trail of attempting to experience the tournament in a wide variety of ways, was to host my own World cup show on TV, radio and the internet. Quite a formidable task, and one that I had been planning for quite some time to put into operation. A number of close friends helped me to achieve it. Constantin and Leonie Schwarz were invaluable. Constantin, with his vast knowledge of new technology, and Leonie as a professional lifestyle photographer. We were brought together by my five year-old daughter Poppy and their blond haired son Xavier.

After several informal chats at the Wentworth tennis club with Constantin, he developed the Hold The Back Page website, while over dinner prior to the NTL launch of my World Cup book This

In a riot of colour and singing, Argentina's fans lit up their team's devastating display of attacking football

Holland 2 v Ivory Coast 1
Group C
Gottlieb-Daimler-Stadion, Stuttgart
Attendance: 52,000
Kick-off: 6pm   Temperature: 25°C

Ruud van Nistelrooy strokes home Holland's winning goal in the 2-1 victory over Ivory Coast

HOLLAND 2 v **IVORY COAST 1**

Referee: Julian Oscar Ruiz Acosta

Scorers

| 23' | van Persie | B Kone | 38' |
| 27' | van Nistelrooy | | |

Teams

Holland	Ivory Coast	
01 van der Sar	Tizie	01
14 Heitinga	Eboue	21
13 Ooijer	Toure	04
04 Mathijsen	Meite	12
05 van Bronckhorst	Boka	03
20 Sneijder	Zokora	05
18 van Bommel	Toure	19
08 Cocu	Romaric	22
17 van Persie	A Kone	09
11 Robben	B Kone	14
09 van Nistelrooy	Drogba	11

Substitutes

45'	> 03 Boulahrouz	10 Yapi Yapo >	61'
	< 14 Heitinga	22 Romaric <	
50'	> 10 van der Vaart	15 Dindane >	62'
	< 20 Sneijder	14 B Kone <	
73'	> 06 Landzaat	02 Akale >	73'
	< 09 van Nistelrooy	09 A Kone <	

Discipline

34'	Robben *diving*	Zakora *foul*	25'
35'	Mathijsen *foul*	Drogba *foul*	40'
58'	van Bommel *foul*	Boka *foul*	66'
90'	Boulahrouz *kicking ball away*		

50%	**Ball Possession**	50%
8	Shots on target	9
2	Shots off target	9
22	Fouls	16
3	Corner Kicks	8
6	Offsides	4

Official FIFA Man of the Match
Arjen Robben

Time, Constantin and myself were in conversation with the NTL hierarchy and the idea popped out to develop a podcast programme for the World Cup with Jason Boswell assigned the seemingly improbable task of putting it all together for them.

A vital link to this wild idea becoming reality were my old friends Jon and Phil Smith who run First Artist Management, and together with our contacts in the game we were able to book guests through Jon's wife Janine who co-runs Splash Events.

Having recorded a dry run the day before the tournament opened, tonight was the first show for real recorded at Markettiers studios in the City. Tonight we pulled off a World Cup coup by netting the first ever UK interview with the world's No.1 football agent, Pini Zahavi. The Israeli super agent was in Germany and agreed to be interviewed while on his mobile in the back of a car on his way to the airport. In the Markettiers studio were controversial Crystal Palace chairman Simon Jordan and former long-serving Charlton manager Alan Curbishley.

Mark Mitchinson from Samsung Mobiles, who had kindly provided Three Lions phones as prizes, was also in to discuss sponsorship issues in the World Cup. The battle of the brands had taken the most amazing twist of all time yesterday when Adidas ordered that all England fans wearing

STATE OF PLAY							GROUP C
	P	W	D	L	F	A	GD Pts
ARGENTINA	2	2	0	0	8	1	+7 6
HOLLAND	2	2	0	0	3	1	+2 6
IVORY COAST	2	0	0	2	2	4	-2 0
SERB & MON	2	0	0	2	0	7	-7 0

Not to be outdone by the massed ranks of Oranje fans, Ivory Coast's supporters brought plenty of colour to the match themselves

Other News

Paraguay boss Anibal Ruiz looked like he could be the first coach to face the axe following his team's departure from the competition, although rumour had it that Poland boss Pawel Janas also faced the chop after his side's dismal exit from the World Cup.

A France press conference experienced muffled laughter as midfielder Florent Malouda said he had missed their opening game with piles. FIFA chose not to punish striker Ivan Kaviedes for donning a Spiderman mask to celebrate his goal against Costa Rica as there was 'nothing specific in the laws of the game that forbid such action'.

Nike caps have the offending head gear removed for the match against Trinidad & Tobago in Nuremburg. Adidas pay a fortune for the branding rights for the 2006 World Cup in Germany, but discovered that the fashion conscious British prefer the Nike brand, and their head gear was far too visible for Adidas liking. Adidas lodged a complaint with FIFA who instructed stewards to remove the caps and issue receipts, so fans could recover their caps after the game.

There are 15 sponsors and partners paying millions to FIFA for endorsements. The tournament had become the biggest branding event in sports history, but the cap confiscation was an issue that Chris Hull of Nationwide, who sponsor the England team, had never heard of before. Hull told me: "I've never seen anything like it. What if those fans without caps had suffered sun stroke? Would FIFA have been culpable?"

Zahavi is the most influential football agent of all time with connections

DID YOU KNOW?
When Angola midfielder Andre Macanga received the second yellow card in this game, (his first) it marked the 1,500th caution in World Cup history.

to owners such as Roman Abramovich and managers like Sir Alex and Eriksson. So he was best placed to reveal the truth about the tug of war between Sir Alex and the England coach over Rooney. Zahavi provided some amazing comments about Sir Alex's attitude toward England's World Cup bid. He told me, "Alex Ferguson will never change, especially in the next part of his life. Alex Ferguson cares only about Manchester United, no doubt. Not the England team, not the Scottish team, although perhaps a little more about the Scottish team. In any case, for him the real important think is to have his 'boy' safe and fit for the league. This is a very crucial league season for Manchester Untied and for him. So of course he prefers that Rooney wouldn't play, but unfortunately for Alex, Eriksson and the player were on the other side in this particular case."

Zahavi also provided an insight into one of his top clients, Rio Ferdinand, who he revealed made special preparations to be in peak condition for this World Cup. Pini told me, "he will be the King of this World cup, he is back to his best and no-one knows how much he prepared for this World Cup, it is so important to him."

Even without pre-publicity such as the massive billboard and newspaper advertising campaign for the Skinner & Baddiel podcast in The Times, NTL's Hold

The Back Page was proving a massive hit. In the trial run the previous week, Harry Redknapp had predicted that Theo Walcott wouldn't get a kick in this World Cup and questioned his true ability. His views made headlines in the national press and featured on a FiveLive phone-in.

After hours of arduous broadcasting, late into the evening, an up-market Thai restaurant near the Markettiers studios provided much needed relaxation and the obligatory TV screen to catch up on World Cup games.

The Argentinians looked sharp, incisive and full of movement and passion as they swept aside a poor Serbia & Montenegro side, for whom striker Savo Milosevic became the first player to win 100 caps. Each of the Argentinian's six goals was beautifully crafted and they look as though they are the team to beat. But have they peaked too soon?

Holland defeated Ivory Coast 2-1 to knock them out of the tournament and set up a fabulous final group match against Argentina to contest the winners and runners-up spots in the group. Didier Drogba's second yellow card of the tournament left him suspended for the Ivorians' final group game.

There was more FIFA sponsorship nonsense as we discovered that before the Dutch game hundreds of fans who had arrived at the stadium wearing orange lederhosen sporting the logo

Mexico 0 v Angola 0
Group D
AWD Arena Niedesacker Stadion, Hanover
Attendance: 43,000
Kick-off: 9pm   Temperature: 19°C

Angola's goalkeeper Joao Ricardo make yet another flying save to preserve his team's clean sheet and pull off one of the results of the tournament as they played the last 11 minutes with ten men

MEXICO 0   v   **ANGOLA 0**

Referee: Shamsul Maidin

Scorers

Teams

Mexico	Angola
01 Sanchez	Joao Ricardo 01
03 Salcido	Jamba 03
04 Marquez	Kali 05
05 Osorio	Delgado 21
14 Pineda	Loco 20
06 Torrado	Figueiredo 07
07 Zinha	Macanga 08
08 Pardo	Mateus 11
16 Mendez	Mendonca 14
10 Franco	Ze Kalanga 17
19 Bravo	Akwa 10

Substitutes

	Mexico	Angola	
52'	21 Arellano / 07 Zinha	09 Mantorras / 11 D Mateus	68'
74'	17 Fonseca / 10 Franco	15 Rui Marques / 07 Figueiredo	72'
78'	11 Morales / 14 Pineda	06 Miloy / 17 Ze Kalanga	83'

Discipline

	Mexico	Angola	
59'	Pineda foul	Delgado foul	13'
		Macanga foul	44'
		Jamba foul	44'
		Ze Kalanga foul	50'
		Macanga handball (second yellow)	80'
		Joao Ricardo time wasting	86'

48%	Ball Possession	52%
14	Shots on target	8
5	Shots off target	11
8	Fouls	20
12	Corner Kicks	4
0	Offsides	8

Official FIFA Man of the Match
Joao Ricardo

of a certain Dutch beer company had been ordered to remove the offending article as FIFA declared it a clear case of 'ambush marketing'. The poor Dutchmen were forced to watch the game wearing nothing but their underpants, making it look like those English fans had had a lucky escape!

Mexico's grand wizard travelled to Germany with the national squad, performing two ceremonies a day to focus players' minds on the task in hand. But it clearly didn't work tonight as his team wasted chance after chance and failed to score against Angola.

Meanwhile Angola chiefs had adopted a more scientific approach, employing a sports psychologist to work with the team, but the players refused to take him seriously. And they proved they didn't need him with a resilient display during which goalkeeper Joao Ricardo became a national hero after pulling off a string of increasingly unorthodox, but fine saves. Mexico's Omar Bravo hit the post in the 88th minute, directly after Joao Ricardo had pulled off a flying save from Marquez' long-range piledriver. But Angola held on bravely.

The Mexican witchdoctor also predicted that Germany would meet Brazil in the final, which looked as bad a prediction as his team's efforts to beat Angola given the performances we've seen so far.

STATE OF PLAY — GROUP D

	P	W	D	L	F	A	GD	Pts
MEXICO	2	1	1	0	3	1	+2	4
PORTUGAL	1	1	0	0	1	0	+1	3
ANGOLA	2	0	1	1	0	1	-1	1
IRAN	1	0	0	1	1	3	-2	0

Day Nine
Saturday 17 June 2006

Big Phil Marches On

Luis Felipe Scolari extended his winning streak as a manager in World Cup finals to an unprecedented nine games as Portugal qualified for the Second Round by defeating battling Iran 2-0

African Dream

Ghana defeat the Czech Republic 2-0 in a rousing encounter, which brings them their first World Cup goal, scored by Asamoah Gyan, their first points and their first clean sheet

Red Sea

The USA end a chaotic game with nine men, while Italy have ten plus one injured passenger, after Daniele De Rossi's elbow sparks a flurry of cards from Uruguayan referee Jorge Larrionda

"It was a vicious elbow and it could have broken his face."
Bruce Arena (USA)

Iran 0 v Portugal 2

Group D
Commerzbank Arena, Frankfurt
Attendance: 48,000
Kick-off: 3pm   Temperature: 25°C

IRAN 0   v   **PORTUGAL 2**

Referee: Eric Poulat

Scorers

Deco	63'
Ronaldo *(pen)*	79'

Teams

01 Mirzapour	Ricardo 01
13 Kaabi	Miguel 13
04 Golmohammadi	Meira 05
05 Rezaei	Ricardo Carvalho 16
20 Nosrati	Nuno Valente 14
06 Nekounam	Costinha 06
02 Mahdavikia	Maniche 18
08 Karimi	Deco 20
14 Teymourian	Ronaldo 17
21 Madanchi	Pauleta 09
09 Hashemian	Figo 07

Substitutes

65'	07 Zandi > / 08 Karimi <	08 Petit > / 18 Maniche <	66'
66'	11 Khatibi > / 21 Madanchi <	19 Tiago > / 20 Deco <	80'
88'	03 Bakhtiarizadeh > / 04 Golmohammadi <	11 Simao > / 07 Figo <	88'

Discipline

20'	Nekounam *foul*	Pauleta *foul*	45'
32'	Madanchi *foul*	Deco *foul*	48'
73'	Kaabi *foul*	Costinha *foul*	61'
87'	Golmohammadi *foul*		

37%	Ball Possession	63%
3	Shots on target	9
4	Shots off target	9
12	Fouls	19
17	Corner Kicks	18
1	Offsides	4

Official FIFA Man of the Match
Deco

Cristiano Ronaldo expresses his relief at slotting from the penalty spot to finally put a tricky game to bed

Well, would you believe it? After all that. It wasn't as bad as everyone was led to believe.

Rooney was back playing football in less than seven weeks because the fracture to the fourth metatarsal of his right foot was not typical of the injury, according to the specialists who passed him fit to play. In a bid to clear any lingering suspicion over the speed of Rooney's recovery, the player and the FA sanctioned a second statement on the nature of his injury. Professors Angus Wallace and Chris Moran flew to Germany before the T&T match at the request of the FA to assess Rooney ahead of his selection. The specialists were invited by the FA, which wanted to make sure that they would be fully covered by their insurance. Rooney's break was actually at the base of the fourth metatarsal bone and under the surface of another small bone, called the lateral cuneiform bone. The fracture was located on the spongy cancellous bone at the base of the metatarsal and this heals three times quicker than the hard bone in the metatarsal shaft. Also, it was not a stress fracture, which take longer to heal.

Senior figures in the England camp were privately worried that Rooney might try to do too much as

DID YOU KNOW?
Portugal successfully navigated a World Cup group for the first time since 1966 when they finished in third place. Iran have now failed to survive the group stage in all three of their World Cups.

STATE OF PLAY   GROUP D

	P	W	D	L	F	A	GD	Pts
PORTUGAL	2	2	0	0	3	0	+3	6
MEXICO	2	1	1	0	3	1	+2	4
ANGOLA	2	0	1	1	0	1	-1	1
IRAN	2	0	0	2	1	5	-4	0

Czech Republic 0 v Ghana 2
Group E
RheinEnergieStadion, Cologne
Attendance: 45,000
Kick-off: 6pm   Temperature: 25°C

Sulley Ali Muntari attempts an overhead kick as Ghana pummel ten man Czech Republic, the surprising thing being they wasted so many chances and only won 2-0

he responded to the public clamour for him to take centre-stage. Although the two professors accepted that declaring Rooney able to play in the T&T game was one "week earlier" than they had anticipated, they both agreed he was "fit to play in the World Cup as from 15 June."

Owen exposed a crack of his own. He had kept a low profile but, after being withdrawn early for the second successive game he delivered a blunt assessment of his form that runs contrary to that offered by the England manager. "We're obviously not firing on all cylinders yet – me or the team and I'm reliant on the team," said Owen. "I'm in the team to be in the box and if the balls come in the box and I'm not on the end of them you can blame me. I've had one chance in

the game, with my head, and I'm kicking myself because I didn't score it. I had one that rebounded off me, but I wouldn't class that as a chance. I'm still a decent finisher. I'm playing well, but if it means bringing me off and putting Wayne on then that's the manager's decision."

Eriksson has plenty to think about after Freddie Ljungberg's late winner against Paraguay denied England guaranteed top place in Group B. "For me Michael Owen is getting better and better," Eriksson said. "I don't think he was tired. I wanted to change something because we hadn't scored a goal. It could have been Peter Crouch, but the only thing they were good at was set pieces and we needed Crouch to mark Lawrence." He denied claims that a disgruntled Owen had refused to shake hands at the end of the game. "He did shake hands."

Beckham was named man of the match in the win over Trinidad & Tobago, clinching the accolade with the superb cross that led to Crouch's goal. By then, he had been switched to right-back and he joked: "I must have looked like Cafu. I have already warned Gary Neville I am after his shirt. I have done it for Manchester United a few times. It gives me options. It gave me more time to cross the ball. I have had better days with my crosses, but I knew at one point I was going to put one on his head and that's all you need. We were nervous after 80 minutes when we hadn't scored, but we finished the game strongly which we haven't done for a while. That's the positive we can take out of it."

The weight of money and weight of expectation that had maintained England at a falsely short price as second-favourites was blown away by Argentina's footballing masterclass. They displaced England as the second favourites at 4-1 with all the leading bookmakers, while Eriksson's men are out to a top-priced 7-1 with Coral. Brazil remain favourites at 3-1, but have been eased after their low-key performance against Croatia and could be deposed from the head of the market by their South American rivals if they give another weak display against Australia on Sunday.

As for the football, it was a wonderful day of exciting games, first Cristiano Ronaldo opened his account as Portugal booked their place in the last 16. The Manchester United winger tucked the ball away from the penalty

spot after 79 minutes to wrap up a vital win over Iran. Phil Scolari's side dominated the game from start to finish, but went in at half-time without scoring. It needed something special to break the deadlock and Deco duly obliged with a stunning right-foot effort after 63 minutes.

Asamoah Gyan netted with a quality left-footed strike after just 68 SECONDS to give the Black Stars three vital points and Africa its first win of this tournament against the Czech Republic. Ghana even missed a penalty against the 10-man Czechs, who had Tomas Ujfalusi sent off midway through the second half. Sulley Muntari finally killed off the game with a second goal eight minutes from time after goalkeeper Petr Cech had turned in a one-man wonder-show to keep them at bay.

Black Stars coach Ratomir Dujkovic had been under pressure going into this match. No longer. He said: "You know as a coach you always have your luggage packed so you are ready to go. This is part of the job and in African countries they are very emotional. If the king dies, there is a new king. But now I am a hero in Ghana."

The final game on Saturday night was a thriller with nine-man USA clinging to a controversial 1-1 with Italy. Daniele De Rossi was guilty of a brutal elbow that floored the blood-splattered McBride and earned the most richly-deserved red card of the tournament. USA's Pablo Mastroeni, for a sliding studs-first challenge, and the twice-booked Eddie Pope soon followed him off.

Before that triple dismissal, Alberto Gilardino's headed opener had

CZECH REPUBLIC 0 v **GHANA 2**

Referee: Horacio Marcelo Elizondo

Scorers

Gyan	1'
Muntari	82'

Teams

01 Cech	Kingston 22
02 Grygera	Pantsil 15
22 Rozehnal	Mensah 05
21 Ujfalusi	Mohamed 13
06 Jankulovski	Shilla 07
08 Poborsky	Essien 08
04 Galasek	Appiah 10
10 Rosicky	Muntari 11
20 Plasil	O Addo 20
11 Nedved	Gyan 03
12 Lokvenc	Amoah 14

Substitutes

45'	19 Polak > 4 Galasek <	9 Boateng > 20 O Addo <	45'
56'	17 Stajner > 8 Poborsky <	18 E Addo > 14 Amoah <	80'
68'	7 Sionko > 20 Plasil <	19 Pimpong > 3 Gyan <	85'

Discipline

49'	Lokvenc foul	O Addo foul	18'
65'	Ujfalusi denying a goalscoring opportunity	Essien foul	37'
		Gyan time wasting	65'
		Boateng foul	75'
		Muntari foul	84'
		Mohamed foul	90'

52%	Ball Possession	48%
8	Shots on target	14
11	Shots off target	5
20	Fouls	8
4	Corner Kicks	12
8	Offsides	0

Official FIFA Man of the Match
Michael Essien

STATE OF PLAY — GROUP E

	P	W	D	L	F	A	GD	Pts
ITALY	1	1	0	0	2	0	+2	3
CZECH REP	2	1	0	1	3	2	+1	3
GHANA	2	1	0	1	2	2	0	3
USA	1	0	0	1	0	3	-3	0

ITALY 1   v   USA 1

Referee: Jorge Larrionda

Scorers

22'	Gilardino	Zaccardo (og)	27'

Teams

01	Buffon	Keller	18
02	Zaccardo	Cherundolo	06
13	Nesta	Onyewu	22
05	Cannavaro	Pope	23
19	Zambrotta	Bocanegra	03
20	Perrotta	Dempsey	08
21	Pirlo	Mastroeni	04
04	De Rossi	Reyna	10
10	Totti	Convey	15
09	Toni	McBride	20
11	Gilardino	Donovan	21

Substitutes

35'	> 8 Gattuso < 10 Totti	13 Conrad > 15 Convey <	52'
54'	> 7 Del Piero < 2 Zaccardo	17 Beasley > 8 Dempsey <	62'
61'	> 15 Iaquinta < 9 Toni		

Discipline

04'	Totti foul	Pope foul	20'
28'	De Rossi foul	Mastroeni foul	44'
70'	Zambrotta foul	Pope foul (second yellow)	46'

54%	**Ball Possession**	46%
4	**Shots on target**	3
6	**Shots off target**	6
13	**Fouls**	23
7	**Corner Kicks**	3
11	**Offsides**	1

Official FIFA Man of the Match

Kasey Keller

Italy 1 v USA 1
Group E
Fritz-Walter-Stadion, Kaiserslautern
Attendance: 46,000
Kick-off: 9pm   Temperature: 20°C

Kasey Keller stretches to fingertip Alessandro Del Piero's effort around the post to keep the USA in the game

been cancelled out by Cristian Zaccardo's own goal equaliser midway through the first period.

All players at the finals signed a pre-tournament agreement stating that they would abstain from betting during the tournament. FIFA's disciplinary committee will now determine whether gambling among team-mates is an offence which warrants punishment or just a reminder of the regulations.

Tim Cahill revealed that several team-mates backed him to score Australia's first World Cup goal, which the Everton player did during the 3-1 win over Japan. A FIFA official said,

DID YOU KNOW?
Daniele de Rossi's red card was the sixth for an Italian player at the World Cup. Eddie Pope became the 10th player to be sent off in this tournament.

DID YOU KNOW?
This was only the fourth occasion in World Cup finals history that a game had seen three red cards, and the first since Denmark met South Africa in Toulouse in France 98.

STATE OF PLAY   GROUP E

	P	W	D	L	F	A	GD	Pts
ITALY	2	1	0	0	2	0	+2	3
CZECH REP	2	1	0	0	3	0	+3	3
GHANA	2	0	0	1	0	2	-2	0
USA	2	0	0	1	0	3	-3	0

Other News

Ismail Bhamjee of Botswana, a member of FIFA's executive committee, was sacked after admitting selling World Cup tickets at three times their face value. He sold 12 tickets for England's match against Trinidad & Tobago for 300 euros each and was told to leave Germany immediately. "I am disappointed about the conduct of a member of the executive committee," said FIFA president Sepp Blatter. "In such a situation, FIFA acts immediately and firmly."

It emerged that FIFA had granted German Evangelical churches the rights to screen World Cup matches free of charge. "Football is a vital part of life," said Bishop Wolfgang Huber.

DID YOU KNOW?
Italy stretched their unbeaten sequence to 20 internationals – the longest streak by the country since 1939.

"I can confirm that the declaration set out by FIFA and signed by all players and staff of each of the 32 nations clearly states that no betting is allowed for the members of the delegations. This includes internal betting within the players of any team, which is also strictly not allowed. The committee has made it very clear that no betting in any form should be taking place and they will investigate any case thoroughly." It is not known what the punishment could be if the Australians are found guilty.

Brian McBride leaves the field for treatment after suffering a horrendous assault from De Rossi's elbow which earned the Italian a deserved red card

Day Ten

Sunday 18 June 2006

Paying The Penalty

Japan keeper Kawaguchi flies to his left to palm away Dario Srna's 23rd minute penalty kick

Golden Goals

Brazil triumph in a tense game against Australia with Adriano netting his first World Cup finals goal

France Blow It

Zinedine Zidane can scarcely believe that France's domination of the game has been wiped away by Park Ji Sung's late equalizer after the officials failed to spot Vieira's header crossing the line

"If you appealed every time you feel a mistake has been made it would be a never-ending story, but video replays would definitely have helped clarify this situation." Raymond Domenech (France)

Croatia 0 v Japan 0

Group F
Franken-Stadion, Nuremburg
Attendance: 41,000
Kick-off: 3pm   Temperature: 26°C

Dada Prso hides his head in shame while full-back Alex celebrates his goalkeeper's flying save from Croatia's first half penalty

CROATIA 0   v   **JAPAN 0**

Referee: Frank De Bleeckere

Scorers

Teams

Croatia		Japan	
01	Pletikosa	Kawaguchi	23
04	R Kovac	Miyamoto	05
03	Simunic	Kaji	21
05	Tudor	Nakazawa	22
07	Simic	Santos	14
02	Srna	Ogasawara	08
08	Babic	Nakata	07
10	N Kovac	Nakamura	10
19	Kranjcar	Fukunishi	15
09	Prso	Takahara	09
17	Klasnic	Yanagisawa	13

Substitutes

69'	18 Olic > / 5 Tudor <	17 Inamoto > / 15 Fukunishi <	45'
78'	14 Modric > / 19 Krancjar <	20 Tamada > / 13 Yanagisawa <	62'
86'	22 Bosnjak > / 2 Srna <	16 Oguro > / 9 Takahara <	85'

Discipline

32'	R Kovac *foul*	Miyamoto *foul*	22'
69'	Srna *foul*	Kawaguchi *time wasting*	42'
		Santos *foul*	72'

49%	Ball Possession	51%
5	Shots on target	4
12	Shots off target	8
19	Fouls	18
12	Corner Kicks	5
6	Offsides	1

Official FIFA Man of the Match
Hidetoshi Nakata

At last France scored! But it was the one that crossed the line and wasn't given that caused such fury, as it could lead to their exit. Thierry Henry scored his first goal of the tournament, but launched a furious attack on ref Benito Archundia after the Mexican official refused to allow a 30th-minute goal from Patrick Vieira – even though the former Arsenal star's header was almost a yard over the line.

That error was magnified when eight minutes from time Manchester United's Park Ji Sung bundled in a late leveller beyond a rather helpless and useless Barthez to cancel out Henry's opener. Henry was clearly upset, "We did not start appealing because it was so obvious. Everyone in the ground could see it. Why he made that decision I do not know, but it was clearly in. The refs are pretty quick to give yellow cards for no reason, but when we wanted a proper decision there was no-one out there to do that."

But Coach Raymond Domenech admitted France should not have been relying on a refereeing decision to see off the plucky Koreans, "I am disappointed that we couldn't carry on the way we started and it was difficult to see why. Like my players I feel disappointed. We prepared so thoroughly, but we did not manage to turn the game around. We did score a second goal, but it was not recognised. If you appealed every time you feel a mistake has been made it would be a never-ending story, but video replays would have helped clarify this situation. It's a pity that at this level we do not use all the technology that we could. We will be depending on other

STATE OF PLAY — GROUP F

	P	W	D	L	F	A	GD	Pts
AUSTRALIA	1	1	0	0	3	1	+2	3
BRAZIL	1	1	0	0	1	0	+1	3
JAPAN	2	0	1	1	1	3	-2	1
CROATIA	2	0	1	1	0	1	-1	1

Australia 0 v Brazil 2
Group F
Allianz Arena, Munich
Attendance: 66,000
Kick-off: 6pm   Temperature: 27°C

Fred taps in after Robinho's shot cannons off Mark Schwarzer's left post leaving him to finish off the robust challenge of the Socceroos

teams now and that's very disappointing for a team of our quality and experience. We really should not find ourselves in a position like this."

Zidane's booking was a sign of frustration. The great man looked a shadow of the 1998 World Cup winning force and will now miss the crucial last match against Togo.

Park, perhaps inspired by the awesome support the Korean fans displayed inside the stadium, believed his team could match their exploits from the last World Cup when they reached the semi-finals, "If we do our best, then we can go anywhere. There's great confidence in our team and also great belief now." The result left France in dire straits, with only two points from two games, needing a win in their final match to ensure qualification.

Carlos Alberto Parreira will continue to stick with the out-of-form Ronaldo as his main attacker despite the huge impression made by substitutes Robinho and Fred during the 2-0 win

over Australia. The victory ensured Brazil qualified with a game to spare, although they will need at least a point in their final group game against Japan to finish on top of Group F if second-placed Australia beat third-placed Croatia in the final group game.

Parreira again substituted Ronaldo, after the star striker again made little impression – although he did set up the opening goal for Adriano. But when he was replaced by Robinho in the 71st minute, Brazil immediately looked more dangerous with Robinho

> **DID YOU KNOW?**
> *Croatia have now failed to score in their last three World Cup matches (losing 0-1 to Ecuador in 2002 and 0-1 to Brazil in this tournament before the stalemate with Japan). In this game Dario Simic became the most capped Croatian in the short history of the country, with 82 appearances, surpassing Robert Jarni.*

> **DID YOU KNOW?**
> *Japan's starting line-up for this game had an average age of 28 years and 210 days, the oldest Japanese team in World Cup history. This goalless draw ended Japan's streak of 17 competitive matches in which they scored at least one goal. Goalkeeper Yoshikatsu Kawaguchi earned his 91st cap and is now joint second most capped player for Japan, behind Masami Ihara (123 caps).*

AUSTRALIA 0 v BRAZIL 2

Referee: Markus Merk

Scorers

48'	Adriano
89'	Fred

Teams

Australia		Brazil	
01	Schwarzer	Dida	01
03	Moore	Cafu	02
06	Popovic	Lucio	03
02	Neill	Juan	04
14	Chipperfield	Carlos	06
07	Emerton	Kaka	08
13	Grella	Emerson	05
21	Sterjovski	Ze Roberto	11
04	Cahill	Ronaldinho	10
05	Culina	Ronaldo	09
09	Viduka	Adriano	07

Substitutes

40'	> 23 Bresciano < 6 Popovic	17 Gilberto Silva > 5 Emerson <	71'
56'	> 10 Kewell < 4 Cahill	23 Robinho > 9 Ronaldo <	71'
69'	> 15 Aloisi < 3 Moore	21 Fred > 7 Adriano <	88'

Discipline

13'	Emerton *dissent*	Cafu *foul*	28'
39'	Culina *foul*	Ronaldo *time wasting*	31'
		Robinho *foul*	83'

47%	**Ball Possession**	53%
4	**Shots on target**	6
10	**Shots off target**	11
23	**Fouls**	9
4	**Corner Kicks**	7
1	**Offsides**	5

Official FIFA Man of the Match
Ze Roberto

setting up the second goal for Fred after crashing a shot against the post. However Parreira defended Ronaldo after the game, saying his performance had been a big improvement on his effort during Brazil's opening win over Croatia. "He is slowly getting his rhythm back. But he needs to play more games to get more rhythm. He is gradually getting fitter but the only way he will continue to get fitter is to play more games." Parreira said Ronaldo would start against Japan, denying he should be replaced by either Robinho or Fred following their key contributions off the bench against the Socceroos.

Yoshikatsu Kawaguchi put in an inspired performance between the posts for Japan as the Asian champions kept their slim World Cup hopes alive with a 0-0 draw with Croatia in Nuremberg. A top class display in the opening 45 minutes from the former Portsmouth goalkeeper – which included a penalty save from Darijo Srna – denied the Croatians and meant both teams had to win their final game to have any chance of progressing to the knockout phase. While the Croatians face Australia in the last day of Group F action, the task is significantly tougher for Japan as they take on defending champions and tournament favourites Brazil.

Michael Owen, nicknamed 'Mo' by his team-mates, had endured a nightmare start to the tournament having been subbed twice before the hour mark. Now he has the chance to start alongside the returning Rooney against Sweden. Owen was frustrated England played long balls up to Crouch against Trinidad & Tobago. He even complained to his Newcastle boss Glenn Roeder about England's playing style.

Owen was anxious to get his point of view across after training, "If we get the ball in better areas of the pitch, then I can make better runs. It is difficult making these good runs if the centre-halves have the ball. If we can get someone just behind me or in midfield with their head up, I come alive. You would think there would not be as many longer balls because Wayne and myself are not that tall. I am sure that, deep down, people aren't doubting me. It is just a story at the minute. We've seen it before with Gary Lineker and Alan Shearer. Everyone goes through patches when they don't score, but it's not like I am having a long drought. Only a few games ago I hardly had a touch against Argentina and scored twice to win the game. Of course I mind being subbed, but if the team play better, I play better and I will look as good as I have ever done. It is just a case of us passing the ball and getting into the right areas for me to come alive. It's simple. It is a large part of my game to

STATE OF PLAY							GROUP F
	P	W	D	L	F	A	GD	Pts
BRAZIL	2	2	0	0	3	0	+3	6
AUSTRALIA	2	1	0	1	3	3	0	3
CROATIA	2	0	1	1	0	1	-1	1
JAPAN	2	0	1	1	1	3	-2	1

France 1 v South Korea 1
Group G
Zentralstadion, Leipzig
Attendance: 43,000
Kick-off: 9pm   Temperature: 17°C

France's Arsenal links give them a great start as Sylvain Wiltord lays the ball off to Thierry Henry for France's opening goal, but they paid the price for failing to kill off South Korea

get in the last third and I need the ball in the box. I'm reliant on team-mates in that respect."

Trinidad & Tobago captain Dwight Yorke intended to plead with as many England players as possible, urging them to win against Sweden and help his country to progress from Group B. If Trinidad & Tobago beat Paraguay in their final group match and England defeat Sweden at the same time, the Caribbean side will reach the second phase at their first finals if they have a better goal difference than the Swedes. "I will be texting or will call the boys, like Rooney, Becks, Rio,

Gary. To be honest I will text them all if I can get their numbers, but certainly most of them anyway."

Yorke is firm friends with many of the England squad, especially those who play or have played for Manchester United. The 34-year-old spent four years at Old Trafford and returned to United recently by invitation to prepare for the finals. "Obviously, after the game we had a good chat and they said they hadn't expected such a tough game, so that is a credit to us. We have done what we wanted so far, we didn't want to be the whipping boys and you know the

tournament is over already for some teams, but it isn't over yet for us."

FIFA intervened to persuade Togo's players not to boycott their game with Switzerland tomorrow as unrest simmers in the Togolese camp. The squad was on its way to Dortmund where Togo play their second Group G match against Switzerland on Monday. The players, due to catch their scheduled morning flight from Friedrichshafen airport to Dortmund, had initially stayed in their base in southern Germany while they discussed the long-running pay dispute. Players from the tiny West African country have

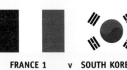

FRANCE 1 v **SOUTH KOREA 1**

Referee: Benito Archundia Tellez

Scorers

| 09' | Henry | Park Ji Sung | 81' |

Teams

16 Barthez	Lee Woon Jae 01
03 Abidal	Kim Young Chul 02
05 Gallas	Kim Dong Jin 03
15 Thuram	Choi Jin Chul 04
19 Sagnol	Lee Young Po 12
07 Malouda	Kim Nam Il 05
04 Vieira	Park Ji Sung 07
06 Makelele	Lee Eul Yong 13
10 Zidane	Lee Ho 17
11 Wiltord	Lee Chun Soo 14
12 Henry	Cho Jae Jin 19

Substitutes

60'	22 Ribery / 11 Wiltord	11 Seol Ki Hyeon / 13 Lee Eul Yong	45'
87'	8 Dhorasoo / 7 Malouda	18 Kim Sang Sik / 17 Lee Ho	69'
90'	20 Trezeguet / 10 Zidane	9 Ahn Jung Hwan / 14 Lee Chun Soo	72'

Discipline

| 79' | Abidal foul | Lee Ho foul | 11' |
| 85' | Zidane foul | Kim Dong Jin foul | 28' |

52%	Ball Possession	48%
4	Shots on target	2
11	Shots off target	3
20	Fouls	10
6	Corner Kicks	2
4	Offsides	1

Official FIFA Man of the Match
Park Ji Sung

demanded 155,000 euros ($196,300) each to play and 30,000 euros for each win, half that for each draw. But officials from the country with an average per capita income of well below $1,000 have repeatedly said those demands are too high. An impasse had been reached once again.

"As far as we understand the team did not want to play," a FIFA spokesman said. "The FIFA delegate there told them it would be extremely serious. He told them to be reasonable and they were," the spokesman said,

adding the team were now on the road. No team that has qualified for a World Cup finals has withdrawn from a match in the 76-year history of the event. Any nation doing so faces a heavy fine and could be banned from subsequent competitions.

"We are on the bus now," coach Otto Pfister told Reuters on the telephone. "I think they have found a solution, but I don't know what it is and I don't want to know," he added.

Fabien Barthez fails to reach Park Ji Sung's looping effort and France somehow are held to a draw

	P	W	D	L	F	A	GD	Pts
SOUTH KOR	2	1	1	0	3	2	+1	4
FRANCE	2	0	2	0	1	1	0	2
SWITZERLAND	1	0	1	0	0	0	0	1
TOGO	1	0	0	1	1	2	-1	0

Day Eleven
Monday 19 June 2006

Swiss On A Role

Swiss goalkeeper Pascal Zuberbühler saves Mohamed Kader's header during Switzerland's 2-0 victory over Togo which puts them on top of Group G

Ukraine Get Going

Sergei Rebrov lashes in the second goal of the game to set Ukraine well on their way to a comprehensive 4-0 win over Saudi Arabia

Spain Triumph In Terrific Tussle

Fernando Torres' penalty defeats Tunisian goalkeeper Ali Boumnijel to guarantee qualification for the Spanish, who made heavy weather of overturning a half-time deficit against a determined Tunisia

"It all crumpled because of one single mistake." Roger Lemerre (Tunisia)

Switzerland 2 v Togo 0
Group G
Signal Iduna Park, Dortmund
Attendance: 65,000
Kick-off: 3pm   Temperature: 29°C

SWITZERLAND 2 v **TOGO 0**

Referee: Carlos Amarilla

Scorers

17'	Frei
88'	Barnetta

Teams

01 Zuberbühler	Agassa 16
20 Müller	Nibombe 02
23 P Degen	Tchangai 05
04 Senderos	A Toure 23
03 Magnin	Agboh 08
16 Barnetta	Dossevi 09
06 Vogel	Cherif-Toure 10
08 Wicky	Romao 15
07 Cabanas	Forson 13
09 Frei	Adebayor 04
10 Gygax	Mohamed 17

Alexander Frei steers home Barnetta's cross to give Switzerland a vital 1-0 lead

Substitutes

45'	> 22 Yakin < 10 Gygax	07 Salifou > 08 Agboh <	24'
77'	> 11 Streller < 07 Cabanas	18 Senaya > 09 Dossevi <	68'
87'	> 18 Lustrinelli < 09 Frei	11 Malm > 10 Cherif-Toure <	86'

Discipline

90'	Vogel foul	Salifou foul	45'
		Adebayor dissent	47'
		Romao foul	52'

49%	Ball Possession	51%
10	Shots on target	5
8	Shots off target	5
13	Fouls	18
8	Corner Kicks	4
5	Offsides	6

Official FIFA Man of the Match
Alexander Frei

Fed up with the same old diet of past-their-sell-by-date pundits on ITV and BBC, I tried out the alternative view...UKTVGold2. While the public seem bored with some of the out of date studio guests on the major channels, over on UKTVGold2, it was most definitely different, off the wall, and at times quite amusing, if low budget and aimed at the Lads who want to know more about the WAGS.

I watched the France versus South Korea game with Ron Atkinson as co-commentator. He may be disgraced after his Marcel Desailly racist remark cost him his lucrative ITV job, but reports that his only TV role these days is his own web-cam from his bedroom with just 63 viewers are way off the mark. Big Ron is one of the smoothest analysts of the game, together with ITV's Davids Pleat. But ITV have more has-beens than anyone else and word reaches me of a post World Cup cull.

DID YOU KNOW?
Frei's effort was Switzerland's first World Cup goal since George Bregy scored in their 4-1 win over Romania in 1994.

DID YOU KNOW?
Goalshy Togo have only scored four goals in their nine internationals in the year of 2006.

STATE OF PLAY — GROUP G

	P	W	D	L	F	A	GD	Pts
SWITZERLAND	2	1	1	0	2	0	+2	4
SOUTH KOR	2	1	1	0	3	2	+1	4
FRANCE	2	0	2	0	1	1	0	2
TOGO	2	0	0	2	1	4	-3	0

Twins In The World Cup

CREDIT SUISSE

23 year-old Swiss twins David (left) and Philipp Degen (born 15 February 1983) are the only twins in this World Cup. David is the eldest by 20 minutes. Philipp is a defender with Borussia Dortmund who appeared in 9 of Switzerland's 12 qualifying matches and had 15 caps before the finals began, while David is a midfielder who had only made 3 appearances at full level for the Swiss (none in World Cup qualifiers) after starring for their Under 21 side.

This was the fifth successive finals to contain a set of twins. In 2002 it was Michal and Marcin Zewlakow of Poland, Frank and Ronald de Boer appeared for the Netherlands in the 1994 and 1998 competitions while Ibrahim and Hossam Hassan played for Egypt in 1990.

The previous occasion that twins appeared in the finals was in 1978 when Willy and Rene van de Kerkhof were in the Netherlands squad.

But over on UKTVGold2, there's a lighter touch. UKTV is half owned by the BBC, and the Beeb paid so much for the World Cup rights, that they 'sold off' simultaneous coverage of the games to UKTV to recoup some of their outlay. However, the details of the commercial deal touch a nerve as the TV station issued me with a statement.

It read: 'UKTV is an independent joint venture between Flextech, the content division of ntl inc. and BBC Worldwide, the BBC's commercial arm.

As such, it operates at arms-length from its shareholders to fund, produce and broadcast its own programming – our World Cup coverage follows a sub-licensing deal between BBC and UKTV. Monies generated by this agreement, together with other commercial activity, are returned to the BBC for the benefit of the licence fee payer.'

Don Perretta, Head of Football, North One Television and Series Editor on UKTVGold2 tells me:

'We are showing 31 or 32 live games from the World Cup, depending on whether England play in the 3rd/4th playoff, essentially the same games as the BBC including the final. We have a one-hour pre-match programme which is designed to provide an entertaining alternative to the more traditional fare offered by ITV and BBC. Our presenter is Andy Goldstein, usually of Sky Sports, who is definitely destined for greater things and he is joined everyday by two guests, one from the world of football and the other from the world of entertainment.'

Football guests are the likes of Dave Bassett, John Fashanu, Ian Holloway, Tony Dorigo and Craig Brown. Showbiz guests include Ainsley Harriott, MC

Harvey, DJ Spoony, Phil Tufnell, Bob Mills, Mike McLean, Rowland Rivron, Brian Blessed, who really knows his football, Steve Pemberton of the League of Gentlemen and Ricky Tomlinson. There's also a studio audience for atmosphere and participation, and various regular items, one of which is a penalty prize in which the showbiz guest is invited to score as many penalties as they can against a masked goalkeeper, whose identity is only to be revealed in the last show.

Don added: 'We also have a Jens Lehmann doll which we use for the item "In Lehmann's Terms", where the German keeper explains the rudiments of German football terminology (e.g. Krank als ein Papagei = sick as a parrot) and has a regular dig at Oliver Kahn.'

French newspapers were left in despair after Les Bleus' embarrassing draw with South Korea. The result left France, who lost the magic that delivered the 1998 World Cup and Euro 2000, needing to beat Togo by two clear goals in their last group game to guarantee a place in the knockout stages. 'Hopeless!' ran the headline of sports daily L'Equipe, with a picture of goalkeeper Fabien Barthez on his knees after Park Ji Sung's late equaliser. 'Dominating and well organised in the first half, Les Bleus nose-dived in the second. It is very worrying,' wrote the paper.

'Les Bleus in danger,' said news daily Le Figaro. 'France fail,' bemoaned Liberation.

Thierry Henry insisted France could qualify even without Zidane who is now suspended for their last group match against Togo. Henry said: "We did it in 1998 without Zidane – he didn't play against Denmark or

---

DID YOU KNOW?
Ukraine's form (i.e losing the first match 0-4 and winning the next by the same margin) is the largest fluctuation since 1982 when Hungary beat El Salvador 10-1 and then lost their next group match to Argentina 1-4.

Saudi Arabia 0 v Ukraine 4

Group H
AOL Arena, Hamburg
Attendance: 50,000
Kick-off: 6pm   Temperature: 28°C

Andrei Shevchenko celebrates his first World Cup finals goal, straight after the restart to put Ukraine 3-0 ahead

SAUDI ARABIA 0 v   UKRAINE 4

Referee: Graham Poll

Scorers

Rusol	04'
Rebrov	36'
Shevchenko	46'
Kalinichenko	84'

Teams

21	Zaid	Shovkovskiy	01
02	Dokhi	Nesmanchniy	02
03	Tukar	Rusol	06
04	Al Montashari	Sviderskiy	22
13	Sulimani	Tymoschuk	08
06	Al Ghamdi	Shelayev	09
07	Ameen	Gusev	11
08	Noor	Rebrov	19
14	Khariri	Kalinichenko	19
16	Aziz	Shevchenko	07
20	Al Kahtani	Voronin	10

Substitutes

55'	> 12 Khathran < 02 Al Dokhi	21 Rotan > 11 Rebrov <	71'
55'	> 23 Mouath < 07 Ameen	14 Gusin > 10 Voronin <	79'
77'	> 09 Al Jaber < 08 Noor	15 Milevskiy > 07 Shevchenko <	85'

Discipline

41'	Al Dokhi *foul*	Nesmanchiy *foul*	22'
56'	Al Ghamdi *diving*	Kalinichenko *foul*	77'
73'	Khariri *time wasting*	Sviderskiy *foul*	89'

49%	**Ball Possession**	51%
2	**Shots on target**	18
6	**Shots off target**	11
21	**Fouls**	20
2	**Corner Kicks**	9
0	**Offsides**	0

Official FIFA Man of the Match
Maxim Kalinichenko

Paraguay; no-one remembers that, but he didn't play in those games. I'm still confident we are going to go through. It should be the easiest game of the group against Togo and we are going to try to take advantage of that."

Henry would never admit it publicly, but Zidane's style of play does not suit the Arsenal striker and a more direct approach may pay dividends for him and for France, who should still progress to the next phase if they beat their former colony in Cologne.

France's problem is so great because Switzerland toiled in the Dortmund sun to pick up a 2-0 Group G win against Togo that put them closer to the knockout stages. The Swiss success ended the hopes of the African side after what has been an extraordinary first appearance on the big stage. Alexander Frei's close-range strike after 16 minutes – the first goal

Switzerland have scored at a World Cup for 12 years – gave Kobi Kuhn's side the perfect start in front of a crowd overwhelmingly in support of the European side.

Tranquillo Barnetta then finished off the World Cup debutants with a late second to secure a win for the Swiss.

Togo played the match despite threatening to boycott it over the ongoing pay dispute. Their players furiously berated Paraguayan referee Carlos Amarilla for spurning a penalty appeal late in the first half. Senderos gave the ball away to substitute Moustapha Salifou who freed Adebayor. The Arsenal player tumbled under a challenge from Patrick Muller, but Amarilla rejected the claims.

Harry Kewell could be about to miss Australia's final group match after being charged by FIFA with insulting referee Markus Merk following

STATE OF PLAY   GROUP H

	P	W	D	L	F	A	GD	Pts
SPAIN	1	1	0	0	4	0	+4	3
UKRAINE	2	1	0	1	4	4	0	3
TUNISIA	1	0	1	0	2	2	0	1
SAUDI ARA	2	0	1	1	2	6	-4	1

the defeat by Brazil. The Liverpool winger was reported by Merk for swearing at him several times after the final whistle and disciplinary proceedings were opened against him.

Andriy Shevchenko scored his first World Cup goal as Ukraine put their dismal display against Spain firmly behind them in Hamburg with a comprehensive 4-0 win over Saudi Arabia. Oleg Blokhin's men bounced back to take a comfortable three points against the outclassed Asians, whose uncertainty at set-pieces was ruthlessly exposed. Midfielder Maksym Kalinichenko set up Andriy Rusol's opener and Shevchenko for the third goal from a corner and free-kick respectively as the Saudi's susceptibility to the high ball fatally wounded their chances of taking anything from the game. Serhiy Rebrov claimed his side's second when his speculative effort from distance sailed into the top corner after Saudi goalkeeper Mabrouk Zaid slipped and Kalinichenko deservedly completed the rout six minutes from time. The win put Ukraine's hopes of progressing to the knockout phase of their first World Cup back on track. Blokhin observed, 'It's a little bit like Cinderella, the pumpkin turned into a beautiful coach and the other animals turned into wonderful horses. That's what happened to us today. We knew it was a decisive match and we turned things around and did a great job.'

The day ended with an exhilarating comeback by Spain that inspired discussion amongst BBC pundits Martin O'Neill and Alan Hansen that this could be THE World Cup of all time. Gary Lineker led the debate and Ian Wright accepted O'Neill and Hansen's verdict that the tournament had been full of goals, attacking football, and few, if any, of the expected dour games in the opening matches.

Spain came from behind with a three-goal second-half blitz. Substitute Raul's 71st-minute goal cancelled out Jaouhar Mnari's seventh-minute effort before Fernando Torres struck home

Spain 3 v Tunisia 1
Group H
Gottlieb-Daimler-Stadion, Stuttgart
Attendance: 52,000
Kick-off: 9pm   Temperature: 22°C

Fernando Torres benefited from the half-time introduction of Cesc Fabregas to notch the second and third goals as Spain managed a late comeback against Tunisia

three minutes later and added a penalty clincher, having himself been held inside the area by Alaeddine Yahia.

Having got their noses in front, Tunisia had seemed content to hold on to their lead, sitting deep and inviting the Spaniards to come onto them.

Aragones had relied on the same starting XI that humbled Ukraine 4-0, with David Villa and Torres leading the attack, but brought on winger Joaquin for Villa and the change reaped dividends. Joaquin's cross from the right found Fabregas, whose strike was

DID YOU KNOW?
Tunisia have not won a World Cup game in ten matches.

This was Tunisia's heaviest defeat in World Cup finals in their 11th game. They have kept only one clean sheet to date.

parried by Boumnijel and the ball fell to Raul, who finished well. The goal inspired the men in red and those two late strikes left Torres as the tournament's top goalscorer with three goals.

"Can you hear the drums, Fernando?" was Lineker's corny pun farewell which he delivered in his best Spanish.

And so to England. Could they now entertain against Sweden tomorrow as well as grind out results?

Joe Cole was confident England would step up a gear, "We are on a nice upward curve and everything is rosy." Gary Neville was still not considered fit enough to return to training. He looked on from the dug-out as England were put through their paces by Eriksson and his coaching staff. Meanwhile, all the cameras were trained on Rooney, who would be resuming his strike partnership with Owen, with Eriksson hoping it will be "like the good old days".

Owen had netted 36 times for his country, but needed to score like never before. He said: "All strikers need goals. Confidence in a striker when he scores is right up high and if they don't score it is the opposite."

Rooney had not scored in a competitive match for his country since Euro 2004, but Eriksson was unconcerned by that fact, "Am I worried about that statistic? No. If I said Rooney concerns me, people would think I am crazy and I hope I'm not crazy! All of us in the camp want to see him on the pitch. We saw him for half an hour in the last game and hopefully we will see him for longer this time. If you are a player or coach,

you want to see him on the pitch. He is very important to us."

FIFA warned England must try to win – even though a defeat could present them with their best chance of avoiding a second-round clash against hosts and old rivals Germany, whose finishing position in Group A will be known by the time England kick off. Section Two of FIFA's Fair Play Code, to which all teams competing at the World Cup must sign up, states: "Winning is the object of playing any game. Never set out to lose. If you do not play to win, you are cheating your opponents, deceiving those who are watching, and also fooling yourself. Play to win, until the final whistle."

FIFA admitted it would be difficult to prove a case where a team deliberately lost a game to avoid playing a particular opponent in the second round, but they said they would be obliged to investigate if there were any suspicions. "Winning the group is best because you have more resting days before the next match," Eriksson pointed out. "Also, we want to win the group because we didn't manage to do that in Euro 2004 or in the last World Cup in 2002. Let's hope we can do it this time."

So the world waited for Rooney's first start, and Adidas were certainly making the most of it with a controversial image of their client plastered over the front and back pages of the national press as well as double page adverts inside the papers.

SPAIN 3   v   **TUNISIA 1**

Referee: Carlos Eugenio Simon

Scorers

72'	Raul	Mnari	8'
76'	Torres		
90'	Torres (pen)		

Teams

01	Casillas	Boumnijel 01
15	Sergio Ramos	Haggui 03
05	Puyol	Jaidi 15
22	Pablo	Ayari 19
03	Pernia	Trabelsi 06
08	Xavi	Mnari 12
14	Alonso	Bouazizi 13
16	Senna	Chedli 14
11	Luis Garcia	Namouchi 20
09	Torres	Nafti 08
21	Villa	Jaziri 05

Substitutes

45'	18 Fabregas ⟩ 16 Senna ⟨	04 Yahia ⟩ 56' 19 Ayari ⟨
45'	07 Raul ⟩ 11 Luis Garcia ⟨	10 Ghodhbane ⟩ 56' 13 Bouazizi ⟨
56'	17 Joaquin ⟩ 21 Villa ⟨	07 Gmamdia ⟩ 79' 14 Chedli ⟨

Discipline

30'	Puyol foul	Ayari foul	32'
90'	Fabregas foul	Trabelsi foul	40'
		Jaidi foul	70'
		Gmamdia foul	80'
		Jaziri dissent	85'
		Mnari foul	90'

64%	**Ball Possession**	36%
10	**Shots on target**	3
14	**Shots off target**	1
10	**Fouls**	21
12	**Corner Kicks**	1
1	**Offsides**	6

Official FIFA Man of the Match
Xabi Alonso

DID YOU KNOW?
Raul's goal brought him level with Butragueno, Hierro and Morientes as the fourth Spanish player to score five World Cup goals. Torres' brace made him top scorer for the 2006 tournament. Arsenal midfielder Cesc Fabregas became the youngest ever Spanish World Cup finals player at 19 years and 46 days old.

STATE OF PLAY							GROUP H
	P	W	D	L	F	A	GD Pts
SPAIN	2	2	0	0	7	1	+6 6
UKRAINE	2	1	0	1	4	4	0 3
TUNISIA	2	0	1	1	3	5	-2 1
SAUDI ARA	2	0	1	1	2	6	-4 1

Day Twelve
Tuesday 20 June 2006

Germany Celebrates Qualification With 100% Record

An estimated 6 million people took to the streets to rejoice at Germany's third successive win, this time thanks to Miroslav Klose's double against Ecuador, who also qualify

England Still Can't Beat Sweden

A last minute goal of comedy proportions ensures England draw against dogged Sweden continues a run stretching back nearly 40 years, despite Joe Cole's stunning first half goal

Trinidad Go Home Goaless

A 2-0 defeat by Paraguay sees Trinidad head for home without having found the back of the net, but having made plenty of friends

"We did not defend very well against set-pieces. We need to work on that before our next game."

Sven-Göran Eriksson (England)

Ecuador 0 v Germany 3
Group A
Olympiastadion, Berlin
Attendance: 72,000
Kick-off: 4pm   Temperature: 29°C

ECUADOR 0   v   GERMANY 3

Referee: Valentin Ivanov

Scorers

Klose	4', 44'
Podolski	57'

Teams

12 Mora	Lehmann 01
04 De la Cruz	Friedrich 03
17 Espinoza	Mertesacker 17
13 Ambrossi	Huth 04
02 Guagua	Lahm 16
16 Valencia	Schwiensteiger 07
20 E Tenorio	Frings 08
15 Ayovi	Ballack 13
08 Mendez	Schneider 19
09 Borja	Klose 11
10 Kaviedes	Podolski 20

Substitutes

45'	> 23 Benitez < 09 Borja	10 Neuville > 11 Klose <	66'
63'	> 07 Lara < 16 Valencia	18 Borowski > 08 Frings <	66'
68'	> 06 Urrutia < 15 Ayovi	14 Asamoah > 19 Schneider <	72'

Discipline

52'	Valencia foul	Borowski persistent fouling	75'

46%	Ball Possession	54%
3	Shots on target	9
4	Shots off target	8
20	Fouls	17
5	Corner Kicks	2
0	Offsides	3

Official FIFA Man of the Match
Michael Ballack

Miroslav Klose rounds Ecuador keeper Cristian Mora to net his second goal in Germany's 3-0 win

It was an eye-opening experience to sample the atmosphere in a Soho pub, The Endurance on Berwick Street, on the night England played Sweden, and realise you cannot fool the fans.

The comments from supporters there were spot on....the lack of depth in Sven's line up of strikers, the problems in defence with Ashley still looking a long way short of his best after his long injury worries, and, of course, there was a collective in-take of breath when Michael Owen crumbled and his knee buckled. And they all spotted the Wayne sulk when he threw his boots to the ground as he skulked off when substituted.

Few took much notice of ITV's so-called panel of experts, who smartened themselves up with collar, suit and ties. Previously Big Sam, El Tel and Pyscho had looked a right bunch of chancers in their open neck shirts, which looked more natural on the Costa Brava. Middlesbrough's new manager Gareth Southgate appeared as co-commentator for ITV, and on the Wayne Rooney substitution tantrum, he said: "He looks just like his mum has told him to come in for tea." Not quite as acidic as Match of the Day host Adrian Chiles, who landed a below-the-belt punch when he told viewers, "Serbia and Montenegro and Ivory Coast now have to play a dead rubber in Munich," adding "Full live coverage of that over on ITV."

The BBC are streets ahead, with Martin O'Neill by far the most entertaining of the pundits and Alan Hansen still a class act. Time for ITV to come up with some more trendy experts and get rid of the old soaks and their endless reliance on complex chalkboard know-it-all comments.

DID YOU KNOW?
Miroslav Klose's first goal on 4 minutes was the second fastest by any German at a World Cup. The record is held by Rudi Abramczik, who scored in the 3rd minute against Holland in 1978.

Thousands cram into Munich's Fan park to watch Germany secure first place in Group A with a 3-0 win against Ecuador

Fans have wisened up and know their holding players from their diamond, and most certainly have had their fill of the Christmas Tree. It all adds up to the same. The best players win World Cups. What we want is some insight into Sven's thinking and less of what the old boys would be doing if they were in the dressing room. My thanks to Bravo TV for the invite, together with a couple of mates, Constantin and Barry, to join the fun.

I am also indebted to my mate Steve, at Hill & Knowlton, for forwarding me this invaluable news item, which I have no doubt would never make the national press.

Sport England has devised a series of World Cup-themed exercises to allow football fans to keep fit whilst watching the match from the comfort of their armchairs. During the tournament, men will spend an estimated fifteen hours a week sitting down watching football, so top sports scientist Alan Pearson has created a series of sofa-based work-outs all themed around England players. As the nation prepares for life beyond the group stages, front room fans can try out everything from the Beckham Bullet and the Gyrating Gerrard to Peter Crouch's robotic dance as part of Sport England's Everyday Sport World Cup Workout.

In 1966, the England team brought the World Cup home to an active nation.

Forty years later activity levels off the pitch are low – 63% of men do not achieve the recommended levels. The reduction in energy expenditure since '66 is estimated at 600kcal/day, causing a negative impact on health and an increase in obesity.

Alan Pearson, a sports scientist who has consulted coaches for all Premiership football clubs and England Rugby said: 'The World Cup is a fantastic opportunity for football fans to get off the sofa and get active. The whole

> **DID YOU KNOW?**
> *Germany have now won each of their last five World Cup groups. The last time they failed to win their group was in 1986 when they finished as runners-up to Denmark. Germany qualified for the second round for the 14th consecutive finals. They have only failed to make the second round once; in 1938, while they did not participate in two finals (1930 and 1950).*

family can benefit from the Everyday Sport World Cup Workout and everyone will feel inspired to go and have a kickabout once the game is finished!' Stephen Baddeley, Interim Chief Executive at Sport England, added: 'The Everyday Sport campaign encourages people to build physical activity into their everyday lives.'

Well, after the Bravo free bar, Pimms, followed by Guinness and a final shot of Drambuie, all I was fit for was a lie in the next morning. I wish.

Far too much to do.

Dear Diary, yes I recall the game, and while I thought it was thrilling enough, the final insult was a late Swedish equaliser from a long throw which it seemed a third of the England team tried to clear without much success.

And let's analyse The Sulk. Wayne reacted angrily after being hauled off with 21 minutes remaining. He was replaced by Gerrard, who scored a goal and cleared a Swedish effort off the line. Not bad. One up to Eriksson.

Rooney said: 'My fitness was never a problem. I feel good and I felt that I could have played on for longer. It was just nice to be out there playing again. I thought the team did well in the first half, but the tempo dropped a bit in the second. Of course it's a big blow for us to lose Michael Owen. He is a very important player, he can score goals for us.'

Eriksson knew one of only four strikers had played his last game of the tournament and played down Rooney's reaction, "I think he was more upset with himself. He thought that he didn't play as well as he did in the first half in the second half but he is getting better and better. He played longer than last time and he will get better and better, but I took him off because I couldn't risk him getting injured."

After Owen's knee went horrifically, whilst turning in the first minute, there was another scare as Rio Ferdinand limped off in the second half with a groin injury. He said: 'I felt it at half-time. I tried to play on, but

Here are the Everyday Sport World Cup Workouts in full.

PRE-GAME WARM-UP

Each exercise should be completed in 45 second intervals

1) The Rooney Run – Seated running on the spot
Seated running on the spot, incorporating an arm drive. Raise the knee only 10-15 cm. Complete five at a slow rhythm on each leg, followed by five at a quick rhythm on each leg.

2) The Gyrating Gerrard – Seated, Two Footed side-to-side Raises with Twist
With feet lightly together, knees slightly apart, bring your feet up and hold arms at 90 degree angle. Raise feet up and twist to the left, with arms and upper torso moving to the right. Return to the centre and place feet on ground. Repeat on the left side.

IN-GAME EXERCISE

To be performed at any time during the game and during natural breaks, e.g. free kicks, half time, penalties and throw-ins

1) The Theo Throw – Maintains shoulder mobility, works shoulder muscles and promotes blood flow
Clasp hands together and rest them on your lap. Raise your arm to a position above your head and then return them to your lap. Complete five at a slow rhythm on each leg followed by five at a quick rhythm on each leg.

2) The Beckham Bullet – Increases range of movement and improves flexibility around the hips
Standing with a chair to one side, place your hand on the chair or table for support (make sure you have space to kick out). Working off the ball of the support foot, swing your inside leg forwards and backwards. Complete six on each leg, three at the Slow Rhythm and three at the Quick rhythm.

GOAL CELEBRATIONS

Impress your mates and celebrate in the style of your heroes with these goal celebration exercises

1) The Jenas Jump For Joy – To raise heart rate, develop power and speed and dynamic balance
On the spot jump up and down with small jumps quickly and punch the arms in the air alternatively. Perform the celebration for 10 seconds

2) The Crouch Robot Dance – To develop positive arm mechanics, improve balance and co-ordination
Jog on the spot with arms at a 90 degree angle at the elbow. Move arms alternatively from the hip to the side of the face. At the same time gradually rotate the hips no more than 90 degrees to the left then 90 degrees to the right. Finally nod your head backwards and forwards.

HALF-TIME EXERCISES

Get to the garden or backyard and re-live the first half action. Play two five minute halves with your kids or your mates. If you don't have access to outdoor space walk up and down the stairs fifteen times with a ten second recovery after each descent. Imagine you are out of your seat at a World Cup game and walking up the steps to the refreshment area for a break

AFTER THE GAME

Re-create the game with your mates, family or neighbours and get outside and get active. Having a kickabout has health benefits for the whole family and helps you to re-live the excitement of the World Cup.

COSTA RICA 1 v **POLAND 2**

Referee: Shamsul Maidan

Scorers

25'	Gomez	Bosacki **33', 66'**

Teams

18 Porras	Boruc **01**
02 Drummond	Baszczynski **04**
12 Gonzalez	Bak **06**
04 Umana	Bosacki **19**
03 Marin	Zewlakow **14**
07 Bolanos	Krzynowek **08**
08 Solis	Szymkowiak **10**
10 Centeno	Smolarek **15**
17 Badilla	Radomski **16**
09 Wanchope	Jelen **21**
11 Gomez	Zurawski **09**

Substitutes

70' > 15 Wallace < 02 Drummond	23 Brozek > 09 Zurawski < 45'
78' > 19 Saborio < 07 Bolanos	18 Lewandowski > 16 Radomski < 64'
82' > 16 Hernandez < 11 Gomez	11 Raziak > 15 Smolarek < 85'

Discipline

17'	Umana foul	Radomski foul	**18'**
45'	Marin foul	Bak foul	**23'**
45'	Gomez dissent	Zewlakow foul	**29'**
56'	Badilla foul	Baszczynski foul	**60'**
76'	Gonzalez foul	Boruc time wasting	**90'**

50%	**Ball Possession**	50%
6	**Shots on target**	8
5	**Shots off target**	6
13	**Fouls**	18
2	**Corner Kicks**	10
4	**Offsides**	1

Official FIFA Man of the Match

Bartosz Bosacki

Costa Rica 1 v Poland 2
Group A
AWD Arena, Hanover
Attendance: 43,000
Kick-off: 4pm   Temperature: 28°C

Bartosz Bosacki scores his first goal against Costa Rica in a 2-1 comeback win which at least gave his nation some small consolation after two opening defeats had put them out

it got worse and worse and I had to come off. We will have to give it a couple of days and I just hope I am OK for the Ecuador game.'

Joe Cole was buzzing after his wonder goal. The Argentineans may have scored a 24 pass spectacular, but this was the individual goal of the tournament so far. The Chelsea star put England ahead with a sensational dipping 30-yard strike and set up Gerrard for the second. It was Cole's sixth international goal and he admitted:

'It was a good moment for me and for England. I caught it right and wanted to test the keeper early. It's a good performance, but there is also a lot for us to work on before the next game. We should have killed them off after playing so well in the first half. Sweden played very well in the second half, but still didn't create any chances from open play.'

Steven Gerrard was more pleased to win the group than avoid hosts Germany, adding: "We were prepared

FINAL TABLE — GROUP A

	P	W	D	L	F	A	GD	Pts
GERMANY	3	3	0	0	8	2	+6	9
ECUADOR	3	2	0	1	5	3	+2	6
POLAND	3	1	0	2	2	4	-2	3
COSTA RICA	3	0	0	3	3	9	-6	0

DID YOU KNOW?
Referee Shamsul Maidin showed ten yellow cards in this match, a total only exceeded on three previous occasions in finals matches.

England 2 v Sweden 2
Group B
RheinEnergieStadion, Cologne
Attendance: 45,000
Kick-off: 9pm   Temperature: 20°C

Steven Gerrard outjumps Sweden's Niclas Alexandersson to head home England's second goal, but it did not prove to be the winner

ENGLAND 2   v   SWEDEN 2

Referee: Massimo Busacca

Scorers

34'	J Cole	Allback	51'
85'	Gerrard	Larsson	90'

Teams

01	Robinson	Isaksson	01
15	Carragher	Lucic	04
05	Ferdinand	Mellberg	03
06	Terry	Edman	05
03	A Cole	Alexandersson	07
07	Beckham	Linderoth	06
16	Hargreaves	Kallstrom	16
08	Lampard	Ljungberg	09
11	J Cole	Jonson	18
09	Rooney	Larsson	11
10	Owen	Allback	20

Substitutes

04'	> 21 Crouch < 10 Owen	21 Wilhelmsson > 18 Jonson <	54'
56'	> 12 Campbell < 05 Ferdinand	17 Elmander > 20 Allback <	74'
69'	> 04 Gerrard < 09 Rooney	19 Andersson > 06 Linderoth <	90'

Discipline

76'	Hargreaves foul	Alexandersson foul	83'
		Ljungberg dissent	87'

54%	Ball Possession	46%
7	Shots on target	6
11	Shots off target	7
12	Fouls	19
6	Corner Kicks	13
1	Offsides	0

Official FIFA Man of the Match
Joe Cole

for whoever we came up against in the last 16, but the most important thing was to top the group. But the most important thing was to top the group so we could get an extra day's rest before the second round and have more time to work on things. I thought our play was a bit better against Sweden but we looked vulnerable on set-pieces, which is unusual for us, and we need to get those sorted on the training ground." That inexcusable defending had allowed Henrik Larsson to pounce late on to deny England a long-awaited success against Sweden.

Ecuador's former Aston Villa defender Ulises de la Cruz had no fear of England, 'We will be no pushovers. Why shouldn't we beat them? We proved in the group we can win games in the World Cup. I don't see any reason why we can't carry on with a shock against England. I know better than anyone the strength of their players.'

Henrik Larsson just beats Olof Mellberg to touch in a loose ball allowed to bounce in England's box for the late, late equaliser which kept Sweden's legendary unbeaten run intact

In Germany's comfortable 3-0 win over Ecuador which saw them win Group A, Michael Ballack was on the receiving end of a harsh tackle from Luis Valencia in the 52nd minute which earned the midfielder his team's only booking. Asked about the injury, Ballack said: "It is not a problem, just a minor bruise, nothing serious. It was good that I jumped (before he hit me)."

After scoring 45 goals in 72 appearances for Costa Rica, Paolo Wanchope finished on a losing note. They opened the scoring through Ronald Gomez, but Poland hit back to record a 2-1 victory thanks to a brace from Barosz Bosacki. Wanchope gave the reason for his decision to retire as the amount of travelling involved for his country. After wearing the colours of, among others, Derby, Manchester City and West Ham, he is anxious to return to Europe. Wanchope, who plays in Costa Rica for Herediano, believes he will be ready for that new challenge because he will be fit and rested as he will not be involved at international level. He said: "I am still young, but I am leaving the squad because of the travelling. It is enough for me. When you have to take a plane and travel 10 to 12 hours it is difficult. Hopefully I can come back to Europe and get a club but we will just have to wait and see. I will be ready because I will be able to rest for domestic games. That will be better for me."

Under-pressure Poland coach Pawel Janas was delighted to record a victory with Bosacki's unlikely contribution. It was the defender's first goals for his country and Janas said: "I am very grateful to him. You expect your strikers and midfielders to get your goals, not defenders. But I have to thank my team for raising their game and giving our marvellous supporters something to cheer about."

Dwight Yorke may end his international career in the aftermath of Trinidad & Tobago's exit in Kaiserslautern. Despite his best efforts, Yorke could not inspire his team to the victory they craved, which ultimately would not have brought them a place in the last 16 following Sweden's draw with England. Instead, Brent Sancho's own goal and a late effort from Nelson Cuevas allowed Paraguay to exit the tournament as winners. Yorke felt the Soca Warriors had made an impact and the 34-year-old said:

'I have played football for over 20 years as a professional and these have been the best times of my life. I can only thank everyone for their support. It is an emotional occasion for me because it may be the last time I play for my country. I will discuss the situation with my family, but I have no problem with that.'

There was a tear in his eye at the final whistle, which brought down the curtain on his country's first World

The atmosphere in the Endurance pub in Berwick Street, Soho was fairly lively during Bravo's party for the match against Sweden. Taking in the game with my friends Constantin (left) and Barry (right) allowed me to get a real feel for what the fans are thinking – and generally they are spot on!

Paraguay 2 v Trinidad & Tobago 0
Group B
Fritz-Walter-Stadion, Kaiserslautern
Attendance: 46,000
Kick-off: 9pm   Temperature: 22°C

Nelson Cuevas celebrates scoring his side's late second goal, but it was not enough for them to reach the knockout stages

PARAGUAY 2 v TRINIDAD & TOBAGO 0

Referee: Roberto Rosetti

Scorers
25' Sancho *(og)*
86' Cuevas

Teams

Paraguay		Trinidad & Tobago	
22	Bobadilla	Jack	21
02	Nunez	A John	03
04	Gamarra	Sancho	05
05	Caceres	Lawrence	06
21	Caniza	Birchall	07
08	Barreto	Whitley	09
10	Acuna	Edwards	11
13	Paredes	Theobald	18
19	dos Santos	Glen	13
09	Santa Cruz	S John	14
18	Valdez	Yorke	19

Substitutes

66'	> 23 Cuevas < 18 Valdez	15 Jones > 03 A John <	31'
78'	> 15 Manzur < 05 Caceres	16 Wise > 13 Glen <	40'
88'	> 14 Da Silva < 21 Caniza	10 Latapy > 09 Whitley <	66'

Discipline

30'	Paredes *foul*	Sancho *foul*	45'
55'	dos Santos *foul*	Whitley *foul*	49'

55%	Ball Possession	45%
7	Shots on target	3
6	Shots off target	7
16	Fouls	21
7	Corner Kicks	1
3	Offsides	3

Official FIFA Man of the Match
Julio dos Santos

Cup finals campaign. They failed to score a goal and picked up just a single point – from the opening 0-0 draw with Sweden – but the reception they received at the end from the neutral fans proved how much their efforts have been appreciated.

DID YOU KNOW?
Coach Leo Beenhakker became the first coach to be in charge of 7 World Cup matches and not achieve a single victory.

Trinidad & Tobago became the eighth country to fail to score in their first World Cup finals tournament.

DID YOU KNOW?
Paraguay have never failed to qualify for the knockout stages of any of their previous three World Cups.

Paraguay skipper Carlos Gamarra made his 110th, and final, international appearance.

FINAL TABLE — GROUP B

	P	W	D	L	F	A	GD	Pts
ENGLAND	3	2	1	0	5	2	+3	7
SWEDEN	3	1	2	0	3	2	+1	5
PARAGUAY	3	1	0	2	2	2	0	3
TRIN & TOB	3	0	1	2	0	4	-4	1

Day Thirteen
Wednesday 21 June 2006

Portugal March On

Portugal's Nuno Maniche opens the scoring against Mexico with a scorching drive as they finished top of their group with three straight wins

Goal Angola!

Angola produce their best performance to score a precious goal and earn a second point against Iran to finish in a creditable third place in Group D

Comeback Kings

Ivory Coast completed a rousing and inspirational comeback against a Serbia team who had been 2-0 ahead before losing Albert Nadj sent off. Aruna Dindane scored the Ivorian's equaliser

"I'm very, very proud of the way my team performed and we can leave Germany with our heads held high."

Luis Oliveira Goncalves (Angola)

Mexico 1 v Portugal 2

Group D
Veltins Arena, Gelsenkirchen
Attendance: 52,000
Kick-off: 5pm   Temperature: 27°C

Portuguese keeper Ricardo watches as Omar Bravo's penalty flies just over the bar as Portugal win 2-1

MEXICO 1	v	PORTUGAL 2

Referee: Lubos Michel

Scorers

29'	Fonseca	Maniche	6'
		Simao *(pen)*	24'

Teams

01	Sanchez	Ricardo 01
14	Pineda	Miguel 13
04	Marquez	Ricardo Carvalho 16
05	Osorio	Meira 05
03	Salcido	Caneira 03
22	Rodriguez	Petit 08
08	Pardo	Maniche 18
23	Perez	Tiago 19
16	Mendez	Figo 07
17	Fonseca	Simao 11
19	Bravo	Postiga 23

Substitutes

45'	> 07 Zinha < 22 Rodriguez	02 Ferreira > 13 Miguel <	61'
69'	> 15 Castro < 14 Pineda	21 Nuno Gomes > 23 Postiga <	69'
80'	> 10 Franco < 16 Mendez	15 Boa Morte > 07 Figo <	80'

Discipline

22'	Rodriguez *foul*	Miguel *foul*	26'
27'	Perez *foul*	Maniche *foul*	69'
61'	Perez *diving (second yellow)*	Boa Morte *foul*	88'
65'	Marquez *foul*	Nuno Gomes *foul*	90'
87'	Zinha *foul*		

50%	Ball Possession	50%
6	Shots on target	6
8	Shots off target	5
15	Fouls	23
5	Corner Kicks	4
2	Offsides	1

Official FIFA Man of the Match
Jose Fonseca

Michael Owen's World Cup is officially over after a scan confirmed he ruptured the anterior cruciate ligament in his right knee.

There was some damage to the medial ligament, but the cruciate injury is by far more serious. Owen went for a scan at the Max Grundig Clinic, near the England team hotel on the edge of the Black Forest. He had been warned to expect the worst and the scan confirmed it. The striker said "goodbye" to his England team-mates and flew home on a private jet, leaving Eriksson to ponder his squad selection. Newcastle refused to put a timescale on his return, but this type of injury usually means at least nine months out, maybe a year. Injury prone Owen had completed just one full game since breaking his foot on New Year's Eve.

In his paid for first-person Times column Owen said, "As I left the team hotel to fly home, I told Sven-Göran Eriksson that I would be back out for the World Cup final. My tournament might be over, but I still want that medal around my neck. My best wishes go with the rest of the lads. When I didn't get up, my family knew it was serious and they were waiting for me by the dressing-room. My mum, wife and sister were obviously upset seeing me lie there with my knee swelling up like a balloon, but I do have the ability to be quite philosophical about these things. I have been called 'cold' in the past and, at times like this, it is a real strength. I can control my emotions and I can honestly say that when I was flat on my back with ice-packs around my knee, it wasn't self-pity I was feeling, but guilt. I was sending text messages apologising to all sorts of people for letting them down. All my dreams were shattered within a minute, but I know that worse things happen to people every day. When I told my little girl that Daddy had hurt his knee, she just asked me to put on Postman Pat."

The FA pay compensation on players wages while out injured of a maximum of £50,000-a-week, which in the case of Owen is a £60,000-a-week short fall.

If Owen is out for nine months, Newcastle's short fall on the FA compensation pay out would be as high as £2.16m. They have been forced to take

DID YOU KNOW?
Luiz Perez's red card meant Mexico became only the second nation after Cameroon to have at least one player dismissed in four successive tournaments.

ANGOLA 1	v	IRAN 1

Referee: Mark Shield

Scorers
60'	Flavio	Bakhtiarizadeh	78'

Teams
01 Joao Ricardo	Mirzapour 01
03 Jamba	Bakhtiarizadeh 03
05 Kali	Rezaei 05
20 Loco	Kaabi 13
21 Delgado	Nosrati 20
06 Miloy	Mahdavikia 02
07 Figueiredo	Zandi 07
11 Mateus	Teymourian 14
14 Mendonca	Madanchi 21
17 Ze Kalanga	Hashemian 09
10 Akwa	Daei 10

Substitutes
23'	> 18 Love < 11 Mateus	23 Shojaei > 20 Nosrati <	13'
51'	> 16 Flavio < 10 Akwa	11 Khatibi > 09 Hashemian <	39'
72'	> 15 Rui Marques < 07 Figueiredo	15 Borhani > 13 Kaabi <	67'

Discipline
21'	Loco *foul*	Madanchi *foul*	37'
45'	Mendonca *delaying restart*	Teymourian *delaying restart*	55'
67'	Ze Kalanga *foul*	Zandi *foul*	90'

46%	**Ball Possession**	54%
8	**Shots on target**	12
8	**Shots off target**	7
21	**Fouls**	18
6	**Corner Kicks**	3
5	**Offsides**	2

Official FIFA Man of the Match
Ze Kalanga

Angola 1 v Iran 1
Group D
Zentralstadion, Leipzig
Attendance: 38,000
Kick-off: 4pm   Temperature: 28°C

Angola's Flavio heads home his country's first ever World Cup goal to spark frenetic celebrations and earn a second World Cup point

out extra insurance cover privately for Owen and are appalled by the FA's failure to recognise that so many of their players now earn more than £50,000-a-week. Owen is in fact the highest paid England international on a staggering £110,000-a-week basic salary.

The FA have a two tier insurance cover. There is a huge pay out if all the squad crashed in a plane accident or terrorist attack. The second tier is for covering wages. It is rare for a players' career

to end as a result of injury while on international duty and then there would be an assessment made of current transfer values. In Owen's case, with modern surgical techniques, there is now absolutely no suggestion this is a career threatening injury. But if he didn't play again there would be a huge row over his valuation as Newcastle paid Real £17m, but I can reveal there has been a secret, private, gentleman's agreement that he could be sold this summer for a fixed

FINAL TABLE						GROUP D		
	P	W	D	L	F	A	GD	Pts
PORTUGAL	3	3	0	0	5	1	+4	9
MEXICO	3	1	1	1	4	3	+1	4
ANGOLA	3	0	2	1	1	2	-1	2
IRAN	3	0	1	2	2	6	-2	1

DID YOU KNOW?
Angola's total of 72 fouls in three matches made them the most offending team of the group stages. Flavio's goal was Angola's first in World Cup finals football and the 17th by a substitute in this World Cup.

Argentina 0 v Holland 0

Group C
Commerzbank Arena, Frankfurt
Attendance: 48,000
Kick-off: 9pm   Temperature: 22°C

*With little action on the pitch to cheer on the gathered hordes of Argentinian
fans found their own way of entertaining themselves in the stands*

ARGENTINA 0   v   HOLLAND 0

Referee: Luis Medina Cantalejo

Scorers

Teams

Argentina		Holland	
01	Abbondanzieri	van der Sar	01
21	Burdisso	Boulahrouz	03
02	Ayala	Ooijer	13
15	Milito	Jaliens	02
17	Cufre	de Cler	15
08	Mascherano	Sneijder	20
18	Rodriguez	Cocu	08
05	Cambiasso	van der Vaart	10
10	Riquelme	van Persie	17
19	Messi	van Nistelrooy	09
11	Tevez	Kuyt	07

Substitutes

24'	> 04 Coloccini < 21 Burdisso	21 Babel > 09 van Nistelrooy <	56'
69'	> 20 Cruz < 19 Messi	06 Landzaat > 17 van Persie <	67'
79'	> 16 Aimar < 10 Riquelme	16 Maduro > 20 Sneijder <	86'

Discipline

57'	Cambiasso foul	Kuyt foul	28'
90'	Mascherano foul	Ooijer foul	43'
		de Cler foul	48'

50%	Ball Possession	50%
2	Shots on target	3
11	Shots off target	7
16	Fouls	23
10	Corner Kicks	7
4	Offsides	1

Official FIFA Man of the Match
Carlos Tevez

price of £11m, although Newcastle chairman Freddy Shepherd has always insisted publicly there is no get out clause of any description.

It is easy to see why Sir Alex Ferguson and Manchester United were in such a crisis mode over Rooney, with so many grey areas about valuation if his career was terminated. But more realistically, if Rooney was out for anywhere near as long as Owen, then United's season would crumble. As for Newcastle, with Owen out for so long and Alan Shearer needing replacing you wouldn't give Glenn Roeder much hope of making a good first of his first full season in charge of a team already looking like they will struggle.

DID YOU KNOW?
This was only the second time in World Cup history that Holland had picked up as good a record as two wins and a draw in their three group matches – ironically the only other occasion was in Germany in 1974.

The injury prompted Newcastle-based Northern Rock to pull a series of adverts featuring Owen. The building society sponsors Owen's club and its ad campaign featured the footballer wrapped in the England flag alongside slogans such as 'One of ours over there' and 'Can we have him back in one piece please?' "Our sympathies are with Michael at this time, it is a really awful thing to have happened,' said a spokeswoman for Northern Rock. 'We thought it was inappropriate in the circumstances to continue with our brand campaign and have decided to withdraw it."

Captain Beckham promised: "The plan now is to win it for Michael. We are all devastated for him because we know how much it meant to him to get fit for the World Cup. In big competitions you want proven goalscorers and Michael has shown he is one of the best in the world. We're all feeling for him deeply. We knew it was a bad injury when we spoke to the doctors and physios at half-time of Tuesday's game. The feeling in the dressing room then was go out and finish the job for him, which is what we eventually did. But that doesn't ease any of the pain for him or for us."

Eriksson was in a self-induced pickle. He had blundered over Owen

Ivory Coast 3 v Serbia & Montenegro 2
Group C
Allianz Arena, Munich
Attendance: 66,000
Kick-off: 9pm   Temperature: 24°C

Bonaventure Kalou slides home the late winning penalty past Serbia & Montenegro's Dragoslav Javric to complete one of the best World Cup recoveries of all time

and was now being rightly criticised for his decision to include only four recognised strikers in his squad – one of those being untried teenager Theo Walcott, who has only 25 minutes of international football experience. Eriksson insisted: "Walcott is ready. It would have been good to put him on against Sweden, but so many things happened and I wanted to be absolutely sure to win the group. That was our big target. Those weeks he has been with us he has been getting better and better, more and more confident. He talks more, he wants the ball more. He has scored fantastic goals in training."

Eriksson received an encouraging injury update on Rio and Gary Neville today. The FA's Director of Communications, Adrian Bevington, said a scan on Ferdinand's groin problem showed no damage at all. The centre-half had a chance of playing against Ecuador on Sunday. Neville, who has missed the last two games with a calf injury, will return to light training tomorrow.

Whenever Germany's top marksman Miroslav Klose has a quiet moment at home, he tries to shoot a ball at the light switches in his house to turn them on or off. Klose's living room practice sessions are part of a homework programme devised by Klinsmann for his squad. 'We have large light switches at home,' Klose said in an interview with local newspapers in Germany. 'When I've got nothing to do I try and turn them on or off with the ball. I've broken one vase and a picture.' Breakages aside, Klinsmann's advice to work on the accuracy of his shooting was working.

The 28-year-old striker has scored four goals already to head the leading scorers list. Since taking over as national coach in August 2004, Klinsmann has stressed the importance of physical and mental fitness. He hired a psychologist and a team of fitness instructors, led by the American Mark Verstegen, and subjected the players to regular checks before raising the workload at pre-World Cup training camps in Sardinia and

Geneva. "I can admit now that the results of the fitness checks were not that good," Klinsmann said at the news conference. "We knew we had work to do and we did it, giving everyone an individual programme. All the hard work we did was worth it."

FIFA President Sepp Blatter and Tony Blair joined forces to help English school pupils who fell foul of a World Cup fake ticket scam. The victims, aged between 11 and 16, were turned away from matches on Saturday after their tickets failed to materialise. They returned home on Monday, many of them devastated that they had missed out on this once in a lifetime opportunity. High-level talks between Minister for Sport, Richard Caborn, and FIFA resolved the issue with the children being flown out to Germany to attend later games. "It was painful for me to hear of the awful fraud the children had innocently fallen victim to," said Blatter. "I am very happy that we found a solution, which reflects the spirit of FIFA and the philosophy of football." The Minister for Sport said, "I am extremely grateful to FIFA for their swift and decisive action in helping us to right this wrong. Going to the World Cup was a dream come true for these youngsters, who bought their tickets in good faith. Now, thanks to the generosity of FIFA and others, these children will have the time of their lives."

Out went Iran and Angola, who played a meaningless 1-1 draw and Iran coach Branko Ivankovic announced that he felt it was time to leave as well.

Ivory Coast celebrated their first ever win in the World Cup finals the only way Africans can, with a dance around the corner flag after Bonaventure Lalou's late winner from the penalty spot in a 3-2 thriller.

The World Cup will at least remember The Elephants for their comeback from a two goal deficit.

Ricardo La Volpe saw his 10-man Mexico side stumble their way into the last 16 after a 2-1 defeat to

Portugal in Gelsenkirchen. Two goals down to strikes by Maniche and Simao, Mexico fought back through Jose Fonseca, but Omar Bravo missed a penalty and then Luis Perez was sent off, forcing them to finish as runners-up. The normally-vociferous Mexican supporters were remarkably quiet given that rivals Angola were running Iran close.

Portugal go forward with confidence after three wins and are headed towards a showdown with England. You just knew Big Phil would be poised for revenge over the FA.

But at least England wouldn't meet mighty Argentina until the Final after their goalless draw with Holland. Pekerman's side have sent shudders through opposition camps in Germany with their explosive displays, but both sides rested key players for the evening game, notably those on yellow cards, and the organised Dutch held out despite outstanding displays from Riquelme, Messi and Tevez. Argentina maintained top spot in the group to set up a last-16 clash with Mexico. Marco van Basten's Dutch now tackle Portugal, with the winners facing England in the quarter-finals.

Van Basten reckons Argentina are playing the best football, "I have seen progress in my team tonight. Argentina are a high-quality team and they are playing Top of the Pops football. But at the end we could have won the game, although that would have been too far. But it was a good performance."

Pekerman was also happy, "We faced a tough opponent and it was a very balanced match. Argentina could have won. We had more scoring opportunities. The players did a good job but there is always a lack of continuity when you change something in a team. I'm satisfied. The team was good and whatever is still lacking we know we can compensate for that in the match in three days time."

IVORY COAST 3 v SERB & MONT 2

Referee: Marco Rodriguez

Scorers

37'	Dindane (pen)	Zigic	10'
67'	Dindane	Ilic	20'
86'	Kalou (pen)		

Teams

23 Barry	Jevric 01
03 Boka	Gavrancic 06
06 Kouassi	N Djordjevic 14
17 Domoraud	Dudic 15
21 Eboue	Krstajic 20
02 Akale	Ergic 02
05 Zokora	Duljaj 04
18 Keita	Stankovic 10
19 G Toure	P Djordjevic 11
09 A Kone	Ilic 22
15 Dindane	Zigic 19

Substitutes

| 60' | > 14 B Kone < 02 Akale | 17 Nadj > 20 Krstajic < | 16' |
| 72' | > 08 Kalou < 18 Keita | 09 Milosevic > 19 Zigic < | 66' |

Discipline

33'	Keita foul	Nadj foul	17'
41'	Domoraud foul	Dudic handball	35'
43'	Dindane diving	Duljaj foul	37'
90'	Domoraud foul (second yellow)	foul (second yellow)	45'
		Gavrancic foul	57'

64%	Ball Possession	36%
19	Shots on target	4
10	Shots off target	4
13	Fouls	19
9	Corner Kicks	1
7	Offsides	1

Official FIFA Man of the Match
Aruna Dindane

FINAL TABLE						GROUP C	
	P	W	D	L	F	A	GD Pts
ARGENTINA	3	2	1	0	8	1	+7 7
HOLLAND	3	2	1	0	3	1	+2 7
IVORY COAST	3	1	0	2	5	6	-1 3
SERB & MON	3	0	0	3	2	10	-8 0

Day Fourteen
Thursday 22 June 2006

Italian Masterpiece

The Italians do an impressive job on the Czech Republic to ensure qualification with Filipo Inzaghi scoring the vital late second goal in a 2-0 win

Ghana Spring A Surprise

The only African nation to truly perform at World Cup 2006 make it through to the second round at the expense of the Czechs and USA, with Haminu Draman scoring the opening goal in a 2-1 win over the States

Poll Axed

English referee Graham Poll faces the chop from the tournament after booking one Croatian player three times in a tempestuous match in which a late Harry Kewell equalizer sent jubilant Australia through

"There'll be a few people missing work in Australia today!"

Guus Hiddink (Australia)

Czech Republic 0 v Italy 2

Group E
AOL Arena, Hamburg
Attendance: 50,000
Kick-off: 4pm   Temperature: 26°C

Early substitute Marco Materazzi rises to head home Italy's opening goal past Petr Cech in the game which put paid to my dark horses, the Czech Republic

CZECH REPUBLIC 0 v   ITALY 2

Referee: Benito Archundia Tellez

Scorers

Materazzi	**26'**
Inzaghi	**87'**

Teams

01	Cech	Buffon	01
02	Grygera	Zambrotta	19
05	R Kovac	Cannavaro	05
22	Rozehnal	Nesta	13
06	Jankulovski	Grosso	03
20	Plasil	Camoranesi	16
19	Polak	Pirlo	21
11	Nedved	Perrotta	20
08	Poborsky	Gattuso	08
10	Rosicky	Totti	10
15	Baros	Gilardino	11

Substitutes

45'	> 17 Stajner < 08 Poborsky	23 Materazzi > 13 Nesta <	17'
64'	> 14 Jarolim < 15 Baros	18 Inzaghi > 11 Gilardino <	60'
78'	> 18 Heinz < 05 R Kovac	17 Barone > 16 Camoranesi <	74'

Discipline

35'	Polak foul	Gattuso foul	31'
45'	Polak foul (second yellow)		

49%	**Ball Possession**	51%
8	**Shots on target**	7
6	**Shots off target**	10
17	**Fouls**	16
4	**Corner Kicks**	5
1	**Offsides**	1

Official FIFA Man of the Match
Marco Materazzi

Pressure was building from some pundits for the axe to fall on the England captain. But Eriksson delivered his strongest rebuttal yet when he insisted that he was "not married to David Beckham, even if you think I am. I'm not even engaged to him. He is treated exactly the same as the other players in every way – at the dinner table, on the bus, tactically, in training, in a match. If I think he's not doing the job I would leave him out. I am prepared to do whatever I need to do if I see things are going wrong."

When told Beckham made only 28 passes in the draw with Sweden compared with Lampard's 56, Eriksson replied: "They are playing different roles. To pass the ball you must first have the ball. Somebody has to pass the ball to him." Eriksson could not remember the last time he had replaced Beckham in a competitive match. But he said: "I'm sure

Ghana 2 v USA 1

Group E
Franken-Stadion, Nuremburg
Attendance: 41,000
Kick-off: 4pm   Temperature: 25°C

USA coach Bruce Arena wipes away a tear after his side bows out of the World Cup propping up Group C

I have done it." With Gary Neville still struggling to recover, it was suggested that Becks could drop to right-back where he finished against Trinidad & Tobago. Eriksson said: "Everything is possible."

More trouble in the camp, according to one back page headline: Beckham and Gerrard rowing as the Liverpool captain criticised the England skipper for hitting too many long balls. Balls!

Well, that's according to the FA spin doctors. England head of communications Adrian Bevington said: "It is absolute rubbish. The players involved don't understand where it has come from." Eriksson is proud of the camaraderie he has fostered within the camp.

After most of the players spent their day off with their families relaxing at the team hotel or wandering around nearby Baden-Baden, they were back on their Buhlertal training pitch to begin preparation for the last-16 clash with Ecuador in Stuttgart.

On whether Rooney will play the whole match against Ecuador, Eriksson said: "It's difficult to say, I hope so, but when the match starts what happens will decide that. He dropped a little bit in the second half (against Sweden) which is normal and I decided to take him off after 70 minutes and that was good for him. There are more practice sessions and he's young and strong."

Ecuador defender Ulises De la Cruz revealed his plans for dealing with young Wayne: "Rooney is a very good player and he is someone I love to play against. But the fact he is not totally fit gives us a boost as well.

Perhaps I can give him a bit of a kick to test it out, although I don't want a red card. But I will certainly be doing my best to see whether he is 100 per cent fit or not."

Branko Ivankovic, who worked for one year as an assistant to former coach Miroslav Blazevic before taking over as head coach in late 2002, will not renew his contract after Iran finished bottom of Group D with just one point from three games. "My contract with the Iranian football federation is going to finish on July 1 and of course we didn't speak about renewing this contract," he said. "We didn't speak about anything." During his time in charge, Ivankovic led Iran's under-23 team to the gold medal at the Asian Games in Busan in 2002 and took them to the semi-finals of the Asian Cup in China two years later. He then helped the senior team qualify for the World Cup after the nation had missed out on the 2002 finals in Japan and South Korea under Blazevic.

Ghana reached the second round for the first time, with a 2-1 defeat of the United States. Haminu Dramani opened the scoring for the Black Stars following a blunder by Claudio Reyna in the 22nd minute, before Clint Dempsey levelled the scores in the 43rd. A controversial penalty from Stephen Appiah just before the break proved decisive, as the USA failed to find a way back into the match. Chelsea midfielder Michael Essien picked up his second yellow card of the tournament after just five minutes to ensure he would be missing from their second round match. Ghana then survived five minutes of injury-time to make history for the country, with a clash against world champions Brazil their reward. Essien must be kicking himself.

With eight of their starting line-up facing the threat of indictment from the ever-growing scandal investigation back home, Marcello Lippi's Italy somehow produced a performance of distinction, ensuring their progress as group winners and maintaining their 21-match unbeaten run. By avoiding Brazil, they have reason to believe that their day of legal reckoning can be delayed until well into July. I have a suspicion they'll be in the final shake-up.

The Czech Republic, though, faced grim reality as the first leading team to take their leave from this World Cup. With Nedved, Poborsky and Koller sure to retire, it was the end of an era for the Euro 2004 semi-finalists, who may never regain their present ranking as No. 2 in the world. Nedved was outstanding in his last international performance, waging a one-man campaign to keep his side in the competition with only the excellence of Buffon denying him several goals.

Lippi was defiant, claiming his players remained unaffected by the scandal at home. "No-one thinks about it any more and the players are completely focussed," he said. "That's

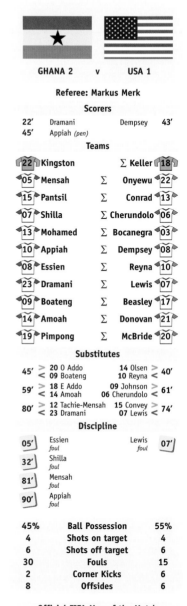

GHANA 2   v   **USA 1**

Referee: Markus Merk

Scorers

| 22' | Dramani | | Dempsey | 43' |
| 45' | Appiah (pen) | | | |

Teams

22	Kingston	Σ Keller	18
05	Mensah	Σ Onyewu	22
15	Pantsil	Σ Conrad	13
07	Shilla	Σ Cherundolo	06
13	Mohamed	Σ Bocanegra	03
10	Appiah	Σ Dempsey	08
08	Essien	Σ Reyna	10
23	Dramani	Σ Lewis	07
09	Boateng	Σ Beasley	17
14	Amoah	Σ Donovan	21
19	Pimpong	Σ McBride	20

Substitutes

45'	> 20 O Addo	14 Olsen >	40'
	< 09 Boateng	10 Reyna <	
59'	> 18 E Addo	09 Johnson >	61'
	< 14 Amoah	06 Cherundolo <	
80'	> 12 Tachie-Mensah	15 Convey >	74'
	< 23 Dramani	07 Lewis <	

Discipline

05'	Essien foul	Lewis foul	07'
32'	Shilla foul		
81'	Mensah foul		
90'	Appiah foul		

45%	**Ball Possession**	55%
4	**Shots on target**	4
6	**Shots off target**	6
30	**Fouls**	15
2	**Corner Kicks**	6
8	**Offsides**	6

Official FIFA Man of the Match
Stephen Appiah

FINAL TABLE						GROUP E	
	P	W	D	L	F	A	GD Pts
ITALY	3	2	1	0	5	1	+4 7
GHANA	3	2	0	1	4	3	+1 6
CZECH REP	3	1	0	2	3	4	-1 3
USA	3	0	1	2	2	6	-4 1

CROATIA 2 v AUSTRALIA 2

Referee: Graham Poll

Scorers

| 2' | Srna | Moore *(pen)* | 38' |
| 56' | N Kovac | Kewell | 79' |

Teams

01	Pletikosa	Kalac	18
07	Simic	Neill	02
05	Tudor	Moore	03
13	Tomas	Chipperfield	14
03	Simunic	Emerton	07
02	Srna	Grella	13
10	N Kovac	Culina	05
08	Babic	Cahill	04
19	Kranjcar	Sterjovski	21
09	Prso	Kewell	10
18	Olic	Viduka	09

Substitutes

65'	> 16 J Leko < 19 Kranjcar	15 Aloisi > 13 Grella <	63'
74'	> 14 Modric < 18 Olic	23 Bresciano > 21 Sterjovski <	71'
83'	> 17 Klasnic < 13 Tomas	19 Kennedy > 14 Chipperfield <	75'

Discipline

32'	Simic foul	Emerton foul	81'
38'	Tudor foul	Emerton foul *(second yellow)*	87'
61'	Simunic foul		
70'	Pletikosa foul		
85'	Simic foul *(second yellow)*		
90'	Simunic dissent *(second yellow)*		

46%	**Ball Possession**	54%
6	**Shots on target**	7
5	**Shots off target**	7
17	**Fouls**	21
5	**Corner Kicks**	10
2	**Offsides**	1

Official FIFA Man of the Match
Harry Kewell

not that what creates any tension, the only thing that generates pressure is the fact that we could be sent home. It's a once in a lifetime chance so we want to play a good championship. Once people go home, alas, they will have to deal with their problems."

Former Everton defender Marco Materazzi gave the Azzurri a 26th-minute lead having only come on as a substitute eight minutes earlier, before another replacement, Filippo Inzaghi, killed the game off four minutes from time. The Czechs were forced to play with 10 men for the entire second half after Nuremberg midfielder Jan Polak was sent off for a second bookable offence. It proved a hammer blow for Karel Bruckner's side, who did have their share of chances.

Ronaldo reportedly weighed just under 15 stone when he began his World Cup preparations. In an interview reproduced in Spanish daily Marca, the team's physical trainer Moraci Sant'Anna admitted the Real Madrid man had scaled 94.7 kilos when he joined up with the squad for the tournament in Germany – around 14st 11lbs. Since then he had shed around four kilos to slim down to just over 14st. But even with that weight loss he has still looked sluggish and overweight during his team's opening two games against Croatia and Japan. Sant'Anna now says Ronaldo is only a kilo over his ideal weight, but says that isn't a massive issue. Ronaldo's weight problems have been put down to the time he missed with Real Madrid due to injuries in the recent La Liga season.

Kawaguchi, a former Portsmouth goalkeeper, was resurrected briefly as a World Cup hero as Japan led briefly thanks to Tamada's smashing strike.

Kawaguchi kept out an early barrage from Brazil and frustrated them almost until half-time. But then the goals started coming in numbers, finished off by a masterpiece from the ever-controversial Ronaldo. His double exchange of passes with Juan was completed with a right-foot shot curled

round Kawaguchi, his second goal of the night, a blast that put him into the record books with 14 goals scored in World Cup finals, equal with Gerd Müller of Germany. Ronaldo also collected the man-of-the-match award and some significant embraces from his team-mates at the final whistle.

After all that criticism, the World Cup's Mr Blobby had come up with two goals. Indeed, the crowd got in on the act, chanting his name.

If the game with Brazil was an astonishing comeback for Ronaldo, the match running parallel in this group spelt the end of Graham Poll's reputation as a ref. Poll saw an astonishing match cascade out of his control as Australia qualified for the second round with an incredible point. A triumph for Australia, but one of the worst of all cock ups for Poll, who showed Josip Simunic, the Croatia defender, a second yellow card near the end, but failed to produce the red. So Simunic stayed on until the last seconds, when he was booked for a third time and at last saw red.

Croatia needed a win and Australia a draw to progress. And with two of Croatia's squad having been born in Australia, while another studied at the Australian Institute of Sport and seven of Australia's players being of Croatian descent it was always going to be tasty.

The choice of Poll as referee was surprising as he is familiar to the Australians who play in the Premiership. Mark Viduka was incandescent early on when the Englishman failed to give a penalty after the Middlesbrough striker was manhandled by Simunic. Poll did point to the spot later in the half when Stjepan Tomas handled a cross. Craig Moore, the Newcastle United defender, thumped home the penalty in the 38th minute, after Darijo Srna's marvellous free-kick gave Croatia a dramatic lead.

Australia coach Guus Hiddink's decision to drop Middlesbrough goalkeeper Mark Schwarzer backfired. In came The Spider, Zeljiko Kalac, one of the Australians with Croatian blood, whom Martin O'Neill

Croatia 2 v Australia 2
Group F
Gottlieb-Daimler-Stadion, Stuttgart
Attendance: 52,000
Kick-off: 9pm   Temperature: 25°C

*Harry Kewell lashes in the late equalising goal which saw Australia pip
Croatia to second spot behind Brazil in Group F*

recalled from his days at Leicester and scoffed at the idea he'd subsequently turned up as a second string keeper in Milan. Kalac had 53 caps, but allowed a miscued long range shot from Niko Kovac to bounce through his gloves and Australia had to chase the match again to preserve their interest in the event.

Croatia, third in 1998, were rocking with 20 minutes left when the ball broke to Kewell, central and close in. He shot fiercely, but straight at Stipe Pletikosa, who tipped it over. Then came a clear mistake by Poll, who failed to spot another handball in the area by Tomas, an even more obvious one than the first. But Kewell lashed the ball in low from the edge of the six-yard box with his right foot with ten minutes to go, just reward for Australia's superiority.

Brazil 4 v Japan 1

Group F
Signal Iduna Park, Dortmund
Attendance: 65,000
Kick-off: 9pm   Temperature: 23°C

Ronaldo nods in the equaliser before later completing the scoring with a rocket to draw level with Gerd Müller as the highest scorer in World Cup finals history

With five minutes left Dario Simic tripped Kewell and received his second yellow card. Croat protests almost turned ugly. Poll then dismissed Brett Emerton for deliberate handball – his second yellow!

Poll now faced the humiliating prospect of being sent home early from a second consecutive World Cup finals. Although FIFA made no comment, and had withdrawn mention of the second booking on its website, its lack of tolerance of such oversights was such that Poll was certain to exit the tournament prematurely. That would be a devastating prospect for

Poll, who was sent home from the 2002 World Cup finals after officiating in only one game. On that occasion, his error was to disallow two 'goals' for Italy against Croatia, both of which were shown to be valid by television replays. Poll tried to make light of that incident, saying that in any case he would not have stayed beyond the last 16 because England had progressed to the quarter-finals. Privately, though, he is said to have been disappointed by the decision. Poll and his assistants, Glenn Turner and Phil Sharp, were praised for their 'low-profile' performance in their first game, between Saudi Arabia and Ukraine, at a referees' meeting on Tuesday, when they were awarded the crucial group F match. The appointment was thought to be an indication that they had a good chance of progressing to the knockout stages, but now, barring an extraordinary reprieve, it seems that another World Cup is over for the self-styled 'Thing from Tring', who in the South Korea v Togo game had sent off Jean-Paul Abalo of Togo for a second yellow card, producing his cards the wrong way round.

Ruud van Nistelrooy spoke out about claims he had fallen out with Cristiano Ronaldo at Old Trafford. "There is no problem between Cristiano and me," stated van Nistelrooy. "I know, he knows and everyone at Manchester United knows that. Nothing has happened between us at all. In fact, we both get along really well." With only one goal to his credit thus far, his coach wants van Nistelrooy to start delivering. "I expect more from a player of his standard," said van Basten.

"Ruud is training well, but I just feel he needs to show a little bit more." Van Basten admitted his statement was partially an attempt to fire van Nistelrooy into life in the same way Ferguson has done on occasion down the years. Van Nistelrooy's form certainly needs to return as, in Portugal, Holland are facing a side which proved too good for them at the semi-final stage of Euro 2004. "We have bad memories from that semi-final," said van Nistelrooy, one of only five members of the Dutch starting line-up that night to retain their places two years on. But this game will be different. We have to go for it."

The prize of a quarter-final meeting with either England or Ecuador set Dutch pulses racing. An appearance against the country in which he currently earns his living is an attractive one, but Van Nistelrooy refused to look too far into the future. "I don't want to think about England," he said. "Portugal are too good a team to start looking beyond them. In Pauleta and Luis Figo, they have a lot of experience, but they also have plenty of younger talent in the likes of Tiago, Miguel and, of course, Cristiano.

We have come through our group well, but I still think we can produce more and the chances are we will have to."

BRAZIL 4 v **JAPAN 1**

Referee: Eric Poulat

Scorers

45', 81'	Ronaldo	Tamada 34'
53'	Juninho	
59'	Gilberto	

Teams

01 Dida	Kawaguchi 23
03 Lucio	Santos 14
04 Juan	Tsuboi 19
13 Cicinho	Kaji 21
16 Gilberto	Nakazawa 22
08 Kaka	H Nakata 07
10 Ronaldinho	Ogasawara 08
17 Silva	Nakamura 10
19 Juninho	Inamoto 17
09 Ronaldo	Maki 11
23 Robinho	Tamada 20

Substitutes

71'	> 20 Ricardinho < 10 Ronaldinho	06 K Nakata > 08 Ogasawara < 56'
71'	> 11 Ze Roberto < 08 Kaka	09 Takahara > 11 Maki < 60'
82'	> 12 Rogerio Ceni < 01 Dida	16 Oguro > 09 Takahara < 66'

Discipline

44'	Gilberto foul	Kaji foul 40'

63%	Ball Possession	37%
16	Shots on target	3
7	Shots off target	6
6	Fouls	10
11	Corner Kicks	3
0	Offsides	4

Official FIFA Man of the Match
Ronaldo

Japanese fans bemoan their team's exit at the hands of the reigning champions

FINAL TABLE							GROUP F
	P	W	D	L	F	A	GD Pts
BRAZIL	3	3	0	0	7	1	+6 9
AUSTRALIA	3	1	1	1	5	5	0 4
CROATIA	3	0	2	1	2	3	-1 2
JAPAN	3	0	1	2	2	7	-5 1

Day Fifteen
Friday 23 June 2006

Spanish Eyes Are Smiling

Spain celebrate a 100% record in the group matches

Ukraine Scrape Through

Andrei Shevchenko's penalty ensures Ukraine make it through to the knockout stages in their first World Cup finals

Allez Les Blues

Patrick Vieira eases French nerves with the opening goal in a 2-0 win over Togo. South Korea's defeat by Switzerland meant the French qualified by the skin of their teeth

"It's stressful when you don't score." Raymond Domenech (France)

Saudi Arabia 0 v Spain 1

Group H
Fritz-Walter-Stadion, Kaiserslautern
Attendance: 46,000
Kick-off: 4pm   Temperature: 28°C

*Juanito celebrates the only goal of the game as Spain qualify
for the second round at a canter*

SAUDI ARABIA 0 v   SPAIN 1

Referee: Coffi Codjia

Scorers
Juanito   **36'**

Teams

21	Zaid	Canizares	19
02	Dokhi	Salgado	02
03	Tukar	Marchena	04
04	Al Montashari	Antonio Lopez	12
12	Khathran	Juanito	20
13	Sulimani	Albelda	06
08	Noor	Reyes	10
14	Khariri	Iniesta	13
16	Aziz	Joaquin	17
09	Al Jaber	Fabregas	18
11	Al Harthi	Raul	07

Substitutes

13'	18 Al Temyat / 16 Aziz	21 Villa / 07 Raul	45'
68'	23 Mouath / 09 Al Jaber	08 Xavi / 18 Fabregas	66'
81'	19 Massad / 13 Sulimani	09 Torres / 10 Reyes	69'

Discipline

27'	Al Jaber *foul*	Albelda *foul*	30'
77'	Al Temyat *diving*	Reyes *foul*	35'
		Marchena *foul*	75'

49%	**Ball Possession**	51%
8	**Shots on target**	7
6	**Shots off target**	10
17	**Fouls**	16
4	**Corner Kicks**	5
5	**Offsides**	0

Official FIFA Man of the Match
Juanito

Beckham admitted failing to understand why England so often lost their way after half-time. "I don't know, to be honest," he said. "It's happened in a few games recently, but it's up to us to put that right. Of course you'd like to win games more easily and go through tournaments more comfortably, but with the English mentality it doesn't happen. I had that with Manchester United and I've had it with England. It's been a long 10 years.

But I'd never change anything about it. We're not kidding ourselves. We've lost players and we've had situations that have not gone right for us, but as a team we are right. There are a few surprised faces at the amount of negativity that's been thrown at certain players and team performances at times, but we're men. We can take that. I've never been in a team that's so positive going into games. The togetherness couldn't be any stronger than it is."

Set pieces deliver an increasing proportion of goals, but can Beckham's

Tunisia 0 v Ukraine 1

Group H
Olympiastadion, Berlin
Attendance: 72,000
Kick-off: 4pm   Temperature: 27°C

The entire Ukrainian nation goes mad as their national team qualify for the knockout stages at the first time of asking

special ability be enough to keep him in the team? Of England's nine goals in their warm-up games against Hungary and Jamaica, he played a part in five. His free-kick induced the own-goal that gave England the win against Paraguay and he centred for Crouch to head England into the lead against T&T. "The best way to get the

best out of me is to give me the ball. If I've got the ball and a yard of space, I can deliver it to someone to score a goal. That's my game, it's what I'm good at. But what's been difficult in the last three games is that I've had two [opposing] players doubling back on me all the way through the game. It's been hard, but when that does

happen it gives other players the free space and the chance to break forward. So there's a positive out of that as well."

According to Beckham, the first half against Sweden gave merely a hint of the football England can produce. "We started to have more confidence in passing the ball about, but we can still play a lot better. The movement is a big part of it. We need to have the confidence to do that more. When we play our football, we become a very attractive team to watch and a good team and a dangerous team."

Surely not! Eriksson lost his temper in the England dressing room! "It surprised me," said John Terry. "Something's changed with Sven. He's been a lot more aggressive than before. He's been raising his voice. He will never knock over tables or scream in your face, but he has certainly been saying a lot more. He has been more demanding than I've ever known him before."

The cause of Eriksson's ire was the second-half performance against Sweden and, specifically, the apparent inability to defend against routine set pieces. Terry explained, "He knows we have a very good side and he knows this is his last chance to win something with a very good group of players. We [the defenders] were disappointed with the way we had played and Sven has singled that out."

He has also been more outspoken in public, describing England's defending as "awful".

Eriksson is more forthcoming with the Press, even letting it be known that he was unimpressed that, midway through a World Cup, news leaked about McClaren's desire to involve Alan Shearer among his staff when he takes over as manager.

More pressing, though, was defending set pieces. A third of England's training session was devoted to practising defending from free-kicks, corners and crosses, with Jenas pumping crosses into the penalty area.

Beckham, who had lost Allback for Sweden's second goal, found that the role of marking the runner had gone to Hargreaves. "We worked hard on it today," said Terry. "No-one really took responsibility. They dominated us in the air and we were disappointed with that. Everyone has to stand up to

their own responsibilities. We have worked alongside each other so often we know there is no excuse for it happening again."

Until now Michael Carrick's only interest seemed to be wondering about a possible move to Manchester United, but now he was in line to play in yet another tactical tweak against Ecuador, a 4-1-4-1 with Hargreaves replacing Carragher at right-back and Rooney a solitary striker. Carrick had never played in a competitive match at international level. He had won only six caps, three as substitute, since his England debut in May 2001.

The 24-year-old had not been involved for a single minute of England's first three games, nor any of the 10 qualifying matches, and he seemed destined for a peripheral role along with Walcott and Jenas after Hargreaves excelled in the holding midfield role against Sweden.

Crouch could consider himself unfortunate to have been omitted in Eriksson's fourth starting formation in as many games, from 4-4-2 against Paraguay, and T&T, a 4-1-3-2 against Sweden and now 4-1-4-1.

Rio was still troubled with a sore thigh. With deep concerns whether Sol Campbell has lost a yard of pace and his confidence with it, Eriksson had issued a public vote of confidence in the Arsenal defender earlier in the week, just in case he was needed.

There were plenty of the usual side issues as well as what might happen in the future with Shearer. Portugal coach Scolari raked up the past by revealing only his World Cup commitments to Portugal had ruled him out of the running to take over from Eriksson. The FA insisted on an appointment before the World Cup, but he wanted to wait. "I desire the best for England, I very much like the people I met from the FA," said Scolari. "I hope people understand the situation and one day, why not, I can coach the English team, when I am free. It is a dream for every coach in the world and I was very happy

TUNISIA 0   v   **UKRAINE 1**

Referee: Carlos Amarilla

Scorers

	Shevchenko *(pen)*	71'

Teams

01	Boumnijel	Shovkovskiy 01
03	Haggui	Nesmachniy 02
15	Jaidi	Rusol 06
19	Ayari	Sviderskiy 22
06	Trabelsi	Tymoschuk 04
12	Mnari	Shelayev 08
13	Bouazizi	Gusev 09
14	Chedli	Rebrov 11
20	Namouchi	Kalinichenko 19
08	Nafti	Shevchenko 07
05	Jaziri	Voronin 10

Substitutes

79'	17 Ben Saada	16 Vorobey	54'
	13 Bouazizi	11 Rebrov	
79'	11 Santos	14 Gusin	75'
	14 Chedli	19 Kalinichenko	
90'	10 Ghodhbane	15 Milevskiy	88'
	08 Nafti	07 Shevchenko	

Discipline

09'	Jaziri *diving*	Sviderskiy *foul*	18'
43'	Bouazizi *foul*	Shelayev *foul*	47'
45'	Jaziri *foul (second yellow)*	Tymoschuk *foul*	61'
90'	Jaidi *foul*	Rusol *foul*	65'

44%	Ball Possession	56%
3	Shots on target	6
5	Shots off target	2
24	Fouls	17
3	Corner Kicks	3
5	Offsides	2

Official FIFA Man of the Match
Anatoliy Tymoschuk

FINAL TABLE							GROUP H
	P	W	D	L	F	A	GD Pts
SPAIN	3	3	0	0	8	1	+7 9
UKRAINE	3	2	0	1	5	4	+1 6
TUNISIA	3	0	1	2	3	6	-3 1
SAUDI ARA	3	0	1	2	2	7	-5 1

SOUTH KOREA 0 v SWITZERLAND 2

Referee: Horacio Marcelo Elizondo

Scorers

Senderos	23'
Frei	77'

Teams

South Korea	Switzerland
01 Lee Woon Jae	Zuberbühler 01
12 Lee Young Pyo	Spycher 17
04 Choi Jin Cheul	Senderos 04
06 Kim Jin Kyu	P Degen 23
03 Kim Dong Jin	Muller 20
17 Lee Ho	Wicky 08
05 Kim Nam Il	Vogel 06
07 Park Ji Sung	Yakin 22
10 Park Chu Young	Cabanas 07
14 Lee Chun Soo	Barnetta 16
19 Cho Jae Jin	Frei 09

Substitutes

62'	09 Ahn Jung Hwan	02 Djourou	53'
	12 Lee Young Pyo	04 Senderos	
65'	11 Seol Ki Hyeon	05 Margairaz	70'
	10 Park Chu Young	22 Yakin	
		19 Behrami	88'
		08 Wicky	

Discipline

23'	Park Chu Young foul	Senderos foul	43'
37'	Kim Jin Kyu foul	Yakin foul	55'
78'	Choi Jin Cheul foul	Wicky foul	69'
78'	Ahn Jung Hwan foul	Spycher foul	82'
80'	Lee Chun Soo foul	Djourou foul	90'

49%	Ball Possession	51%
7	Shots on target	5
9	Shots off target	6
19	Fouls	7
6	Corner Kicks	8
3	Offsides	3

Official FIFA Man of the Match

Alexander Frei

DID YOU KNOW?
South Korea have never beaten a European side in World Cup finals outside their own country.

---

when it happened. They were very correct about everything. Everything happened in a very good atmosphere, the FA did everything officially, and they contacted the Portuguese Federation asking them if they can talk with me. Everything was going well but we stopped at a crucial point for both. They needed to announce the new England coach in a period that was impossible for me. I have a contract until July 31 with Portugal."

Speculation that Shearer would be invited to become part of McClaren's back room team along with Terry Venables could not have come at a more inconvenient time, with both working as television pundits during the World Cup finals, Shearer for the BBC and Venables for ITV. The former England No. 9, who scored 30 times in 63 appearances for his country, recently attended a residential course in Largs, Ayrshire to complete his UEFA A licence and working with the national team would enhance his coaching credentials for when he does, inevitably, head into full-time management. Brian Barwick, the FA Chief Executive, was expected to sit down with both as soon as the present tournament finished.

Shearer is seen by McClaren as an imposing presence around the dressing-room who could relate to the multi-million pound earners and celebrity status. McClaren had considered other options for his backroom team including Stuart Pearce, the Manchester City manager. The five candidates for Eriksson's position were all told at interview that they would be expected to work behind the scenes to develop young English managers.

As for the day's action, Les Bleus scrambled into the knockout stages as the final team to qualify. The champions of 1998 recorded their first win since they hosted the final at the Stade de France with a comfortable 2-0 victory over limited opponents in Togo. That will not be the case with Spain in the knock out stage. Patrick Vieira, a towering presence on his 30th birthday, forced his side ahead with his fifth goal in 90 appearances.

Supporters booed coach Raymond Domenech's name as it was announced over the tannoy before kick-off, a reminder of the pressures and the failures.

Zidane sat out his own birthday, his 34th, suspended. Qualification temporarily prolonged his international career.

David Trezeguet could have marked his first start of this tournament with a hat-trick, but ended with nothing, not helped by the cancelling of a perfectly good goal just after the quarter-hour, the linesman flagging for offside as Ribéry squared his pass and Trezeguet tapped in. The mistake did not have the same demoralising effect as previous refereeing blunders in the games against South Korea and Switzerland. Ribéry was guilty of two dreadful misses before he made amends. Driving through the centre, the Marseille midfielder slipped a neat pass inside for Vieira to spin and arc a fine shot into the far corner. Some six minutes later, Willy Sagnol's centre was flicked on by the French captain for Thierry Henry, edging away from Tchangai, to slide in his 35th international goal.

Togo supporters were conga-ing around the stadium before the end, their first taste of the finals having been embraced with enthusiasm. This was perhaps their most admirable performance, their players relishing the occasion with a long-running pay dispute behind them. FIFA will investigate the Togolese FA's conduct. Mohamed Kader, one of five of their starters who play in France, forced Barthez to save in the first half and Salifou impressed.

Another Arsenal star performer, Swiss defender Philippe Senderos, had blood pouring from a head wound after scoring a goal that eased his country's passage to a second round meeting with Ukraine. Senderos was later taken off with a shoulder injury which is almost certain to force him to

South Korea 0 v Switzerland 2

Group G
AWD Arena, Hanover
Attendance: 43,000
Kick-off: 9pm   Temperature: 23°C

Alexander Frei scores the controversial second goal after referee Elizondo correctly overruled his assistant's flag to allow the Swiss forward to round Lee Woon Jae and net

miss out on the opportunity to mark Andriy Shevchenko. His 19 year-old Arsenal team-mate Johan Djourou is set to stand in after replacing him in this match.

After his shaky performance against Togo, Senderos's tournament appeared to be taking a turn for the better after scoring and he battled bravely, coming off on another occasion in the first half for attention to his cut, until his shoulder gave way.

Switzerland are the only team not to have conceded a goal so far and deservedly completed victory over South Korea, whose elimination follows a run to the 2002 semi-finals. With France winning they would have needed a victory to progress, but failed to take the handful of chances they created before Alexander Frei sealed their fate amid the latest bout of officiating controversy after Poll.

An Argentinean assistant raised an offside flag before lowering it. He initially thought Frei was offside when latching on to a ball from Margairaz, but corrected himself, shortly before Frei hit the net, when he realised the pass had diverted off Korea's Lee Ho. Several Korea players stopped, but not the goalkeeper Lee Woon Jae, who attempted to stop Frei from sidestepping him. "Most of the decisions were not on our side, but sometimes that happens," said Korean coach Dick Advocaat.

"Switzerland deserved to win because of their first-half performance."

Spain extended their unbeaten run to 25 games and finished on top of Group H with a maximum nine points for the second World Cup in a row. With the luxury of knowing they had already secured a place in the last 16, Spain fielded their reserves against the Saudis, who needed to win by three goals to have any chance of staying on. Luis Aragonés made 11 changes to the side that beat Tunisia. The first half was played to a steady rhythm of slow drumbeats and quickening handclaps, and there was a Mexican wave as early as the seventh minute. After 36 minutes the breakthrough finally came. Reyes hit a swirling, inswinging free-kick, Juanito evaded his marker and headed into the top corner from 10 yards. "The game didn't have a lot of importance because we had already qualified, but it was a chance for the other players to impress," Juanito admitted afterwards. The Spanish players were whistled off the pitch by their fans.

Andriy Shevchenko scored for the second game in a row to send Ukraine into the last 16, but in reality they had beaten two poor teams to finish runners-up to Spain. Ukraine were unable to impose themselves on a Tunisia team reduced to 10 men for the entire second half after the dismissal of Ziad Jaziri. Shevchenko was particularly disappointing and Chelsea will surely hope for much better for their £60m investment!

Only the Bayer Leverkusen midfielder Andriy Voronin could leave the field satisfied with his contribution. Twice in the last three minutes Voronin almost scored the goal his

France 2 v Togo 0
Group G
RheinEnergieStadion, Cologne
Attendance: 45,000
Kick-off: 9pm   Temperature: 21°C

DID YOU KNOW?
This was France's first win at a World Cup finals since the 1998 Final against Brazil.

Lilian Thuram won his 117th cap to break the record held by Marcel Desailly.

Thierry Henry's goal was his fifth in World Cup finals and ranks him equal second along-side Michel Platini in France's goalscoring list, which is lead by Just Fontaine with 13 goals.

Patrick Vieira became the 6th player in World Cup finals history to score on his birthday.

Thierry Henry gets back into the scoring groove by netting the vital second goal which would have seen France qualify whatever the result in the South Korea versus Switzerland game

performance deserved. But twice he was foiled and Ukraine had to rely on the most dubious of penalties, created and converted by Shevchenko in the 71st minute.

In one of the few disappointing games of the tournament, there was appropriately a bad referee in Carlos Amarilla from Paraguay. In awarding Ukraine a penalty Amarilla was guilty of failing to see the most obvious lack of contact on Shevchenko from either Karim Haggui or goalkeeper Ali Boumnijel, when Shevchenko rushed on to the ball and knocked it between

them. Both held back from challenging, fearful of a penalty no doubt, but Shevchenko went to ground. Señor Amarilla pointed to the spot and Shevchenko steered the ball past Boumnijel. That proved to be enough for Ukraine to claim the points.

On the final whistle Ukraine celebrated exuberantly with their many fans in the stadium. It was probably relief. The other big decision the referee got wrong also benefited Ukraine. Having been correct in booking Jaziri for an outrageous ninth-minute dive in the Ukraine box, he got it completely wrong at the end of the first half and a second caution followed. Jaziri was understandably baffled by it. A small striker, Jaziri lunged lazily at Voronin after tracking back, but made no contact with the ball or with Voronin and a generous reading of Amarilla's thought process would be that Jaziri showed intent.

Oh no, just when everyone had said how marvellous our fans had been, can we spot trouble ahead? More than 1,800 police were on duty in Stuttgart to prevent disorder breaking out between German fans and some 50,000 England supporters who were expected in the city for Sunday's second round game.

Plain-clothes intelligence officers were deployed to identify German football hooligans, who police feared would try to provoke disorder.

Siegfried Stumpf, the head of Stuttgart police, said it would be the "hardest day" for his force, with up to 60,000 German fans expected to watch their team's early-evening match against Sweden on big screens at the same time as England fans pour into the city. Stumpf said: "We have intelligence officers who know the football scene and those troublemakers are known to them... we do not know if anything is planned. It might be a difficult situation, but we are well prepared for that, with very many officers working. We hope it will be peaceful."

Spotters from Cologne, who identified 50 German hooligans who were arrested to prevent trouble after England's match against Sweden, were on duty. Assistant Chief Constable Stephen Thomas, gold commander of the British policing operation in Germany, said 3,783 hooligans had been prevented from travelling from the UK and said that of 3,842 arrests during the tournament only 135 were English, of which 50 were for criminal offences and 85 preventive arrests.

Sir Peter Torry, British ambassador to Germany, praised a visit by 150 England fans, together with German and Polish supporters, to the former Dachau concentration camp, near Munich. They took part in a wreath-laying ceremony. The FA acquired an extra 580 tickets for the match against Ecuador, bringing the official allocation for members of England's supporters' club to 4,200.

My ntlworld.com World Cup Hold The Back Page debates were now in full swing, and how fortuitous to have Jeff Winter, former controversial Premiership referee, appearing. As we went through the scripts for the podcast, Jeff was the first to arrive. That gave me plenty of time for a chat. Jeff told me that Graham Poll is one of the most despised referee in English football and players, managers, rival refs, and even one Premiership club Chief Executive gloated at his three yellow card trick by sending Jeff text messages saying "it couldn't happen to a nicer chap".

Jeff also handed out his business card, which just happened to be in yellow and red and the appropriate size. That gave me an idea, and when I asked Jeff the first question on air, I first delivered three yellows and one red!

On the show Winter said: "As a ref, I think he is a very good one. As a person... Poll wouldn't speak highly of me. He has great deal of ability – does he know it. He did not have a terrible game for 89 minutes, but he forgot to send a player off. You have got to get the big decisions right.

He has gone from a very good game, to a holocaust. His credibility in world game is shot and its going to be hard in the Premiership next season. Australia would have had a case – had Croatia won – to have had the game rearranged. FIFA must be thankful that Australia went through.

Someone should have got the message through. The fourth official should have got involved. Even the player himself started to walk off."

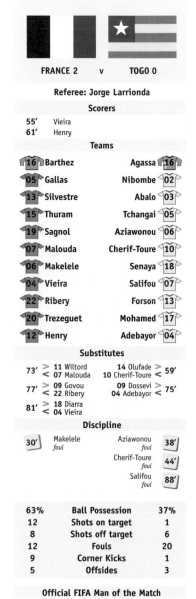

FRANCE 2 v **TOGO 0**

Referee: Jorge Larrionda

Scorers

55'	Vieira
61'	Henry

Teams

16 Barthez	Agassa 16
05 Gallas	Nibombe 02
13 Silvestre	Abalo 03
15 Thuram	Tchangai 05
19 Sagnol	Aziawonou 06
07 Malouda	Cherif-Toure 10
06 Makelele	Senaya 18
04 Vieira	Salifou 07
22 Ribery	Forson 13
20 Trezeguet	Mohamed 17
12 Henry	Adebayor 04

Substitutes

73'	11 Wiltord / 07 Malouda	14 Olufade / 10 Cherif-Toure	59'
77'	09 Govou / 22 Ribery	09 Dossevi / 04 Adebayor	75'
81'	18 Diarra / 04 Vieira		

Discipline

30'	Makelele foul	Aziawonou foul	38'
		Cherif-Toure foul	44'
		Salifou foul	88'

63%	Ball Possession	37%
12	Shots on target	1
8	Shots off target	6
12	Fouls	20
9	Corner Kicks	1
5	Offsides	3

Official FIFA Man of the Match
Patrick Vieira

FINAL TABLE							GROUP G	
	P	W	D	L	F	A	GD	Pts
SWITZERLAND	3	2	1	0	4	0	+4	7
FRANCE	3	1	2	0	3	1	+2	5
SOUTH KOR	3	1	1	1	3	4	-1	4
TOGO	3	0	0	3	1	6	-5	0

section four

second round

Day Sixteen
Saturday 24 June 2006

Germany 2 v Sweden 0
Allianz Arena, Munich
Attendance: 66,000
Kick-off: 5pm   Temperature: 30°C
Referee: Carlos Eugenio Simon

Podolski's The Man

Two goal Lukas Podolski celebrates as the hosts win through easily to the quarter-finals. Are the Germans finally beginning to believe?

	Scorers		
4', 12'	Podolski		

Team

	Germany	Sweden	
01	Lehmann	Isaksson	01
03	Friedrich	Alexandersson	07
21	Metzelder	Mellberg	03
17	Mertesacker	Lucic	04
16	Lahm	Edman	05
07	Schweinsteiger	Ljungberg	09
08	Frings	Linderoth	06
13	Ballack	Kallstrom	16
19	Schneider	Jonson	18
20	Podolski	Ibrahimovic	10
11	Klose	Larsson	11

Substitutes

Germany:
72'	> 18 Borowski < 07 Schweinsteiger
74'	> 10 Neuville < 20 Podolski
85'	> 05 Kehl < 08 Frings

Sweden:
13 Hansson > 16 Kallstrom <	39'
21 Wilhelmsson > 18 Jonson <	52'
20 Allback > 10 Ibrahimovic <	72'

Discipline

Germany:
| 27' | Frings *foul* |

Sweden:
Lucic *foul*	28'
Lucic *foul (second yellow)*	35'
Jonsson *foul*	48'
Allback *foul*	78'

Official FIFA Man of the Match
Miroslav Klose

Germany		Sweden
63%	Ball Possession	37%
13	Shots on target	2
16	Shots off target	2
15	Fouls	20
4	Corner Kicks	4
3	Offsides	2

Lukas Podolski slides home the second of his goals to see Germany through

The England team moved under police escort from their tournament base in the spa resort of Baden-Baden into Stuttgart's Steisenberger Graf Zeppelin Hotel, where they were greeted by about 100 fans when they arrived at 10.45am. Players did not stop to sign autographs or pose for pictures.

"This isn't the time for that. After the game, maybe," explained an FA official.

As David Beckham prepared for his 93rd cap and his 57th appearance as captain in his fifth major tournament with England, Eriksson told his players to consume as much liquid as possible around the clock to help avoid dehydration leading to fatigue. The players' drinking regime was water and energy-replenishing sports drinks to cope with temperatures predicted to reach 35C degrees, Eriksson explained, "You have to try to prepare as good as you can. Of course drinking is extremely important, but not that you start one hour before the game. You start today to drink as much as you possibly can. Go on tomorrow morning, when they wake up start them drinking, drinking, because we want to get as much fluid as possible into the body, and you can't do that in half an hour, to drink one or two litres of water and some sports drinks."

The Swede described the first knockout round contest as a 'life or death' situation. He cited as evidence that the players were heeding his advice, the sight of them all arriving at their training session in the afternoon clutching bottles, and doing the same as they left just over an hour later.

Eriksson let slip just how much the unyielding sun over southern Germany was making him fret over England's chances when, asked if the conditions are more likely to suit their opponents, he replied sombrely: "Maybe. Maybe." He also disclosed that England players are immersing themselves in baths of ice after both training sessions and matches in a bid to improve their circulation and so reduce their chances of getting cramp or suffering an injury.

England wanted to avoid suffering a repeat of the painful lesson they

"It's great for the world to see that Germany can party."
Jürgen Klinsmann (Germany)

learned in their opening game at the World Cup, two weeks earlier; afterwards players cited the sticky, unrelenting heat as the reason for their customary second-half decline. That was another afternoon kick-off.

England, too, had cited the oppressive heat as a factor in their disappointing quarter-final capitulation to Brazil in Shizuoka in 2002 and, while Ecuador might be an easier task than the world champions, the predicted match-time temperature was far from the cooler European conditions England had hoped for. Joe Cole had other worries as he fretted over a missing piece of kit, "I was only last off the pitch [against Sweden] because I had lost one of my lucky shinpads in the game and I was desperately trying to find it. It came off in the 75th minute and there was no way I was stopping to put it back on. But after the game I went to find it because they are extremely lucky for me. I got them sent over by my sponsors Nike because I left them at home. I didn't wear them in any of the England friendlies and I wasn't firing on all cylinders, so I needed to get them back. I've worn them throughout the World Cup and I've been happy with my performance, so I wasn't about to let someone pick it up as a souvenir and chance my form going out the window. I won the league with Chelsea wearing them, but to be honest with you I've got so many superstitions I wouldn't even know where to begin. We would be here all day talking about them. I know people will think I'm mad, but it's silly things really. Like I won't kick a ball in the changing-room and at Chelsea I have to use the same toilet."

Further evidence of a new formation arrived when Michael Carrick spoke of his delight at playing his first competitive international at such an important juncture. "The manager took me aside and said, 'This is the position that I want you to play and this how you are going to play.' Then we went out and trained with the system. I would describe it pretty much as a midfield position, probably holding more than the other two. It's pretty much as I've played for Tottenham all season, so I'm comfortable with it. This will the biggest game of my career by far."

Ecuador's training HQ was, like England's, a genteel spa town, of Bad Kissingen "What we have done is not all," said coach Suárez. "There is more to come. The World Cup has not ended for Ecuador. There is no reason for Ecuador to feel defeated beforehand. If we are going to lose, let it be during the match, not before." A heavy defeat against Germany in the last group match did not worry the coach. "That's in the past, forgotten," Suárez said. "It's good to have a bad memory in cases like this one."

Suárez prepared for the biggest game of his career by reading the works of Argentinean psychologists and the former US secretary of state Colin Powell, and is neither shocked nor awed by his opponents. "England are the favourites, there's no doubt about that. When you see the names on the team sheet and look at their players most people would say that England will beat Ecuador, but we know what we are capable off and we know who we have beaten. We are in the second round because we deserve to be and we have earned the right to fight."

But history was on England side, as they had beaten Ecuador 2-0 in a warm-up match for the 1970 World Cup finals. Ecuador, for whom 23 of 28 qualifying points were won in the rarified atmosphere of Quito, their capital city which is 9,250ft above sea level, would be playing in the Gottlieb-Daimler Stadion in Stuttgart; nearly 8,500ft lower.

Germany were also in the clouds. Heading for Berlin and the quarter-finals with a decent chance of returning there for the final, perhaps for another momentous night against England.

Klinsmann's victory so far has been one of conviction, winning over

Argentina 2 v Mexico 1
*after extra time
Zentralstadion, Leipzig   Attendance: 43,000
Kick-off: 9pm   Temperature: 27°C
Referee: Massimo Busacca

To The Maxi!

Maxi Rodriguez's classy volley put paid to plucky Mexico who took an early lead and pushed Argentina all the way

Scorers

10'	Crespo
98'	Rodriguez

Team

01	Abbondanzieri
02	Ayala
06	Heinze
13	Scaloni
03	Sorin
05	Cambiasso
10	Riquelme
18	Rodriguez
08	Mascherano
07	Saviola
09	Crespo

Substitutes

75'	>	11 Tevez
	<	09 Crespo
76'	>	16 Aimar
	<	05 Cambiasso
84'	>	19 Messi
	<	07 Saviola

Discipline

45'	Heinze *foul*
112'	Sorin *foul*

Scorers

Marquez	6'

Team

Sanchez	01
Salcido	03
Marquez	04
Guardado	18
Osorio	05
Castro	15
Mendez	16
Pardo	08
Borgetti	09
Morales	11
Fonseca	17

Substitutes

06 Torrado	>	38'
08 Pardo	<	
14 Pineda	>	66'
18 Guardado	<	
07 Zinha	>	74'
11 Morales	<	

Discipline

Marquez *foul*	70'
Castro *foul*	82'
Torrado *foul*	118'
Fonseca *kicking the ball away*	119'

Official FIFA Man of the Match
Maxi Rodriguez

51%	Ball Possession	49%
6	Shots on target	9
4	Shots off target	5
19	Fouls	26
7	Corner Kicks	6
8	Offsides	2

Mexican goalkeeper Oswaldo Sanchez leaps in vain to keep out Maxi Rodriguez's extra time wonder strike which clinched victory for Argentina

the doubters who said he could not marry the obvious attacking potential of young Podolski and the dynamic Klose. Even captain Michael Ballack wondered – publicly and for a little too long – if Klinsmann could put all the pieces together in time. "Each individual player who is on the pitch and the extraordinary support from everyone means it was a lot of fun watching this team play, especially in the first half-hour," said Klinsmann. "It was out of the ordinary. Everything we set out to do, to play with a lot of pressure and get goals quickly was achieved. Strangely, we lost our rhythm after the Swedish player's expulsion, so we had some good opportunities. But then there was the penalty which also took some concentration. We played all the way to the end and created a lot of opportunities and it was amazing and we can be very proud. It's really forming now, how the

team gets better with ever game, closer as a unit."

Sweden coach Lars Lagerback conceded that his team were outplayed and outpaced. "Germany are a good team," he said. "They controlled the game. They have a fair chance to go on in the tournament. It's difficult to say what happened in the first 10 minutes. I think we were a little passive and at the same time the goals were a little coincidental. I think it was a little bit of bad luck as well as the quality of the German forwards."

Sweden's coach was not as enamoured of the referee, Carlos Simon of Brazil, who gave the excitable Lucic two yellow cards, both for fouls on Klose – the second one, not long before the break, extremely marginal for a shirt-pull. "Both yellow cards for Teddy Lucic were not the worst things I have seen players do, especially the second one. Anyway, it's always

difficult against Germany." However, the damage was done before Lucic marched. Two stunning goals, crisply executed by the man Germans hoped would form the nucleus of their attack not only at this World Cup but for years to come. Podolski's first finish was clinical. After Isaksson halted the advancing Klose, he eased away from Mellberg's challenge to follow up with predatory instinct. Podolski struck again only eight minutes later, as Klose shimmied across the line until he laid off the simplest of passes. The Cologne striker rammed the ball home and the stadium acclaimed him with something approaching hysteria. As Klinsmann observed: "It was great for the world to see that Germany can party as well."

Henrik Larsson woefully overstruck a penalty in the 53rd minute, after Metzelder's clumsy foul on the striker.

But what was the Swedish coach's thinking, holding up Larsson while he made a substitution?

Ballack, who had so many goes at goal it was hard to keep up, hit a post with a scorching right-footer. British bookmakers immediately cut Germany's odds by a point to 6-1. England are now 11-2.

So to Argentina, who will now need to recover after the sapping 120-minutes to eliminate Mexico. The Argentinians' status as the most assured team of the World Cup was challenged when they fell behind and needed a flash of brilliance in extra-time from Maxi Rodriguez finally to place them in the quarter-finals. Argentina possessed the superior resources, able to revamp the forward line for the final, decisive half-hour with Messi, Tevez and Aimar. But there are weaknesses. Surely Argentinian football possesses finer full-backs than Lionel Scaloni, the right-back who spent several months on loan at West Ham and who made his first World Cup start? His first competitive touch of a football since the FA Cup final was a hoofed clearance that spiralled up for a corner.

Ayala and Heinze did not look comfortable as the centre-backs. Why was the towering Walter Samuel left at home? Against as agile a jumper as Borgetti, they looked vulnerable and when he outleapt Heinze to meet a Pardo free-kick, Mexico had their breakthrough. Borgetti flicked the cross on so it fell to Marquez and the Mexican captain stretched to turn the ball in.

Borgetti, though, failed to get his forehead to a Riquleme corner in the 10th minute. Marking at the near post, Borgetti stooped to clear and made contact with the ball at the same time as Crespo's boot. It was 1-1.

Messi, on his 19th birthday, had a small part in the winner, laying off a pass to Sorin, who crossed, left to right, to the edge of the Mexico penalty area. Rodriguez cushioned the ball on his chest, let it drop to volley

and watched the effort plunge beyond Sanchez's leap. A glorious winner.

Sad news. Philippe Senderos was out of the World Cup. A scan revealed he dislocated his right shoulder and the team doctor, Rudolf Roder, said: "He will be out for a minimum of two weeks. There is a 50 per cent chance he will require an operation, but the most important thing is rest for now."

Senderos should be fit for the start of Arsenal's Premiership season.

Coach Kobi Kuhn said: "Of course, it is a big blow for us, but we have already seen his friend Johan standing in well in the defence. One of our strengths is that we can replace almost everybody in the team without losing too much."

Worse news as a brawl began when an English fan clutching an England flag jumped into a crowd of Germans and the Germans pulled it off him. Punches between both sides were exchanged by a handful of yobs, but when bottles and chairs were thrown riot police armed with batons and CS sprays moved in. There was a tense stand-off between around 300 English fans and around 400 Germans, but it was calmed down by police. A police spokesman said:

"We had to move in as a preventative measure. Both sides were attacking each other and now we will stay here to stop it getting worse." The German fans had been watching their team beat Sweden on a big screen in Stuttgart's Schlossplatz main square.

It later emerged that around 122 England supporters, including three women, would miss the big game after they were arrested under "preventative powers". They appeared in front of five German judges who issued 48-hour detention orders, ensuring they missed the match against Ecuador. Two of the men were being investigated for the assault of a Tunisian man. This was still the first sign of trouble, but had the unpleasantness, so often associated with England internationals begun?

DID YOU KNOW?
Rafael Marquez's opening goal marked the 16th match at the 2006 World Cup in which a goal was scored in the first 10 minutes. No other World Cup finals has contained so many early goals.

DID YOU KNOW?
Hernan Crespo has scored in the last four World Cup matches in which he has played. The last game in which he did not score was on 7 June 2002 against England. Jairzinho and Just Fontaine both scored in six consecutive World Cup matches played.

Crespo is the first player to score in three different matches at this tournament. In 2002, Ronaldo scored in six of Brazil's seven matches.

To be fair most of the estimated 70,000 England fans were mingling merrily with the thousands of Germans, who were noisily celebrating their team's win over Sweden. Jens Grittner, spokesman for the German World Cup organising committee, said "These incidents have nothing to do with hooliganism – it was not people who were known to the police. We are not that worried – if you consider the huge amount of people partying peacefully in Germany you must regard this as an exception. This can happen at any kind of party. We don't want to reduce the seriousness of this but we must compliment the police for their immediate intervention."

Day Seventeen
Sunday 25 June 2006

England 1 v Ecuador 0
Gottlieb-Daimler-Stadion, Stuttgart
Attendance: 52,000
Kick-off: 5pm   Temperature: 28°C
Referee: Frank De Bleeckere

Another Becks Please

Captain Beckham swoops from a free-kick once again to save England's blushes and send Sven's men into the quarter-finals

England		
Scorers		
60'	Beckham	
Team		
01	Robinson	
16	Hargreaves	
06	Terry	
05	Ferdinand	
03	A Cole	
07	Beckham	
18	Carrick	
04	Gerrard	
08	Lampard	
11	J Cole	
09	Rooney	

Substitutes		
77'	15 Carragher > < 11 J Cole	
87'	19 Lennon > < 07 Beckham	
90'	20 Downing > < 04 Gerrard	

Discipline	
18'	Terry *foul*
78'	Robinson *time wasting*
82'	Carragher *time wasting*

Ecuador		
Scorers		
Team		
Mora	12	
De la Cruz	04	
Hurtado	03	
Espinoza	17	
Reasco	18	
Valencia	16	
E Tenorio	20	
Castillo	14	
Mendez	08	
Delgado	11	
C Tenorio	21	

Substitutes		
07 Lara > < 20 E Tenorio	69'
10 Kaviedes > < 21 C Tenorio	71'

Discipline	
Valencia *delaying restart of play*	24'
C Tenorio *foul*	37'
De la Cruz *foul*	67'

Official FIFA Man of the Match
John Terry

England		Ecuador
51%	Ball Possession	49%
4	Shots on target	4
4	Shots off target	8
13	Fouls	22
5	Corner Kicks	7
3	Offsides	6

Ashley Cole's knee deflects Carlos Tenorio's shot onto the bar to spare England the ignominy of going a goal behind to Ecaudor

> **"I think it was about time that we got a bit of luck in a game. Yes, we could have scored more goals, but in the end we had to rely on Beckham"**
> **Sven-Göran Eriksson (England)**

Ecuador stood between Sven and any future with England. They had reached the knock-out stage for the first time and, until their capitulation against Germany, prompted comparisons with the Colombia sides that so discomforted European opponents in the 1990s. Coach Luis Fernando Suárez is the second successive Colombian to take charge of the team and has adapted the close-passing patience of his countrymen to fit a 4-4-2 based on width, pace and a high tempo. They would be tricky opponents.

And so they proved, but England's 1-0 victory in Stuttgart set-up a quarter-final showdown with either Holland or Portugal in Gelsenkirchen.

England fans might have been sick of poor performances. Beckham was simply sick. But England were through. And this is now a results orientated industry.

Beckham revealed a ribbing from Rooney and text message from Roberto Carlos inspired his match-winning free-kick. The skipper curled home a second-half long distance free-kick with remarkable precision

to see his team past the South Americans with Posh punching the air in delight, Romeo giving the thumbs up and Brooklyn equally chuffed for his dad. The Captain told BBC1's Garth Crooks immediately afterwards, "To be honest I have not scored for a while and I haven't scored many free-kicks this season. But last night Wayne said to me I have been terrible in the last few games and Roberto Carlos texted me to score a goal for him, so I am more than happy."

Beckham stuck a finger down his throat to make himself sick after scoring the winner, "I didn't feel very well before the game and then in the second half and it just came out." He did not mind who England got in the next round, "I don't care. We have done our job. We were ugly at times but we are through."

Asked by Crooks about his controversial formation, Eriksson said: "I think it worked. We should have scored more goals, but I am rather happy that we are in the quarter-finals again. I hope we will have a better result in the quarters this time." Asked if he took Beckham off because he had been sick on the field, the Swede said: "I think he was gone

physically and Aaron Lennon came on and played very well."

Wayne Rooney treated critics of this England side with contempt. After going the full distance for the first time despite the sweltering conditions, he rounded on those who question England's performances. "I don't think we've struggled to play well. Four games and it's three wins and a draw. I don't think that's too bad. You lot [the media] have made out that our performances have been terrible, but the main thing is that we keep finding a way and we're through to the quarter-final. We've reached the next stage of the competition and this is where life will get really tough, so we have to be at our very, very best on Saturday. We've not really played our best stuff, but we're still in the quarter-final. But we all know we have to raise our game to get a result against Portugal or Holland."

Deployed as the spearhead in England's formation Rooney was tireless in his first full game since April. Lampard blazed over after Rooney beat two defenders to present him with the sort of chance he usually buries. Poor old Frank really doesn't look like he has any of his usual confidence when striking at goal.

Eriksson was on the verge of introducing Crouch when Beckham scored the free-kick that took England through, but with England ahead the coach had enough confidence in Rooney's fitness to hold back.

Rooney's comments about his improving fitness will hearten Eriksson and his team-mates. "It was difficult on my own up front but I got a lot of support from midfield and it worked for us in the end. I feel myself getting fitter all the time. In the last 30 minutes I did better than in the first 60. That's a positive sign for me. Hopefully it will stand me in good stead for the next game."

Ecuador's defender Ulises de la Cruz declined to praise England's per-formance, instead claiming his team had more respect for Brazil.

"Ecuadorean people fear England a bit because in my homeland they can watch Premiership matches, but we respect Brazil more." Goalkeeper Cristian Mora admitted Beckham's free-kick had been too good for him. "I managed to touch the ball, but it was a perfect shot."

Could England win the World Cup? Not on this performance. But surely it's how you finish that counts.

For the present it was Oh so painful to watch, despite the BBC pundits declining to make any real hard-hitting observations, in truth it was agonising for half the nation watching this back home on TV. Now Alan Shearer was being tipped for a role within the coaching set up, he too, lost his appetite for any biting comment.

Carrick did play well, but the Hansen-Shearer-Wright team had been pushing for his inclusion and wanted to be proved right. Again in reality he was superb on the ball, but his covering left a lot to be desired.

For me Ashley Cole was the real man of the match, Carrick not too far behind, though, and Beckham produced a long-overdue piece of free-kick magic to sink Ecuador and book his team into the last eight. We were all left still waiting for the team to click and fulfil their potential – but so far England could only be described as the worst of the last eight.

And, it might not have happened but for a moment of vintage Beckham on the hour.

Lampard won a free-kick and the skipper stepped up. Gerrard was screaming for it at the back-post where he was unmarked, but Beckham ignored him and sent the ball curling over the wall. Mora reached it with an outstretched hand, but could not keep it from touching the post and squeezing into the bottom corner. There was even a split second delay in the cele-brations as it seemed unlikely it could have made it into such a small window of opportunity.

It was Beckham's first successful free-kick in more than a year for his country and a reminder of the days when he seemed to win England games on his own.

It made history, as he became the first England player to score in three different World Cup finals and he could not hide his delight. Beckham had been a target for criticism before the game. He was sick, but his critics probably felt sicker! Sir Geoff Hurst was one who thought he should have been replaced by Lennon.

Ecuador should have stolen the lead in 11th minute when Terry miscued a simple header. Carlos Tenorio latched onto Terry's mistake and burst through on goal but Cole sprinted back 30 yards and threw himself in front of his shot. The Arsenal full-back, winning his 50th cap, did enough to divert it off his knee onto the bar and out for a corner.

England breathed again, but they struggled to find any rhythm at all, despite the extra man in midfield. Easy passes were misdirected and Beckham's dead-ball delivery was ter-rible before the break. Rooney suf-fered alone up front in only his second start after injury. He was a victim of the dreadful service, all too often having to challenge for a long punt from Robinson with no support any-where near him.

The team disappeared back into the dressing to a chorus of jeers from their own fans.

Eriksson made no major tactical changes during the interval. England came out in the same shape, but Beckham's free-kick changed the game in the 60th minute.

Ecuador hit back briefly and Robinson was forced to make a full-length save from Luis Valencia.

Eriksson had to fend off hostile questioning in the after match media briefing. He acknowledged victory had been another unsatisfactory per-formance but he also accused his detractors of having unreasonable expectations. "If we expected to be

Holland 0 v Portugal 1
FrankenStadion, Nuremburg
Attendance: 41,000
Kick-off: 9pm   Temperature: 26°C
Referee: Valentin Ivanov

Fight Night

Portugal and Holland battle out the most brutal World Cup finals match in history with 16 cards being dished out by referee Ivanov

Scorers

Team

01	van der Sar
05	van Bronckhorst
04	Mathijsen
13	Ooijer
03	Boulahrouz
08	Cocu
20	Sneijder
18	van Bommel
11	Robben
07	Kuyt
17	van Persie

Substitutes

56'	> <	10 van der Vaart 04 Mathijsen
67'	> <	14 Heitinga 18 van Bommel
84'	> <	19 Vennegoor of Hesselink 08 Cocu

Discipline

02'	van Bommel *foul*
08'	Boulahrouz *foul*
59'	van Bronckhorst *foul*
63'	Boulahrouz *foul*
73'	Sneijder *kicking the ball away*
74'	van der Vaart *kicking the ball away*
90'	van Bronckhorst *foul*

Official FIFA Man of the Match
Nuno Maniche

Scorers

Maniche	23'

Team

Ricardo	01
Nuno Valente	14
Ricardo Carvalho	16
Meira	05
Miguel	13
Maniche	18
Deco	20
Costinha	06
Figo	07
Pauleta	09
Ronaldo	17

Substitutes

11 Simao 17 Ronaldo	> <	34'
08 Petit 09 Pauleta	> <	45'
19 Tiago 07 Figo	> <	84'

Discipline

Maniche *foul*	20'
Costinha *foul*	31'
Costinha *foul*	45'
Petit *foul*	50'
Figo *foul*	60'
Deco *foul*	73'
Ricardo *foul*	76'
Nuno Valente *foul*	76'
Deco *foul*	78'

Holland		Portugal
49%	**Ball Possession**	51%
8	**Shots on target**	6
14	**Shots off target**	4
12	**Fouls**	9
5	**Corner Kicks**	3
2	**Offsides**	4

Nuno Maniche slots the only goal of the game to end Holland's unbeaten record and send Portugal through to face England in another quarter-final

DID YOU KNOW?
The 16 cards shown were a record for a World Cup encounter, equalling those shown in the Cameroon v Germany fixture at the 2002 tournament.

DID YOU KNOW?
Costinha's dismissal was the third for a Portuguese player at a World Cup. Deco's was the fourth. Both Joao Pinto and Beto were sent off in 2002 against South Korea.

The four dismissals in this game took the 2006 total of red cards to 23, breaking the record set in 1998.

DID YOU KNOW?
Luiz Felipe Scolari has taken his perfect record at the World Cup to 11 matches. This victory means the Portuguese now hold the best current unbeaten run in competitive matches by a European nation with 16, having ended the Dutch streak of 15.

controlling games for 90 minutes and creating 20 chances then we are in the wrong place. Today we were among the best 16 teams in the world. Next week it is the best eight. Of course there are going to be times in matches when we are going to suffer. I've also seen Mexico make life extremely difficult for Argentina. This is the World Cup and it can happen that way. The important thing is that we are getting better and better with each game. This was certainly better than how we played against Sweden and I can assure you we will be better again in our quarter-final. So, no, I

am not concerned. I would be if we had lost two or three games and were heading out of the competition but the fact is we are now in the quarter-finals, among the best eight teams in the world. I am actually rather proud."

Graham Poll eat yer heart out. The Russian ref of the evening's Portugal versus Holland game made World Cup history with FOUR reds and 16 yellows.

And, yes, it was fate. Just as in Shizuoka at the 2002 World Cup and Lisbon in Euro 2004, Scolari and Eriksson will go head to head at the quarter-final stage, with the Swede desperately hoping it will be third time lucky, thanks to a farce of a game.

For once, fortune seems to favour Eriksson as Portugal will be deprived of Costinha and, much more crucially, chief playmaker Deco, after the pair were dismissed in a stormy affair as both sides finished with nine men.

The game was settled by Maniche's first-half strike. By the time it ended, under-pressure referee Valentin Ivanov had produced an incredible 16 yellow cards – equalling the all-time tournament record – plus

four reds and been forced to intervene in countless skirmishes.

Through it all, Ruud van Nistelrooy remained on the bench, axed now by his country as well as his club, and not even invited to come on to try to save the game. Van Nistelrooy's omission provided the first talking point an hour before kick-off. Having dumped Davids, Seedorf, Kluivert and Makaay from his squad altogether, van Nistelrooy was paying for a series of indifferent performances. His absence cost him an anticipated match-up with Manchester United team-mate Cristiano Ronaldo, the man with whom a training ground bust-up is said to have led to his Old Trafford exile. Not that Ronaldo lasted long, 34 minutes to be precise. Marc van Bommel had already been cautioned for chopping down the winger when Boulahrouz caught him with a vicious high tackle which warranted more than the yellow card it received. The deep gash to Ronaldo's thigh forced him to the touchline for treatment on two separate occasions, he eventually left the field for good in streams of tears. The 21-year-old had already made a positive contribution, darting between van Bronckhorst and Sneijder to seize possession before releasing Deco with an inspired pass. The Barcelona man quickly crossed low, allowing Pauleta to lay a pass off to Maniche. No longer wanted by Jose Mourinho at Chelsea, the midfielder skipped inside Ooijer and beat van der Sar with an impressive finish.

Ronaldo was not alone in being on the wrong end of crude tackles. Robben's shoulder was the point of impact when Valente flew in to make a high, studs-first challenge. Costinha ridiculously stuck his arm out to intercept a pass bound for Van Persie. Having already been booked, a red card was automatic. A flurry of activity around the Portugal goal at the start of the second half saw Cocu smash a shot against the underside of the bar. Figo was fortunate to escape with just a caution when he shoved his head – albeit with minor contact – into Van Bommel's face. Figo was also involved in the next incident, the one which sparked a mass confrontation between both sets of players by the dug-outs, as he went down after being caught in the face by Boulahrouz's

arm, prompting Ivanov to produce another red card.

Deco swiftly followed, booked twice in five minutes as chaos reigned, with van Bronckhorst also departing early in stoppage time. Portugal's remaining nine players, marshalled by the outstanding Ricardo Carvalho, somehow survived, although in the end they were indebted to keeper Ricardo, who brilliantly denied Kuyt. It could get worse for Portugal if FIFA launches disciplinary proceedings against Figo for that butt on van Bommel. Ivanov showed Figo a yellow card and the Internazionale player was likely to escape action on video evidence if the card was for the butt because the incident will have been dealt with at the time. If the caution was for another reason, Figo could be

charged and banned. FIFA president Sepp Blatter ominously said afterwards: "I consider that today the referee was not at the same level as the participants, the players. There could have been a yellow card for the referee."

Scolari showed how adept he is at reorganising in difficult situations as his team held on when, twice, they had a man fewer than Holland. His Brazil finished with 10 men when beating England in 2002. Deploying a touch of kidology, he remarked, "There's no advantage of one coach in relation to another. I would like to have the ability and quality of Eriksson. Just because I beat him once or twice doesn't mean I'm better than him. We respect each other and winning again or losing to England will not make me better or worse than Eriksson."

Other News

Holland's Khalid Boulahrouz sees red to become the second of a record four players dismissed by referee Valentin Ivanov

Day Eighteen
Monday 26 June 2006

Italy 1 v Australia 0
Frtitz-Walter-Stadion, Kaiserslautern
Attendance: 46,000
Kick-off: 5pm   Temperature: 30°C
Referee: Luis Medina Cantalejo

Sucker Punch

Francesco Totti celebrates his match-winning, last minute goal with his own unique thumb-sucking routine

	Scorers				Scorers	
90'	Totti *(pen)*					

	Team				Team	
01	Buffon			Schwarzer	01
19	Zambrotta			Chipperfield	14
05	Cannavaro			Neill	02
23	Materazzi			Moore	03
03	Grosso			Culina	05
07	Del Piero			Wilkshire	20
20	Perrotta			Cahill	04
08	Gattuso			Grella	13
21	Pirlo			Bresciano	23
11	Gilardino			Sterjovski	21
09	Toni			Viduka	09

Substitutes

45'	> 15 Iaquinta < 11 Gilardino			15 Aloisi > 21 Sterjovski <	81'
55'	> 06 Barzagli < 09 Toni				
75'	> 10 Totti < 07 Del Piero				

Discipline

29'	Grosso *foul*
51	Materazzi *denying a goalscoring opportunity*
89'	Gattuso *foul*
90'	Zambrotta *time wasting*

Discipline

Grella *foul*	23'
Cahill *foul*	49'
Wilkshire *foul*	61'

Official FIFA Man of the Match
Gianluigi Buffon

58%	Ball Possession	42%
4	Shots on target	7
5	Shots off target	5
24	Fouls	17
2	Corner Kicks	2
2	Offsides	2

> "A penalty shoot-out is like Russian roulette. I didn't watch it. I went back into the changing rooms, I just couldn't take it any more. Watching 120 minutes of a match like that was too much for me. I just said to them, 'Lads, you decide. Whoever wants to take a penalty, go for it'."
>
> Oleg Blokhin (Ukraine)

Lucas Neill trips Fabio Grosso in the area to give Italy a last gasp penalty which Francesco Totti converted to win the game. The Aussies had other ideas about the validity of the spot-kick

Eriksson advised the English nation to trust him to take them to the World Cup final. Asked why, the Swede smiled. "You have to," he said. "You don't have any choice."

Eriksson again tried to dismiss concerns, "I don't remember any team who started the World Cup in a perfect way and won all seven games and did it with style every time. I think you have to suffer in a tournament like this." He has certainly made us do that.

Five days of preparation gave him a good opportunity to eradicate the flaws.

Comparisons with Scolari have not often been flattering. "I don't play, I don't score goals," the Brazilian said, "but I have participation with the team that the athletes accept. Maybe I can give the extra yard to a player on the field that wins the game. That's the spirit that I have. They give me that opportunity of working with them and that small part sometimes helps.

I give them a lot of human warmth, a lot of vibration, because they are living that on the field. We want to be close to them and hold them, we want to participate in the game. That's why we adopt certain attitudes of being by the sideline, of being with them, telling them what they have to do, that they can go forward, that they can reduce space. Sometimes they look outside and they see their group through the face of their coach and they know that even all those on the bench are playing. Maybe I can give the extra yard to a player on the field that wins the game. That's the spirit that I have. That is what I've done with Portugal."

Scolari is convinced that he is an ever-present source of inspiration to his team and, damned Eriksson with faint praise as a "competent coach."

It is believed to have been Gareth Southgate who remarked privately that Eriksson resembled Iain Duncan Smith, when England needed some Churchillian rhetoric in the dressing-room as Brazil came from behind to win the World Cup quarter-final in Shizuoka four years ago. While Eriksson remains a skilled diplomat, Scolari, now being lauded as the 'king of Portugal', prefers to use Churchillian language of war. "For many years Portugal did not see a team to dignify the name of Portugal, fighting so much

and doing so much for Portugal," he said. "So we have to congratulate our team, our athletes, on a heroic victory. We have heard, and read in the papers, that Portugal has the capacity to suffer. It doesn't win 3-0 and everybody suffers, here and in Portugal and throughout the world with our diaspora of immigrants. In South American championships there are a lot of victories like this, with a lot of suffering and a lot of fighting, so it's part of my life. It's part of my career. My life is trying to get better things even with some difficulties."

But problems were mounting for Portugal even more so than England. Scolari's plans were disrupted by suspension after their bruising victory over Holland and the losses of Deco – an appeal against his red card unlikely to succeed – and Costinha are considerable blows. Tiago, the former Chelsea player, and Petit seem likely to deputise. Figo was fortunate to be cleared to play after his head-butt on Mark van Bommel.

England fans would dominate the 52,000-capacity stadium in Gelsenkirchen, but it also had happy memories for Portuguese travellers given that it was where José Mourinho's

Australia's dejected players applaud their fans in the stadium after their agonising late defeat

Switzerland 0 v Ukraine 0
*after extra time, Ukraine won 3-0 on penalties
RheinEnergieStadion, Cologne   Attendance: 45,000
Kick-off: 9pm   Temperature: 22°C
Referee: Benito Archundia Tellez

Scorers

Team

01	Zuberbühler	
02	Djourou	
03	Magnin	
20	Muller	
23	P Degen	
06	Vogel	
07	Cabanas	
08	Wicky	
16	Barnetta	
22	Yakin	
09	Frei	

Substitutes

33'	13 Grichting	>
	02 Djourou	<
64'	11 Streller	>
	22 Yakin	<
116'	18 Lustrinelli	>
	09 Frei	<

Discipline

59'	Barnetta foul

Swiss Pay The Penalty

Tranquillo Barnetta is one of three Swiss players to fail to score from the spot as his team go out despite having not conceded a goal

Scorers

Team

Shovkovskiy	01	
Vashchuk	17	
Nesmachniy	02	
Tymoschuk	04	
Shelayev	08	
Gusev	09	
Gusin	14	
Kalinichenko	19	
Voronin	10	
Vorobey	16	
Shevchenko	07	

Substitutes

21 Rotan	>	75'
19 Kalinichenko	<	
11 Rebrov	>	93'
16 Vorobey	<	
15 Milevskiy	>	110'
10 Voronin	<	

Discipline

Official FIFA Man of the Match
Oleksandr Shovkovskiy

Switzerland		Ukraine
51%	Ball Possession	49%
5	Shots on target	2
7	Shots off target	13
22	Fouls	19
5	Corner Kicks	6
0	Offsides	1

Ukraine's Oleg Gusev strokes home the decisive penalty which clinches a 3-0 shootout win to put his nation through to the quarter-finals at the first time of asking

FC Porto lifted the European Cup in May 2004.

For England's part, Frank Lampard is convinced it is only a matter of time before he breaks his World Cup duck after having more shots than any other player in Germany without scoring, "I'm getting into the right positions, but I'm not scoring and that is frustrating. Four games is a long time for me to go without a goal, so I'm hoping one will come in the most important game of all. The most important thing is that England are winning games and we've made it through to the quarter-finals. But on a personal note I do want to score at the World Cup and I could have wrapped the Ecuador game up with the one I sent over the bar. I'm hoping that the quarter-final game against Portugal will be a bit more open because, even though it was a knockout match, Ecuador sat so deep and did not come out from midfield in any numbers."

Germany captain Michael Ballack recovered from a minor foot injury and will be fit to play against Argentina. "It's all healed," coach Klinsmann told

a news conference. "Ballack is of great importance to this team. He reads the game well and is prepared to sacrifice himself. He has a key role."

Klinsmann said he was not interested in any other job, dousing speculation he might be the next United States coach. "That doesn't interest me at all," Klinsmann said when asked at a news conference in Berlin about his interest in coaching the U.S. team, who were eliminated at the group stage. "At the moment, I'm only interested in my job and that has to continue to the final." His two-year contract with Germany expires after the World Cup. Klinsmann, who has an American wife, has lived for years in California and cherishes his anonymous lifestyle there. He spent a few weeks working as an observer with the U.S. team several years before he took the Germany job in 2004.

Marcello Lippi hailed 10-man Italy's determination to beat Australia 1-0 and insisted their controversial winning penalty was rightly given. Defender Marco Materazzi was sent off

in the 50th minute – a straight red for a foul on Marco Bresciano – but substitute Francesco Totti converted a penalty in stoppage-time to book them into the quarter-finals. The turning point came when defender Fabio Grosso fell over Lucas Neill's challenge in the area. "When in the 92nd minute, our defender headed into the area and was taken down for a nailed-on penalty, I think it was something fantastic," Lippi said. "And Totti converted it with real skill."

Pressed about the penalty decision, Lippi said: "There were two fouls on him. He didn't go down under the first and he carried on dribbling and then sustained another clear foul. Why?" he asked the news conference. "Does anyone have any doubts about the penalty?"

As for his team's performance, he said: "In the first half we didn't let them have anything during open play, not even a long shot, and we had four really clear scoring chances. In the second half, down to 10 men against 11 we suffered – but still gave very

DID YOU KNOW?
Ukraine became only the third country in World Cup history to reach the quarter-finals despite losing a group match by a margin of at least four goals. In 1954, West Germany actually claimed the title after losing 8-3 to Hungary, while Cameroon reached the quarter-finals in 1990 despite a 4-0 defeat against the Soviet Union.

DID YOU KNOW?
Switzerland became the first team ever to go out of the tournament without conceding a goal. They are also the first country to miss all their spot-kicks in a World Cup penalty shoot-out. Ironically these were the first penalties any Swiss player has had to take, as they have not been awarded a regular penalty in their previous 26 World Cup matches.

little away. There was a real desire to succeed and real determination – plus a bit of organisation because it is not easy to defend in 10. It's an indescribable joy. I'm really delighted. These lads showed great heart, great character and also great quality."

Hiddink was less convinced about the decision to award a penalty, "Overall you can have doubts about the penalty. We are very disappointed because we were so close, but I can be very proud of the team. I think the only thing we can blame ourselves for is that we did not get a goal."

Defeat left a bitter taste for Australia's players. "I think we dominated the match for many parts and with an extra player it made it easier for us but it's a really bad way to go out," said captain Mark Viduka. "We're obviously happy we've got this far, but it is so disappointing to go out in the fashion we did."

Midfielder Tim Cahill was also very down, "It's a feeling of disbelief. We're trying to break them down and then they get a lucky break, he falls over in the box and gets a penalty."

Hiddink said his team also had themselves to blame for their downfall through their failure to make more of their control of the game. Hiddink felt Australia tried to attack too much

down the centre of the park and did not have enough width to their game, which he said the Socceroos would have to learn if they were to continue to improve on the enormous gains they have made at this tournament. "Our crosses weren't good enough in the ultimate phase and as a consequence we didn't score any goals," he said. "We had to use the wings more and the move the ball more laterally."

The Socceroos were not helped in that regard by the loss of Liverpool winger Harry Kewell. Hiddink revealed after the game that the injury-prone Kewell, who came into this tournament lacking fitness after injuring his groin in the FA Cup final while playing for Liverpool, had again succumbed to injury during the Croatia match. This time the problem is to his ankle, which resulted in Kewell watching the clash against Italy on crutches from the bench.

Andrei Shevchenko missed a penalty, but Ukraine still won the shootout after a dismal 0-0 draw in Cologne, for my money the worst match of the finals so far. Chelsea's big money buy stepped up first in the spot-kick shootout, but saw his weak attempt easily saved by Swiss goalkeeper Pascal Zuberbühler. Fortunately for Shev, three appalling Swiss penalties in a row handed the tie to Ukraine. Streller and Cabanas saw their attempts saved and Barnetta hit the top of the bar.

The Eastern Europeans advance to a last eight meeting with Italy in their first finals after Milevskiy, Rebrov and Gusev all held their nerve.

Shevchenko came close to a goal in normal time when he beat Djourou to Kalinichenko's dead-ball, but his header came back off the bar. Then it was Switzerland's turn to strike the woodwork. Shelayev fouled Barnetta 25 yards out and Frei's free-kick rattled the bar with Shovkovskiy rooted to the spot.

The only ones laughing at the end of this poor game were the Italians.

Other News

Chelsea goalkeeper Petr Cech underwent arthroscopic surgery on both shoulders. The Czech Republic international opted to go under the knife following his country's elimination at the group stage. "The operation was successful and lasted more than two hours. Petr feels well," said Petr Travnicek, the player's media spokesman. "Petr will have a rest and intensive rehabilitation in the following weeks."

Day Nineteen
Tuesday 27 June 2006

Brazil 3 v Ghana 0
Veltins Arena, Dortmund
Attendance: 65,000
Kick-off: 5pm   Temperature: 30°C
Referee: Lubos Michel

	Scorers
5'	Ronaldo
45'	Adriano
84'	Ze Roberto

	Team
01	Dida
02	Cafu
03	Lucio
04	Juan
06	Carlos
05	Emerson
11	Ze Roberto
08	Kaka
10	Ronaldinho
07	Adriano
09	Ronaldo

Substitutes
45'	> <	17 Silva / 05 Emerson
61'	> <	19 Juninho / 07 Adriano
83'	> <	20 Ricardinho / 08 Kaka

Discipline
13'	Adriano *diving*
44'	Juan *foul*

Record Breaker

Ronaldo celebrates becoming the World Cup's all-time highest scorer after notching his fifteenth goal in the 3-0 win over Ghana

Official FIFA Man of the Match
Ze Roberto

Scorers	

Team	
Kingston	22
Pantsil	15
Shilla	07
Mensah	05
Pappoe	06
Dramani	23
E Addo	18
Appiah	10
Muntari	11
Amoah	14
Gyan	03

Substitutes
08 Boateng 18 E Addo	> <	60'
12 Tachie-Mensah 14 Amoah	> <	69'

Discipline
Appiah *foul*	07'
Muntari *foul*	11'
Pantsil *foul*	29'
E Addo *foul*	38'
Gyan *dissent*	48'
Gyan *diving (second yellow)*	81'

51%	Ball Possession	49%
11	Shots on target	9
2	Shots off target	12
16	Fouls	22
3	Corner Kicks	4
5	Offsides	4

The goal which earned Ronaldo his place in history, a left-footed shot low past Pantsil on the line after waltzing round goalkeeper Richard Kingston

The media coverage of the WAGS intensified as Joe Cole insisted the presence of wives and girlfriends in Germany had not been a distraction.

"It's a long time to be away from home and to be stuck away in a hotel. For most of our lives, we are stuck in hotels. To give us a little break when we can go and see the family – just to talk about things you can't talk about with the other lads like who is looking after the dogs – is great. It's just normal things. It just gets your mind off it. That's very important. Anyone who thinks it's a distraction is mad because when we are playing three games a week at home, you don't go and lock yourself away in a hotel room. You need to get a bit of normality. It's nice to see them enjoying it as well. It's good for me to see my girlfriend, my mum and dad and friends being really excited and enjoying it. I'm happy then that I've been able to give them that."

Here was a new one....Paul Robinson claimed the dry German pitches were inhibiting England's passing game, "The conditions have made it hard for us. I think we are finding the pitches particularly difficult because they are not putting water on them. It's slowing our passing game down. We are finding it hard to get a rhythm."

Rio was off his chair, heading for the door at the close of a media briefing, when he was asked to give his preference: Rooney or Cristiano Ronaldo? "Rooney," he replied instinctively. That choice might yet have to be made back at Ferdinand's club as Manchester United were forced to intervene as speculation escalated that Ronaldo wanted to go to Real. The Reds were staggered when Real Madrid Presidential candidate Villar Mir not only backed up Ronaldo's version of events, but also stated talks with United had been held to clear the path towards a deal, saying, "Manchester United know we are talking with him," he said. "We have gone in 'through the front door'."

Mir's allegation was tantamount to revealing an intention by the Red Devils to sell one of the cornerstones of Sir Alex's current rebuilding work,

> "We won because we were patient, worked hard, stuck together and were intelligent. We started slowly, but we were in top gear by the end."
> **Raymond Domenech (France)**

just months into a contract extension which is due to run until 2010. Condemnation from United was swift and to the point. "(We) are astonished with Juan Miguel Villar Mir's comments," said a senior club spokesman. "There has been no contact between Manchester United and Villar Mir's election team or Real Madrid, and any suggestion there has been is incorrect. Unfortunately, these tactics seem to be a common occurrence in elections of this nature."

England had still to convince the rest of the footballing world they had the credentials to be world champions. 'The home of football could be thankful,' a Brazilian paper declared, that the WAGs, 'anorexics addicted to shopping with hollow lobotomised heads', were there to 'detract from their team's poor football skills'.

Brazil's Folha de São Paulo carried the derogatory headline 'Worsening with each match, England eliminate the Ecuadoreans'. Portugal, the Folha claims, could consider themselves favourites for a quarter-final against 'the weary, lethargic English'.

Stefan Effenberg, the former Germany player turned TV pundit, rounded on England, with a widely quoted: 'I wouldn't call this football – it's a botch job.' Bild declared that 'the only hot thing in the game was the air'. Die Welt noted: 'Sven-Göran Eriksson announced that the match was a matter of life and death, an obvious exaggeration. But since he brought the subject up, it's worth noting that the English are still alive.'

For Ecuador's El Nacional it was 'easy to believe Sven when he said the best is yet to come because the white flag with the cross of Saint George suffered in the face of lesser rivals...unlike the subjects of Queen Elizabeth...England's was 'an embarrassing performance from the country that invented football'.

Portugal's Diario de Noticias, recalling what happened at the European Championships two years

ago, delivered a chilling prediction ahead of the quarter-final: 'Here come the penalties against England again.'

And so to the last of the action for the remaining two quarter-final places....

Ronaldo became the most prolific scorer in World Cup history as Brazil saw off a spirited Ghana and progressed through to the quarter-finals with relative ease. Africa's last remaining representatives were made to pay for some cavalier defending and waywardness in front of goal as they went down to a Brazil side still lacking their traditional samba-style and swagger.

On five minutes Ronaldo collected a delightful slide rule pass from Kaka, bamboozled an exposed Kingston with a trademark step-over and calmly toe-poked the ball into the net to become the World Cup's highest ever goalscorer with a tally of 15. Ronaldo could have added a second. Clear through on goal following another deft pass from deep, Adriano chose to delay and allow Kingston to pounce instead of making a simple lay off to Ronaldo. To try to save his blushes, Adriano elaborately threw himself to the floor and was rightly booked.

With half-time looming and Brazil hanging on, Ghana's buccaneering forays forward were undermined by a combination of raw defending, breathtaking Brazilian play and some inept officiating from the assistant referee.

During a sweeping counterattack, Adriano was clearly offside on two occasions. Firstly as Lucio fed Cafu down the right and then as the rampaging right-back cut the ball across the six yard box for Adriano to knee high fortuitously into the net.

Gyan was sent off on 80 minutes for a second yellow card after foolishly going to ground under a non-existent challenge from Juan. A third goal from Ze Roberto originated from another dinked ball over a flat-footed defence.

"That was never my goal, it's just something that's happened," Ronaldo told reporters. "I'm happy to have broken this record; for seven World Cups it has not been broken. It's a

France 3 v Spain 1

AWD Arena, Hanover
Attendance: 43,000
Kick-off: 9pm   Temperature: 27°C
Referee: Roberto Rosetti

French Inspiration Sees Off Spain

Will Spain ever get it together in a major tournament? Not this one – as a late French flurry, rounded off by Zinedine Zidane's deserved goal, sees the 1998 Champions step up a gear and win through to the quarters

Scorers (France)

41'	Ribery
83'	Vieira
90'	Zidane

Team (France)

16	Barthez
19	Sagnol
15	Thuram
05	Gallas
03	Abidal
22	Ribery
10	Zidane
06	Makelele
04	Vieira
07	Malouda
12	Henry

Substitutes (France)

| 74' | > 09 Govou
< 07 Malouda |
| 88' | > 11 Wiltord
< 12 Henry |

Discipline (France)

68'	Vieira *foul*
87'	Ribery *time wasting*
90'	Zidane *foul*

Scorers (Spain)

| Villa *(pen)* | 28' |

Team (Spain)

Casillas	01
Pablo	22
Puyol	05
Sergio Ramos	15
Pernia	03
Fabregas	18
Xavi	08
Alonso	14
Villa	21
Torres	09
Raul	07

Substitutes (Spain)

17 Joaquin > 21 Villa <	54'
11 Luis Garcia > 07 Raul <	54'
16 Senna > 08 Xavi <	72'

Discipline (Spain)

| Puyol
foul | 82' |

Official FIFA Man of the Match
Patrick Vieira

France		Spain
44%	Ball Possession	56%
7	Shots on target	5
3	Shots off target	4
22	Fouls	28
5	Corner Kicks	8
8	Offsides	2

French players pile on top of goalscorer Patrick Vieira whose goal gave France a late and vital lead

determine the sex of poultry". Aragonés was caught on camera calling Henry a "black shit" in October 2004 as he attempted to motivate Reyes, the Frenchman's Arsenal team-mate. He subsequently apologised publicly to Henry, though never privately, with the Spanish football federation handed a paltry £2,000 fine – the equivalent of a day's wages – last March.

This was the first meeting between the 67-year-old Spaniard and the France striker since the incident, and Henry had the last laugh, although he was forced to deny accusations of cheating to win the free-kick that led to France's decisive second goal. Seven minutes from time the Arsenal striker was barged in the chest by Puyol as the pair clashed for a loose ball however as the Arsenal striker went down he clutched his face in howled anguish, as if he had been pole-axed by a flying elbow. But afterwards Henry denied any suggestion of trying to con the referee Roberto Rosetti and claimed that Puyol had committed a "basketball block" on him. "Puyol came up to me afterwards and apologised so how is that cheating?" he said. "Spain's left-back Mariano Perina was going to win the ball, so I don't know why Puyol cut across me, but he did. I don't cheat. People can say whatever they want to say but if any team has been cheated since the beginning of the tournament it's France," he added, referring to Vieira's disallowed goal against South Korea. "Look at the replay, their left-back was going to take the ball and Puyol came across me and blocked me. If that's basketball that's a good block, but we're not playing basketball. In my head I'm not a guy who does go down or cheats."

Spain's coach Luis Aragones did not agree, "For me the referee blew for a non-existent foul for the second goal. However I don't blame the referee because we also made two mistakes late on. They killed us on the counter-attack, but that's football. The players have done their very best, but we wanted more."

great satisfaction to make this record, but let's not forget our main objective is to reach the final."

Brazilian players were simply relieved their much-criticised defence managed to keep a powerful Ghanaian attack at bay. "The Brazilian defence was very good. It was a worry and today there was great calm. We knew the second half would be very difficult, as it was. It was a team playing against Brazil with nothing to lose," Arsenal midfielder Gilberto Silva told reporters.

Ghana coach Ratomir Dujkovic paid tribute to his own side, 'I'm very proud of our players, they fought from

the first minute of the first match to the last minute today. We missed some important chances, they scored three goals. They are a fantastic team and if you give them a fraction of a second they will finish you.'

Dujkovic was banished to the stands at the end of the first half by the Slovakian referee Lubos Michel. "I said it would be better for us if he put on a yellow jersey," he explained.

Spain coach Luis Aragonés refused to apologise before the evening's game for racially abusing Henry, insisting he has "black, Gypsy and Japanese friends, including one whose job is to

DID YOU KNOW?
This was the 700th match in the history of World Cup finals. The French were one of the combatants in the very first game and they also featured in the 600th match four years ago.

France ended Spain's 10 match unbeaten run at the World Cup. It was also a first defeat in 26 international matches for the Spaniards, in a sequence stretching back to a 1-0 loss to Portugal at Euro 2004.

Raul celebrated his 29th birthday on the day of the match. The Real Madrid striker is Spain's all-time leading scorer with 44 goals and made his 99th international appearance against France.

Thierry Henry's goal against Spain marked the first occasion at international level that he had scored following a cross or pass by Zinedine Zidane.

Frank Ribery rounds Iker Casillas to put the French level after Villa's early penalty had given Spain the lead

The France coach Raymond Domenech neatly side-stepped questions about the Henry's play-acting and instead boldly predicted that his side could win the World Cup. "There were a few difficult moments, but we took control as the match went on, I can't predict the future, but all I know is that we want to go further. We want to be in Berlin on July 9. It's our project, that's our plan. We have enormous potential and we can get better. The Brazil game will be the most important of my life. Not many coaches have led a team into the quarter-finals of a World Cup, so I'm satisfied. But we will give them a game."

Zinédine Zidane finished off the night with his late strike to prolong his illustrious career by at least one more game. Despite the pundits being convinced Spain were going to make history with their first competitive win over the French, and with that it would be history for Zizou, it didn't

turn out quite that way. Taking a third-minute corner in front of the Spanish fans, Zidane was greeted with waving hands and a chorus of au revoir.

Some 87 minutes later he was in the opposite corner of a fascinated stadium cutting inside Puyol to drill in France's third past his Bernabéu team-mate Iker Casillas for one of those magic World Cup moments.

The 83rd-minute free-kick that eventually found the head of Vieira was also Zidane's. He departed with

an arm around Fabien Barthez and a massive smile.

So onto Brazil for the French, Zidane's most glorious game in the Final. "That is a memory for the French people. We were very well prepared for this match. We wanted to accomplish something and show the people that we had the qualities, even if in the group stage there were difficult matches. The Spanish made it very difficult for us. The adventure continues. It was a celebration today."

Other News

FIFA confirmed Portuguese midfielder Deco had no case to appeal against his sending off against Holland. Coach Scolari had claimed that the first of Deco's two yellow cards was unjust. In that incident, the midfielder chased after Heitinga and scythed him down from behind after Holland refused to return the ball to the Portuguese. FIFA communications director Markus Siegler confirmed that the governing body had been contacted by the Portuguese Football Federation. "There was a phone call and they were clearly told 'forget it'," he said.

Luis Figo, however, escaped suspension after FIFA said it could not take retrospective action against him despite his headbutt on Mark van Bommel, because the referee saw the incident and only deemed it worthy of a yellow card.

section
five

quarter finals

Day Twenty
Wednesday 28 June 2006

FIFA president Sepp Blatter bullishly declared this summer's finals to be the greatest ever. In an interview to be published in Berlin's Der Tagesspiegel newspaper, Blatter claimed: "This is the best World Cup of all time. Never before has an event been presented in such an emotional and global manner. And from a sporting point of view we're also getting the highest quality." Blatter also said domestic fervour regarding the Germany team was giving coach Jürgen Klinsmann's players a major lift.

"The Germany team is being carried by the enthusiasm in the country," added Blatter. "I'm beginning to ask myself: 'Who can stop these Germans?' Today, all the critics have to say 'Chapeau Herr Klinsmann'. I say that too."

Graham Poll paid the price for his yellow-card blunder by being named among the 14 referees sent home as FIFA's referees committee announced the 12 match officials retained to be in contention to take charge of the remaining eight games of the tournament. Poll, who later announced his international retirement, was not among them and neither was Russian Valentin Ivanov, who presided over the Portugal versus Holland cardfest.

Argentina's Horacio Elizondo was named as the referee in charge of England's quarter-final. He cut short Beckham's involvement in the infamous 2000 FIFA World Club Championship showing him a straight red for a reckless thigh-high challenge on Joe Milian during Manchester United's 1-1 draw with Mexican club side Necaxa, and the dismissal marked the low point of a disastrous competition for United.

Elizondo's selection is controversial given his nationality – Beckham's most high-profile dismissal came against Argentina in the 1998 World Cup. The

Sepp Blatter (left) tipped Franz Beckenbauer's home nation to go all the way in today's press conference

Euro 2004 game between these two nations was soured by the reaction to a decision by Swiss referee Urs Meier, who disallowed what would have been a winning goal from Sol Campbell for a foul by John Terry. Meier was hounded from the game after English newspapers published his email address and he received death threats.

An international referee since 1994, Elizondo is a former PE teacher who lists his hobbies as poetry and golf. He has so far officiated in three World Cup games and dished out 18 yellow cards and one red.

German official Markus Merk was retained despite his flawed handling of Ghana's 2-1 defeat of the USA. Merk drew criticism from both managers after incorrectly awarding a yellow card to Essien and giving the softest penalty of the tournament. It proved to be Ghana's winner. Lubos Michel, the Slovakian who will take charge of Argentina v Germany was favourite to take charge of the final.

Rooney arrived from England's training session to talk about his rapid recovery since April 29, when he stumbled under Paulo Ferreira's tackle He might find himself facing Ferreira

again, with Portugal also a reminder of the quarter-final of Euro 2004 when he left the ground midway through the first half, also with a broken metatarsal, and sat with his girlfriend and his agent in his Lisbon hotel room, watching the television as England went out on penalties. "You don't know what would have happened," he replied when someone suggested his injury had changed the course of that game in Portugal's favour. "I think you've got to try and forget it, really, and look forward. I certainly won't be going into the game thinking about revenge. But it would be nice to beat them."

Rooney was still awaiting his first goal, "Hopefully that first goal will come, but I'm not too worried as long as we can keep winning. I'd go through the tournament not scoring if we can win it."

Rooney conceded it would boost England's chances if his Manchester United colleague Cristiano Ronaldo did not recover from a thigh injury, "Although I want him to be fit it would be nice if he could just miss our game. He's a great player, if he plays it will be a tough job for us. He's a handful for any team but hopefully we can keep him quiet on the day."

Gary Neville looked poised to start the quarter-final after joining his team-mates for full training for the first time in a fortnight. Eriksson would not divulge any details about the formation or make-up of his team to start in Gelsenkirchen, although he revealed he had already made his mind up.

England had used four right-backs so far and it transpired that one of those, Beckham, had talked Eriksson out of using him there against Ecuador. The Swede had been toying with playing him behind Lennon, but the captain was uncertain as to whether his defensive qualities were good enough.

Eriksson, who gave his players a second successive day off training, called the squad to a 7pm meeting to run through the strengths and weaknesses of the team who knocked them out of Euro 2004. The players were briefed the previous night on the underhand tactics that Portugal might employ. Eriksson warned his players about their gamesmanship. Gary Guyan, the FA's video technician, put together a montage of Portugal's games, particularly the defeat of Holland when 16 yellow cards were shown and both teams finished with nine men. England had three on yellow cards from the Ecuador game – Terry, Carragher and Robinson – and Eriksson was anxious not to lose anyone to suspension. His message was to apply good sense. Robinson was booked for wasting time in the second half of the Ecuador game and the FIFA official was asked to define exactly what it takes to commit such an offence.

Scolari, using one of the oldest tricks to motivate his players, tapped into the pride Portuguese players have for their country, stoking up a siege mentality in his squad when his team's head of media, Afonso Melo, accused English newspapers of disrespecting Portugal and its squad. Flanked by Pauleta and Nuno Valente in the media conference, Melo berated English newspapers for their treatment of Portugal. He took one paper to task for publishing what he described as fabricated Pauleta quotes criticising Robinson as their team's weak link, and said English papers had caused great offence by accusing the squad of being "violent and insubordinate".

Big Phil Scolari was beginning to adopt Alex Ferguson's siege mentality approach to motivating his team

Wayne Rooney tells Frank Lampard where he's been going wrong with his shooting, during England's training session

English papers were restricted to three questions after a lengthy portion of the conference in Portuguese. Scolari is known to exploit any detail to achieve victory, and was famous at club level in Brazil for gamesmanship such as ordering ballboys to delay returning the ball.

Deco reiterated his belief that his dismissal against Holland was "unfair" with Scolari publicly wondering whether his side were being punished for the actions of their predecessors. "Portugal is known for what happened in 2002, which is always brought up," said the coach, recalling that Joao Pinto punched a referee after his dismissal against South Korea, was then suspended from all football for three months and never played for his country again.

During Euro 2000, Abel Xavier, Nuno Gomes and Paulo Bento picked up hefty bans for harassing a referee after he awarded a penalty to France in the quarter-final. "The country's record over 2003, 2004, 2005 and 2006 is never shown," claimed Scolari, a disciplinarian who went three years and 46 games without seeing one of his players sent off. "Portugal are not a violent team, but sometimes we are given the image of being undisciplined.

We have to ask whether we played in a disgraceful way, with play-acting, or whether what happened against Holland was brought about by refereeing issues."

However the facts do not back up Scolari's assertion in this instance. FIFA statistics suggest that only Mexico, Holland and Ecuador committed more fouls in this tournament, Portugal's tally currently standing at 78.

In a classic piece of intercontinental tabloidese, it was discovered that an expatriate British academic living in the northern German city of Bremen was the uncle of none other than England's star striker Wayne Rooney! Not only that, but Martin Rooney, 57, spoke fluent German and was more than happy to co-operate with journalists, posing for pictures in an England shirt with his famous surname on the back. ARD, the equivalent of BBC1, broadcast a prime-time feature of Mr Rooney watching his nephew in action against Ecuador from the comfort of his sofa.

However, if he was, as he claimed, Wayne's uncle from the side of his mother, Jeanette, he should have the surname Morrey! Intrigued by ARD's exclusive, journalists quizzed the player at a press conference the next day and were answered simply by a raise of the eyebrows. Wayne's grandmother, Pat Morrey, 75, said, "I haven't heard of him. I think I'd know if he was one of the family. I don't know anyone by that name. I've never heard of him and I doubt any of the family has. I don't know why this man would say such a thing."

Day Twenty-One
Thursday 29 June 2006

Saturday's match could be David Beckham's last at a World Cup should England lose, but the 31-year-old argued: "I wouldn't say it's my biggest game because I've been lucky enough in my career to have be involved in big matches before. Seeing the way the fans are at home, we've always said when we've won big games that to see the fans' reaction is incredible."

Eriksson believed Wayne Rooney was almost back to his best and could handle the expectations of leading England to glory, "All of our players are important and they have to show that on Saturday if we want to win that game. Of course, Wayne Rooney is very special – but all of them are important with a big part to play. It is a pity about the expectation levels everyone places on Wayne Rooney, because I don't think it is fair.

He has been away for a long time. But he is doing a good job and I think he is doing better and better. The expectations will not be too much for him. No."

Rooney was waiting for his first World Cup goal, but was so confidence he considered one day breaking Ronaldo's goal record: "I hope so, yes. You never know what's going to happen. Ronaldo's been some player, one of the best players ever over the past 10 years, and it's great to see him scoring those goals. I'm hungry to score and the sooner I do the better, whether that's the next game or the game after." Rooney also marvelled at the enduring skills of Zidane as he watched France beat Spain on television from the comfort of England's team hotel, "I thought he was brilliant. Zidane and Ronaldo have some critics at this World Cup, which is embarrassing really because they're both world-class players."

Wayne Rooney and partner Coleen McLoughlin stroll through Baden-Baden as the WAGs were allowed into the England camp for one last time before the team face Portugal on Saturday

Captain Beckham warned of the threat of his former Real Madrid team-mate Luis Figo who would operate in a central role in the absence of the suspended Deco. "Luis is one of the best players in the world and has been for many years. He's played for many big clubs and has performed well at the highest level. He is one of the best players around and could cause problems to any team. He is one player you always have to watch."

Asked about comments from FIFA President Sepp Blatter, who accused England of playing negative football against Ecuador, Beckham was diplomatic. "We feel under pressure to perform and win games, and that's what it's all about – winning games. We do it our way. It's up to us to enjoy ourselves and win football matches."

Gary Neville declared himself ready for action, "The calf is fully fit and I'm available for selection. I am certainly more happy than I was a week ago. It has been frustrating for me to be injured during the World Cup, but that can happen to a football player. But I am looking forward. I have enjoyed the last two days training and I am ready."

Neville believed victory against Portugal would mark Eriksson's men down as one of the country's greatest teams matching the accomplishments of Sir Bobby Robson's Italia 90 team. Defeat would condemn them to the massed ranks of under-achievers, as Neville said: "If we fail you as a country on Saturday then we have to hold our hands up and say: 'We haven't delivered, the talk of us actually being potential world champions was rubbish'. We have to respond to the challenge if we want to be recognised as a great England team. Otherwise we will be recognised as a nearly team – a team that promised and had potential but didn't deliver. It's how you are perceived in years to come. The measure of the team will be in this tournament." It was a fiercely positive message, designed to dispel any negative vibes about the team spluttering through their early games, delivered with passion.

But as one injury subsided, so another one occurred. Frank Lampard injured an ankle in a practice match and left the training pitch with an ice pack attached and underwent some intensive treatment with England's medical staff. His ankle was badly swollen, although he was said to be positive about his chances of winning his 45th international cap. England's team doctor Leif Sward and the physiotherapist Gary Lewin would inspect the level of swelling as Lampard tweaked ankle ligaments and may need an injection to relieve the pain. He was limping when he returned to the team hotel. Lampard had a good record of shaking off injuries; Sir Alex once describing him as a "freak" because of the way he never seemed to miss a match.

In-form Germany striker Miroslav Klose pitied Argentina for their 'bad luck' in having to play the hosts. The 1990 finalists are preparing for what could be one of the most thrilling and hard-fought matches of the whole tournament. Backed by a euphoric home crowd, Germany have won all their first four matches – while unbeaten Argentina looked especially

Miroslav Klose takes aim during a session with the German national archery team, another one of coach Jürgen Klinsmann's innovative techniques to improve co-ordination and focus

Who's the real Daddy? Ray Winstone motivates Gary Neville, Steven Gerrard and David Beckham prior to the quarter-final against Portugal

impressive in a 6-0 thrashing of Serbia and Montenegro.

Klose, who has four goals to his name, insisted there was no reason for his country to be 'nervous' about tomorrow's match in Berlin. "We know they are a strong team and were considered favourites to win it all," said the 28-year-old. "But it's bad luck for them to meet us, because we want to reach the next round – and therefore we will beat them. If we keep them under pressure for 90 minutes they will commit mistakes – and then we will capitalise." Germany twice drew 2-2 against Argentina in the first half of 2005.

Arsenal's teenage midfielder Cesc Fabregas admitted Spain's second-round elimination was a double heartbreak. He broke down in tears after the Spaniards slipped to a 3-1 defeat against France. Fabregas had hoped to have better luck with his national team after Arsenal's defeat to Barcelona in last month's Champions League final. "Once again I walk out

as a loser," said the 19-year-old. "It has already happened in the Champions League final and it's painful. I know that I am young and that there will be other tournaments, but time flies and you need to take advantage of these opportunities. We didn't do that against France."

Portugal captain Luis Figo said of England, "We have a deep knowledge of their team. We saw them in the World Cup, we know the way they play and we have to be prepared for anything that could happen on the pitch. We've seen their videos and we have a deep knowledge about them." Figo has particularly strong knowledge of David Beckham after playing with him at Real Madrid for two seasons. "David first is a very good friend of mine. I spent very good time with him in Madrid. I respect him a lot as a player and for me it doesn't matter too much what critics say about him because he always gives his best for his team. He is the captain of England, he is one of the great players right now in football. I just expect Saturday night I will be more happy than him, but in the rest I wish him the best luck, like he did for me."

Beckham missed a penalty in the shoot-out that decided the teams' meeting in Lisbon two years ago. Figo expected Portugal to practise for a similar scenario and did not believe his team-mates would be overawed by anything. "I'm one of the oldest players, but the younger ones are also in great European teams, they do not need my advice. They are experienced and mature." The 33-year-old described this Portugal squad as one that was "still making history" as it sought to at least emulate the achievements of the 1966 team that reached the semi-finals.

Tough guy actor Ray Winstone recorded a message, borrowing from Winston Churchill's wartime orations and stirring scenes from Shakespeare's Henry V, to be played in the England dressing room ahead of the clash with Portugal. BAFTA-winner Ray, whose screen hits include Scum, Cold Mountain, Nil By Mouth and Sexy Beast, filmed his patriotic talk for the FA. He had shared lunch with the squad at the England team hotel after meeting them at a Buhlertal training session and will be in Gelsenkirchen to cheer them on the pitch.

Ray, 49, was in Germany helping the FA as an unofficial fans' liaison officer. The East End hardman, a former amateur boxer, also wrote a motivational letter before the win over Ecuador. It was pinned to a changing room wall and read to the players. Ray said, "I've talked to our players and they have a real air of confidence about them. We have a duty to keep backing them. We're all Englishmen together and the players have a pride and a passion to win this World Cup for England. I've known some of them a while, Rio Ferdinand, Frank Lampard, Joey Cole, David James, John Terry. It's vital we give them our full support. We're creeping through this tournament very nicely. We can march quietly through to the final and then bash someone 5-0. Now we've got Wayne Rooney back to fitness, Ashley Cole was fantastic against Ecuador and Owen Hargreaves is the worker that every great team needs. I've talked to a lot of fans and the feeling on the street is that they're happy with the way our team's going."

Ray planned to mingle with England fans in Düsseldorf and Dortmund urging them to be on best behaviour. He said: "I've been travelling for years with England and West Ham and seen a lot of things. But at the European Championships in Portugal two years ago I sensed a real change in attitude among our supporters. Society is changing, football has become a much bigger spectacle and there's no room for bad behaviour. I don't want to see it and the real fans don't want to see it. England fans still get the blame for a lot of stuff and my priority is to help clear our name."

Winstone had witnessed the trouble which led to more than 200 England fans being arrested in Stuttgart. But he insisted: "Those disturbances centred round one bar. It was an isolated incident. You can't pin it on 40,000 fans when 200 misbehave. Those fans who have been arrested have already had their reminder. The message is we don't want them here if they're going to behave like that."

Ray defended his involvement in the anti-violence campaign despite the brutal nature of many of his roles, "I've played a man who beats his wife and a man who rapes his kids. That's what I do for a job. It does not mean I'm like that. I've never had a fight at a football match in my life."

DID YOU KNOW?

The +Teamgeist ball, which was used in the World Cup finals brought much criticism from goalkeepers deceived by the flight of the ball. Right from Philipp Lahm's opening goal of the tournament, the ball, made of 14 panels and constructed using thermal bonding rather than stitching to hold it together, when struck off centre swerved in flight in unpredictable fashion. England keeper Paul Robinson had been so worried by the new ball he had been practising with it for the last month of the domestic season.

Portugal's Cristiano Ronaldo was voted pin-up boy of the year by Dutch gay magazine Krant.

Each of the competing nations travelled in a coach with a message of encouragement emblazoned on the side. The French coach borrowed from their famous constitutional phrase to espouse 'Liberté, Egalité, Jules Rimet'.

Day Twenty-Two
Friday 30 June 2006

Argentina 1 v Germany 1
*After extra time, Germany won 4-2 on penalties
Olympiastadion, Berlin   Attendance: 72,000
Kick-off: 5pm   Temperature: 31°C
Referee: Lubos Michel

Fisticuffs As Germany Bid Adios To Argentina

A tense quarter-final ends with a victory for Germany on penalties, which sparks a confrontation between both sets of players and benches including Germany coach Jürgen Klinsmann

Argentina Scorers		Germany Scorers	
49'	Ayala	Klose	80'

Team

Argentina		Germany	
01	Abbondanzieri	Lehmann	01
03	Sorin	Friedrich	03
02	Ayala	Mertesacker	17
04	Coloccini	Metzelder	21
06	Heinze	Lahm	16
18	Rodriguez	Schweinsteiger	07
22	Gonzalez	Frings	08
10	Riquelme	Ballack	13
08	Mascherano	Schneider	19
09	Crespo	Klose	11
11	Tevez	Podolski	20

Substitutes

Argentina		Germany	
71'	> 12 Franco < 01 Abbondanzieri	22 Odonkor > 19 Schneider <	62'
72'	> 05 Cambiasso < 10 Riquelme	18 Borowski > 07 Schweinsteiger <	74'
78'	> 20 Cruz < 09 Crespo	10 Neuville > 11 Klose <	85'

Discipline

Argentina		Germany	
46'	Sorin *foul*	Podolski *foul*	03'
60'	Mascherano *foul*	Odonkor *foul*	90'
88'	Rodriguez *diving*	Friedrich *foul*	114'
96'	Cruz *foul*		
	Cufre *(post match) violent conduct*		

Official FIFA Man of the Match
Michael Ballack

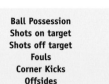

Argentina		Germany
53%	Ball Possession	47%
5	Shots on target	7
8	Shots off target	7
30	Fouls	23
6	Corner Kicks	4
3	Offsides	3

"Today was a match-up between the two best teams in the tournament so far. I told them that they should just remain patient. Roberto Ayala's header for their goal was a beauty, but I was never worried about the fact that we were behind." Jürgen Klinsmann (Germany)

Jens Lehmann makes his second save of the penalty competition, this time from Esteban Cambiasso, to send Argentina home and Germany into the semis

David Beckham, seven appearances from the international century mark, declared it would give him immense pride if he managed to achieve the caps tally of two of his heroes in Bobby Charlton and 1966 World Cup-winning skipper Bobby Moore.

Beckham said, "To reach a hundred caps would be an incredibly proud moment for me because the players who are above 90 and a hundred are those I have always looked up to in my career. When I went above Bryan Robson, who was one of my heroes, I was very proud to do that but there are other heroes, Sir Bobby Charlton who has 106 caps and Bobby Moore with 108. To think I started as a youngster at Bobby Charlton's soccer school, it's been an incredible journey for me."

Scolari stirred it up when he said he was 'proud' to be considered for the England job and if the FA approached him again in the future he might be willing to 'do a deal'.

Scolari, speaking at Portugal's Marienfeld training camp commented, "I have been very proud about the proposal of the English FA, but the timing was not correct. I have some ideals in my life and I try to show those to my players so I cannot break them. In the future who knows? If the English FA comes with another proposal perhaps we can do a deal, but who knows what the future holds."

Injury doubt Frank Lampard took part in the afternoon's final training session in Gelsenkirchen. Eriksson trusted him to recapture his goal touch. "I think he's been unlucky," said the Swede. "He's had a lot of shots so far and that is good. It will come for him. The important thing in football is you create chances and are

> "Am I going to stay on as Argentina manager? No, I think it's time for me to go. It's the end of an era."
>
> José Pekerman
> (Argentina)

Berlin erupts in celebration after the host nation reaches the semi-final

DID YOU KNOW?
Germany's progress continues a trend since 1984 that the hosts have reached at least the semi-finals in a major championship on European soil. Germany retain their perfect record in World Cup penalty shoot-outs, recording their fourth straight triumph. The only German ever to miss a spot-kick in 18 attempts in World Cup shoot-outs is Uli Stielike in 1982 against France.

For Argentina it was their first World Cup penalty shoot-out defeat, having won their previous three. Roberto Ayala had earlier become the first player to beat the German defence in 336 minutes of play in this World Cup since Paolo Wanchope's second goal in the opening game.

The dismissal of unused Argentine substitute Leandro Cufre in the scuffle that directly followed the penalty shoot-out made him a record 10th Argentine to be sent off at the World Cup finals and the second to be dismissed whilst not officially on the field of play following Claudio Cannigia's red card in 2002 against Sweden for abusing the referee from the touchline.

on the end of them. Sooner or later, if that happens you will score goals."

But Steven Gerrard believed his midfield partner could be suffering from self doubt, "There is that fine line between not scoring and scoring. I think scoring goals gives you confidence and because Frank has scored so many goals for Chelsea and England over the last couple of years, because he hasn't scored in this competition he is maybe doubting himself."

Look, it wasn't only England introspectively worried about performance. "We're doing our best to improve," said Henry on behalf of France. "We've got to raise our level," Mario Zagallo, Brazil's veteran assistant coach, remarked. "What's most important for a team that wants to win the title," he added, "is to know how to give more at the key moment."

Gerrard denied Scolari had the psychological upper hand, "Do we feel Scolari has the edge over us? No. You see this kind of stuff on television and think about it beforehand. But once that whistle goes for the start of the game, we are not going to be worried about their manager or who they have got missing. All we will be focused on is who we are up against and trying to get that right result. I think it helps as a player, knowing that their manager has beat us a couple of times in the past. We need to put a stop to

that and make sure our manager gets one over on him. We would like to achieve that."

Gerrard had a score to settle with the Portuguese after the experience of two years ago as well as Liverpool's Champions League exit at the hands of Benfica last season, "I have had a couple of bad experiences against Portuguese opposition. Obviously, Simao ruined our Champions League run this year and I am still hurting from the Euros two years ago. I don't want to say the word `revenge', but it will be nice to get one over on them."

Forgotten man Theo Walcott was making a video diary of his own adventure, to show his friends and family, "I'm filming myself every day on my camcorder, how I'm feeling and how training has gone. I may even interview a couple of the lads, it's good fun to do. I'm saying things into the camcorder about training, how well I'm doing, how the game went the other day, the heat. That kind of stuff. My dad wants to know how I'm doing in training but I'm not really telling him because I'm putting it on the camcorder – so he'll see soon!"

Walcott's incredible pace was the first thing to catch the eye of his England team-mates, "In this squad my pace is up there and it's a good thing for defenders to train against because they are going to find it a lot

Italy 3 v Ukraine 0

AOL Arena, Hamburg
Attendance: 50,000
Kick-off: 9pm   Temperature: 22°C
Referee: Frank De Bleeckere

Italy Turn On The Style

With the Argentinians
packing their bags,
Italy look like potential
winners as they clinically
dispose of Ukraine

Scorers

| 6' | Zambrotta |
| 59', 69' | Toni |

Team

01	Buffon
19	Zambrotta
05	Cannavaro
06	Barzagli
03	Grosso
20	Perrotta
21	Pirlo
08	Gattuso
16	Camoranesi
09	Toni
10	Totti

Substitutes

68'	>	17 Barone
	<	21 Pirlo
68'	>	22 Oddo
	<	16 Camoranesi
76'	>	02 Zaccardo
	<	08 Gattuso

Discipline

Scorers

Team

Shovkovskiy	01
Nesmachniy	02
Sviderskiy	22
Rusol	06
Tymoschuk	04
Shelayev	08
Gusev	09
Gusin	14
Kalinichenko	19
Milevskiy	15
Shevchenko	07

Substitutes

16 Vorobey	>	
22 Sviderskiy	<	20'
17 Vashchuk	>	
06 Rusol	<	45'
20 Byelik	>	
15 Milevskiy	<	72'

Discipline

Sviderskiy *foul*	16'
Kalinichenko *foul*	21'
Milevskiy *persistent fouling*	67'

Official FIFA Man of the Match
Gennaro Gattuso

59%	Ball Possession	41%
9	Shots on target	6
3	Shots off target	9
14	Fouls	24
1	Corner Kicks	3
2	Offsides	2

in the World Cup – including Cristiano Ronaldo coming up. A few people have talked about my pace, finishing and my touch. I'm trying to improve all of those as you do when you are a young player. Hopefully I'll develop into a very good player one day."

And so to the games.

Players of both teams clashed on the pitch after Germany beat Argentina 4-2 on penalties, the match having finished 1-1 after extra-time. German team manager Oliver Bierhoff was at the centre of the on-pitch fracas and incurred the wrath of the Argentina players in the seconds that followed their exit. FIFA officials and referee Lubos Michel were all caught up in the melée; punches and kicks were thrown in chaotic scenes which went on for 90 seconds in front of a 72,000 crowd and a massive global TV audience.

Italy's Gianluca Zambrotta scores the opening goal of the match

The trouble started when Tim Borowski gestured towards the Argentina players to "keep quiet" having scored his penalty to make it 4-2 in Germany's favour. Several of the South American players walked towards him and when the final Argentina spot-kick was saved, Coloccini approached Neuville and punches were thrown.

German captain Ballack said the hosts deserved to beat Argentina. "That was sensational. The match was maybe not so interesting for spectators but it was a match at a very high level. The team fought to the end. Of

course, there's always luck when it comes to penalties, but I think the team really deserved to win."

Klinsmann added: "It's difficult to find words. I'm incredibly happy, proud and thankful. The fantastic crowd carried us, they believed in us. We knew that even down a goal we'd come back. We were convinced that if we got to penalties we'd advance. The belief we have in ourselves is really strong. This is a team that's grown together over the past six weeks and we want to be world champions."

José Pekerman quit as coach at his post-match press conference, remarking, "It was a very exciting match. Argentina also played like favourites and gave of their best although they lost. The penalties were a consequence of a very even match. It's a shame for Argentina who played very well today and in the whole championship."

Lehmann, who saved two penalties in the shootout from Ayala and Cambiasso to become an instant national hero, was embraced by rival keeper Oliver Kahn before the spot-kicks. He responded by keeping out Argentina's second and fourth penalties, saying: "To win the quarter-final is fantastic for us. We had super shots.

And it's just expected that a German goalkeeper makes the saves."

Ballack, referring to Argentina's opening goal scored by Ayala after 49 minutes, said: 'It was their first chance on that set piece. We knew how they'd do their set pieces. It was a super header from him but our team fought back hard and scored a beautiful goal."

FIFA would inevitably hold an inquiry as the ugly scenes at the end dominated events. At least one German player was left lying on the grass after being kicked. Thorsten Frings condemned Argentina's behaviour, "It was typical Argentinian. They are bad losers and the pictures just show it. They completely lost their minds. We tried to calm them down, but I just saw them being all over Per Mertesacker. It just shows they are bad sports and are badly behaved. I hope their players get suspended."

Argentina's Leandro Cufre, an unused substitute, was shown the red card by the referee for his part in the melée after he was seen kicking Mertesacker, who commented, "They are no choirboys, that's for sure. One of their players attacked me even though I did not do anything, and he got the red card. I have three or four

Other News

Italy's players dedicated their victory to Gianluca Pessotto a recently retired former Italian international, who had fallen from a window at Juventus' club headquarters in what was believed to be a suicide bid as he struggled to cope with life after playing in his new job as a team administrator for his former club. Pessotto was seen throwing himself 10 metres into the club's car park from the second floor whilst holding a rosary. Alessandro Del Piero, Gianluca Zambrotta and assistant manager Ciro Ferrara had left the Azzurri camp prior to the quarter-final to rush to see the stricken Pessotto in his hospital bed. Doctors reported that his multiple fractures were serious, but not life threatening.

red marks on my thigh and then he kicked me again in the groin. I cannot understand that it turned into so much aggression. He behaved in a very unsportsmanlike way and I asked him why he did that and then he completely lost it again."

Bierhoff said he had intervened after seeing Mertesacker targeted, "Per was angry about what was a very unsporting thing to do and the players started going at each other. I saw that and wanted to put myself between them so the players didn't do anything stupid."

Marcello Lippi won four Champions League finals and five Italian titles with Juventus, but leading his country to a World Cup semi-final against

Germany felt particularly special. "The fact that we've made it to the semi-finals is a great move forward. I've taken teams to four Champions League finals but the emotions I'm having in the World Cup I've never had before."

He hopes the adventure will not end there, saying "everything is possible now". Parallels are being inevitably drawn with 1982, when Italy won the World Cup amid a match-fixing scandal, having started the tournament slowly.

"I hope there are parallels, but I can't find any right now," Lippi said. "Every team that wins the World Cup starts out slowly, except Brazil, who

always win all their matches. No-one wants to play them. Good teams build their confidence slowly and improve as they go along... Each team has its own traits, its own features. We will never play like Brazil, but Brazil will never play like we do."

Two sharp saves from Buffon and a goalline clearance from the impressive Zambrotta kept Italy ahead before Toni scored the first of his two goals.

A sense of Italian destiny was completed when the bar came to their rescue at 2-0. The only goal they have so far conceded at this World Cup was an own-goal by Cristian Zaccardo.

Zambrotta scored an early goal with the aid of poor goalkeeping, set up the third and cleared off the line in between. Gattuso was eye-catching in midfield. There were flashes from Totti; from his cross Toni headed in at a vital moment. Less than 60 seconds earlier Buffon had saved well from Gusev. Then Zambrotta intervened when Kalinichenko sent a loose ball goalwards. That came during Ukraine's most dangerous period, with Buffon earlier pushing a downward header from Gusin on to a post.

Shevchenko did not pose the danger Italy may feared, getting scant service in surely his last World Cup game. He blew kisses to celebrating Italy supporters at the end, saying 'farewell' as he prepared for a new career at Chelsea.

Lippi was delighted with Luca Toni's first goals of the tournament. "He came close to scoring before and missed by a matter of centimetres. I told him this morning I thought he would score, maybe twice."

Italy will now take on the hosts on the back of a 23-game unbeaten run. One of those matches was a 4-1 win over Germany in March, though they will expect a tougher test from Jürgen Klinsmann's team on Tuesday.

Having defeated West Germany in the final of the 1982 World Cup, Italy hope for similar success against the hosts in Dortmund, although the Germans have famously never lost there.

Luca Toni (second left) stoops to nod in Italy's vital second past Shovkovskyi in the Ukraine goal

Day Twenty-Three
Saturday 1 July 2006

England 0 v Portugal 0
*After extra time, Portugal won 3-1 on penalties
Veltins Arena, Gelsenkirchen   Attendance: 52,000
Kick-off: 5pm   Temperature: 30°C
Referee: Horacio Marcelo Elizondo

Scorers

	Team			Scorers	
01	Robinson		Ricardo	01	
02	Neville		Miguel	13	
06	Terry		Meira	05	
05	Ferdinand		Ricardo Carvalho	16	
03	A Cole		Nuno Valente	14	
16	Hargreaves		Figo	07	
07	Beckham		Maniche	18	
04	Gerrard		Petit	08	
08	Lampard		Tiago	19	
11	J Cole		Ronaldo	17	
09	Rooney		Pauleta	09	

England's Penalty Misery Continues

Tears greet yet another failure from the penalty spot as England bow out

Substitutes

			Substitutes	
51'	> 19 Lennon < 07 Beckham		> 11 Simao < 09 Pauleta	64'
65'	> 21 Crouch < 11 J Cole		> 10 Viana < 19 Tiago	74'
119'	> 15 Carragher < 19 Lennon		> 23 Postiga < 07 Figo	86'

Discipline

			Discipline	
30'	Terry *foul*		Petit *foul*	44'
62'	Rooney *violent conduct*		Ricardo Carvalho *foul*	111'
106'	Hargreaves *dissent*			

Official FIFA Man of the Match
Owen Hargreaves

49%	Ball Possession	51%
7	Shots on target	15
4	Shots off target	11
18	Fouls	10
6	Corner Kicks	4
0	Offsides	3

I wasn't quite doing my own camcording like Theo, but in the Hold The Back Page studio, I spent this week pre-recording, as PR guru Max Clifford could only make it into the studios on Tuesday lunch time, while the Minister of Sport Richard Caborn was only available at Wednesday at 9am.

The Minister was in fine form in the webcast alongside George Cohen, with Max's clips on the big screen. During the chat I asked the Minister what we could expect if England actually won the World Cup? Caborn, who supports Sheffield United, remarked, "I think the boys of 66 have been recognised in many ways. As for this one, we will just have to wait and see. There's all sorts of ideas flying around, such as to have a day's holiday. If we win it, I tell you the nation will erupt, productivity will go up, I think Gordon Brown might even give us tax relief."

I also interviewed Sir Geoff Hurst on his mobile phone out in Germany, and, while George Cohen was sticking to his guns that Beckham should be dropped to inject pace down the right, the World Cup hat-trick hero back tracked on comments attributed to

him before the Ecuador game that he too would axe the captain.

Cohen told me: "Alf Ramsey dropped Jimmy Greaves who was the greatest goalscorer I'd ever seen. In fact he didn't bring Jimmy back when he had recovered from injury and kept faith with Geoff Hurst. Nobody would have contemplated going into that World Cup of dropping Jimmy. It takes big people to make big decisions and they also make big mistakes, but they are big enough to rectify them. Eriksson is not big enough to rectify his mistakes and I don't know what advice, if any, he is getting from Steve McClaren. So, yes I am afraid I would drop Beckham even though he scored that goal that took us through."

Sir Geoff, an ambassador for World Cup sponsors McDonalds, was at pains to clarify the hitherto public perception that he would also drop Beckham, "You know what it's like in the media, Harry. You say something on radio and then it's picked up in the papers. I said that when Aarron Lennon came on as a substitute England played well and he gave them pace in the side. My point is that he should come on in the latter stages of games when players are tired, and I felt David Beckham was physically

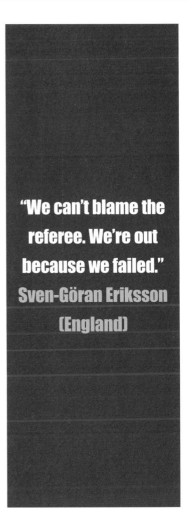

"We can't blame the referee. We're out because we failed."
Sven-Göran Eriksson (England)

(left) Was it a stamp? (right) Referee Elizondo thought so. Wayne Rooney looks in disbelief as the Argentinean referee wields a red card in his direction

PR guru Max Clifford came into the Hold The Back page studios to reveal the incredible story of four star players who had bet on their own team against Premiership rules

DID YOU KNOW?
This was Portugal's first draw in the World Cup in their 17th game. They are now unbeaten in 17 competitive internationals and have gone 301 minutes of World Cup football since conceding a goal against Mexico in the final group match.

Ricardo became the first goalkeeper to save 3 penalties in a World Cup shoot-out.

The Minister for Sport, Richard Caborn, revealed that there would probably be a public holiday if England were to win the World Cup

sick, so should have come off. I want to make it clear that I feel that David Beckham is an important and integral part of the squad that can win the World Cup. But when it comes to tactical substitutions it would help to inject some pace into the side, but I didn't suggest dropping Beckham.'

Caborn praised the England fans out in Germany and believed their general good behaviour will enhance England's chances of staging the World Cup in 2018. "They've been absolutely fantastic," argued the Minister, who has been out to the finals in Germany to watch England. Caborn was not sweeping under the carpet the isolated incident, but he insisted: "Let's keep this in proportion, and make it clear we are not going back to the dark days a decade or so ago. The reason for that is we have taken 3,500 of these thugs out of circulation with the banning orders preventing them from travelling. Go back to Euro 2004 and the policing was successful and again in the last World Cup in Korean and Japan. Yes, there were 300 or 400 arrests in Stuttgart, but there were only three charged and compare that to 25 charged for a brawl in the car park at Ascot! Of course there are a few idiots on the fringes who get arrested and they get onto the back pages, but there were 60,000 in that square and only three arrested, and that's not bad by any stretch of the imagination."

England football fans travelled in unprecedented numbers to watch

Cristiano Ronaldo celebrates the penalty which disposed of England

their team take on Portugal, with 100,000 fans, the largest movement of supporters for a sports event involving a British team, descending on Gelsenkirchen, a mining town in the industrial Ruhr area and one of the smallest World Cup host cities, with a population of 270,000.

But nothing could have prepared England's massed phalanx of fans for yet another day of drama and intrigue.

Was it Rooney to blame for the stamp? Or, perhaps, his United team-mate Ronaldo for goading him into the push? The Ronaldo wink to the bench said it all.

Little wonder Alan Shearer suggested that Rooney might 'put one on him' when they re-unite at the Carrington training ground. Probably Ronaldo will end up at Real to avoid the inevitable confrontation.

It was a limp exit...penalties again. But this time it was a feeble excuse. England should have beaten Portugal – and even with 10-men looked the better side. It was a waste. A pity. A mixture of anger and frustration.

So let's blame Sven.

No guile, but plenty of guts. Heroics for hanging on to the shootout.

But England, and Eriksson in particular, could expect an avalanche of criticism, and he wasn't to be disappointed. It was vastly justified. For England's first foreign coach departs shouldering the blame for the catalogue of errors that lie underneath the surface of yet another tearful shootout calamity.

When Lampard stepped up to take England's first spot kick, you couldn't help wondering whether the Chelsea midfield player had been picked out for such duty by the luck of some per-verted draw. Frank has had something like 30 shots in this tournament without once finding the net and even Gerrard was moved to point out in the build up to England's downfall that his midfield partner might just be suffering a confidence crisis. So, pick Lampard for the first penalty? Well, what an own goal.

But it was not the first, and by no means the worst. England had three key penalty takers missing when it came to write down those first five names.

Rooney sent off, Michael Owen back home and Beckham off injured. It merely compounded the first and the biggest blunder in selecting the squad....one injured striker (Rooney), one injury prone striker (Owen), one who isn't a prolific scorer (Crouch), and one Eriksson hadn't even seen and didn't give a kick to in the entire tournament (Walcott).

England were overloaded with midfield players and not enough genuine goalscorers. Sven had told us it would be alright, that he knew what he was doing. He didn't.

He should have picked Defoe. Pace frightens defenders and that was evident the moment Lennon came on. His tactics switched back and forth, confused rather than clarified, and in this game he went for a defensive midfielder in Hargreaves when every-one wanted a more positive approach with Carrick.

So England's 'Golden Generation' leave the World Cup without ever impressing. No-one would have minded, but once again any chance of

Victoria Beckham hugs her tearful son Brooklyn following England's defeat

England's massed army of fans watching on the big screen in Gelsenkirchen experience that all too familiar feeling

coming good at the end was derailed by a penalty shoot out. At least Hargreaves scored. Well, he does play in Germany!

Sven had risked all on Rooney, and in truth the boy wasn't up to it when it mattered. He left the World Cup without a goal. Worse still, after all the fuss over his broken metatarsal, it was his short fuse that let him and the country down. Rooney is a beautiful artist with the ball, but a brute without it, with a tendency to want to do harm. All he achieved was to spoil England's chances.

Ok, it was bravery beyond the call of duty for the 10-men, but the wound was self-inflicted.

I am not saying 'point an accusing finger at Wayne', because look at the repercussions Beckham suffered when he was shown the red against Argentina in 98. No-one wants a repetition of such nastiness.

So, farewell the Swede, who has failed now in three big tournaments to get past the last eight. And welcome to Steve McClaren who has been sitting beside Sven for so many years. Let's hope he hasn't learned a single thing.

Funny, the thought haunts me that I just wish it was Big Phil taking over instead of Big Mac.

At least Eriksson immediately admitted it was 'just not good enough' after his five-year reign came to an end as Lampard, Gerrard and Carragher all missed penalties allowing Ronaldo to score the crucial spot-kick which saw Portugal into only their second World Cup semi-final.

It all came after Rooney's red following a tangle which ended with him stamping on the groin of Chelsea defender Ricardo Carvalho. I thought the Argentine ref wasn't going to take any action until Ronaldo turned up and Rooney reacted with a shove. The nation will take sides on who is the villain. Eriksson apportioned blame to Rooney, when he observed, "I don't think we can complain about the red card from what I saw on the TV. Maybe we should have had a free-kick when there was a tangle, but it went on and on and the referee was there."

Sven knew England had blown the chance of reaching a final he believed was there for the taking. "I

DID YOU KNOW?

Out of 14 penalties taken by Englishmen in World Cup shoot-outs, they have scored from 7, had six saved and missed one. By contrast, England's opposition have scored 11 out of their 14 attempts with David Seaman saving one spot-kick against Argentina, while the two others were missed by Portuguese players in this shootout.

Rooney became the third England player to be sent off in a World Cup match, following Ray Wilkins' dismissal against Morocco in 1986 and David Beckham's against Argentina in 1998.

Eriksson ended his reign with an unbeaten run of 11 games (9 wins and two draws).

David Beckham made his tenth appearance as England captain in the World Cup finals equalling the England record held by Billy Wright and Bobby Moore.

Brazil 0 v France 1
Commerzbank Arena, Frankfurt
Attendance: 48,000
Kick-off: 9pm   Temperature: 24°C
Referee: Luis Medina Cantalejo

Vive La France

Scorers

Team

01	Dida
02	Cafu
03	Lucio
04	Juan
06	Roberto Carlos
19	Juninho
17	Silva
11	Ze Roberto
08	Kaka
10	Ronaldinho
09	Ronaldo

Substitutes

63'	> 07 Adriano < 19 Juninho
76'	> 13 Cicinho < 02 Cafu
79'	> 23 Robinho < 08 Kaka

Discipline

25'	Cafu *foul*
45'	Juan *foul*
45'	Ronaldo *dissent*
75'	Lucio *foul*

Thierry Henry's goal rounds off a World class display from the French, who disposed of Brazil and look to be changing up the gears in readiness for the semi-finals

Scorers

Henry   57'

Team

Barthez	16
Sagnol	19
Thuram	15
Gallas	05
Abidal	03
Ribery	22
Makelele	06
Vieira	04
Zidane	10
Malouda	07
Henry	12

Substitutes

09 Govou > 22 Ribery <	76'
11 Wiltord > 07 Malouda <	81'
14 Saha > 12 Henry <	85'

Discipline

Sagnol *foul*	73'
Saha *foul*	87'
Thuram *time wasting*	88'

Official FIFA Man of the Match
Zinedine Zidane

44%	**Ball Possession**	56%
5	**Shots on target**	6
6	**Shots off target**	7
17	**Fouls**	21
5	**Corner Kicks**	7
2	**Offsides**	5

An unmarked Thierry Henry steers Zidane's free-kick past Dida to earn France a place in the semi-finals

opportunities. We were forced to shoot from long-distance and that is not something the Portugal players do very well. England did well to close the space.'

Scolari knew the shoot-out could have gone either way. "I could not imagine winning or losing. I was just waiting to see what happens. Ricardo has developed very well in terms of saving spot-kicks in the past years and he stopped three penalties today. If I had to select a player it would have been Ricardo because he saved three penalties. He was happy to be in the right place. You have to give him more merit for saving than the English players (for not scoring). But they can select any one of the opponents as long as we win."

Ricardo said his exploits were down to more than luck. "Penalty shootouts are a lottery, but I train well too, but I'm not going to tell you my secrets, then you will know everything," he said. The normally jovial keeper became visibly irate at a reporter who suggested he was just lucky and insisted: "It wasn't luck – watch the television. I'm not a hero. The hero is the whole Portugal team, the great player is everybody."

So how do the Germans do it? Apparently Germany's painstaking preparation gave goalkeeper Jens Lehmann a crucial advantage in the penalty shootout.

Few people at the Olympiastadion on Friday noticed, but before each of the Argentina penalties Lehmann was handed a slip of paper by the coaching

feel sad and a bit angry because we should be in the tournament. But we are not and we can't blame the referee or somebody else. I'm sorry for the team, the squad and the fans who were fantastic. They deserve to have a team in the semi-final or the final. The quarter-finals four years and two years ago was OK. This time it is not good enough. These players should at least have been in the final. It's more our fault rather than the force of Portugal."

Ironically, Hargreaves. who has taken so much flak, was the Man of the Match, the only England player to score in the

shoot-out, and England fans chanted: 'There's only one Owen Hargreaves.'

Frank Lampard broke down in tears along with most of his team-mates. He said: "It is the worst feeling I've ever experienced. I don't want to talk too much and I am devastated. I cried a couple of times at the end of the game. The World Cup is the ultimate. Deep down I really believed we could go all the way."

Scolari paid tribute to England for the way they fought with 10 men.

"I want to value the attitude of the English players. It looked like 11 against 11. They did not give us many

"We can only really say we have succeeded if we win on July 9, so none of us are saying 'cockadoodle-doo'."
Raymond Domenech (France)

Quarter-Final Stats

This is only the fourth time in World Cup history that the four semi-finalists are all-European, and the first since 1982. Coincidentally, three of those same four are in the 2006 semi-finals (France, Germany and Italy) with Poland failing to make it in this tournament.

After the four quarter finals, bookings now total a competition record of 332, with another record of 27 red cards.

The total goals tally of 138 at this stage is the lowest since the increase of matches in 1998, while we still await the first hat-trick.

staff with an analysis of where each player usually put his shot. Lehmann saved two of the penalties and Germany won the shootout 4-2, after the match had finished 1-1 at the end of 120 minutes.

The preparation was done, as usual, by Germany's chief scout Urs Siegenthaler, a Swiss who may well be the hardest working man at this World Cup. "Before both our knockout games against Sweden and Argentina we gave Lehmann information on the possible penalty takers," team manager Oliver Bierhoff said at a news conference. "Lehmann saw videos of all the penalties Argentina have taken in the past two years, with a list of the specific types of penalty the players usually take. He then had to briefly consult the notes with (goal-keeping coach) Andreas Köpke, because you never know until the shootout who will be on the list.' Bierhoff added: "We then just told him to save two penalties, in case he forgot."

More shocks as Brazil crashed out and struggled to come to terms with a 1-0 quarter-final defeat by France that ended their dreams of winning a sixth World Cup.

Brazil, who are the World, Copa America and Confederations Cup champions, were hot favourites to win the tournament with their embarrassing array of talent. Instead, they made a relatively early exit after their third successive defeat to France at a World Cup finals. Brazil lost on penalties after a 1-1 draw at the same stage of the

1986 World Cup and a 3-0 defeat in the 1998 final. "There's no describing our disappointment," said Ronaldinho, who failed throughout the tournament to live up to his billing as the World Player of the Year. "It's an enormous sadness especially after a long period in which we've become used to winning all the competitions. When you get used to winning and take a knock like this, it's very sad. I wanted to make Brazil champions." Midfielder Kaka said: "You prepare for four years and it's sad to go out this way, it's frustrating. It's a sad day for Brazilians. We never managed to impose our rhythm on the game at any moment."

Fellow midfielder Juninho Pernambucano appeared braced for the reception back home. "We played badly and we didn't deserve to win. We have to accept the criticisms."

The Brazilians were generous in their praise for France captain Zinedine Zidane, who is retiring after the finals. "Unfortunately, he had a great game today and he's a great player," said Kaka. Brazil captain Cafu added:

"It was Zidane who tipped the balance of the game. We left him free for the whole game and leaving Zidane free is very dangerous. He was, without doubt, the Man of the Match."

Zidane said France produced a great performance when they had to. "We needed a great match and we delivered. We fought closely together for a well-deserved victory. Now we'll try to win a place in the final. We don't

want to stop now. This is so beautiful, we want it to carry on."

Goalscorer Thierry Henry said the win was deserved. "We played well. We didn't steal anything from anybody. We had a tactical plan and it worked perfectly. We wanted to prove after what happened in 2002 that we were not rubbish," he added, referring to France's early exit four years ago.

Coach Raymond Domenech again praised his team and reiterated what has been his mantra throughout the tournament – that only victory in the final would satisfy him. "To play Brazil you have to know how to defend because they know how to attack. We had to stake out the field and play, stay strong and battle. If we didn't do that we would die peacefully. They made us suffer a bit at the end when they had some chances, so I would not say we dominated the match – but I would say that we controlled it in the terms of how to play a match against Brazil. Our objective remains the final on July 9, but first we have a tough match with Portugal. We can only really say we have succeeded if we win on July 9 so none of us are saying `cockadoodle-doo'. But we are still in the tournament and that's a good thing.

Maybe we started the tournament slowly, but the teams who were playing well at the start of the tournament are now watching it on TV."

section six

final stage

Day Twenty-Four
Sunday 2 July 2006

A tearful David Beckham quit as England captain after five-and-a-half years at the helm.

He strolled into the media conference, smartly attired in England blazer shirt and tie, hair neatly waxed, held up his hand to halt a premature question and started to read from a pre-prepared script. "I wrote this last night after talking to my family and close friends," he said.

Beckham revealed he had taken the decision some time ago after consulting with his family. He said: "It was the greatest honour of my career when Peter Taylor made me England captain and I fulfilled the England dream. Now I feel is the right time to pass on the armband as we enter a new era. I stress that I want to continue to play for England and help the new manager Steve McClaren and the new captain. This is the most difficult decision of my career, but I hoped to leave on the back of a successful World Cup. Sadly it was not to be. After discussing it with my family, I feel the time is right. I would like to thank all the players and manager for my support as captain, the media and England supporters. For me to do this job has been an absolute honour. I am so proud I lived the dream."

With that Beckham left the stage with tears in his eyes without making any further comment.

Beckham, by his own standards, had a mediocre World Cup and had been in tears when a knee injury forced him to be substituted early in the second half against Portugal. Already there were signs that Lennon would be pushing hard to replace him on the right flank in the near future. Could this be the end for the most famous man in football?

Beckham was a fine England captain, in my opinion. In a two-way street he was proud to wear the armband, and

David Beckham relinquishes the captaincy with the emotions of England's exit from the World Cup still plain to see

he was a stylish ambassador for our game. I recall how Peter Taylor gave him the captaincy in Italy to lead a new vibrant young England team. I can also recall how Sven-Göran Eriksson sat on the fence thinking about whether Beckham should retain the captaincy, and put him on trial for a series of games. I also can reveal that at that time he was leaning toward Sol Campbell as his captain.

Beckham, by his own admission, didn't think of himself as captaincy material when he first got the job, but he grew into the role and had his moment, and in my book can be regarded, for a variety of reasons, as one of the best. Not the best, and actually nowhere near the best, as he never really came close to lifting a trophy for England. But that shouldn't be held against him too much as only Bobby Moore has managed that feat. But looking at what the captaincy did for Beckham leads me to argue the case for considering Rooney as the next captain of England.

What! I can just sense the reaction to that one. 'Surely Harry's had far too much of this blistering heat!'

But think about it. Giving Beckham the captaincy changed his personality on the field. He grew up quickly, grew out of that temperamental streak that got him red carded in the World Cup against Argentina in France in similar circumstances to Rooney in Germany. Rooney is England's future. He can be the pivotal player in the real Golden Generation to come, but only if he curbs that character defect which haunted Beckham.

In his farewell press conference Eriksson must have said 'sorry' nine times in just a few minutes, confessing his final game was his darkest hour. But he also begged leniency for Rooney, "I think that you, much more than me, need Wayne Rooney. He is the golden boy of English football, so don't kill him. If he did it with intention or not, leave it – you need him for the qualification games and to win Euro 2008."

England made Eriksson one of the best-paid football managers in the world, with a salary of £5million, but Eriksson said: "If you talk about other managers at this level, I think they are paid very well. Why shouldn't an international manager be as well paid as a club manager? I'm not the best-paid manager in the world. There are others earning more money than I do. But if you want people in the future to take this job for honour, or whatever it is, I think you will have difficulties to find the right manager."

Whoops, that didn't sound like a ringing endorsement for McClaren.

It later emerged that Beckham has had scans on his injured knee and ankle which showed a tear in his right Achilles tendon and a small "lesion" in the ligaments of his left knee. A spokesman confirmed the England star will undergo a second scan on the injuries with the Real Madrid club doctors present. Beckham had planned to have three weeks' rest before returning to pre-season training with Real, but the injuries could change his schedule.

The two obvious candidates in most people's minds to succeed Beckham as England skipper gave their version of events surrounding Wayne Rooney's dismissal against Portugal. John Terry believed Rooney had been fouled in the lead-up to the red card, "Wayne should have had the free-kick 15-20 seconds beforehand. With any other team, the players go down and then the ref gives a foul, but we are honest players. Wayne tries to stay on his feet and tries to win the ball. He's got two people fighting against him. That's the honesty we show."

Steven Gerrard was livid with Ronaldo provoking the Rooney red, "I saw that, and if it was one of my team-mates I'd be absolutely disgusted in him because there's no need for that. I've seen Ronaldo going over giving the card and I think he's bang out of order."

Of Ronaldo's infamous wink to his team-mates, Gerrard said: "I think that sums him up as a person." Personally, I can't wait until Liverpool meet Manchester United in the Premiership on 22 October – that is if Ronaldo is still a United player by then.

England's team bus had been branded with the large slogan: ONE NATION, ONE TROPHY, ELEVEN LIONS. But the Lions had only whimpered, cried and were on their way home.

England supporters await the arrival of the team's plane at Stansted airport, but the handful present merely reminded everyone of the team's failure to deliver

At 2.15pm three coaches carrying 22 players and the largest retinue in English football history set out from the schloss for the airport, where equal complements of journalists and well-wishers awaited their departure. As the buses passed through the gates of the private terminal, a single St. George's flag fluttered in a child's hand, someone shouted "Auf Wiedersehen Victoria" and the former captain's wife, son Romeo sitting on her knee, waved back.

At 3.42pm local time a BA jet left the tarmac at Baden-Baden carrying the bruised egos and battered reputations of England's beaten squad, the 28th side to leave Germany. Flight BA9200C took 71 minutes, but for so many so-called world class footballers who arrived in Germany with such high aspirations to lift the trophy it was the longest journey back.

Only around 150 die-hard supporters were at Stansted's Business Aviation terminal in the afternoon, to wait patiently in the sweltering heat, peering through the perimeter fences for what turned out to be a mere fleeting glimpse of Eriksson's men, who landed on the far side of the tarmac, around a quarter of a mile away.

Only the southern-based players – and the departing manager – disembarked, along with out-going captain Beckham. The only people lucky enough to get a memento of the occasion were the waiting ground staff, a few of whom picked up autographs and the odd cheeky snap of a Premiership star on a mobile phone.

The plane closed its doors as Rooney and company departed for Manchester, leaving the waiting fans, many of them children, some of whom dashed across the road to try to head off their heroes at the exit, standing. A pitiful ending.

"There are not many of us here, but they should have come off the plane and signed autographs and posed for photos," said Matt Ogilvie, a 17-year-old from Bishop Stortford who is in the England Supporters club. "We are all as disappointed as they are. They are sad – well the whole country is sad, people have been crying too and the players should have come back here to talk to everybody. We had thousands of fans out in Germany, and we all thought this was going to be the year as well."

Frank Lampard, Aaron Lennon and families board the plane at Baden-Baden airport as England say 'Auf Wiedersehen'

Day Twenty-Five
Monday 3 July 2006

Aaron Lennon replaces David Beckham against Portugal as he surely will do on a more permanent basis in the near future

Four years ago as England crashed out tamely to Brazil, my assignment was to seek a mystical crystal ball and predict the line up for the next World Cup. Carrick and Defoe figured prominently in my 2006 Team of the Future, and for a variety of reasons Defoe was left at home (grave error by Sven) and Carrick was edged out of the holding role by Hargreaves (grave error by Sven).

Of course I am allowed one error myself....I picked David Dunn as my wild card extravagant player, but, of course, in my defence, he did suffer a series of injury set backs.

So, let's start again, and look forward to South Africa 2010. In goal, Paul Robinson, who is rapidly developing into a top class goalkeeper. Far too young and inexperienced to be rated world class in 2006, but with a European Championships to come, he will be ready for the next World Cup.

Ashley Cole will still be young enough in four years' time, in fact he should be at his peak, with a step up from Arsenal to Real Madrid, the preferred choice if he wants to get even better. The knowledge and experience gained from playing in La Liga with one of the world's greatest sides will benefit England.

A right-back successor to Gary Neville is a tough call, and I am working on that, but I would love Glen Johnson to learn how to defend to augment his wonderful athleticisim and ability to rampage down the flank.

Rio and Terry would not be my choice for the bid to end 44 years of hurt. England need another solid back line if we are not going to be looking at 48 years of hurt. Terry has been touted as a future England captain,

perhaps sooner rather than later, and Beckham once handed the Chelsea skipper the coveted England armband in this tournament. But Terry showed some shortcomings at times and his swashbuckling, braveheart style cannot hide deficiencies that are exposed at the highest level. Rio has had his time, and so to the new golden generation, and perhaps Spurs manager Martin Jol will be key to England's development.

Ledley King and Michael Dawson have the potential to forge the new generation of centre-backs. With Carrick and Robinson also involved, White Hart Lane might be the home of half of the future England team. England's future depends, in my view, on an injection of pace and penetration into the national side. Aaron Lennon has both, and across North London at the new Emirates Stadium we shall also thrill to the development of Theo Walcott. Walcott and Lennon have pace to burn that can frighten any defence in the world once they gain vital experience, and that is the trick for McClaren, who will be tempted to keep the old guard to qualify for the European Championships.

In four years time Gerrard can still be the influential driving force we all hope for. Rooney will figure for World Cups to come, but English football still has an uncut diamond. Beautiful with the ball, a brute without it, Rooney is the ugly face of English football at the moment, stamping, pushing, spitting mad as he went off reluctantly with a torrent of swear words. Sir Alex is the man to guide English football's No. 1 talent, but I believe there are other young players who can truly become the Golden Generation.

This version looked extremely tarnished with all the glamour belonging to the WAGs. A near-deserted Garibaldi's restaurant and bar will never quite be the same without the Wives and Girlfriends. Only a few days ago Frank Lampard's partner Elen Rives leapt atop its wooden surface, clutching a champagne and Amaretto cocktail. The small spa town of Baden-Baden was back to its sleepy self.

Garibaldi's staff were in philosophical mood at the prospect of losing their best customers. "We survived before they arrived," Norbert the barman said wryly. "And we will survive after they have gone. I am sure they will come back some time."

With the press staying in the same hotel, it was a curious mix enabling Joanne Beckham to take journalists to task in the hotel bar for perceived slights against her brother and Neville Neville – father of Gary – leading impromptu karaoke singsongs, for which he was taken to task by his son after being snapped looking worse for wear at the WAGs' piss-up holding a replica World Cup. It was, at least, the nearest England came to lifting any sort of trophy.

The WAGs 'circus' will be curtailed on FA orders. The FA picked up the £300,000 bill for the wives, girlfriends and children to spent a luxurious week in the Algarve along with the players and entire FA entourage. But the WAG's continual presence in Baden-Baden has raised more than a few eyebrows above the gin and tonics from the FA blazers. One FA insider told me, 'I am not telling you how much the FA spent on that week in the Algarve, and you will probably never find out. We have budgeted for it, but it will be under Operating Costs in the FA accounts. However much we spent isn't the point, because we accepted Sven's explanation that the players deserved, in the way as a bonus, the week in the Algarve with their families to unwind before all the serious training for the World Cup. Well, that was fine, but then we discover all of them turn up in Baden

2006 marked a zenith for the glamourpusses of the WAGs, such as Joe Cole's partner Carly Zucker. Their antics will be curtailed by the FA in future tournaments

Baden. Of course we did not pay a penny toward any of that. But it turned into a circus. Look, we are all saying within the FA that no-one takes their wives and kids to work, so why should the England players?

Will we see this happen again? I doubt it very much. But it needs someone strong to put a stop to it. We shall be looking to see what the new head coach Steve McClaren has to say about it and we are looking for someone bold to take some tough decisions on this one.'

It was hard to assess who drank the most, the WAGs or the fans. In their farewell appearance in these finals, Police estimated that English supporters made up 40,000 of the 45,000 saleable capacity of the Veltins-Arena, with a further 40,000 watching on big screens in two separate public viewing arenas. The total beat the previous record of 70,000 who travelled to Frankfurt for England's opening match.

More than 350,000 supporters attended the venues of England's five matches and Stephen Thomas, assistant chief constable of Greater Manchester, who was in charge of the British policing operation in Germany said: "I think our fans, the real football fans, have been absolutely superb."

There were 224 arrests in Gelsenkirchen, of which 105 were English, held under Germany's preventative detention laws, mostly for minor disorder, including throwing beer over performers on a concert stage. Some showed no interest in watching the match against Portugal, and had spent the duration of the game singing "10 German Bombers".

Out of 6,000 arrests during the tournament about 700 were English supporters, mostly preventative detentions. Thomas said the government, fans' groups and the police had worked hard over the past six years to ensure that hooligan scenes that almost led to England's expulsion from Euro 2000 after riots in Charleroi were never repeated. "Now our reputation as the hooligans of Europe can be finally laid to rest," he said.

A fight of another sort has been predicted between Rooney and Ronaldo when they returned to Manchester. But Ronaldo insisted there is no ill-feeling between the pair and that they had been in contact since the end of the match. Despite some reports suggesting the Portuguese star would be forced to leave United because of the bust-up, Ronaldo says the air has been well and truly cleared. "The things that have been said regarding me and my team-mate and friend Rooney are incredible. Between me and Rooney, there is absolutely no problem. I reiterate, no problem. At the end of the game, we sent each other some text messages and also today. Between the two of us everything has been cleared. He wasn't angry with me and moreover, he told me to completely ignore what the English press has said, that all they wanted was to create confusion but we are already used to that."

Ronaldo shrugged off suggestions that he was responsible for the red card, saying, "I am not a referee."

The inquests were not peculiar to England. There was also plenty of soul searching going on in Brazil and Argentina.

In 2002, Emerson was named his country's skipper, but injury forced him out of the tournament just before it started and he had to watch stand-in skipper Cafu lift the trophy in Japan. On Saturday evening, Emerson, considered the toughest midfielder in the Brazil side, was again reduced to the role of spectator as injury ruled him out of the 1-0 quarter-final defeat to France in Frankfurt, in which Les Bleus dominated the midfield. The loss means that for the first time since 1990, the World Cup final will not feature Brazil and Emerson admitted he was numbed by the biggest failure for the South Americans since that summer in Italy. "I'm just lost at the moment and I don't want to think about the future," said Emerson. "I'm sad because we've made a lot of people cry, including members of my own family. We have to think about putting our club teams on a solid footing again so the national team can do well again."

When Argentina left their base in Herzogenaurach for a flight home from

An England 'fan' is arrested by Gelsenkirchen police on the night of the team's exit, but the level of violence was low amongst generally well-behaved supporters

France's Claude Makelele had proved, alongside Zidane and Vieira, that France's midfield was not the ageing, spent force many thought

Nuremberg, Roberto Ayala told reporters: "I'm sorry for having disillusioned the Argentinean people. Also for not having reached our goal of being among the top four teams in the tournament. I'm sorry for leaving Germany empty-handed when we believed we could have won the game in the 90 minutes." Ayala and Cambiasso were the two Argentina players to have their penalties saved by Lehmann. "I feel a huge anger inside," Ayala revealed. "There's no consolation from scoring the goal during the match because the last thing remains on the mind."

It emerged Diego Maradona was not in Berlin's Olympiastadion to see Argentina's quarter-final defeat because a member of his entourage was not allowed in. FIFA said Maradona had been given four VIP tickets for the match, but wanted to bring in a fifth person whom FIFA had already declared was not welcome. "It has been reported that Diego Maradona arrived at the stadium and then left again because not all of his entourage was allowed in," FIFA spokesman Markus Siegler said. "This was the decision of Diego

Maradona alone. Maradona's delegation was told in advance that one particular person would not get a ticket because this person has been rude repeatedly during the World Cup and even became almost physically aggressive. We're sorry if Diego Maradona didn't want to accept that. He and a certain number of companions are welcome at any time."

Many pundits believed the all-conquering French heroes who won the tournament eight years ago were finished as an international force, but Chelsea midfielder Claude Makelele insisted he had always dismissed such a notion, "In football there's no age, I have always said it. We are proving in football there's no age."

Veterans like Makelele, 33, and 34 year-old Zidane were key to beating Spain and Brazil after a stuttering start. Henry was back to his peak and Marseille's Franck Ribery emerged as one of the stars of the tournament. "Henry is a player that works well," said Makelele. "He accelerates in any time and is a pleasure to have him up front. We all know Zidane, I think his CV speaks for itself."

Next up are Portugal, and Makelele is under no illusions, "We must keep our heads down because we face a serious team that plays very well. There's a place up for grabs for the final and we are in a beautiful position. It's going to be a difficult game and we just have to prepare for it in the same manner we prepared for our previous games."

Jürgen Klinsmann was confident Thorsten Frings would be cleared to play against Italy. FIFA was investigating Frings's role in the melée at the end of Germany's quarter-final victory over Argentina and requested Germany submit a repoort. "I think that he's innocent and he has pleaded not guilty," said Klinsmann. "We shouldn't forget that this was all started by Argentina." FIFA had initially said it was taking no action against any Germany player, but later re-opened the case, citing new evidence. Television executives from Italy said they had found evidence that Frings threw a punch at Cruz in the fracas.

FIFA rejected claims that the belated citing of Frings had anything to do with lobbying from Italy. The Bild newspaper carried a front-page headline, saying "Italians want Frings suspended!"

FIFA communications director Markus Siegler responded: "Let me make it clear, there was no attempt whatever from the Italian federation to incite FIFA into doing something. The footage was not presented to us from Italian TV stations, it was shown in Germany."

The news eventually came that FIFA's disciplinary committee decided Frisk was guilty of violent conduct, ruling that Frings was an 'active participant in the incidents following the final whistle,' and imposed a one-match suspension, with another suspended ban that would come into force should he misbehave again in the next six months. Thus Frings would be available for the final, should Germany beat Italy, or the third-place play-off, but would miss the semi-final.

Germany was most displeased.

Day Twenty-Six
Tuesday 4 July 2006

Germany 0 v Italy 2
*After extra time
Signal Iduna Park, Dortmund   Attendance: 65,000
Kick-off: 9pm   Temperature: 24°C
Ref: Benito Archundia Tellez

Forza Italia

Scorers

Team

01	Lehmann
03	Friedrich
21	Metzelder
17	Mertesacker
16	Lahm
18	Borowski
13	Ballack
05	Kehl
19	Schneider
11	Klose
20	Podolski

Substitutes

72'	> <	07 Schweinsteiger 18 Borowski
83'	> <	22 Odonkor 19 Schneider
111'	> <	10 Neuville 11 Klose

Discipline

40'	Borowski *foul*
56'	Metzelder *foul*

Alessandro Del Piero clinches Italy's place in the World Cup final with a wondrously slick goal

Scorers

Grosso	119'
Del Piero	120'

Team

Buffon	01
Zambrotta	19
Cannavaro	05
Materazzi	23
Grosso	03
Camoranesi	16
Perrotta	20
Gattuso	08
Pirlo	21
Totti	10
Toni	09

Substitutes

11 Gilardino 09 Toni	> <	74'
15 Iaquinta 16 Camoranesi	> <	90'
07 Del Piero 20 Perrotta	> <	104'

Discipline

Camoranesi *foul*	90'

Official FIFA Man of the Match
Andrea Pirlo

42%	Ball Possession	58%
6	Shots on target	11
12	Shots off target	6
19	Fouls	19
4	Corner Kicks	12
2	Offsides	11

Semi-Final

Gennaro Gattuso celebrates Italy's dramatic victory

Rooney broke his silence to plead his innocence, claiming he did not deliberately stamp on Carvalho.

In a carefully prepared statement, he said, "I want to say absolutely categorically that I did not intentionally put my foot down on Ricardo Carvalho. He slid in from behind me and unfortunately ended up in a position where my foot was inevitably going to end up as I kept my balance. That's all there was to it. If you ask any player – and indeed almost any fan – they will tell you that I am straight and honest in the way I play. From what I've seen in the World Cup, most players would have gone to ground at the slightest contact, but my only thought then was to keep possession for England. When the referee produced the red card I was amazed – gob-smacked."

Rooney was "disappointed" with Ronaldo, but promised not to hold a grudge, "I bear no ill feeling to

Cristiano, but am disappointed that he chose to get involved. I suppose I do, though, have to remember that on that particular occasion we were not team-mates."

Players union leader Gordon Taylor was critical of Ronaldo, "It's always disappointing to see players from one team looking to get players from another sent off, be it the Premier League, be it the Football League, be it a World Cup. But it's doubly disappointing when they are colleagues from the same club side. From my point of view, that was hard to stomach."

Slippery Sven will be paid by the FA for the next TWO YEARS for doing absolutely nothing. Eriksson's critics believe he has actually been doing nothing, or very little for English football, for the past five years, so imagine the extent of the outage when in The Express this morning I broke the story of how Eriksson will be paid for two more years by English football. The FA, the fans, and the media might have

> "Our game was on a higher level to Germany's tonight – we hit the post and the bar, and we had the better of the play. The hosts can have no complaints."
> **Marcello Lippi (Italy)**

seen the back of the first foreign coach to the England team – but to still be paying him for two more years is really the final insult.

My FA insider told me, "Sorry I am not prepared to discuss with you the deal that we struck with Sven. It's private and this is not the right time to talk about it. Put it this way, we are honourable people and Sven has still got two more years left on his existing contract."

The absurdity of this 'exit strategy' devised by FA chief executive Brian Barwick will only serve to heighten the belief that greedy Eriksson has been taking English football for a very expensive ride. Barwick and Eriksson, together with an army of lawyers and advisors, thrashed out a severance agreement six months go. Eriksson's contract ran until 2008, but after a series of indiscretions the FA wanted Eriksson out, although he wasn't going to go quietly. Eriksson agreed to wave the compensation on his final two

years, in return for the FA making up the short fall from his lavish £5m a year contract for the first two. In year one, the FA agreed to give Eriksson the full amount, his basic £3m tax free, if he didn't find a new job in the first 12 months. If Eriksson is re-employed the shortfall in his new salary will be paid by the FA up to a maximum of £3m. Any shrewd club hiring Eriksson would give him a low salary for the first two years, knowing the FA will have to foot the rest of the bill.

So English football hasn't really rid itself of Sven – there's two more years of paying him for doing what he does best – nothing.

But Eriksson should have been sacked for the team's incompetence in Germany, the players' failure to match their reputations as some of the best players in the world, his own ineptitude in devising the right formula, or switching to so many different ones. No-one really knew the strategy. Worse still, the suspicion lingers that

he was de-mob happy, so out went all that calculating ice-cool devotion to detail to be replaced by a maverick decision to pick Theo Walcott and gamble on the fitness of Rooney and the injury prone Owen.

Most coaches who failed in Germany were booted out, and if they didn't like it they can sue. Eriksson surely would be ashamed to take legal action against the FA for two more years' money after the summer's events.

Anyway, Barwick argues that three times qualifying is good, three times going past the qualifying groups is even better, and, for most nations, reaching the quarter-finals is acceptable, but perhaps not for England. Well as one FA insider told me, 'Brian has a lot to learn.'

But the man in control at Soho Square has been very economical with the truth. He told us on the appointment of McClaren that it was the unanimous choice of the FA when it was clearly not, he said SuperMac was his first

Eriksson will still be paid up to £3m a year, without the hassle of the press following his every move, thanks to his severance deal with the FA

Jens Lehmann flails in trying to reach Fabio Grosso's wonderstrike which put Italy ahead in the dying seconds

choice, when we all knew it was O'Neill, and he told us he had not offered the job to Big Phil when he had. Now, surely no-one will swallow his warped assessment of Sven, who had the next room to his and so Barwick knew just how motivated and committed Sven was to England's cause.

Out go the hosts. With the semi-final goalless in the last minute of extra-time Italy faced the daunting prospect of a penalty shoot-out with Germany. But for a change the heart-break belonged to the Germans. Lehmann reached Pirlo's drive, but from the corner the playmaker slipped a pass to Grosso and the full-back curled home a beautiful shot from the right with his left foot. In the seconds that were left Alessandro del Piero gathered a reverse pass from a fellow substitute, Gilardino, to curl in a first time shot into the top corner.

Italy needed a measure of luck after 81 minutes when the referee awarded a free-kick some 20 yards out

for an offence that Cannavaro had committed on Podolski inside the area.

It had taken camaraderie, organi-sation and the vocal backing of home crowds to get them this far. But class prevailed and Germany lost an interna-tional in Dortmund for the first time.

Marcelo Lippi felt justice was done and praised the performance of his players and the way they dealt with a vibrant home crowd. "It would have been unjust if we had not won the game or had to go to a penalty shoot-out," Lippi declared. "I think we deserved to win tonight. We were a little better than the German team. We were not that much superior, but we were better. We hit the bar twice and were close a couple of times and in the end we deserved to win. I don't think anyone will doubt that. We are very happy to win such an important match in a ground full of 60,000 cheering Germany supporters and we were able to play such a great match in this atmosphere. The team was

> "A dream has died. It really hurts when the other side delivers a knockout punch right before the final whistle – that takes some coming to terms with."
> Jürgen Klinsmann (Germany)

DID YOU KNOW?
This was the 50th World Cup match to require extra time – the first was a Preliminary Round encounter between Austria and France in 1934 which Austria won 3-2 after the two teams were level at 1-1 after 90 minutes. It was Germany's first international defeat in Dortmund.

Italy reached their sixth World Cup final, denying Germany a record eighth final appearance. Italy have now kept five clean sheets and have conceded only one goal (an own goal by Cristian Zaccardo) in the tournament. Their five shut-outs equals a record for a nation in a World Cup campaign. Italy are now unbeaten in 24 internationals, their best run since 1939. Alessandro del Piero's goal was the 22nd goal scored by a substitute in the current tournament – a new World Cup record beating the 21 set in 2002.

composed on the ball, but we haven't reached the end of the road yet. We want to try to complete the task and we will await to see who our opponents will be in the final."

Among the first to congratulate Lippi and his team was Italian Prime Minister Romano Prodi, who attended the game. "I'm sure all hell broke lose in Italy and everyone was cheering and jubilant because to beat the Germany in their back yard is an amazing achievement," Lippi said.

Prior to travelling to Dortmund, Prodi sent an open letter to the German Chancellor Angela Merkel. In it Prodi congratulated Germany for the enthusiastic way it has staged the World Cup, stating that Germany is now a 'reference point' for Italy culturally and economically. Prodi added, mainly for domestic consumption it has to be said, that Italian football had to rid itself of 'criminal elements' and required 'profound reform' regardless of last night's result. However, on the day it emerged that Juventus might be demoted TWO divisions due to the match-fixing scandal, Italy reached another World Cup final.

The former Juventus coach made attacking substitutions in an attempt to secure victory, ending with Del Piero, Iaquinta, Gilardino and Totti on the field. Gilardino set up Del Piero for the clinching goal, a sequence that did not surprise Lippi. "We were able to use quite a few of the weapons at our disposal in the last 20 minutes. When I sent on Del Piero I told my friends on the bench that he would score the decisive goal. I was pretty sure he would make an impact. I had looked at how he warmed up before the match and I knew he was very keen to come on and he played a very important role and decided the match. These are the assets we have on our side. It's important the substitutes also contribute to the team spirit and are not disappointed if they don't play for the full 90 minutes."

Del Piero said it was hard to describe his feelings, "It was fantastic

German fans clung to every possible vantage point to see if their heroes could win through to the final

Italy fans rejoice around Rome's Coliseum

to be part of a match like that. To win in their own backyard -- there aren't any words that describe what I'm feeling right now... I've had some criticism recently, but today I demonstrated that my desire is as great as anyone else's."

Italy had hit the woodwork twice in extra-time, after all, as well as beating Lehmann twice so late.

Germany had no cause for complaint. Instead they played You'll Never Walk Alone as their team did a lap of honour. The fans know Germany have over-achieved. A German team that contains players such as Bastian Schweinsteiger, who struggles to keep a place at Bayern Munich, knocked out the favourites, Argentina.

Klinsmann went off to think about his future, rightly proud to say, "It's fantastic what we've seen in Germany, it's wonderful that football can stir these emotions, bring people together, create these moods. We had two aims at the beginning, to go as far as we could as a team and to be good hosts. I think these players can be proud, they have gone up to their limits, and again tonight."

A tearful Michael Ballack claimed 'it just isn't meant to be' for him to play in a World Cup final. Four years after he missed out on Germany's 2-0 loss to Brazil after being banned following receiving a second yellow card in the semi-final, he could not hold

back his tears after the final whistle. "It is very bitter for us to get eliminated like this, one minute from time. The game was well-balanced. The Italians had the better chances in extra-time as they hit woodwork twice. But we also had some good opportunities afterwards."

Klinsmann acknowledged that the Italians "had been more cold-blooded in front of goal than we were." Germany defender Christoph Metzelder claimed Pirlo's 'moment of brilliance' made the difference. "Everyone was expecting him to shoot, but he just passed," Metzelder said. "That was a moment of brilliance."

Day Twenty-Seven
Wednesday 5 July 2006

France 1 v Portugal 0
AllianzArena, Munich
Attendance: 66,000
Kick-off: 9pm   Temperature: 25°C
Referee: Jorge Larrionda

Zidane On The Spot

Zinedine Zidane outwits Portugal's Ricardo from the penalty spot to win the semi-final for France

Scorers			Scorers	
33'	Zidane *(pen)*		Ricardo	01

Team (France)

No	Player
16	Barthez
19	Sagnol
15	Thuram
05	Gallas
03	Abidal
22	Ribery
04	Vieira
10	Zidane
06	Makelele
07	Malouda
12	Henry

Team (Portugal)

Player	No
Ricardo	01
Miguel	13
Meira	05
Ricardo Carvalho	16
Nuno Valente	14
Costinha	06
Maniche	18
Deco	20
Ronaldo	17
Pauleta	09
Figo	07

Substitutes (France)

69'	> 11 Wiltord	< 07 Malouda
72'	> 09 Govou	< 22 Ribery
85'	> 14 Saha	< 12 Henry

Substitutes (Portugal)

02 Paulo Ferreira > 13 Miguel <	62'
11 Simao > 09 Pauleta <	68'
23 Postiga > 06 Costinha <	74'

Discipline

87'	Saha *foul*		Ricardo Carvalho *foul*	83'

Official FIFA Man of the Match
Lilian Thuram

France		Portugal
49%	Ball Possession	51%
3	Shots on target	6
3	Shots off target	4
10	Fouls	16
3	Corner Kicks	8
0	Offsides	4

Semi-Final

Despite desperate attempts to win penalties and free-kicks with 'simulation', the impressive referee, Jorge Larrionda, saw through all Portugal's attempts to con him

Rooney's plea of innocence over his red card was backed by the FA who wrote to FIFA to stress Rooney did not mean to stamp on Carvalho. So, there was no written apology from the player or the FA. FIFA's disciplinary chiefs would consider England's version of events before imposing Rooney's punishment. He can expect a fine and a suspension, which will force him to miss the start of the Euro 2008 qualifying campaign.

The feeling within the England camp is that Elizondo was pressurised into the red card by Portuguese players. They believe he showed no intention of reaching for his cards until Ronaldo rushed over to lead the complaints. The FA wanted FIFA to take into account the rough treatment Rooney was getting from several Portugal players in the seconds before the flashpoint. England would settle for a two-match ban, but anything more than three would seem excessive.

FIFA would have preferred a show of contrition from England similar to the way Italy dealt with Daniele de Rossi's elbow on Brian McBride, earlier in the World Cup. It was a much more clear-cut offence than the Rooney dismissal, but De Rossi wrote an apology and was rewarded with a four-match ban rather than five games.

> "We've been playing every match knowing we could be eliminated, but that's the true essence of football."
>
> **Raymond Domenech (France)**

Sepp Blatter, for once, backed referee Elizondo and cleared Ronaldo, "The referee was touching distance from the players and he took the decision according to what he witnessed. I can only say that the referee's decision is final and I have not seen any protest from fans or even team-mates on the field of play."

He admitted the trend of players waving imaginary cards had to be stopped, but then stressed Ronaldo had not actually done this, "I was at the match and I have not seen any wrongdoing that has not been sanctioned by the referee."

Jamie Carragher wants Steven Gerrard to be named as the new England skipper, "The captain has to be someone who is one of the first names on the team-sheet, someone who has the respect of the other players and someone who has good leadership qualities," Carragher told Liverpoolfc.tv: "Stevie and John Terry have got all that. But, from my own point of view, having played under Stevie at Liverpool and seen how well he captains the side, I'd like it to be him. When you look back at the way he played in Cardiff in the FA Cup final and in Istanbul in the Champions League final, you'd have to say there can't be too many players around who are more inspirational than him."

Carragher is aiming to put his World Cup horror behind him, "What happened in the shoot-out is one of those things that happens in football

The decisive moment saw Ricardo Carvalho's trailing left leg swing through and chop down Thierry Henry to give away a penalty

Within seconds of the game ending, Scolari was striding out to the centre of the pitch to berate the referee, although this time it was he who had lost the plot

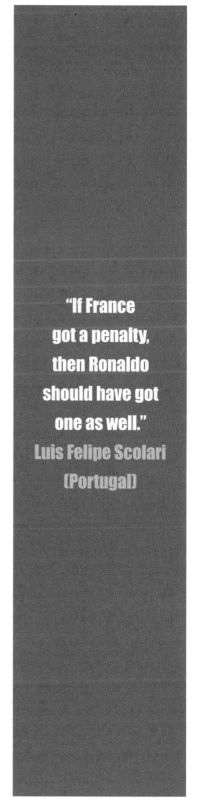

and you just have to get on with it. Of course I wish my penalty had gone in and I wish Stevie's and Frank's had and I wish England were still in the tournament. But it didn't turn out like that, so you just have to accept it and move on.

The fact is we didn't go out because we lost on penalties. We went out because we didn't do enough to win the game during the 90 minutes. Even when we had 11 men we hadn't taken the lead and when it comes down to penalties anything can happen."

Not content with encouraging foul play by suggesting that players should not be suspended until they have received three yellow cards in future tournaments, FIFA Chief Sepp Blatter wants to pursue the idea of using two referees in matches in the near future. Blatter believes bringing in a second referee will help eradicate mistakes and reduce controversy. "At the beginning there was a reluctance to consider the system. Then we had tests conducted in Malaysia and Sao Paulo, Brazil, with encouraging results, but an unsatisfactory reaction in Norway and Italy. But now we are facing a situation in the game where the pace is such that we must ask if there should be a further experiment. We observe the situation in ice hockey, for instance, with two referees and two assistants on a much smaller arena and they have no [personality] clashes with the players because they know the game."

What price two Graham Poll's at the next World Cup?

France reached the Final via Zinedine Zidane's serenely dispatched penalty, showing how to beat the Portuguese keeper, a feat that England found so tough.

The 1998 winners were the second oldest team ever to reach the semi-finals

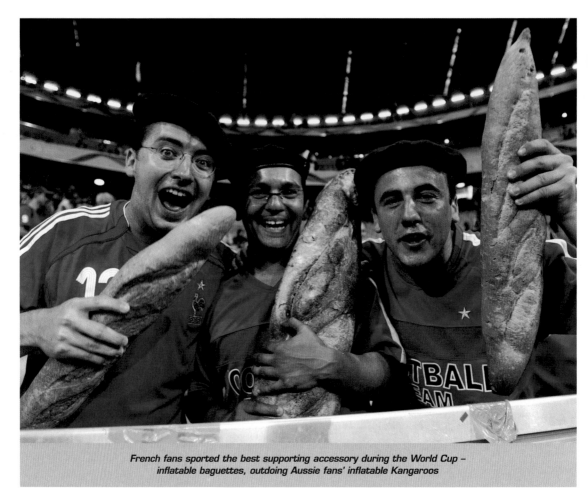

French fans sported the best supporting accessory during the World Cup –
inflatable baguettes, outdoing Aussie fans' inflatable Kangaroos

and now the OAPs made it all the way to Berlin. The penalty was awarded when Henry moved elusively and Carvalho, off balance, jutted out a left boot and the Arsenal forward went down. Ricardo's specialist skill as a penalty-stopper proved England's downfall, but Zidane, with a two step run-up, was too crisp in his execution for the goalkeeper to have any hope. The playmaker raised his hands to the skies in a gesture of gratitude. His career appropriately ends with the Final itself.

Substitute Louis Saha was shown yellow shortly after coming on ruling him out of the final. Portugal, searching for an equaliser, scared France when Barthez fumbled and spooned into the air a Ronaldo free-kick with 12 minutes left and Figo headed over

from close range. Scolari removed Pauleta, his usual disappointing self, and introduced Sabrosa, so that Ronaldo, who was booed throughout, could play through the middle.

Ronaldo has made himself the most hated man in football with his blatant diving and other associated antics in these finals. Wonderful footballer that he is, you can't help but think he has made a rod for his own back reminiscent of that which whacked Beckham across the back of the legs for a season or so following his red card at France 98.

Ronaldo and Scolari laid the blame for defeat at the feet of the Uraguayan referee Jorge Larrionda. The incidents that sent the Portuguese camp scowling towards Stuttgart for a third-place play-off

against Germany came within five first-half minutes as Larrionda first awarded France a penalty and then denied Ronaldo a similar prize as he flew theatrically to the ground in a crowded French box.

Ronaldo claimed after the game that he was pushed by Sagnol as he attempted to reach a Figo cross. "He was a very bad referee, I should have had a penalty." His coach agreed that a foul went unpunished, a sentiment demonstrated when he led most of the Portuguese bench to the edge of the technical area in protest at Larrionda's decision to wave play on. "It was a penalty, they had to give a penalty, and against Ronaldo it didn't happen," Scolari said before implying that the officials had conspired against his made a mistake when he did not give a penalty when Ronaldo was fouled. The referee knows exactly what he is doing. We know South American referees know how to kill the game."

Ronaldo added, "We played well and did our best, but the referee didn't help us. Everyone who saw the match could see that the referee wasn't fair. He should have shown yellow cards, but he did not because Portugal is a small country. We just have to carry on working and then we will be a big country.

Portugal showed that they can play good football. France were no better than we were. They got a penalty, but not much else"

Ronaldo was greeted by a thunderstorm of catcalls every time he touched the ball, but he insisted the harassment only made him stronger. "I was pleased about being booed. I am a dangerous player. And maybe the French fans were upset to see a dangerous player. I am not worried at all."

A raging Scolari accused French players of insulting his team during confrontations after the final whistle. "The French players made some absurd comments about our country and our athletes that I cannot repeat, and they did not show respect to our country."

Television replays, however told a different story, showing that Sagnol made only the slightest contact with Ronaldo, who needed little persuasion to go to ground having realised that the centre was beyond his reach.

Scolari conceded France deserved a penalty when Carvalho went to ground when turned by Henry. The contact was minimal but Henry opted not to go for the shooting opportunity he had fashioned for himself in favour of going to ground.

France's coach Raymond Domenech paid tribute to ZZ, "Zidane is a world champion, it is as simple as that. He has got his photograph on walls across France and he is a hero to the French public. He has brought something permanent and wonderful to French football and to his team. He has afforded the French public real dreams this month, but this has always been the case, he has been doing this for 10 years. Of course it will be the last game

for him, but for us it is not Zinedine Zidane's last game, it's a World Cup final, and Zizou is thinking about it in the same way. This is not a victory tour for him and Lilian and Claude. It is a World Cup, and we want to win it."

For Thuram, the prospect of a second World Cup final is now reality after he came out of international retirement. The central defender would line up against several of his Juventus team-mates in Berlin. "It is my second final and I confess it is something I could not possibly have imagined. The World Cup remains a dream of my childhood. It is something quite fantastic. I wasn't going to be there because I decided not to play for the French team any more, but the coach picked me against my own will and now I am going to the final. Football is fantastic. It is beautiful and I hope it will go on."

The World Cup was expected to provide a festival of youth, but Kaka, Messi and Rooney self-destructed and the old men, led by Alessandro Del Piero and Zidane, have grabbed the stage for a final parade. But which one has an appointment with destiny?

DID YOU KNOW?
Portugal's undefeated run of 17 competitive matches stretching back to Euro 2004 ended. It was also the first World Cup defeat for coach Phil Scolari in 13 games.

DID YOU KNOW?
France have won all three competitive internationals against Portugal; the last two have been semi-finals and on both occasions Zidane has scored the winning goal. The previous occasion was in Euro 2000 when his "golden goal" gave France a 2-1 win to put them in the final against... Italy.

This was France's 50th World Cup finals match.

The average age of France's starting line-up, 30 years and 10 days, was the second oldest ever for a World Cup Semi-Final.

Day Twenty-Eight
Thursday 6 July 2006

Cheryl Tweedy told how she was shocked by the WAGS' vanity as she met them for the first time.

The Girls Aloud singer commented, "It's like a comedy. Everyone's so flash. It's like, 'Who's got the best watch on, who's got the best bag, which wife is dressed the best, which wife's got the best hair?' I'm like, 'I've got my own career'." Cheryl, who weds Ashley Cole a week on Saturday, criticised footballers' wives and girlfriends for 'living off their man's money'. The 23-year-old pop star was in Baden-Baden socialising with the WAGs, "It really annoys me when people try to call me a footballer's wife. Footballers' wives have no careers and live off their husbands' money. I was in Girls Aloud before I met Ashley and have my own successful career. I'm not going to quit the band and sit around in the sun all day or go shopping with Ashley's plastic. If I'm going shopping I'll pay with the money I've worked hard for. I'd die of embarrassment if I had to resort to taking boyfriends' cards. You see girls in clubs making a beeline for the footballers and it makes me sick.' Cheryl, however, does use Ashley's credit card, keeping hers as back-up, "I've got my own money, so if my husband's card is declined I whip out mine." Victoria, though, was an exception. Cheryl said: "I love Victoria. She's very ambitious, so we have a lot in common."

Cheryl Tweedy and Ashley Cole take a turn round Baden-Baden town centre

But many of the WAGs earn their wedge. Coleen signed as the new face of Asda's George range and runs her own PR company. Carly is a personal fitness instructor and 29-year-old Elen is a supermodel and mum. Lisa teaches pilates and 20-year-old Michaela Henderson-Thynne (Stewart Downing's girl) is studying law.

Klinsmann's contract was due to expire at the end of the tournament, but the decision-makers and fans hoped he would stay on. "He has woken this national team up and I certainly hope Jürgen Klinsmann and his team can continue taking this side into the future," said DFB president Gerhard Mayer-Vorfelder. "Having achieved what he has, I am sure he feels some kind of responsibility to carry the job through." Mayer-Vorfelder not only praised Klinsmann for leading an unfancied Germany to the last four, he thanked him for breathing new life into the nation, which has witnessed "a wonderful World Cup experience."

It was only in the early hours of the morning following their exit to Italy that team manager Oliver Bierhoff was able to close his eyes and try to get some sleep. "It felt like a bottomless pit of disappointment," he explained. "It was a once-in-a-lifetime opportunity which we have been working two years for and for the last seven weeks of intense work to be all over is a huge disappointment, particularly since we wanted to have the cup in our hands. In the dressing room afterwards, it was very quiet. Nobody wanted to discuss what had happened, and that was the case on the plane and into the hotel. Only at about 3.30am did we start to try to realise what had happened and I wasn't in bed until five. Let's not forget we have achieved lots of small aims, even if the big one eluded us. I think throughout the first round, Germany played the most attractive football of all the nations.

Brazil's Roberto Carlos quit international football following the 1-0 defeat to France, in which he was widely blamed for failing to mark goalscorer Henry. "On the Brazilian national team, my story has ended," he said on his official Web site. "I want to open space for new blood. I hope I can give this number six jersey to someone who might carry on this victorious history. I thank my team-mates and the supporters who were always on my side. A big hug to everyone."

Carlos, famous for his booming left-footed shot and renowned for the one great free-kick he scored at Le Tournoi in 1997, played at the 1998, 2002 and 2006 World Cups and won 125 caps for Brazil in full internationals. He had a chequered history with the national side. He was much criticised for his performances in 1998, when Brazil finished as runners-up to France, and was also criticised after being quoted as saying he could not understand how anyone could live on less than several thousand dollars a month. "I wear an apartment on my arm," he added in a newspaper interview, referring to a watch worth thousands of dollars. Brazilians – most of whom scrape by on around $100 a month – replied by giving him a new nickname: 'O mascarado' (the masked one). In this context, it meant big-headed. Carlos claimed he had been misinterpreted, that he was always proud to represent his country and that he has not changed since his humble upbringing in the state of Sao Paulo.

Mind you he got away scot free compared to poor old Ronaldinho. The twice World Footballer of the Year returned home to discover that a 7 metre tall statue of him in the Southern town of Chapeco in Santa Catarina state, was burnt the night of Brazil's disappointing exit to France.

Gary Neville insisted he would never voluntarily quit international football, despite admitting he may have played in his last World Cup as he will be 35 when the next finals take place in South Africa in 2010, "Perhaps I have played in my last World Cup finals, but I have said always I will never retire from international foot-

Roberto Carlos departs the international stage after defeat by France

ball. It's not Gary Neville's right to retire from international football. While I'm still playing football for any club then I will be available for my country. That is the way it has always been and always will be with me."

If he can recapture his fitness Neville is still the best right-back in the country, but surely McClaren needs to look to the future. Neville is adamant there is still the possibility of the so called 'Golden Generation' achieving glory in the future, although by 2010 many of the squad will be in their 30s, "I still think there is a little bit left in the golden generation. I don't think it is the end, but we all know this World Cup was a big chance for us. It was on European soil and we cruised through to the quarter-final without even having to perform. It is another lost opportunity – one of many because we have got good players. We start again with a new manager in four or five weeks' time and a friendly against Greece. We are suffering now, but we have to pick ourselves up and go again."

Ronaldinho can't believe Brazil's exit or the arson of his statue back home in Chapeco

Day Twenty-Nine
Friday 7 July 2006

At least one little piece of England will be in the World Cup Final.

Roma midfielder Simone Perrotta was born in Lancashire at Ashton-under-Lyne. Parents Francesco and Annamaria emigrated to England in the early 1960s where they had three sons, Simone being the youngest. The family then returned to Italy in 1982, the year the Azzurri last won the World Cup by beating West Germany 3-1. Perrotta, speaking in Italy's World Cup base in Duisburg, said: "I have vague memories of England as a little boy. I remember the park and the garden and I also remember the school where I used to play football in the playground with my friends. Although my parents are Italian and I've spent most of my life in Italy, I still feel I have a little bit of England in me. I was born there and I spent five years there. I only wish I could speak better English because, after so many years, I've forgotten how. I could have played for England and I remember my friends and family said I could, but there was no doubt in my mind I wanted to play for Italy. I am so proud to be Italian and so delighted to be playing in the World Cup final as it is every player's ultimate dream."

Del Piero was a football icon for his country for more than a decade, yet his misses against France in the Euro 2000 final tarnished his reputation. The Juventus captain failed to hit the target late in the game against Les Bleus and France claimed a narrow triumph. "No-one suffered more than I did in that game," said Del Piero. "I was criticised a lot, even described as being half a player. I don't feel guilty and for a simple reason, whenever I play I give everything, my head, my legs and my heart on the pitch. That defeat is already in the past, Sunday's game is a new story and a new battle."

Simone Perrotta takes on Sebastien Kehl in the semi-final as the last 'Englishman' standing in the competition

If Italy's 2-0 triumph over Germany in the semi-final was an epic one, Sunday's encounter against France, according to Del Piero, will not be for the faint hearted.

"There could have been other teams to have reached this final. I believe that this is the best possible final, between two great teams that have incredible champions. There couldn't have been any other team more adapted to this final than France and it's going to be a fantastic final."

One of the big reasons France made it this far is because of Del Piero's former Juve team-mate Zidane, who wanted to retire in style. Del Piero has fond memories of Zizou from the time together in Turin. "There's little that can be said about Zizou, he is simply number one. I have very fond memories of our time together at Juve. We experienced great adventures and we have a friendship and respect that goes above the greatness of him as a player. I am very happy that he has been able to crash those criticisms he received at the start of the tournament, but I'm afraid he may not be able to have his dream finish."

France's veteran side is full of quality including two of Del Piero's current team-mates at Juve in Vieira and Thuram. "We cannot think only about Zidane," he said. "France have very good and strong players and they can punish us if we give them a chance. We really have to play a perfect match in every respect."

Vieira, Del Piero and Thuram all had the spectre of the football scandal back at their club Juventus, the club faced relegation if found guilty of match fixing or other serious infractions. "The fact that there could be at least eight Juve players in this final highlights the quality of our club team. It's inevitable not to think a little bit about what is happening back home, but my priority is Sunday's final. I think Juve will be well represented on Sunday and I hope that the Italians and the Juve fans will be able to smile. After Monday I can think about my future and the club's situation."

So far, the scandal has galvanised Lippi's side, who also have had to deal with other problems along the way. "So far, the scandal has stimulated us. We are well aware that it could have brought us down. I think a World Cup final represents something unique, you don't need any extra motivation because we know what we are fighting for."

Del Piero nevertheless believed France, who had beaten Italy twice in their last two meetings in major tournaments, had the upper hand. "I think France has less stress going into the final. We have the scandal back home, the pressure from the media. Then there was the incident with (Juve team-manager) Gianluca Pessotto which was dramatic and really affected us. But, in a final, anything can happen."

With Lippi unlikely to continue coaching the national team having been linked with a return to Juve and this morning with succeeding Sir Alex Ferguson at Manchester United, this could be the last chance for Del Piero. "I would define it as a great opportunity for this group. It's a great chance. I don't know what the plans of the other players are, but I'm not thinking about the future, my future is on Sunday."

A hearty rendition of O Sole Mio was booming out in Italy's dressing room when Prime Minister Romano Prodi came to congratulate the team on beating Germany. "Even he joined in," captain Fabio Cannavaro revealed. "It was great." Cannavaro was a ball boy at his hometown stadium in Naples in 1990 when Italy's dream was crushed by Argentina in a penalty shoot-out.

Now, Marcello Lippi dubbed him the world's best centre-back. Fittingly, the Final marks the skipper's 100th cap. "We were joking about how many caps he needed to overtake this player and that player," Lippi said, "and I told him: 'Do you know, with this World Cup if you get to the final, seven games will take you to 100?' And now we are there it is a fantastic thing. Cannavaro is having a fantastic World Cup. He is without question the strongest defender at this tournament and the absolute No. 1 in the world."

The 32-year-old is described in the Italian football federation guide as "the footballing Neapolitan street urchin". It sums up what he brings that a former national coach, Cesare Maldini, called him 'Canna', meaning cane or reed – something that bends, but does not break.

Cannavaro has been unbreakable as Italy have conceded only once, and that an own-goal. A relative lack of height does not prevent him being

Frank Beckenbauer holds aloft the Golden Ball trophy awarded to FIFA's most valuable player of the 2006 World Cup at the announcement of the nominated ten players in Berlin

World Cup 2006 Best Players

FIFA's Technical Study group drew up a shortlist of 10 players for the Adidas Golden Ball award made up of four Italians, three Frenchmen, two Germans and one Portuguese to succeed German keeper Oliver Kahn, who was chosen in 2002.

THE NOMINEES ARE

Ballack (Germany)
Buffon (Italy)
Cannavaro (Italy)
Henry (France)
Klose (Germany)
Maniche (Portugal)
Pirlo (Italy)
Vieira (France)
Zambrotta (Italy)
Zidane (France)

Of the six candidates for the Gillette best young player award, three were chosen by fans in an internet poll and three selected by FIFA's technical study group.

FANS SELECTIONS

Ronaldo (Portugal)
Valencia (Ecuador)
Messi (Argentina)

TECHNICAL STUDY GROUP SELECTIONS

Podolski (Germany)
Barnetta (Switzerland)
Fábregas (Spain)

*Players had to be under 21 on January 1 this year in order to qualify.

strong in the air, his positioning is excellent and his tackling well timed.

When Cannavaro reflected on this team's accomplishments he alluded to failure in Euro 2004 and the 2002 World Cup. "We stored up a lot of anger about how we hadn't performed or qualified for the later stages, and we have taken that anger out on the pitch here."

Italy team physicians ruled out key defender Alessandro Nesta, Cannavaro's usual partner. "He's definitely not available," announced Dr. Enrico Castellacci. It is the third straight time that Nesta, who suffered a groin setback against the Czech Republic, has missed time due to injury in a World Cup.

Argentinean referee Horacio Elizondo, who sent off Rooney, was put in control of the World Cup final. FIFA clearly agreed with Elizondo's decision and his overall performance in Gelsenkirchen and selected him to referee the Berlin showpiece.

Franz Beckenbauer called for a summit meeting of players, coaches and referees in a bid to stop the increasing trend towards play-acting and feigning injury which blighted matches at the World Cup. Beckenbauer, president of the German organising committee said it was time for players to stop cheating in a bid to gain an unfair advantage. "I think it is time to get the players, the coaches and the referees around the table and try to find some sort of solution to this problem. None of us in the game wants these incidents. The players are seeking to gain an unfair advantage and attempt to exploit every situation. The referees are there to correct this kind of misconduct, but the players do not make it easy for the referees. If I was a referee I would also show the yellow card to any player who signalled to the ref with an imaginary card to get an opponent booked. That is also cheating."

FIFA and UEFA planned a technical convention with coaches, referees and players' representatives in Berlin in September to discuss the World Cup with cheating and play-acting on the agenda. Beckenbauer was also disappointed with the number of goal attempts at the finals, adding, "as the old German coach Sepp Herberger used to show, if you don't shoot, you won't score. Well there have not been enough shots on goal as far as I am concerned."

Speaking six years to the day after Germany was awarded the right to stage the finals by FIFA, Beckenbauer said the World Cup had been an astonishing success and had brought people together in a way the organisers could only have dreamed of. "The Fan Miles have been a spectacular success and Germany has celebrated the World Cup in a way few thought was possible."

England players unsurprisingly failed to make the shortlists for either the World Cup's outstanding player or the inaugural award for best young player of the tournament.

Rooney and Lennon were both eligible for the Gillette sponsored youngest player prize, but did not get near the top three of the fans' vote list, which was headed by Cristiano Ronaldo. Ecuador's Luis Valencia and Argentina's Luis Messi, who finished second and third, both benefited from worldwide campaigns to vote for them as the nearest challengers to the new biggest villain in football – Ronaldo. The Portuguese winger had held a seemingly unassailable lead in the fans vote until his histrionic performance in the semi-final prompted a co-ordinated campaign on website www.ihateronaldo.com, which was reportedly receiving over 300,000 hits a day.

And that cost him the award as Germany striker Lukas Podolski lifted the prize for scoring three goals in his six matches so far.

Podolski said: "I would have liked to have taken home the World Cup – but this is a great honour and is a great motivation to become more successful."

Holger Osieck, head of the FIFA technical study group that chose the winner, said: "We want to have decent behaviour and I admit we were critical of this. We had a number of criteria, but we have to admit players of that age do have their weaknesses and are not fully developed. Players should be role models and fair play is a consideration. But we have to admit young players are not always mature tactically and they also have difficulties in handling stressful situations."

Germany legend Lothar Matthäus, who is patron of the award, added: "You will never have 100% fair play and maybe looking at Cristiano he was obviously doing something here."

Cristiano Ronaldo became a hate figure across the globe after his antics in the quarter and semi-finals which cost him the inaugural Gillette Young Player of the World Cup award

Day Thirty
Saturday 8 July 2006

Germany 3 v Portugal 1
Gottlieb-Daimler-Stadion, Stuttgart
Attendance: 52,000
Kick-off: 9pm   Temperature: 21°C
Referee: Toru Kamikawa

Schweinsteiger Strikes

Bastian Schweinsteiger, dropped for the semi-final, returns with a bang, scoring twice and making the third goal as Germany finish on a high

Official FIFA Man of the Match
Bastian Schweinsteiger

Scorers	
56′, 78′	Schweinsteiger
60′	Petit (og)

Team	
12	Kahn
02	Jansen
06	Nowotny
21	Metzelder
16	Lahm
19	Schneider
05	Kehl
08	Frings
07	Schweinsteiger
11	Klose
20	Podolski

Substitutes		
64′	> 10 Neuville	< 11 Klose
71′	> 09 Hanke	< 20 Podolski
79′	> 15 Hitzlsperger	< 07 Schweinsteiger

Discipline	
07′	Frings *foul*
79′	Schweinsteiger *pulling shirt over head*

Scorers	
Nuno Gomes	88′

Team	
Ricardo	01
Paulo Ferreira	02
Ricardo Costa	04
Meira	05
Nuno Valente	14
Costinha	06
Maniche	18
Deco	20
Ronaldo	17
Pauleta	09
Simao	11

Substitutes		
08 Petit >	06 Costinha <	45′
21 Nuno Gomes >	14 Nuno Valente <	69′
07 Figo >	09 Pauleta <	77′

Discipline	
Ricardo Costa *foul*	24′
Costinha *foul*	29′
Paulo Ferreira *foul*	61′

48%	Ball Possession	52%
5	Shots on target	10
8	Shots off target	5
15	Fouls	15
2	Corner Kicks	7
1	Offsides	3

Third/Fourth Place Play-off

Cristiano Ronaldo is confirmed as football's biggest villain as boos ring around Stuttgart's Gottlieb-Daimler-Stadion with his every touch

"It's impossible to put into words what happened here this evening. You can't top that. The fans were fantastic, and the team played like men possessed. I'm so incredibly proud."
Jürgen Klinsmann (Germany)

Chelsea defender John Terry is the only England player to have made it into the World Cup squad of the tournament. FIFA's technical study group chose 23 players in total, including seven players from Italy and four from fellow finalists France. Terry makes it in even though most commentators believe central defensive partner Ferdinand had a more impressive tournament.

Only one Brazilian makes it into the Mastercard all-star squad, Bayern Munich midfielder Ze Roberto and there is no room for Brazil's Ronaldo, who scored three goals. No players from the African or Asian nations made the squad.

It looked unlikely at the start of the tournament that Thierry Henry would get a second chance to play in football's most prestigious match. Just three weeks ago, France looked dead and buried following two sluggish performances in the opening draws against Switzerland and South Korea. But Henry, who missed out on a substitute appearance in the 1998

FIFA'S World Cup Squad Of The Tournament

GOALKEEPERS

Gianluigi Buffon (Italy)
Jens Lehmann (Germany)
Ricardo (Portugal)

DEFENDERS

Roberto Ayala (Argentina)
Fabio Cannavaro (Italy)
Ricardo Carvalho (Portugal)
Philipp Lahm (Germany)
John Terry (England)
Lilian Thuram (France)
Gianluca Zambrotta (Italy)

MIDFIELDERS

Michael Ballack (Germany)
Luis Figo (Portugal)
Gennaro Gattuso (Italy)
Maniche (Portugal)
Andrea Pirlo (Italy)
Patrick Vieira (France)
Ze Roberto (Brazil)
Zinedine Zidane (France)

STRIKERS

Hernan Crespo (Argentina)
Thierry Henry (France)
Miroslav Klose (Germany)
Luca Toni (Italy)
Francesco Totti (Italy)

John Terry, displaying the sort of passion which got him into FIFA's squad of the tournament

final when Desailly's dismissal forced coach Jacquet to rethink, has got a second chance after France made a wonderful recovery in Germany.

But Henry admitted France desperately needed to "step up their game" to defy their critics, "It is true that we were not playing well at the start of the tournament, and people were saying we were too old. That was pretty harsh, but as soon as we stepped it up it started to work for us."

A convincing victory over Togo then set the pace for glorious performances against Spain, Brazil and Portugal. "We were not listening to what people were saying," Henry added. "We were just concentrating on playing as a team. That is what the team is all about. We never cared about our critics – we just got it done. We defended like lions. It was not at all an easy victory. It was very difficult, but we were very efficient."

Henry predicts a tight encounter against Italy. "It will be a close match – nobody expected anything

from them either. We saw what they did to the Germans and how they worried them. They are a very good team. We don't know what will happen in the final."

Patrick Vieira insisted France were oozing with confidence. Vieira believed the side's "fantastic team spirit" and "physical fitness" has made the difference as the tournament has progressed. "We did not play our best football, but I am very happy about how things have progressed. Everyone is doing very well physically and that is the reason why we keep getting better and better. And the team spirit is fantastic – everyone is having a good time. We've improved throughout the competition. I think when you beat Spain, Brazil and now Portugal, the confidence is very high. Both teams can win it. You have to be patient and make your first chance count. We will just keep believing in ourselves and do it."

Vieira admitted the returns of Zidane, Thuram and Makelele – all of whom had announced their retirement after the Euro 2004 – had given France a major boost. "When you have three of the best players of the world in your team that makes it very easy. They give us belief and make us a stronger team. We got one step closer and [winning the World Cup] would be a great finish for the older players."

Lyon manager Gerard Houllier made a toast to France's previously questioned group of old-timers for their influence in the current World Cup title drive. "What I have loved about this World Cup is the elder players," he told L'Equipe. "If you take stock, Vieira was very important against Spain, Makelele has been a jewel, a gold mine, Zidane – obviously against Brazil – and against Portugal. I don't think Thuram has lost a single challenge. For the final, man of the day could be Thierry Henry, or maybe a Zizou free-kick."

Oasis star Noel Gallagher is Italy star Alessandro del Piero's lucky mascot for the final. Gallagher is friends with the Italian striker and was asked by Del Piero to turn up to the final in exactly the same clothes he wore for the semi-final against Germany.

The Oasis songwriter commented, "The semi-final was the first time I'd seen Italy play and before the game we went to the hotel and Del Piero was a bit upset because he wasn't starting, but he then said, "I'm going to come off the bench and score". After the game he said I'd become his lucky mascot, so I've got to go to the final and wear the exact same clothes and underwear and socks to bring him good luck."

Del Piero is a big Oasis fan and once gave the Gallagher brothers a pair of his boots. "I had to split them with Liam – he's got one boot and I've got the other," said Gallagher, "I've been to a lot of big football matches in my time, but I have to say the atmosphere there was just sensational. If I never see another game in my entire life, that will do for me."

Gallagher was confident Italy would win, "I think Zidane has played his great game against Brazil because Brazil let him play. He is not going to be allowed to play on Sunday night.

Germany coach Klinsmann, celebrating finishing third, emerged as many people's man of the tournament

"There was nothing to choose between the teams in the first half, but in the second, we let two goals in one after the other. Germany's third goal was a beauty though. We had chances ourselves, but we just couldn't put them away."
Luis Felipe Scolari (Portugal)

German fans in Castle Square, Stuttgart relish their team's victory

As for Henry, this is going to either be the defining moment in his career where he is going to be absolutely amazing or, as I think, he won't actually get a kick."

FIFA found Rooney guilty of violent conduct despite the FA and the striker arguing his case. He misses England's Euro 2008 qualifiers against Andorra on September 2 at Old Trafford and Macedonia away on September 6. Rooney and new England coach Steve McClaren were relieved FIFA did not impose a three-match ban or worse.

Cristiano Ronaldo, whose Cheshire house had reportedly been targeted by vandals reacting to the part he played in Rooney's sending-off, commented after Portugal's defeat to Germany. "I think I should get out of Manchester. The circumstances are not right to keep playing in Manchester. In two or three days I will decide where to go. I always said I wanted to play in Spain. Nobody stood up for me at Manchester, although I did not do anybody any harm." Ronaldo, a £12.24m signing from Sporting Lisbon in August 2003, had been linked with

Real Madrid. When new Real manager Fabio Capello was asked about Ronaldo he said: 'He is a Manchester player. But he really wants to play here and that is good news for me. We will have to wait and see.'

Another player moving on was Sol Campbell, who left Arsenal in search of a 'fresh challenge', following speculation linking the 31-year-old with a move to Portsmouth or Fenerbahce. His final match for the club was May's Champions League final against Barcelona, in which he gave Arsenal a first-half lead before they lost to two late goals.

Marcello Lippi dismissed the idea of a move to Manchester United after the World Cup, after reports suggested he would work alongside Sir Alex for a while before replacing him as manager. The Italy coach, who had yet to confirm if he would remain in charge of the national team after the final, said: "How can you work in a place where you don't even know the language? All I am interested in is winning the World Cup and I find it useless to speak about the rest."

Italy were in danger of losing out on their bid to stage the European Championship in 2012 as a result of the Serie A match-fixing scandal, an unnamed member of Uefa's executive committee told a news agency. "Although the scandal will obviously have blown over by the time the championship is held. Uefa cannot now support the Italian FA unless it is completely reorganised by the time we decide. We find ourselves in a very difficult position. If the vote was being taken tomorrow, I am not sure who would win it, but it could not be Italy."

Jürgen Klinsmann again asked for more time to decide whether he will stay on as Germany coach even as a crowd of 52,000 chanted his name and one-time critic Franz Beckenbauer pleaded with him to continue. "The 'Kaiser' said 'you'd better keep going", Klinsmann told a news conference when asked what the man who captained and later coached West Germany teams to World Cup wins said to him on the pitch after Germany beat Portugal 3-1 for third place. "I told him 'let's wait and see what happens','" Klinsmann added to laughter as he borrowed Beckenbauer's favourite 'Schaun 'mer mal' phrase and turned it against his mentor. "But seriously, I'm delighted that he holds our work in such high esteem," Klinsmann said. "Those words came from his heart. For me as a young guy and young coach to get such a compliment like that from Franz Beckenbauer, it's a special moment."

Even FIFA President Sepp Blatter said he thought Klinsmann should stay on. "I hope that he'll stay longer, they've achieved something here. With their beautiful and attacking style, they've done something for football. I'll tell him to stay, but he has to decide. The whole country wants him to stay but he has to decide himself."

Oliver Kahn, given one last hurrah by Klinsmann for the Third/Fourth match, announced he was retiring from international football, "That was my last international match. It was a beautiful time, but you have to know when it's all over. The atmosphere was overwhelming. You have to stop and think for a moment what it would have been like if we had won the World Cup. It was one of the biggest, if not the biggest, emotional moment that I can remember. You could hardly ask for a better match to go out on." Kahn, who had 86 caps for Germany, was captain of the team that went to the World Cup final in 2002, where they lost to Brazil 2-0. He won the Golden Ball award given to the most valuable player of the 32-team tournament.

Dropped for the semi-final, Bastian Schweinsteiger missed out on what would arguably have been the biggest game of his short footballing career. But back in the side for the third-place play-off the Bayern Munich midfielder played the game of his life to give Germany the bronze medal. Two stunning goals and a third shot which Petit deflected into his own net made 'Schweini' the obvious choice for Man of the Match and the 21-year-old explained how much he enjoyed the occasion. "I was so happy with the game in Stuttgart in front of a great crowd," he said. "From when we were welcomed in the hotel, it was like we had won the World Cup."

Having opened the scoring with a fizzing 25-yard effort which bent one way and the other on its way past Ricardo's flailing hand, Schweinsteiger revealed how he hoped his free-kick would take a fortunate deflection in for the second, as it did. "We had done a lot of free-kicks and none had gone how we had wished. I saw they put just one man in the wall, so I thought I would try and hit the ball powerfully towards the far post and maybe one of our players could get a leg in. Luckily, a Portugal player did that."

After celebrating finishing third, the focus turned to the future, which Schweinsteiger believes is very bright for Germany. "We have a young team and that is always a good sign. We have all got room for improvement and we all will get better. Of course we want to qualify for the European Championships, but I think if things continue like this, then we could be tasting success at the next World Cup."

Armando Petit deflects in Schweinsteiger's free-kick to give Germany a two goal lead

Germany As Hosts

German supporters greeted the World Cup with an incredible gusto, which changed the way the World viewed them and their country, possible for ever

Harry Says

With the World Cup having provided such a fantastic jamboree of football, I wanted to find out more about how the whole event had affected the host nation and changed attitudes both within Germany itself and about the country and its people across the globe. So I asked 13 year-old Marie Schulte-Bockum, who prior to the tournament had managed to interview the great German Franz Beckenbauer, to sum up what the tournament meant to her and her country.

My father said to me that there are three terrible things in the life of an Englishman – the loss of a great friend, the death of a relative and England losing in a penalty shoot-out during a World Cup.

The final was a great ending to what I think was the best World Cup ever. We have seen great games that will be written and talked about for years to come. The final, the match of the yellow and red cards Portugal against Holland, the quarter-final between Germany and Argentina, which made a whole country go crazy, and the last match with David Beckham as the English captain, England against Portugal.

It was an especially bitter experience because England could have won against Portugal, and were unable to do so even though they had the best players in their team since their first and only World Cup win 1966.

Even I, as a German was upset and surprised to see England go out of the World Cup so early. They have great players with the same or an even better quality than the two teams in the World Cup Final, but unlike his opposite Scolari, Sven-Göran Eriksson was unable to build up a great team with a mixture of the right players.

But although England was now out of the World Cup, it had to carry on. Jürgen Klinsmann and his young German team with its goalscoring attackers, Podolski and Klose, didn't manage to score a goal against Italy, and while they were already getting ready for penalties, received two

goals against in the last two minutes. Two very nice goals I have to say, but this did not interest me or anybody else German, our country was out of its own World Cup.

Winning 3-1 against Portugal and claiming the Bronze Medal was Germany's own little Final, and 700,000 Germans welcomed the team back to Berlin on the morning of the Final, celebrating it and its achievements – not many people thought the German team could win against Sweden, Argentina and Portugal before the World Cup. Klinsmann had been heavily criticised in the months leading up to the tournament and our warm-up matches were only so-so. But the team came right when it mattered and united our whole nation behind them.

The Germans can be proud of their own team, their own country, the great atmosphere during the World Cup and, of course, being great hosts. Half a billion people across the globe watched the final in Berlin and saw my nation truly united in its love for this wonderful game.

Millions of those people had come from all over the world to Germany to see the World Cup with their own eyes, many of who didn't even have a ticket. Public viewing events in the towns and cities around the country, especially in the huge 'Fan Miles' in the cities hosting matches, were a huge success. 15 million people are said to have watched the World Cup at these events alone, 8 million of these on the Fan Mile in Berlin.

Before they visited us, Brazilian, Argentinean, African, English, Costa Rican and Japanese fans, they all thought Germans were very serious and unfriendly, but Germany proved them all wrong. If their own country wasn't playing, they even turned up on the streets wearing a Holland or England Shirt. The South American and African guests danced Samba and celebrated Carnival throughout the whole country and young (and older) German volunteers were always able

to help when someone had lost their tickets or children, needed advice on a good hotel to spend the night at, or needed to know how to get to the nearest Stadium.

I have to say as a German that I am proud of my team and my country more than ever before, and that I think the World Cup was a huge success. It really was "a time to make friends". It will be hard for every World Cup and the country it is held in to fill the World with as much enthusiasm and inspire it as well as this tournament has. It has shown how much happiness and joy football can create and how it can bring people of all nations, colours and religions together.

By Marie Schulte-Bockum
13 years-old

German fans threw themselves into the true spirit of the World Cup and came out as the true winners in many ways

The German team visited Berlin's Fan Mile on the morning of the final to say 'thank you' to the wonderful fans who had supported them so heartily throughout the competition

Day Thirty-One
Sunday 9 July 2006

France 1 v Italy 1
*after extra time, Italy won 5-3 on penalties
Olympiastadion, Berlin   Attendance: 69,000
Kick-off: 8pm   Temperature: 24°C
Referee: Horacio Marcelo Elizondo

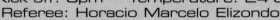

Italy Win Fourth World Cup

Scorers			Scorers		
7′	Zidane (pen)		Materazzi	19′	

Team		Team	
16	Barthez	Buffon	01
19	Sagnol	Zambrotta	19
15	Thuram	Cannavaro	05
05	Gallas	Materazzi	23
03	Abidal	Grosso	03
22	Ribery	Camoranesi	16
04	Vieira	Pirlo	21
06	Makelele	Gattuso	08
10	Zidane	Perrotta	20
07	Malouda	Totti	10
12	Henry	Toni	09

Substitutes

56′	> 18 Diarra		15 Iaquinta >	61′	
	< 04 Vieira		20 Perrotta <		
100′	> 20 Trezeguet		04 De Rossi >	61′	
	< 22 Ribery		10 Totti <		
107′	> 11 Wiltord		07 Del Piero >	86′	
	< 12 Henry		16 Camoranesi <		

**Captain Fabio Cannavaro
lifts the Jules Rimet
trophy into the Berlin sky**

Discipline

12′	Sagnol foul		Zambrotta foul	05′	
76′	Diarra foul				
110′	Zidane violent conduct				
111′	Malouda dissent				

Official FIFA Man of the Match
Andrea Pirlo

49%	Ball Possession	51%	
7	Shots on target	2	
7	Shots off target	3	
24	Fouls	15	
7	Corner Kicks	5	
2	Offsides	4	

Fabio Grosso and Gianluigi Buffon celebrate Grosso's winning penalty

"We always had hope, even though we were up against great players. We stayed cool, and I would also like to thank the Italian supporters for their support."
Marcello Lippi (Italy)

So, Italy can overcome their penalty shoot out phobia. Why couldn't England? And, in a World Cup year when there wasn't really an outstanding team, why didn't England finally end 40 years of hurt? Those questions well haunt English football until the Finals in South Africa in 2010.

The tournament lacked quality, but made up for it with sheer drama. The Final in Berlin epitomised the rawness of the entire competition, the equality that existed as the football flowed from one end to the other, and apart from glimpses of brilliance from Argentina, the under-achieving England team left an even more frustrating and bitterly disappointing taste.

As it turned out Italy won the World Cup on penalties as Zinedine Zidane ended his wonderful career with a red card for a shameful head-butt. Fabio Grosso smashed the winning kick past Fabien Barthez as the Azzurri claimed their first world title since 1982. It is their first ever win on penalties in the World Cup and heals the scars of their shoot-off defeat in the 1994 final to Brazil.

David Trezeguet was the only player to miss, firing his shot against the crossbar and Italy skipper Fabio Cannavaro then lifted the World Cup to celebrate his 100th cap for his country. It was a wonderful moment to mark a brilliant tournament by the Juventus skipper just a few hours before the Italian courts passed sentance on Juve and the other clubs trapped in the match fixing trial.

But sadly the final will be remembered most for Zidane's moment of madness in his last game before retirement. He charged at Italy defender Marco Materazzi and butted him in the chest in the second period of extra-time. Referee Horacio Elizondo, who sent off Rooney, reached for the red card after consulting with an assistant, who had been informed of Zidane's idiotic act by the fourth official. Zidane made his way slowly down the tunnel in tears, symbolically passing the World Cup on his way off the World stage for the final time. Sadly the enduring image of one of the greatest footballers of his generation will be of him ramming his bald head into Materazzi. The Italian defender fell to the floor and his team-mates reacted furiously. Both players had been involved in a tussle for possesson with the defender rapping his arms around the French skipepr and grabbing a fist full of flesh around the chest area. Initially Zidane laughed it off, but as they trotted away from the scene, the former Everton defender clearly mouthed some obscenity toward Zidane, who turned on his heels, the smile vanishing from his face, replaced by venom, and he brutally attacked his opponent. Clearly, Zidane's temper had snapped after something Materazzi said.

Zidane and Materazzi had been the key actors in the drama all night.

France went ahead through Zidane in the seventh minute when Materazzi was adjudged to have fouled Florent Malouda as he made a clumsy challenge inside the area.

The France skipper stepped up and copied Peter Crouch's cheekily chipped penalty – with one vital difference. Where Crouch landed his kick in Old Trafford's Stretford End against Jamaica, Zidane's made it into the goal – just. His dink hit the underside of the bar, bounced down a yard over the line and spun out. Argentinian ref Elizondo and his assistant were on the ball and gave the goal. Zidane jogged

> "It's a huge disappointment. You could see that in how we were a notch above our opponents in extra time."
> Raymond Domenech (France)

Zinedine Zidane departs the final, past the trophy he so coveted, after headbutting Marco Materazzi and receiving a deserved red card

Marco Materazzi's header equalises Zidane's early penalty

away with an arm raised as he joined Pel?, Vava and Paul Breitner as the only players to score in two World Cup finals.

It was a breathless start and Materazzi made amends for conceding the penalty when he climbed above Patrick Vieira to level the scores. In the team because of an injury to Alessandro Nesta, the defender now met Andrea Pirlo's out-swinging corner and headed in his second goal of the tournament.

Luca Toni then hung in the air and rattled the bar with a header before the break as France struggled to cope from corner kicks. Again it was Pirlo's expert delivery which caused the problem and Barthez was relieved to have the woodwork on his side.

France opened the second-half well. A typical burst of Thierry Henry's pace and power down the inside left channel sliced open Cannavaro and Gianluca Zambrotta. The striker opened up his body for a right-foot shot, but struck it tamely, straight at Gianluigi Buffon. Zambrotta then hacked clear from Henry in front of goal and the Arsenal captain dithered over a chance moments later.

France lost Vieira in the 55th minute. He limped off holding his hamstring and was replaced by Alou Diarra. Marcello Lippi made two changes on the hour, removing play-maker Francesco Totti and fellow midfielder Simone Perrotta, in a bid to halt the French charge. Within seconds, Toni found the net with a

header from a Pirlo free-kick, but one of his team-mates had drifted offside and it was ruled out.

Pirlo shaved the post with a curling free-kick and Lippi played his final card in the 86th minute when he sent on Alessandro del Piero. Just like the Euro 2000 final between the countries, extra-time was needed. Trezeguet, who scored the golden goal in Rotterdam six years ago, came on, but this time he would be the villain not the hero.

Buffon made a fingertip save to keep out a powerful header from Zidane in extra-time before the France captain did more damage by sinking his head into Materazzi. Henry, who was knocked out in a first-minute clash with Cannavaro, limped out of

DID YOU KNOW?
Italy's fourth World Cup title, following victories in 1934, 1938 and 1982. Brazil are the only country to have won the competition five times.

The Squadra Azzurra conceded only two goals during Germany 2006, equalling France's record set in 1998, for least goals conceded by World Cup winners.

Zinedine Zidane became the fourth player to be sent off in a World Cup final, joining countryman Marcel Desailly (1998), and Argentines Pedro Monzon and Gustavo Abel Dezotti (1990).

Zidane's goal ended Italy's clean sheet streak of four matches, one short of the World Cup best. This record was also set by Italy in 1990. Italy are unbeaten in 25 international matches, their longest such sequence since 1939. Their 12 goals at this tournament were scored by 10 different players. This equals France's record set in 1982.

the final in extra-time. Italy had trusted in fate all the way to Berlin. The Azzurri have reached the World Cup final every 12 years since 1970. And their domestic football was in the midst of a corruption scandal, just as it was when they last conquered the world, 24 years ago. And so, in the stadium where Jesse Owens won four gold Olympic gold medals, Italy won the World Cup for the fourth time.

Italy coach Marcello Lippi was naturally estatic, "I have to say thanks to the players. This is the most satisfying moment of my life. We are very happy. I dedicate the victory to my family. The players have unlimited heart, character and personality. This is the greatest satisfaction that any coach or footballer can feel. I've had the fortune to win the Champions League – a kind of world title for clubs – and lots of Serie A titles, but I've never felt anything like this."

But the shadow of Zidane hung heavily over France coach Domenech. The most Domenech would say was "it is a pity" before accusing Materazzi of play-acting, although television pictures clearly showed he was butted fiercely in the chest. "It should not have happened, but the referee was not on our side," he said. "I don't know what Materazzi said to Zidane. All I know is that the man of the match was not Andrea Pirlo, but Marco Materazzi because he scored the equaliser and had Zidane sent off. It is a pity. He really put on a great show when he went down and we know how

The Trevi fountain in Rome is bedecked in celebrating Italian fans

Rome's Circus Maximus is a riot of celebratory colour

these things work."

Domenech understood Zidane's loss of control, "There are moments when you take blows for 80 minutes. I'm not saying I'm excusing it, but I can understand. We missed Zinedine Zidane a lot in the last 10 minutes. His absence weighed heavily on the match. Yes, we can say that Zidane being sent off was the killing moment of the game. Especially in extra time -- the Italian team were obviously waiting for the penalty shootout. We can only be disappointed, not by our run, but by the final match and the way it ended. Really, from the game we played, we would have deserved to win. I've said it from the start, only victory is pretty. There will always be something missing. You can say what we did wasn't bad but it's Italy who are the champions."

France's 1998 World Cup-winning coach Aime Jacquet told Canal Plus TV: "A penalty shootout is always a lottery. I'm deeply disappointed because I was expecting a goal for France at any moment. Zizou's sending off was a terrible moment. They gave it all they had, physically and mentally. Maybe he was provoked. It's awful to see him leave that way because I sincerely believed he would lift that trophy."

The Italian victory sparked incredible scenes around the globe, stretching from Palestine to Boston, USA. In London, thousands of Italian fans turned Soho into a sea of red, white and green. Waving flags, blowing whistles and sounding klaxons, the Azzurri supporters spilled out of pubs and bars to celebrate.

But of course, the biggest celebration of all came in the capital city, Rome. Hundreds of thousands of delirious fans gathered in the ancient chariot-racing track of the Circus Maximus and, under instructions from Totti, celebrated with Italian sparkling wine rather than champagne.

Italian fans around the world celebrated in style and en masse. In London's Soho, at renowned cafe, Bar Italia, hundreds gather to witness the World Cup being won together

Day Thirty-Two
Monday 10 July 2006

The Italian airforce's acrobatic squadron greet the returning heroes with a tre colore fly-past at Rome's Pratica di Mare airport

There were a record 29 red cards and the lowest goals per game ratio on par with 1990, but for all of the negatives, I actually enjoyed a World Cup full of intrigue, penalty shoot outs and a poetic victory for a nation whose domestic football was in a complete state of turmoil.

Sure, there could have been more goals and less reds, but actually the stats, as usual, can paint a false picture. The games were more evenly matched in general, and if anything there should have been more yellows and red for the cheats and divers. Here is an element that urgently needs eradicated form

the game, not just globally, but more specifically in the Premiership. And the challenge for Keith Hackett and those who run the domestic game, is to instruct the refs to be bolder in flashing the cards at the divers. Naturally there is an element of doubt. And thats why I have been an advocate of using new technology to aid the officials. Whether or not monitors by the touchline were used to determine the Zidane headbutt, it must be time for those monitors to be utilised by the fourth and fifth officials to give a more definitive view of such major incidents.

I would have loved Thierry Henry to be a World Cup winner. There were more fouls committed on Henry than

any other player, but this was not the tournament where the big reputations shone. All the leading lights, notably the star strikers, never made much of an impact, with Klose finishing with the Golden Shoe with five goals.

However Italy were refreshingly attacking and were caught offside the most, which also meant that their keeper Gianluigi Buffon made by far the most saves in the competition.

My main frustration was the inexplicable failure by the England players to match their club reputations by underperforming in Germany. There were flashes of genius from Argentina, fewer from Brazil, lovely football at times from Spain and Mexico.

But the real World Cup winners were Germany. Tony Blair made the point that the national team might not have been in the final, but the tournament was still a triumph for the hosts.

The German economy has enjoyed a 0.3 per cent increase in GDP, two million visitors revised their idea of the country and Germans are again proud. Günter Grass, the Nobel-winning novelist, spoke of a "spontaneous embrace of the national colours." After Germany beat Portugal to take third place, a million fans packed streets near the Brandenburg Gate chanting: "Germany is the world champion of our hearts." Angela Merkel, the Chancellor, said: "It pleases me more than I can say that Germany is capable of rejoicing, even though it has not come first."

There had been fears of terrorism, hooligans, neo-Nazi marches and the diplomatic disaster of a visit by the Iranian leadership. And of course our own fans. But even England support-ers behaved, by and large, thanks in part to the relaxed way that police handled them.

Controversy followed the tournament right to the end, when Zidane won the FIFA Golden Ball award as the outstanding player of the World Cup despite being sent off in the second half of the final. The prize was decided by media votes, cast before Zidane was shown the red card. Zidane received 2,012, Cannavaro second (1,977) and his team-mate Pirlo third (715). Brazil and Spain shared the fair play award.

Zidane's mark on the 18th World Cup finals will never be forgotten – for good and bad reasons. His successful seventh minute penalty for France against Italy meant he became the fourth player to score three goals in the history of the showpiece final.

But his sending off in the 111th minute meant he also became only the fourth player to be sent off in a World Cup final. Zidane also scored in

FIFA Awards From The World Cup Finals

GOLDEN SHOE (top scorer)
Miroslav Klose (Germany)

GOLEN BALL
Zinedine Zidane (France)

MOST ENTERTAINING TEAM
Portugal

BEST GOALKEEPER
Gianluigi Buffon (Italy)

BEST YOUNG PLAYER
Lukas Podolski (Germany)

Zidane remained tight-lipped about what Materazzi had said to him during his official appearance with the French team to meet President Chirac

Zambrotta and Luca Toni fight over the Jules Rimet trophy on board the Italian open-top bus

France's second-round 3-1 victory over Spain and he netted from the penalty spot in their 1-0 semi-final victory over Portugal.

To cap a vintage World Cup – until the final itself – Zidane, 34, set up Henry's winner in the 1-0 victory over champions Brazil in the quarter-finals.

Despite media speculation, FIFA insisted video replays played no part in Zidane sending off. The off-the-ball incident was missed by Argentinean referee Horacio Elizondo and his assistants, but was spotted by the fourth official Luis Medina Cantalejo from Spain. France coach Domenech suggested that the fourth official only took action after seeing a video replay

– something that is not permitted under the rules of the game. But FIFA spokesman Andreas Herren said: "The fourth referee saw the incident with his own eyes and told the referee and the assistant referee directly though their headsets." FIFA said, although the fifth official does have a TV monitor, he is not permitted to intervene, and the fourth official has no access to video replays.

What Marco Materazzi may or may not have said to Zidane to cause the headbutt which had been the subject of endless column inches and phone-in shows, including even Channel 4's Richard and Judy, became the matter of intense speculation. Zidane's cousin

hined at a racial slur, or something akin to Materazzi having called Zidane a 'terrorist'. Whatever the words used, Zidane was saying nothing – yet.

The Italian media struggled to come to terms with the victory, barely able to believe they had overcome scandal and setbacks to win. "It's all true! Champions of the World," screamed the front page headline of sports daily Gazzetta dello Sport. "We are the champions of the world, although no-one thought we would be and no one wanted us to be," columnist Mario Sconcerti wrote in Corriere della Sera.

Before the tournament pundits expected they would be distracted by the prospect of relegation of their

"It's all true! Champions of the World,"
Gazzetta dello Sport

teams by a sporting tribunal. Some commentators celebrated what they saw as a return to innocence for the Italian game. "The cynics will say that the stars looking for new contracts after their clubs are relegated were running around in the search of new contracts," wrote Gianni Riotta in a front-page column in Corriere della Sera. "Not us. We think that after the phone taps, the accusations, the intrigue and the fraud, each one of the Azzurri returned for a month to what they were when they were lads on the street, when football was a dream, not a racket."

A sports prosecutor leading the investigation in the match-fixing case recommended the toughest punishments for Juventus – relegation to the third division or beyond, the annulment of the club's last two Italian titles and a deduction of points at the start of next season. He also wanted AC Milan, Fiorentina and Lazio to be sent to the second division, also with points deducted.

Amidst all this, the victorious team arrived back in Rome on Monday evening determined to enjoy the celebrations of an incredulous nation, forgetting entirely, for the moment, the unravelling of their national game, which must surely follow. For this one night Italy lived the dream – worthy winners of the 2006 World Cup.

Victorious captain Fabio Canavarro presents the World Cup to a breathless Italian nation

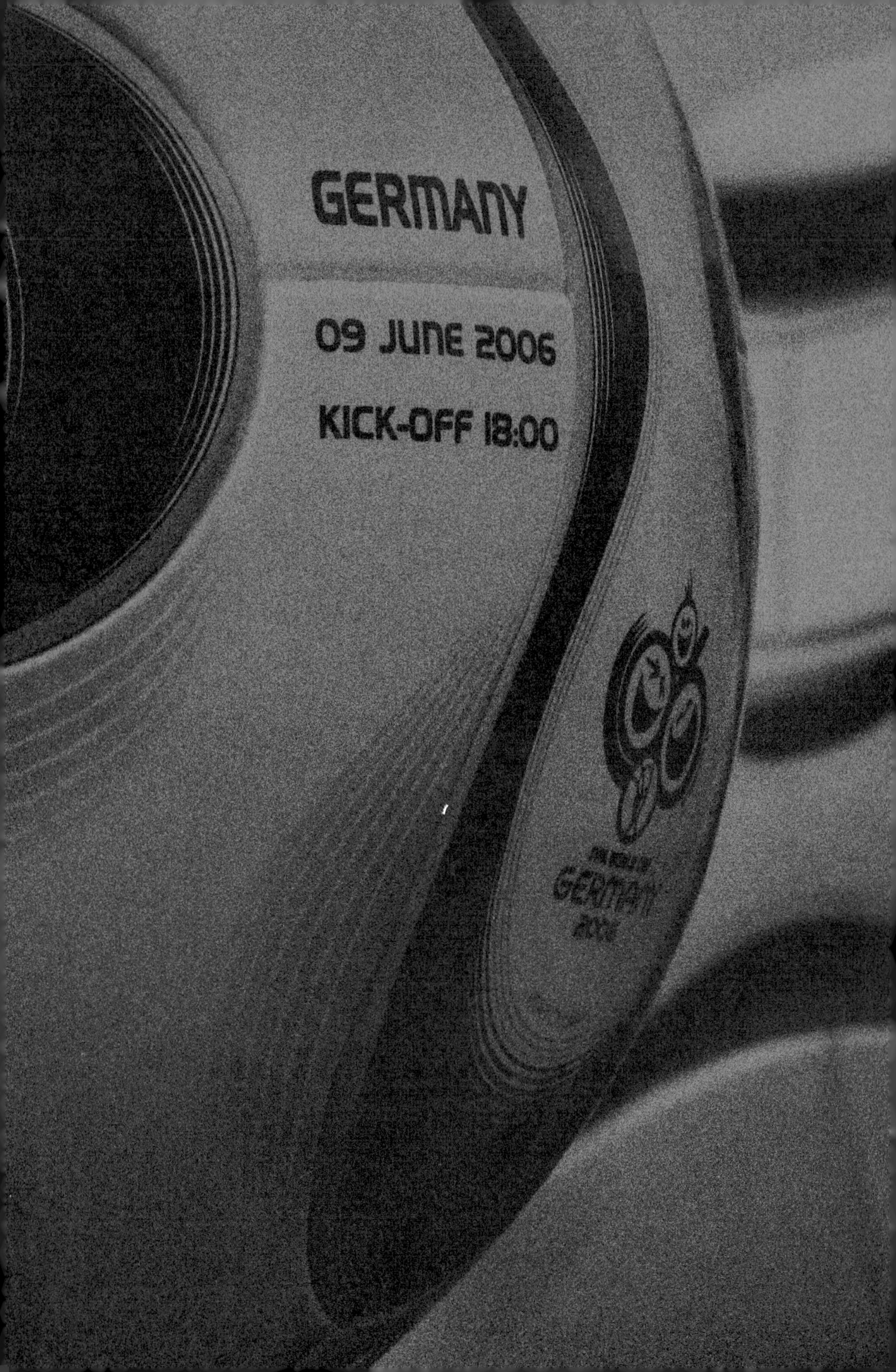
GERMANY
09 JUNE 2006
KICK-OFF 18:00

section
seven

statistics

Every Goal, Every Game, Every Fact!

Miroslav Klose celebrates his equaliser against Argentina, his fifth goal in the 2006 World Cup

LEADING GOALSCORERS

Miroslav Klose	Germany	5
Hernan Crespo	Argentina	3
Thierry Henry	France	3
Lukas Podolski	Germany	3
Maxi Rodrigues	Argentina	3
Ronaldo	Brazil	3
Fernando Torres	Spain	3
David Villa	Spain	3
Zinedine Zidane	France	3

MOST ASSISTS

Juan Riquelme	Argentina	4
Luis Figo	Portugal	3
Bastian Schweinsteiger	Germany	3
Francesco Totti	Italy	3

LEADING GOALKEEPERS

		Conceded	Games	Per Game
Pascal Zuberbühler	Switzerland	0	5	0
Gianluigi Buffon	Italy	2	7	0.29
Paul Robinson	England	2	5	0.40
Dida	Brazil	2	5	0.40
Fabien Barthez	France	3	7	0.42
Edwin van der Sar	Holland	2	4	0.50

DISCIPLINE

		Yellow Cards	Red Cards
Francisco Costinha	Portugal	4	1
Asamoah Gyan	Ghana	4	1
Khalid Boulahrouz	Holland	3	1
Deco	Portugal	3	1
Brett Emerton	Australia	3	1
Zied Jaziri	Tunisia	3	1
Teddy Lucic	Sweden	3	1
Andre Macanga	Angola	3	1
Albert Nadj	Serbia & Montenegro	3	1
Giovanni van Bronckhorst	Holland	3	1
Zinedine Zidane	France	3	1

TEAM DISCIPLINE				
	Yellow Cards	Red Cards	Games	Cards Per Game
Portugal	24	2	7	3.71
Ghana	18	1	4	4.75
Holland	16	2	4	4.50
France	16	1	7	2.43
Tunisia	14	1	3	5.00
Croatia	11	2	3	4.33
Serbia & Montenegro	12	1	3	4.33
Argentina	12	1	5	2.60
Ukraine	12	1	5	2.60
Australia	11	1	3	4.00

MOST GOALS IN A GAME

Argentina 6 v Serbia & Montenegro 0

MOST CARDS IN A GAME

16, Holland v Portugal (including 4 red cards for receiving two yellows)

Key to Squad Statistics

Due to the practice, in many cases, of players using names other than their 'surname' or in fact using a soubriquet, capitals are used for the name which each player used on his shirt during the World Cup finals

PLAYER POSITIONS

GK   Goalkeeper
DEF   Defender
MID   Midfielder
FOR   Forward

'Caps' column is correct up to, but not including, the county's first game in the World Cup finals. Any caps earned in World Cup 2006 are only listed on the right, under 'Games'.

'Assists' can total more than goals scored, where two players combine to create the goalscoring opportunity. They may also be lower where goals are scored direct from penalties or free-kicks or without the key assistance of another player.

statistics

ANGOLA

Coach: Luis de Oliveira Goncalves

In World Cup 2006

Squad No.	Player	Date of Birth	Club	Position	Caps	Games	Minutes played	%age	Goals	Assists	Yellow cards	Red cards
1	JOAO RICARDO Pereira	7/1/1970	Unaffiliated	GK	28	3	270	100%	0	0	0	0
2	Marcos AIROSA	6/8/1984	Barreirense (POR)	DEF	2	0	0	0%	0	0	0	0
3	JAMBA	10/7/1977	AS Aviacao (ANG)	DEF	37	3	270	100%	0	0	1	0
4	Antonio LEBO-LEBO	29/5/1977	Petro Atletico (ANG)	DEF	15	0	0	0%	0	0	0	0
5	KALI	11/10/1978	Barreirense (POR)	DEF	23	3	270	100%	0	0	0	0
6	MILOY	27/5/1981	Inter de Luanda (ANG)	MID	13	3	109	40%	0	0	0	0
7	Paulo FIGUEIREDO	28/11/1972	Varzim (POR)	MID	24	3	223	83%	0	0	0	0
8	Andre MACANGA	14/5/1978	Al Kuwait (KUW)	MID	35	2	168	62%	0	0	3	1
9	Pedro Manuel MANTORRAS	18/3/1982	Benfica (POR)	FOR	13	2	54	20%	0	0	0	0
10	AKWA	30/5/1977	Unaffiliated	FOR	79	3	199	74%	0	0	0	0
11	MATEUS Galiano da Costa	18/6/1984	Gil Vicente (POR)	MID	6	3	179	66%	0	0	0	0
12	LAMA	1/2/1981	Petro Atletico (ANG)	GK	9	0	0	0%	0	0	0	0
13	EDSON de Jesus Nobre	2/3/1980	Pacos Ferreira (POR)	MID	8	1	21	8%	0	0	0	0
14	Antonio MENDONCA	9/10/1982	Varzim (POR)	MID	36	3	270	100%	0	0	1	0
15	Manuel RUI MARQUES	3/9/1977	Hull City (ENG)	DEF	2	2	36	13%	0	0	0	0
16	FLAVIO Amado	30/12/1979	Al Ahly (EGY)	FOR	46	1	40	15%	1	0	0	0
17	ZE KALANGA	12/10/1983	Petro Atletico (ANG)	MID	25	3	241	89%	0	1	2	0
18	LOVE	14/3/1979	AS Aviacao (ANG)	FOR	35	1	68	25%	0	0	0	0
19	Andre TITI BUENGO	11/2/1980	Clermont (FRA)	FOR	2	0	0	0%	0	0	0	0
20	LOCO	25/12/1984	Primeiro de Agosto (ANG)	DEF	13	3	270	100%	0	0	2	0
21	Luis DELGADO	1/11/1979	Petro Atletico (ANG)	DEF	19	3	270	100%	0	0	1	0
22	Hipolito MARIO	1/6/1985	Inter de Luanda (ANG)	GK	1	0	0	0%	0	0	0	0
23	MARCO Abreu	8/12/1974	Portimonense (POR)	DEF	3	0	0	0%	0	0	0	0
								Team Totals	1	1	10	1

ARGENTINA

Coach: José Pekerman

In World Cup 2006

No.	Player	Date of Birth	Club	Position	Caps	Games	Minutes played	%age	Goals	Assists	Yellow cards	Red cards
1	Roberto ABBONDANZIERI	19/08/1972	Boca Juniors (ARG)	GK	22	5	460	90%	0	0	0	0
2	Roberto AYALA	14/04/1973	Valencia (ESP)	DEF	98	5	510	100%	1	0	0	0
3	Juan Pablo SORIN	05/05/1976	Villarreal (ESP)	DEF	71	4	420	82%	0	1	2	0
4	Fabricio COLOCCINI	22/01/1982	Deportivo La Coruna (ESP)	DEF	23	2	187	37%	0	0	0	0
5	Esteban CAMBIASSO	18/08/1980	Internazionale (ITA)	MID	22	5	378	74%	1	0	1	0
6	Gabriel HEINZE	19/04/1978	Manchester United (ENG)	DEF	29	4	420	82%	0	0	2	0
7	Javier SAVIOLA	11/12/1981	Sevilla FC (ESP)	FOR	31	3	215	42%	1	2	1	0
8	Javier MASCHERANO	08/06/1984	Corinthians (BRA)	MID	15	5	510	100%	0	0	2	0
9	Hernan CRESPO	05/07/1975	Chelsea (ENG)	FOR	55	4	305	60%	3	1	1	0
10	Juan RIQUELME	24/06/1978	Villarreal (ESP)	MID	31	5	449	88%	0	4	0	0
11	Carlos TEVEZ	05/02/1984	Corinthians (BRA)	FOR	21	4	288	56%	1	1	0	0
12	Leonardo FRANCO	20/05/1977	Atletico Madrid (ESP)	GK	3	1	50	10%	0	0	0	0
13	Lionel SCALONI	16/05/1978	West Ham United (ENG)	DEF	6	1	120	24%	0	0	0	0
14	Rodrigo PALACIO	05/02/1982	Boca Juniors (ARG)	FOR	2	1	27	5%	0	0	0	0
15	Gabriel MILITO	07/09/1980	Zaragoza (ESP)	DEF	15	1	90	18%	0	0	0	0
16	Pablo AIMAR	03/11/1979	Valencia (ESP)	MID	40	3	57	11%	0	0	0	0
17	Leandro CUFRE	09/05/1978	AS Roma (ITA)	DEF	2	1	90	18%	0	0	0	1
18	Maxi RODRIGUEZ	02/01/1981	Atletico Madrid (ESP)	MID	13	5	494	97%	0	0	1	0
19	Lionel MESSI	24/06/1987	Barcelona (ESP)	FOR	7	3	122	24%	1	1	0	0
20	Julio CRUZ	10/10/1974	Internazionale (ITA)	FOR	15	2	63	12%	0	0	1	0
21	Nicolas BURDISSO	12/04/1981	Internazionale (ITA)	DEF	8	3	203	40%	0	0	0	0
22	Luis GONZALEZ	19/01/1981	Porto (POR)	MID	27	3	152	30%	0	0	1	0
23	Oscar USTARI	03/07/1986	Independiente (ARG)	GK	0	0	0	0%	0	0	0	0
								Team Totals	8	10	12	1

AUSTRALIA

Coach: Guus Hiddink

In World Cup 2006

No.	Player	Date of Birth	Club	Position	Caps	Games	Minutes played	%age	Goals	Assists	Yellow cards	Red cards
1	Mark SCHWARZER	06/10/1972	Middlesbrough (ENG)	GK	37	3	270	75%	0	0	0	0
2	Lucas NEILL	09/03/1978	Blackburn Rovers (ENG)	DEF	25	4	360	100%	1	0	0	0
3	Craig MOORE	12/12/1975	Newcastle United (ENG)	DEF	33	4	308	86%	2	0	1	0
4	Tim CAHILL	06/12/1979	Everton (ENG)	MID	16	4	273	76%	0	0	2	0
5	Jason CULINA	05/08/1980	PSV Eindhoven (HOL)	MID	13	4	360	100%	0	0	1	0
6	Tony POPOVIC	04/07/1973	Crystal Palace (ENG)	DEF	56	1	40	11%	0	0	0	0
7	Brett EMERTON	22/02/1979	Blackburn Rovers (ENG)	MID	48	3	266	74%	0	0	3	1
8	Josip SKOKO	10/12/1975	Wigan Athletic(ENG)	MID	46	0	0	0%	0	0	0	0
9	Mark VIDUKA	09/10/1975	Middlesbrough (ENG)	FOR	33	4	360	100%	0	0	0	0
10	Harry KEWELL	22/09/1978	Liverpool (ENG)	FOR	20	3	215	60%	1	0	0	0
11	Stan LAZARIDIS	16/08/1972	Birmingham City (ENG)	MID	59	0	0	0%	0	0	0	0
12	Ante COVIC	13/06/1975	Hammarby (SWE)	GK	1	0	0	0%	0	0	0	0
13	Vince GRELLA	05/10/1979	Parma (ITA)	MID	17	4	332	92%	0	0	2	0
14	Scott CHIPPERFIELD	30/12/1975	Basel (SUI)	DEF	46	4	344	96%	0	0	0	0
15	John ALOISI	05/02/1976	Alaves (ESP)	FOR	41	4	76	21%	1	2	1	0
16	Michael BEAUCHAMP	08/03/1981	Central Coast Mariners (AUS)	DEF	2	0	0	0%	0	0	0	0
17	Archie THOMPSON	23/10/1978	PSV Eindhoven (HOL)	FOR	20	0	0	0%	0	0	0	0
18	Zeljko KALAC	16/12/1972	AC Milan (ITA)	GK	52	1	90	25%	0	0	0	0
19	Joshua KENNEDY	20/08/1982	Dynamo Dresden (GER)	FOR	1	2	46	13%	0	0	0	0
20	Luke WILKSHIRE	02/10/1981	Bristol City (ENG)	MID	8	2	164	46%	0	0	1	0
21	Mile STERJOVSKI	27/05/1979	Basel (SUI)	MID	22	3	240	67%	0	0	0	0
22	Mark MILLIGAN	04/08/1985	Sydney FC (AUS)	DEF	1	0	0	0%	0	0	0	0
23	Marco BRESCIANO	11/02/1980	Parma (ITA)	MID	24	4	212	59%	0	0	0	0
								Team Totals	5	2	11	1

BRAZIL

Coach: Carlos Alberto Parreira

In World Cup 2006

No.	Player	Date of Birth	Club	Position	Caps	Games	Minutes played	%age	Goals	Assists	Yellow cards	Red cards
1	DIDA	07/10/1973	AC Milan (ITA)	GK	86	5	441	98%	0	0	0	0
2	CAFU	07/06/1970	AC Milan (ITA)	DEF	138	4	345	77%	0	2	2	0
3	LUCIO	08/05/1978	Bayern Munich (GER)	DEF	50	5	450	100%	0	0	1	0
4	JUAN	01/02/1979	Bayer Leverkusen (GER)	DEF	38	5	450	100%	0	1	2	0
5	EMERSON	04/04/1976	Juventus (ITA)	MID	70	3	206	46%	0	0	1	0
6	ROBERTO CARLOS	10/04/1973	Real Madrid (SPA)	DEF	121	4	360	80%	0	0	0	0
7	ADRIANO	17/02/1982	Internazionale (ITA)	FOR	32	4	265	59%	2	0	1	0
8	KAKA	22/04/1982	AC Milan (ITA)	MID	38	5	410	91%	1	1	0	0
9	RONALDO	22/09/1976	Real Madrid (SPA)	FOR	92	5	409	91%	3	1	2	0
10	RONALDINHO	21/03/1980	Barcelona (SPA)	FOR	63	5	430	96%	0	1	0	0
11	ZE ROBERTO	06/07/1974	Bayern Munich (GER)	MID	79	5	380	84%	1	0	0	0
12	Rogerio CENI	22/01/1973	Sao Paulo (BRA)	GK	15	1	9	2%	0	0	0	0
13	CICINHO	24/06/1980	Real Madrid (SPA)	DEF	10	2	105	23%	0	1	0	0
14	LUISAO	13/02/1981	Benfica (POR)	DEF	19	0	0	0%	0	0	0	0
15	CRIS	03/06/1977	Lyon (FRA)	DEF	16	0	0	0%	0	0	0	0
16	GILBERTO	25/04/1976	Hertha Berlin (GER)	DEF	9	1	90	20%	1	0	1	0
17	GILBERTO SILVA	07/10/1976	Arsenal (ENG)	MID	36	4	244	54%	0	0	0	0
18	MINEIRO	02/08/1975	Sao Paulo (BRA)	MID	2	0	0	0%	0	0	0	0
19	JUNINHO Pernambucano	30/01/1975	Lyon (FRA)	MID	37	3	182	40%	1	0	0	0
20	RICARDINHO	23/05/1976	Corinthians (BRA)	MID	19	2	28	6%	0	1	0	0
21	FRED	03/10/1983	Lyon (FRA)	FOR	3	1	3	1%	1	0	0	0
22	Julio CESAR	03/09/1979	Internazionale (ITA)	GK	11	0	0	0%	0	0	0	0
23	ROBINHO	25/01/1984	Real Madrid (SPA)	FOR	23	4	143	32%	0	0	1	0
								Team Totals	10	8	11	0

statistics

COSTA RICA

Coach: Alexandre Guimaraes

In World Cup 2006

No.	Player	Date of Birth	Club	Position	Caps	Games	Minutes played	%age	Goals	Assists	Yellow cards	Red cards
1	Alvaro MESEN	24/12/1972	Herediano (CRC)	GK	38	0	0	0%	0	0	0	0
2	Jervis DRUMMOND	08/09/1976	Saprissa (CRC)	DEF	56	2	94	35%	0	0	0	0
3	Luis MARIN	10/08/1974	Alajuelense (CRC)	DEF	120	3	270	100%	0	0	2	0
4	Michael UMANA	16/07/1982	Brujas (CRC)	DEF	18	3	270	100%	0	0	1	0
5	Gilberto MARTINEZ	01/10/1979	Brescia (ITA)	DEF	57	1	65	24%	0	0	0	0
6	Danny FONSECA	07/11/1979	Cartagines (CRC)	MID	22	2	118	44%	0	0	1	0
7	Cristian BOLANOS	17/05/1984	Saprissa (CRC)	MID	16	2	90	33%	0	0	0	0
8	Mauricio SOLIS	13/12/1972	Comunicaciones (GUA)	MID	107	3	257	95%	0	0	1	0
9	Paulo WANCHOPE	31/07/1976	Herediano (CRC)	FOR	69	3	270	100%	2	0	0	0
10	Walter CENTENO	06/10/1974	Saprissa (CRC)	MID	93	3	263	97%	0	1	0	0
11	Ronald GOMEZ	24/01/1975	Saprissa (CRC)	FOR	80	3	260	96%	1	1	1	0
12	Leonardo GONZALEZ	21/11/1980	Herediano (CRC)	DEF	36	3	235	87%	0	0	1	0
13	Kurt BERNARD	08/12/1977	Puntarenas (CRC)	FOR	3	1	7	3%	0	0	0	0
14	Randall AZOFEIFA	30/12/1984	Saprissa (CRC)	MID	5	1	1	0%	0	0	0	0
15	Harodl WALLACE	07/09/1975	Alajuelense (CRC)	DEF	78	2	111	41%	0	0	0	0
16	Carlos HERNANDO	09/04/1982	Alajuelense (CRC)	MID	17	2	44	16%	0	0	0	0
17	Gabriel BADILLA	30/06/1984	Saprissa (CRC)	DEF	7	1	90	33%	0	0	1	0
18	Jose PORRAS	08/11/1970	Saprissa (CRC)	GK	16	3	270	100%	0	0	0	0
19	Alvaro SABORIO	25/03/1982	Saprissa (CRC)	FOR	23	2	75	28%	0	0	0	0
20	Douglas SEQUEIRA	23/08/1977	Real Salt Lake (USA)	MID	29	2	180	67%	0	0	0	0
21	Victor NUNEZ	15/04/1980	Cartagines (CRC)	FOR	3	0	0	0%	0	0	0	0
22	Michael RODRIGUEZ	30/12/1981	Alajuelense (CRC)	DEF	3	0	0	0%	0	0	0	0
23	Wardy ALFARO	31/12/1977	Alajuelense (CRC)	GK	2	0	0	0%	0	0	0	0
								Team Totals	3	2	8	0

CROATIA

Coach: Zlatko Kranjcar

In World Cup 2006

No.	Player	Date of Birth	Club	Position	Caps	Games	Minutes played	%age	Goals	Assists	Yellow cards	Red cards
1	Stipe PLETIKOSA	08/01/1979	Hajduk Split (CRO)	GK	50	3	270	100%	0	0	1	0
2	Darijo SRNA	01/05/1982	Shakhtar Donetsk (UKR)	MID	36	3	266	99%	1	0	1	0
3	Josip SIMUNIC	18/02/1978	Hertha Berlin (GER)	DEF	42	3	270	100%	0	0	2	1
4	Robert KOVAC	06/04/1974	Juventus (ITA)	DEF	56	2	180	67%	0	0	2	0
5	Igor TUDOR	16/04/1978	Siena (ITA)	DEF	52	3	249	92%	0	0	2	0
6	Jurica VRANJES	31/01/1980	Werder Bremen (GER)	MID	24	0	0	0%	0	0	0	0
7	Dario SIMIC	12/11/1975	AC Milan (ITA)	DEF	80	3	264	98%	0	0	2	1
8	Marko BABIC	28/01/1981	Bayer Leverkusen (GER)	MID	33	3	270	100%	0	0	0	0
9	Dado PRSO	05/11/1974	Rangers (SCO)	FOR	29	3	270	100%	0	0	0	0
10	Niko KOVAC	15/10/1971	Hertha Berlin (GER)	MID	58	3	220	81%	1	0	1	0
11	Mario TOKIC	23/07/1975	Austria Vienna (AUT)	DEF	28	0	0	0%	0	0	0	0
12	Joe DIDULICA	14/10/1977	Austria Vienna (AUT)	GK	4	0	0	0%	0	0	0	0
13	Stjepan TOMAS	06/03/1976	Galatasaray (TUR)	DEF	48	1	82	30%	0	0	0	0
14	Luka MODRIC	09/09/1985	Dinamo Zagreb (CRO)	MID	5	2	30	11%	0	0	0	0
15	Ivan LEKO	07/02/1978	Club Brugge (BEL)	MID	13	0	0	0%	0	0	0	0
16	Jerko LEKO	09/04/1980	Dynamo Kiev (UKR)	MID	36	2	76	28%	0	0	0	0
17	Ivan KLASNIC	29/01/1980	Werder Bremen (GER)	FOR	20	3	153	57%	0	0	0	0
18	Ivica OLIC	14/09/1979	CSKA Moscow (RUS)	FOR	36	3	129	48%	0	0	0	0
19	Niko KRANJCAR	13/08/1984	Hajduk Split (CRO)	MID	21	3	231	86%	0	0	0	0
20	Anthony SERIC	15/01/1979	Panathinaikos (GRE)	MID	14	0	0	0%	0	0	0	0
21	Bosko BALABAN	15/10/1978	Club Brugge (BEL)	FOR	27	0	0	0%	0	0	0	0
22	Ivan BOSNJAK	06/02/1979	Dinamo Zagreb (CRO)	FOR	13	1	4	1%	0	0	0	0
23	Tomislav BUTINA	30/03/1974	Club Brugge (BEL)	GK	28	0	0	0%	0	0	0	0
								Team Totals	2	0	11	2

CZECH REPUBLIC

								In World Cup 2006					
No.	Player	Date of Birth	Club	Position	Caps	Games	Minutes played	%age	Goals	Assists	Yellow cards	Red cards	
1	Petr CECH	20/05/1982	Chelsea (ENG)	GK	41	3	270	100%	0	0	0	0	
2	Zdenek GRYGERA	14/05/1980	Ajax (HOL)	DEF	41	3	270	100%	0	1	1	0	
3	Pavel MARES	18/01/1976	Zenit St Petersburg (RUS)	DEF	10	0	0	0%	0	0	0	0	
4	Tomas GALASEK	15/01/1973	Ajax (HOL)	MID	29	2	135	50%	0	0	0	0	
5	Radoslav KOVAC	27/11/1979	Spartak Moscow (RUS)	MID	6	1	77	29%	0	0	0	0	
6	Marek JANKULOVSKI	09/05/1977	AC Milan (ITA)	DEF	48	3	370	100%	0	0	0	0	
7	Libor SIONKO	01/02/1977	Glasgow Rangers (SCO)	FOR	17	1	23	9%	0	0	0	0	
8	Karel POBORSKY	30/03/1972	Ceske Budejovice (CZE)	MID	115	3	181	67%	0	0	0	0	
9	Jan KOLLER	30/03/1973	Borussia Dortmund (GER)	FOR	68	1	44	16%	1	0	0	0	
10	Tomas ROSICKY	04/10/1980	Borussia Dortmund (GER)	MID	54	3	265	98%	2	0	1	0	
11	Pavel NEDVED	30/08/1972	Juventus (ITA)	MID	87	3	270	100%	0	1	0	0	
12	Vratislav LOKVENC	27/09/1973	Austria Salzburg (AUT)	FOR	72	2	136	50%	0	0	2	0	
13	Martin JIRANEK	25/05/1979	Spartak Moscow (RUS)	DEF	24	0	0	0%	0	0	0	0	
14	David JAROLIM	17/05/1979	Hamburg (GER)	MID	3	1	27	10%	0	0	0	0	
15	Milan BAROS	28/10/1981	Aston Villa (ENG)	FOR	49	1	63	23%	0	0	0	0	
16	Jaromir BLAZEK	29/12/1972	Sparta Prague (CZE)	GK	11	0	0	0%	0	0	0	0	
17	Jiri STAJNER	27/05/1976	Hanover 96 (GER)	MID	21	3	85	31%	0	0	0	0	
18	Marek HEINZ	04/08/1977	Galatasaray (TUR)	FOR	28	1	13	5%	0	0	0	0	
19	Jan POLAK	01/3/1981	Nuremberg (GER)	MID	18	3	99	37%	0	0	2	1	
20	Jaroslav PLASIL	05/01/2019	Monaco (FRA)	MID	14	3	24	9%	0	0	0	0	
21	Tomas UJFALUSI	24/03/1978	Fiorentina (ITA)	DEF	48	2	154	57%	0	0	0	1	
22	David ROZEHNAL	05/07/1980	Paris Saint-Germain (FRA)	DEF	22	3	270	100%	0	0	0	0	
23	Antonin KINSKY	31/05/1975	Saturn Moscow Region (RUS)	GK	5	0	0	0%	0	0	1	0	
								Team Totals	3	2	7	2	

ECUADOR

								In World Cup 2006					
No.	Player	Date of Birth	Club	Position	Caps	Games	Minutes played	%age	Goals	Assists	Yellow cards	Red cards	
1	Edwin VILLAFUERTE	12/03/1979	Deportivo Quito (ECU)	GK	15	0	0	0%	0	0	0	0	
2	Jorge GUAGUA	28/09/1981	El Nacional (ECU)	DEF	18	3	134	37%	0	0	0	0	
3	Ivan HURTADO	16/08/1974	Al Arabi (QAT)	DEF	130	3	248	69%	0	0	1	0	
4	Ulises DE LA CRUZ	08/02/1974	Aston Villa (ENG)	DEF	84	4	360	100%	0	0	2	0	
5	Jose PERLAZA	06/10/1981	Olmedo (ECU)	DEF	3	0	0	0%	0	0	0	0	
6	Patricio URRUTIA	15/10/1977	LDU Quito (ECU)	MID	6	3	49	14%	0	0	0	0	
7	Christian LARA	27/04/1980	El Nacional (ECU)	MID	19	2	50	14%	0	0	0	0	
8	Edison MENDEZ	16/03/1979	LDU Quito (ECU)	MID	64	4	360	100%	0	2	1	0	
9	Felix BORJA	02/04/1983	El Nacional (ECU)	FOR	6	1	45	13%	0	0	0	0	
10	Ivan KAVIEDES	24/10/1977	Argentinos Juniors (ARG)	FOR	44	4	180	50%	1	1	0	0	
11	Agustin DELGADO	23/12/1974	LDU Quito (ECU)	FOR	68	3	262	73%	2	1	0	0	
12	Christian MORA	26/08/1979	LDU Quito (ECU)	GK	12	4	360	25%	0	0	1	0	
13	Paul AMBROSI	14/10/1980	LDU Quito (ECU)	DEF	24	1	90	75%	0	0	0	0	
14	Segundo CASTILLO	15/05/1982	El Nacional (ECU)	MID	11	3	270	19%	0	0	1	0	
15	Marlon AYOVI	27/09/1971	Deportivo Quito (ECU)	MID	74	1	67	87%	0	0	0	0	
16	Luis VALENCIA	04/08/1985	Recreativo Huelva (ESP)	MID	17	4	314	94%	0	1	2	0	
17	Giovanny ESPINOZA	12/04/1977	LDU Quito (ECU)	DEF	56	4	338	94%	0	0	0	0	
18	Neicer REASCO	23/7/1977	LDU Quito (ECU)	DEF	31	3	270	75%	0	0	0	0	
19	Luis SARITAMA	20/10/1983	Deportivo Quito (ECU)	MID	15	0	0	0%	0	0	0	0	
20	Edwin TENORIO	16/06/1976	Barcelona (ECU)	MID	68	4	338	94%	0	0	0	0	
21	Carlos TENORIO	14/05/1979	Al Sadd (QAT)	FOR	29	3	180	50%	2	0	1	0	
22	Damian LANZA	10/04/1982	Aucas (ECU)	GK	5	0	0	0%	0	0	0	0	
23	Cristian BENITEZ	01/05/1986	El Nacional (ECU)	FOR	5	1	45	13%	0	0	0	0	
								Team Totals	5	5	9	0	

statistics

ENGLAND

Coach: Sven-Göran Eriksson

In World Cup 2006

No.	Player	Date of Birth	Club	Position	Caps	Games	Minutes played	%age	Goals	Assists	Yellow cards	Red cards
1	Paul ROBINSON	15/10/1979	Tottenham Hotspur (ENG)	GK	21	5	480	100%	0	0	1	0
2	Gary NEVILLE	18/02/1975	Manchester United (ENG)	DEF	79	2	210	44%	0	0	0	0
3	Ashley COLE	20/12/1980	Arsenal (ENG)	DEF	46	5	480	100%	0	0	0	0
4	Steven GERRARD	30/5/1980	Liverpool (ENG)	MID	42	5	411	86%	2	0	1	0
5	Rio FERDINAND	07/11/1978	Manchester United (ENG)	DEF	47	5	445	93%	0	0	0	0
6	John TERRY	07/12/1980	Chelsea (ENG)	DEF	24	5	480	100%	0	0	2	0
7	David BECKHAM	02/05/1975	Real Madrid (SPA)	MID	89	5	407	85%	1	2	0	0
8	Frank LAMPARD	20/06/1978	Chelsea (ENG)	MID	40	5	480	100%	0	0	1	0
9	Wayne ROONEY	24/10/1985	Manchester United (ENG)	FOR	29	4	252	53%	0	0	0	1
10	Michael OWEN	14/12/1979	Newcastle United (ENG)	FOR	77	3	115	24%	0	0	0	0
11	Joe COLE	08/11/1981	Chelsea (ENG)	MID	32	5	386	80%	1	1	0	0
12	Sol CAMPBELL	18/09/1974	Arsenal (ENG)	DEF	68	1	35	7%	0	0	0	0
13	David JAMES	01/08/1970	Manchester City (ENG)	GK	34	0	0	0%	0	0	0	0
14	Wayne BRIDGE	05/08/2001	Fulham (ENG)	DEF	23	0	0	0%	0	0	0	0
15	Jamie CARRAGHER	28/1/1978	Liverpool (ENG)	DEF	25	4	163	34%	0	0	1	0
16	Owen HARGREAVES	20/01/1981	Bayern Munich (GER)	MID	30	4	308	64%	0	0	2	0
17	Jermaine JENAS	18/02/1983	Tottenham Hotspur (ENG)	MID	15	0	0	0%	0	0	0	0
18	Michael CARRICK	28/07/1981	Tottenham Hotspur (ENG)	MID	6	1	90	19%	0	0	0	0
19	Aaron LENNON	16/04/1987	Tottenham Hotspur (ENG)	MID	1	3	104	22%	0	0	0	0
20	Stewart DOWNING	22/07/1984	Middlesbrough (ENG)	MID	2	3	52	11%	0	0	0	0
21	Peter CROUCH	30/01/1981	Liverpool (ENG)	FOR	7	4	323	67%	1	0	1	0
22	Scott CARSON	03/09/1985	Liverpool (ENG)	GK	0	0	0	0%	0	0	0	0
23	Theo WALCOTT	16/03/1989	Arsenal (ENG)	FOR	1	0	0	0%	0	0	0	0
								Team Totals	5	3	9	1

FRANCE

Coach: Raymond Domenech

In World Cup 2006

No.	Player	Date of Birth	Club	Position	Caps	Games	Minutes played	%age	Goals	Assists	Yellow cards	Red cards
1	Michael LANDREAU	14/05/1979	Nantes (FRA)	GK	3	0	0	0%	0	0	0	0
2	Jean-Alain BOUMSONG	14/12/1979	Newcastle (ENG)	DEF	19	0	0	0%	0	0	0	0
3	Eric ABIDAL	11/09/1979	Lyon (FRA)	DEF	8	6	570	86%	0	0	2	0
4	Patrick VIEIRA	23/6/1976	Juventus (ITA)	MID	87	7	585	89%	2	2	1	0
5	William GALLAS	17/08/1977	Chelsea (ENG)	DEF	40	7	660	100%	0	0	0	0
6	Claude MAKELELE	18/02/1973	Chelsea (ENG)	MID	43	7	660	100%	0	0	2	0
7	Florent MALOUDA	13/06/1980	Lyon (FRA)	MID	13	6	501	76%	0	0	1	0
8	Vikash DHORASOO	10/10/1973	Paris St-Germain (FRA)	MID	16	2	10	2%	0	0	0	0
9	Sidney GOVOU	27/07/1979	Olympique Lyonnaise (FRA)	FOR	19	4	64	10%	0	0	0	0
10	Zinedine ZIDANE	23/06/1972	Real Madrid (SPA)	MID	102	6	558	85%	3	1	3	1
11	Sylvain WILTORD	10/5/1974	Lyon (FRA)	FOR	80	7	208	32%	0	1	0	0
12	Thierry HENRY	17/08/1977	Arsenal (ENG)	FOR	78	7	632	96%	3	0	0	0
13	Mikael SILVESTRE	09/08/1977	Manchester United (ENG)	DEF	39	1	90	14%	0	0	0	0
14	Louis SAHA	08/08/1978	Manchester United (ENG)	FOR	9	3	32	5%	0	0	2	0
15	Lilian THURAM	01/01/1972	Juventus (ITA)	DEF	114	7	660	100%	0	0	1	0
16	Fabien BARTHEZ	28/06/1971	Marseille (FRA)	GK	80	7	660	100%	0	0	0	0
17	Gael GIVET	09/10/1981	Monaco (FRA)	DEF	11	0	0	0%	0	0	0	0
18	Alou DIARRA	15/07/1981	Lens (FRA)	MID	9	2	75	11%	0	0	0	0
19	Willy SAGNOL	18/03/1977	Bayern Munich (GER)	DEF	38	7	660	100%	0	0	3	0
20	David TREZEGUET	15/10/1977	Juventus (ITA)	FOR	63	3	112	17%	0	0	0	0
21	Pascal CHIMBONDA	21/2/1979	Wigan Athletic (ENG)	DEF	1	0	0	0%	0	0	0	0
22	Frank RIBERY	07/04/1983	Marseille (FRA)	MID	3	7	512	78%	0	0	0	0
23	Gregory COUPET	31/12/1972	Lyon (FRA)	GK	18	0	0	0%	1	1	1	0
								Team Totals	9	5	16	1

GERMANY

Coach: Jürgen Klinsmann | In World Cup 2006

No.	Player	Date of Birth	Club	Position	Caps	Games	Minutes played	%age	Goals	Assists	Yellow cards	Red cards
1	Jens LEHMANN	10/11/2001	Arsenal (ENG)	GK	32	6	600	87%	0	0	0	0
2	Marcell JANSEN	04/11/1985	Borussia Moenchengladbach (GER)	DEF	7	1	90	13%	0	0	0	0
3	Arne FRIEDRICH	29/05/1979	Hertha Berlin (GER)	DEF	36	6	573	83%	0	0	1	0
4	Robert HUTH	18/08/1984	Chelsea (ENG)	DEF	16	1	90	13%	0	0	0	0
5	Sebastian KEHL	13/02/1980	Borussia Dortmund (GER)	MID	27	4	235	34%	0	0	0	0
6	Jens NOWOTNY	11/01/1974	Bayer Leverkusen (GER)	DEF	46	1	90	13%	0	0	0	0
7	Bastian SCHWEINSTEIGER	01/08/1984	Bayern Munich (GER)	MID	28	7	526	76%	2	3	1	0
8	Torsten FRINGS	22/11/1976	Werder Bremen (GER)	MID	52	6	539	78%	1	0	2	0
9	Mike HANKE	05/11/1983	Wolfsburg (GER)	FOR	6	1	20	3%	0	0	0	0
10	Oliver NEUVILLE	01/05/1973	Borussia Moenchengladbach (GER)	FOR	55	7	145	21%	1	0	0	0
11	Miroslav KLOSE	09/06/1978	Werder Bremen (GER)	FOR	55	7	582	84%	5	1	0	0
12	Oliver KAHN	15/06/1969	Bayern Munich (GER)	GK	85	1	90	13%	0	0	0	0
13	Michael BALLACK	26/09/1976	Bayern Munich (GER)	MID	65	5	510	74%	0	1	1	0
14	Gerald ASAMOAH	03/10/1978	Schalke 04 (GER)	FOR	40	1	18	3%	0	0	0	0
15	Thomas HITZLSPERGER	05/04/1982	VfB Stuttgart (GER)	MID	15	1	12	2%	0	0	0	0
16	Philipp LAHM	11/11/1983	Bayern Munich (GER)	DEF	18	7	690	100%	1	0	0	0
17	Per MERTESACKER	29/09/1984	Hanover 96 (GER)	DEF	23	6	600	87%	0	0	0	0
18	Tim BOROWSKI	02/05/1980	Werder Bremen (GER)	MID	20	6	248	36%	0	1	2	0
19	Bernd SCHNEIDER	17/11/1973	Bayer Leverkusen (GER)	MID	64	7	574	83%	0	1	0	0
20	Lukas PODOLSKI	04/06/1985	FC Cologne (GER)	FOR	25	7	633	92%	3	0	1	0
21	Christoph METZELDER	05/11/1980	Borussia Dortmund (GER)	DEF	22	6	600	87%	0	0	2	0
22	David ODONKOR	21/02/1984	Borussia Dortmund (GER)	MID	1	4	125	18%	0	0	2	0
23	Timo HILDEBRAND	05/04/1979	VfB Stuttgart (GER)	GK	0	0	0	0%	0	1	0	0
								Team Totals	13	8	12	0

GHANA

Coach: Ratomir Dujkovic | In World Cup 2006

No.	Player	Date of Birth	Club	Position	Caps	Games	Minutes played	%age	Goals	Assists	Yellow cards	Red cards
1	Sammy ADJEI	01/09/1980	Ashdod (ISR)	GK	31	0	0	0%	0	0	0	0
2	Hans SARPEI	28/06/1976	Wolfsburg (GER)	DEF	7	0	0	0%	0	0	0	0
3	Asamoah GYAN	22/11/1985	Modena (ITA)	FOR	13	3	252	70%	1	1	4	1
4	Samuel KUFFOUR	03/09/1976	AS Roma (ITA)	DEF	58	1	90	25%	0	0	0	0
5	John MENSAH	29/11/1982	Rennes (FRA)	DEF	33	4	360	100%	0	0	1	0
6	Emmanuel PAPPOE	03/03/1981	Hapoel Kfar Saba (ISR)	DEF	27	2	135	38%	0	0	0	0
7	Illiasu SHILLA	26/10/1982	Asante Kotoko (GHA)	DEF	2	4	315	88%	0	0	1	0
8	Michael ESSIEN	03/12/1982	Chelsea (ENG)	MID	17	3	270	75%	0	0	2	0
9	Derek BOATENG	02/05/1983	AIK Solna (SWE)	MID	11	3	121	34%	0	0	1	0
10	Stephen APPIAH	24/12/1980	Fenerbahce (TUR)	MID	42	4	360	100%	1	1	2	0
11	Sulley MUNTARI	27/08/1984	Udinese (ITA)	MID	16	3	270	75%	1	0	3	0
12	Alex TACHIE-MENSAH	15/02/1977	St Gall (SUI)	FOR	5	3	34	9%	0	0	0	0
13	Habib MOHAMED	10/12/1983	King Faisal (GHA)	DEF	1	2	180	50%	0	0	1	0
14	Matthew AMOAH	24/10/1980	Borussia Dortmund (GER)	FOR	16	4	273	76%	0	0	0	0
15	John PANTSIL	15/06/1981	Hapoel Tel-Aviv (ISR)	DEF	21	4	360	100%	0	0	1	0
16	George OWU	07/07/1982	AshantiGold (GHA)	GK	6	0	0	0%	0	0	0	0
17	Daniel QUAYE	25/12/1980	Hearts (GHA)	DEF	7	0	0	0%	0	0	0	0
18	Eric ADDO	12/11/1978	PSV Eindhoven (HOL)	MID	6	4	192	53%	0	0	1	0
19	Razk PIMPONG	30/12/1982	Copenhagen (DEN)	FOR	4	3	119	33%	0	0	0	0
20	Otto ADDO	09/06/1975	Mainz 05 (GER)	MID	13	2	90	25%	0	0	1	0
21	Ahmed ISSAH	24/05/1982	Randers FC (DEN)	DEF	10	0	0	0%	0	0	0	0
22	Richard KINGSTON	13/06/1978	Ankaraspor (TUR)	GK	33	4	360	100%	0	0	0	0
23	Haminu DRAMANI	01/04/1986	Crvena Zvezda (SCG)	MID	7	2	169	47%	1	0	0	0
								Team Totals	4	2	18	1

statistics

HOLLAND

Coach: Marco van Basten   In World Cup 2006

No.	Player	Date of Birth	Club	Position	Caps	Games	Minutes played	%age	Goals	Assists	Yellow cards	Red cards
1	Edwin VAN DER SAR	29/10/1970	Manchester United (ENG)	GK	109	4	360	100%	0	0	0	0
2	Kew JAIENS	15/09/1978	AZ Alkmaar (HOL)	DEF	1	1	90	25%	0	0	0	0
3	Khalid BOULAHROUZ	28/12/1981	Hamburger SV (GER)	DEF	11	4	202	56%	0	0	3	1
4	Joris MATHIJSEN	05/04/1980	AZ Alkmaar (HOL)	DEF	8	3	230	64%	0	0	1	0
5	Giovanni VAN BRANCKHORST	05/02/1975	Barcelona (SPA)	DEF	57	3	270	75%	0	0	3	1
6	Danny LANDZAAT	06/05/1976	AZ Alkmaar (HOL)	MID	23	3	73	20%	0	0	0	0
7	Dirk KUYT	22/07/1980	Feyenoord (HOL)	FOR	19	3	202	56%	0	0	1	0
8	Phillip COCU	29/10/1970	PSV Eindhoven (HOL)	MID	97	4	353	98%	0	0	0	0
9	Ruud VAN NISTELROOY	01/07/1976	Manchester United (ENG)	FOR	51	3	195	54%	1	0	0	0
10	Rafael VAN DER VAART	11/02/1983	Hamburger SV (GER)	MID	35	3	166	46%	0	0	1	0
11	Arjen ROBBEN	23/01/1984	Chelsea (ENG)	FOR	20	3	270	75%	1	1	1	0
12	Jan KROMKAMP	17/08/1980	Liverpool (ENG)	DEF	11	0	0	0%	0	0	0	0
13	Andre OOIJER	11/07/1974	PSV Eindhoven (HOL)	DEF	19	4	360	100%	0	0	1	0
14	John HEITINGA	15/11/1983	Ajax (HOL)	DEF	18	3	159	44%	0	0	1	0
15	Tim DE CLER	08/11/1978	AZ Alkmaar (HOL)	DEF	3	1	90	25%	0	0	1	0
16	Hedwiges MADURO	13/02/1985	Ajax (HOL)	MID	11	1	5	1%	0	0	0	0
17	Robin VAN PERSIE	06/08/1983	Arsenal (ENG)	FOR	10	4	336	93%	1	1	0	0
18	Mark VAN BOMMEL	22/04/2019	Barcelona (SPA)	MID	37	3	215	60%	0	0	2	0
19	Jan VENNEGOOR OF HESSELINK	07/11/1978	PSV Eindhoven (HOL)	FOR	7	1	7	2%	0	0	0	0
20	Wesley SNEIJDER	09/06/1984	Ajax (HOL)	MID	23	4	314	87%	0	0	1	0
21	Ryan BABEL	19/12/1986	Ajax (HOL)	FOR	6	1	35	10%	0	0	0	0
22	Henk TIMMER	03/12/1971	AZ Alkmaar (HOL)	GK	2	0	0	0%	0	0	0	0
23	Maaren STEKELENBURG	22/09/1982	Ajax (HOL)	GK	2	0	0	0%	0	0	0	0
							Team Totals		3	2	16	2

IRAN

Coach: Branko Ivankovic   In World Cup 2006

No.	Player	Date of Birth	Club	Position	Caps	Games	Minutes played	%age	Goals	Assists	Yellow cards	Red cards
1	Ebrahim MIRZAPOUR	16/09/1978	Foolad Ahvaz (IRN)	GK	64	3	270	100%	0	0	0	0
2	Mehdi MAHDAVIKIA	24/07/1977	Hamburger SV (GER)	MID	89	3	270	100%	0	1	0	0
3	Sohrab BAKHTIARIZADEH	11/09/1977	Saba Battery Tehran (IRN)	DEF	31	2	93	34%	1	0	0	0
4	Yahya GOLMOHAMMADI	19/03/1971	Saba Battery Tehran (IRN)	DEF	69	2	177	66%	1	0	1	0
5	Rahman REZAEI	20/02/1975	Messina (ITA)	DEF	43	3	270	100%	0	0	0	0
6	Javad NEKOUNAM	07/09/1980	Al Sharjah (UAE)	MID	71	2	180	67%	0	0	2	0
7	Ferydoon ZANDI	26/4/1979	Kaiserslautern (GER)	MID	10	2	116	43%	0	0	1	0
8	Ali KARIMI	08/11/1978	Bayern Munich (GER)	MID	90	2	126	47%	0	0	0	0
9	Vahid HASHEMIAN	21/07/1976	Hanover 96 (GER)	FOR	28	3	218	81%	0	0	0	0
10	Ali DAEI	21/03/1969	Saba Battery Tehran (IRN)	FOR	147	2	180	67%	0	0	0	0
11	Rasoul KHATIBI	22/09/1978	Pas Tehran (IRN)	FOR	12	2	77	29%	0	0	0	0
12	Hassan ROUDBARIAN	06/07/1978	Pas Tehran (IRN)	GK	3	0	0	0%	0	0	0	0
13	Hossein KAABI	23/09/1985	Foolad Ahvaz (IRN)	DEF	44	3	246	91%	0	0	1	0
14	Andranik TEYMOURIAN	06/03/1983	AbooMoslem (IRN)	MID	7	3	270	100%	0	0	1	0
15	Arash BORHANI	14/09/1983	Pas Tehran (IRN)	FOR	20	2	34	13%	0	0	0	0
16	Reza ENAYATI	23/09/1976	Esteghlal Tehran (IRN)	FOR	15	0	0	0%	0	0	0	0
17	Javad KAZEMEIAN	23/04/1981	Pirouzi (IRN)	FOR	25	0	0	0%	0	0	0	0
18	Moharram NAVIDKIA	01/11/1982	VFL BOCHUM 01 (GER)	MID	24	0	0	0%	0	0	0	0
19	Amir Hossein SADEQI	06/09/1981	Esteghlal Ahvaz (IRN)	DEF	1	0	0	0%	0	0	0	0
20	Mohammad NOSRATI	11/1/1982	Pas Tehran (IRN)	DEF	44	3	182	67%	0	0	0	0
21	Mehrzad MADANCHI	10/01/1985	Pirouzi (IRN)	MID	6	3	183	68%	0	0	2	0
22	Vahid TALEBLOO	26/05/1982	Esteghlal Tehran (IRN)	GK	1	0	0	0%	0	0	0	0
23	Masoud SHOJAEI	09/06/1984	Saipa Karadj (IRN)	MID	3	1	78	29%	0	0	0	0
							Team Totals		2	1	8	0

ITALY

Coach: Marcello Lippi — In World Cup 2006

No.	Player	Date of Birth	Club	Position	Caps	Games	Minutes played	%age	Goals	Assists	Yellow cards	Red cards
1	Gianluigi BUFFON	28/01/1978	Juventus (ITA)	GK	60	7	690	100%	0	0	0	0
2	Cristian ZACCARDO	21/12/1981	Palermo (ITA)	DEF	12	3	157	23%	0	0	0	0
3	Fabio GROSSO	28/11/1977	Palermo (ITA)	DEF	17	6	600	87%	1	0	1	0
4	Daniele DE ROSSI	24/07/1983	AS Roma (ITA)	MID	17	3	177	26%	0	0	1	1
5	Fabio CANNAVARO	13/09/1973	Juventus (ITA)	DEF	93	7	690	100%	0	0	0	0
6	Andrea BARZAGLI	08/05/1981	Palermo (ITA)	DEF	8	2	125	18%	0	0	0	0
7	Alessandro DEL PIERO	09/11/1974	Juventus (ITA)	FOR	74	5	172	25%	1	0	0	0
8	Gennaro GATTUSO	09/01/1978	AC Milan (ITA)	MID	41	6	552	80%	0	1	2	0
9	Luca TONI	26/5/1977	Fiorentina (ITA)	FOR	18	6	479	69%	2	0	0	0
10	Francesco TOTTI	27/09/1976	AS Roma (ITA)	MID	51	7	465	67%	1	3	1	0
11	Alberto GILARDINO	05/07/1982	AC Milan (ITA)	FOR	15	5	304	44%	1	1	0	0
12	Angelo PERUZZI	16/02/1970	Lazio (ITA)	GK	31	0	0	0%	0	0	0	0
13	Alessandro NESTA	19/03/1976	AC Milan (ITA)	DEF	74	3	196	28%	0	0	0	0
14	Marco AMELIA	02/04/1982	Livorno (ITA)	GK	1	0	0	0%	0	0	0	0
15	Vincenzo IAQUINTA	21/11/1979	Udinese (ITA)	FOR	12	5	192	28%	1	0	1	0
16	Mauro CAMORANESI	04/10/1976	Juventus (ITA)	MID	21	5	350	51%	0	0	2	0
17	Simone BARONE	30/04/1978	Palermo (ITA)	MID	13	2	40	6%	0	0	0	0
18	Filippo INZAGHI	09/08/1973	AC Milan (ITA)	FOR	49	1	31	4%	1	0	0	0
19	Gianluca ZAMBROTTA	19/02/1977	Juventus (ITA)	DEF	52	6	600	87%	1	1	3	0
20	Simone PERROTTA	17/09/1977	AS Roma (ITA)	MID	24	7	613	89%	0	0	0	0
21	Andrea PIRLO	19/05/1979	AC Milan (ITA)	MID	24	7	667	97%	1	3	0	0
22	Massimo ODDO	14/06/1976	Lazio (ITA)	DEF	20	1	23	3%	0	0	0	0
23	Marco MATERAZZI	19/08/1973	Internazionale (ITA)	DEF	28	4	363	53%	2	0	0	1
								Team Totals	**12**	**9**	**11**	**2**

IVORY COAST

Coach: Henri Michel — In World Cup 2006

No.	Player	Date of Birth	Club	Position	Caps	Games	Minutes played	%age	Goals	Assists	Yellow cards	Red cards
1	Jean-Jacques TIZIE	07/09/1972	Esperance (TUN)	GK	24	2	180	67%	0	0	0	0
2	Kanga AKALE	07/03/1981	Auxerre (FRA)	MID	22	3	138	51%	0	0	0	0
3	Arthur BOKA	02/04/1983	Strasbourg (FRA)	DEF	23	3	270	100%	0	1	1	0
4	Kolo TOURE	19/03/1981	Arsenal (ENG)	DEF	42	2	180	67%	0	0	0	0
5	Didier ZOKORA	14/12/1980	Saint-Etienne (FRA)	MID	38	3	270	100%	0	0	1	0
6	Blaise KOUASSI	02/02/1975	Troyes (FRA)	DEF	36	1	90	33%	0	0	0	0
7	Emerse FAE	24/01/1984	Nantes (FRA)	MID	14	0	0	0%	0	0	0	0
8	Bonaventure KALOU	12/01/1978	Paris St-Germain (FRA)	FOR	49	2	72	27%	1	0	0	0
9	Arouna KONE	11/11/1983	PSV Eindhoven (HOL)	FOR	17	3	176	65%	0	0	0	0
10	Gilles YAPI YAPO	30/01/1982	Young Boys (SUI)	MID	26	1	29	11%	0	0	0	0
11	Didier DROGBA	11/03/1978	Chelsea (ENG)	FOR	32	2	180	67%	1	0	2	0
12	Abdoulaye MEITE	06/10/1980	Marseille (FRA)	DEF	18	2	180	67%	0	0	0	0
13	Marc ZORO	27/12/1983	Messina (ITA)	DEF	13	0	0	0%	0	0	0	0
14	Barkary KONE	17/09/1981	Nice (FRA)	FOR	16	3	121	45%	1	0	0	0
15	Aruna DINDANE	26/11/1980	Lens (FRA)	FOR	34	3	155	57%	2	0	1	0
16	Gerard GNANHOUAN	12/02/1979	Montpellier (FRA)	GK	6	0	0	0%	0	0	0	0
17	Cyrille DOMORAUD	22/07/1971	Creteil (FRA)	DEF	50	1	90	33%	0	0	2	1
18	Kader KEITA	06/08/1981	Lille (FRA)	MID	26	2	148	55%	0	1	1	0
19	Yaya TOURE	13/05/1983	Olympiakos (GRE)	MID	14	3	270	100%	0	0	0	0
20	Guy DEMEL	13/06/1981	Hamburger SV (GER)	MID	7	0	0	0%	0	0	0	0
21	Emmanuel EBOUE	04/06/1983	Arsenal (ENG)	DEF	11	3	270	100%	0	0	1	0
22	ROMARIC N'Dri	04/06/1983	Le Mans (FRA)	MID	8	1	61	23%	0	0	0	0
23	Boubacar BARRY	30/12/1979	Beveren (BEL)	GK	6	1	90	33%	0	0	0	0
								Team Totals	**5**	**2**	**9**	**1**

JAPAN

Coach: Zico

In World Cup 2006

No.	Player	Date of Birth	Club	Position	Caps	Games	Minutes played	%age	Goals	Assists	Yellow cards	Red cards
1	Seigo NARAZAKI	15/04/1976	Nagoya Grampus Eight (JPN)	GK	50	0	0	0%	0	0	0	0
2	Teruyuki MONIWA	08/09/1981	FC Tokyo (JPN)	DEF	8	1	34	13%	0	0	1	0
3	Yuichi KOMANO	25/07/1981	Sanfrecce Hiroshima (JPN)	DEF	8	1	90	33%	0	0	0	0
4	Yasuhito ENDO	28/01/1980	Gamba Osaka (JPN)	MID	40	0	0	0%	0	0	0	0
5	Tsuneyasu MIYAMOTO	07/02/1977	Gamba Osaka (JPN)	DEF	69	2	180	67%	0	0	2	0
6	Koji NAKATA	09/07/1979	Basel (SUI)	DEF	55	1	35	13%	0	0	0	0
7	Hidetoshi NAKATA	22/01/1977	Bolton Wanderers (ENG)	MID	74	3	270	100%	0	0	0	0
8	Mitsup OGASAWARA	05/04/1979	Kashima Antlers (JPN)	MID	51	2	145	54%	0	0	0	0
9	Naohiro TAKAHARA	04/06/1979	Hamburger SV (GER)	FOR	41	3	180	67%	0	0	1	0
10	Shunsuke Nakamura	24/06/1978	Celtic (SCO)	MID	60	3	270	100%	1	0	0	0
11	Seiichiro MAKI	07/08/1980	JEF United Chiba (JPN)	FOR	10	1	59	22%	0	0	0	0
12	Yoichi DOI	25/07/1973	FC Tokyo (JPN)	GK	4	0	0	0%	0	0	0	0
13	Atsushi YANAGISAWA	27/05/1977	Kashima Antlers (JPN)	FOR	56	2	138	51%	0	0	0	0
14	Alessandro SANTOS	20/07/1977	Urawa Red Diamonds (JPN)	DEF	72	3	270	100%	0	1	1	0
15	Takashi FUKUNISHI	01/09/1976	Jubilo Iwata (JPN)	MID	62	2	135	50%	0	0	0	0
16	Masashi OGURO	04/05/2001	Grenoble (FRA)	FOR	18	3	32	12%	0	0	0	0
17	Junichi INAMOTO	18/09/1979	West Bromwich Albion (ENG)	MID	63	2	135	50%	0	0	0	0
18	Shinji ONO	27/09/1979	Urawa Reds (JPN)	MID	54	1	12	4%	0	0	0	0
19	Keisuke TSUBOI	16/09/1979	Urawa Red Diamonds (JPN)	DEF	33	2	145	54%	0	0	0	0
20	Keiji TAMADA	11/04/1980	Nagoya Grampus Eight (JPN)	FOR	39	2	120	44%	1	0	0	0
21	Akira KAJI	13/01/1980	Gamba Osaka (JPN)	DEF	43	2	180	67%	0	0	1	0
22	Yuji NAKAZAWA	25/02/1978	Yokohama Marinos (JPN)	DEF	50	3	270	100%	0	0	0	0
23	Yoshikatsu KAWAGUCHI	15/08/1975	Jubilo Iwata (JPN)	GK	89	3	270	100%	0	0	1	0
								Team Totals	2	1	7	0

MEXICO

Coach: Ricardo La Volpe

In World Cup 2006

No.	Player	Date of Birth	Club	Position	Caps	Games	Minutes played	%age	Goals	Assists	Yellow cards	Red cards
1	Oswaldo SANCHEZ	21/09/1973	Guadalajara (MEX)	GK	70	4	390	100%	0	0	0	0
2	Claudio SUAREZ	17/12/1968	Chivas (USA)	DEF	178	0	0	0%	0	0	0	0
3	Carlos SALCIDO	02/04/1980	Guadalajara (MEX)	DEF	32	4	390	100%	0	0	1	0
4	Rafael MARQUEZ	13/02/1979	Barcelona (SPA)	DEF	65	4	390	100%	1	0	2	0
5	Ricardo OSORIO	30/03/1980	Cruz Azul (MEX)	DEF	39	4	390	100%	0	0	0	0
6	Gerardo TORRADO	30/04/1979	Cruz Azul (MEX)	MID	56	3	218	56%	0	0	2	0
7	ZINHA	23/05/1976	Toluca (MEX)	MID	32	4	188	48%	1	1	1	0
8	Pavel PARDO	26/07/1976	America (MEX)	MID	125	4	307	79%	0	1	0	0
9	Jared BORGETTI	14/08/1973	Bolton Wanderers (ENG)	FOR	75	2	171	44%	0	0	0	0
10	Guillermo FRANCO	03/11/1976	Villarreal (SPA)	FOR	7	3	129	33%	0	1	0	0
11	Ramon MORALES	10/10/1975	Guadalajara (MEX)	FOR	46	2	86	22%	0	0	0	0
12	Jose CORONA	26/01/1981	Tecos UAG (MEX)	GK	6	0	0	0%	0	0	0	0
13	Guillermo OCHOA	13/07/1985	America (MEX)	GK	1	0	0	0%	0	0	0	0
14	Gonzalo PINEDA	19/10/1982	Guadalajara (MEX)	DEF	30	4	290	74%	0	0	1	0
15	Jose Antonio CASTRO	11/08/1980	America (MEX)	DEF	12	2	142	36%	0	0	1	0
16	Mario MENDEZ	01/06/1979	Monterrey (MEX)	DEF	32	4	379	97%	0	2	0	0
17	Jose FONSECA	02/10/1979	Cruz Azul (MEX)	FOR	29	4	266	68%	1	0	1	0
18	Andres GUARDADO	28/09/1986	Atlas (MEX)	DEF	7	1	65	17%	0	0	0	0
19	Omar BRAVO	04/03/1980	Guadalajara (MEX)	FOR	33	3	270	69%	2	0	0	0
20	Rafael GARCIA	14/8/1974	Atlas (MEX)	MID	52	0	0	0%	0	0	0	0
21	Jesus ARELLANO	08/05/1973	Monterrey (MEX)	FOR	69	1	39	10%	0	0	0	0
22	Francisco RODRIGUEZ	20/10/1981	Guadalajara (MEX)	DEF	32	1	45	12%	0	0	1	0
23	Luis PEREZ	12/01/1981	Monterrey (MEX)	MID	52	2	105	27%	0	0	2	1
								Team Totals	5	5	12	1

PARAGUAY

Coach: Anibal Ruiz

In World Cup 2006

No.	Player	Date of Birth	Club	Position	Caps	Games	Minutes played	%age	Goals	Assists	Yellow cards	Red cards
1	Justo VILLAR	30/06/1977	Newells Old Boys (ARG)	GK	39	1	7	3%	0	0	0	0
2	Jorge NUNEZ	22/01/1978	Estudiantes (ARG)	DEF	15	3	189	70%	0	0	1	0
3	Delio TOLEDO	10/02/1976	Zaragoza (ESP)	DEF	30	1	81	30%	0	0	0	0
4	Carlos GAMARRA	17/02/1971	Palmeiras (BRA)	DEF	106	3	270	100%	0	0	0	0
5	Julio Cesar CACERES	05/10/1979	River Plate (ARG)	DEF	32	3	256	95%	0	0	0	0
6	Carlos BONET	02/10/1977	Libertad (PAR)	MID	29	2	147	54%	0	0	0	0
7	Salvador CABANAS	05/08/1980	Jaguares Chiapas (MEX)	MID	15	0	0	0%	0	0	0	0
8	Edgar BARRETO	15/07/1984	NEC Nijmegen (HOL)	MID	15	2	100	37%	0	0	1	0
9	Roque SANTA CRUZ	16/08/1981	Bayern Munich (GER)	FOR	42	3	242	90%	0	1	0	0
10	Roberto ACUNA	25/03/1972	Deportivo La Coruna (ESP)	MID	93	3	270	100%	0	0	1	0
11	Diego GAVILAN	01/03/1980	Newells Old Boys (ARG)	MID	39	0	0	0%	0	0	0	0
12	Derlis GOMEZ	02/11/1972	Sportivo Luqueno (PAR)	GK	5	0	0	0%	0	0	0	0
13	Carlos PAREDES	16/07/1976	Reggina (ITA)	MID	68	3	270	100%	0	0	2	0
14	Paulo DA SILVA	01/02/1980	Toluca (MEX)	DEF	33	1	2	1%	0	0	0	0
15	Julio MANZUR	22/01/1981	Santos (BRA)	DEF	13	1	14	5%	0	0	0	0
16	Cristian RIVEROS	16/10/1982	Libertad (PAR)	MID	9	2	151	56%	0	0	0	0
17	Jose MONTIEL	19/03/1988	Olimpia Asuncion (PAR)	MID	6	0	0	0%	0	0	0	0
18	Nelson VALDEZ	28/11/1983	Werder Bremen (GER)	FOR	11	3	245	91%	0	0	1	0
19	Julio DOS SANTOS	07/05/1983	Bayern Munich (GER)	MID	17	2	119	44%	0	0	1	0
20	Dante LOPEZ	16/08/1983	Genova (ITA)	FOR	7	1	28	10%	0	0	0	0
21	Denis CANIZA	29/8/1974	Cruz Azul (MEX)	DEF	74	3	268	99%	0	0	0	0
22	Aldo BOBADILLA	20/04/1976	Libertad (PAR)	GK	5	3	263	97%	0	0	0	0
23	Nelson CUEVAS	10/01/1980	Pachuca (MEX)	FOR	35	2	48	18%	1	0	0	0
								Team Totals	1	1	7	0

POLAND

Coach: Pawel Janas

In World Cup 2006

No.	Player	Date of Birth	Club	Position	Caps	Games	Minutes played	%age	Goals	Assists	Yellow cards	Red cards
1	Artur BORUC	20/02/1980	Celtic (SCO)	GK	17	3	270	100%	0	0	2	0
2	Mariusz JOP	03/08/1978	FK Moscow (RUS)	DEF	12	1	90	33%	0	0	0	0
3	Seweryn GANCARCZYK	22/11/1981	Metalist Kharkiv (UKR)	DEF	2	0	0	0%	0	0	0	0
4	Marcin BASZCZYNSKI	07/06/1977	Wisla Krakow (POL)	DEF	32	3	270	100%	0	0	1	0
5	Kamil KOSOWSKI	30/08/1977	Southampton (ENG)	MID	45	1	13	5%	0	0	0	0
6	Jacek BAK	24/03/1973	Al Rayyan (QAT)	DEF	72	3	270	100%	0	0	1	0
7	Radoslaw SOBOLEWSKI	13/12/1976	Wisla Krakow (POL)	MID	19	2	140	52%	0	0	2	0
8	Jacek KRZYNOWEK	15/05/1976	Bayer Leverkusen (GER)	MID	58	3	243	90%	0	1	1	0
9	Maciej ZURAWSKI	12/09/1976	Celtic (SCO)	FOR	50	3	217	80%	0	1	0	0
10	Miroslav SZYMKOWIAK	12/11/1976	Trabzonspor (TUR)	MID	29	2	180	67%	0	0	0	0
11	Grzegorz RASIAK	12/1/1979	Southampton (ENG)	FOR	30	1	6	2%	0	0	0	0
12	Tomasz KUSZCZAK	20/03/1982	West Bromich Albion (ENG)	GK	4	0	0	0%	0	0	0	0
13	Sebastian MILA	10/07/1982	Austria Vienna (AUT)	MID	27	0	0	0%	0	0	0	0
14	Michal ZEWLAKOW	22/04/1976	Anderlecht (BEL)	DEF	56	3	262	97%	0	0	1	0
15	Ebi SMOLAREK	09/01/1981	Borussia Dortmund (GER)	MID	13	3	264	98%	0	0	1	0
16	Arkadiusz RADOMSKI	27/06/1977	Austria Vienna (AUT)	MID	20	3	243	90%	0	0	1	0
17	Dariusz DUDKA	09/12/1983	Wisla Krakow (POL)	DEF	7	1	8	3%	0	0	0	0
18	Mariusz LEWANDOWSKI	18/05/2001	Shakhtar Donetsk (UKR)	DEF	25	2	41	15%	0	0	0	0
19	Bartosz BOSACKI	20/12/1975	Lech Poznan (POL)	DEF	11	2	180	67%	2	0	0	0
20	Piotr GIZA	28/02/1980	Cracovia (POL)	MID	4	0	0	0%	0	0	0	0
21	Ireneusz JELEN	09/04/1981	Wisla Plock (POL)	FOR	9	3	203	75%	0	0	0	0
22	Lukasz FABIANSKI	18/04/1985	Legia Warsaw (POL)	GK	2	0	0	0%	0	0	0	0
23	Pawel BROZEK	21/04/1983	Wisla Krakow (POL)	FOR	4	3	54	20%	0	0	0	0
								Team Totals	2	2	10	0

statistics

PORTUGAL

Coach: Luis Felipe Scolari

No.	Player	Date of Birth	Club	Position	Caps	Games	Minutes played	%age	Goals	Assists	Yellow cards	Red cards
1	Alexandro RICARDO	11/02/1976	Sporting Lisbon (POR)	GK	49	7	660	100%	0	0	1	0
2	Renato Paulo FERREIRA	18/01/1979	Chelsea (ENG)	DEF	30	3	149	23%	0	0	1	0
3	Marco CANEIRA	09/02/1979	Sporting Lisbon (POR)	DEF	14	1	90	14%	0	0	0	0
4	Miguel Ricardo COSTA	16 May 1981	Porto (POR)	DEF	3	1	90	14%	0	0	1	0
5	Fernando MEIRA	05/06/1978	VfB Stuttgart (GER)	DEF	30	7	660	100%	0	0	0	0
6	Francisco COSTINHA	01/12/1974	Unaffiliated	MID	44	5	285	43%	0	0	4	1
7	Luis FIGO	04/11/1972	Internazionale (ITA)	MID	120	7	528	80%	0	3	1	0
8	Armando PETIT	25/09/1976	Benfica (POR)	MID	36	6	395	60%	0	0	2	0
9	Pedro PAULETA	28/04/1973	Paris St-Germain (FRA)	FOR	82	6	430	65%	1	1	1	0
10	Hugo VIANA	15/01/1983	Valencia (SPA)	MID	21	2	55	8%	0	0	0	0
11	Sabrosa SIMAO	31/10/1979	Benfica (POR)	FOR	43	7	411	62%	1	1	0	0
12	Silva QUIM	13/11/1975	Benfica (POR)	GK	24	0	0	0%	0	0	0	0
13	Luis MIGUEL	04/01/1980	Valencia (SPA)	DEF	28	6	511	77%	0	0	1	0
14	Jorge NUNO VALENTE	12/09/1974	Everton (ENG)	DEF	23	6	548	83%	0	0	2	0
15	Luis BOA MORTE	04/08/1977	Fulham (ENG)	FOR	24	1	11	2%	0	0	1	0
16	Alberto RICARDO CARVALHO	18/05/1978	Chelsea (ENG)	DEF	24	6	570	86%	0	0	2	0
17	Cristiano RONALDO	05/02/1985	Manchester United (ENG)	MID	32	6	482	73%	1	0	1	0
18	Nuno MANICHE	11/11/1977	Chelsea (ENG)	MID	31	7	565	86%	2	0	2	0
19	Cardoso TIAGO	02/05/1981	Lyon (FRA)	MID	22	5	263	40%	0	0	0	0
20	Anderson DECO	27/08/1977	Barcelona (SPA)	MID	35	4	336	51%	1	0	3	1
21	Miguel NUNO GOMES	05/07/1976	Benfica (POR)	FOR	53	2	44	7%	1	0	1	0
22	Jorge Paulo SANTOS	11/12/1972	Braga (POR)	GK	1	0	0	0%	0	0	0	0
23	Helder POSTIGA	02/08/1982	Saint-Etienne (FRA)	FOR	24	3	119	18%	0	0	0	0
						Team Totals			7	5	24	2

SAUDI ARABIA

Coach: Paqueta

No.	Player	Date of Birth	Club	Position	Caps	Games	Minutes played	%age	Goals	Assists	Yellow cards	Red cards
1	Mohammed AL DEAYEA	02/08/1972	Al Hilal (KSA)	GK	181	0	0	0%	0	0	0	0
2	Ahmed DOKHI	25/10/1976	Al Ittihad (KSA)	DEF	68	3	234	87%	0	0	1	0
3	Redha TUKAR	29/11/1975	Al Ittihad (KSA)	DEF	37	3	270	100%	0	0	0	0
4	Hamad AL MONTASHARI	22/06/1982	Al Ittihad (KSA)	DEF	32	3	270	100%	0	0	0	0
5	Naif AL QADI	03/04/1979	Al Ahli (KSA)	DEF	28	0	0	0%	0	0	0	0
6	Omar AL GHAMDI	11/04/1979	Al Hilal (KSA)	MID	38	2	180	67%	0	0	1	0
7	Mohammed AMEEN	29/04/1980	Al Ittihad (KSA)	MID	16	2	70	26%	0	0	0	0
8	Mohammed NOOR	26/02/1978	Al Ittihad (KSA)	MID	63	3	240	89%	0	1	0	0
9	Sami AL JABER	11/12/1972	Al Hilal (KSA)	FOR	160	3	90	33%	1	0	1	0
10	Mohammad AL SHLHOUB	08/12/1980	Al Hilal (KSA)	MID	48	0	0	0%	0	0	0	0
11	Saad AL HARTHI	03/02/1984	Al Nasr (KSA)	FOR	15	1	90	33%	0	0	0	0
12	Abdulaziz KHATHRAN	31/07/1973	Al Hilal (KSA)	DEF	19	2	126	47%	0	0	0	0
13	Hussein SULIMANI	21/01/1977	Al Ahli (KSA)	DEF	97	3	260	96%	0	0	0	0
14	Saud KARIRI	08/07/1980	Al Ittihad (KSA)	MID	34	3	270	100%	0	0	1	0
15	Ahmed AL BAHRI	18/09/1980	Al Shabab (KSA)	DEF	11	0	0	0%	0	0	0	0
16	Khaled AZIZ	14/07/1981	Al Hilal (KSA)	MID	14	3	192	71%	0	0	0	0
17	Mohamed AL BISHI	03/05/1987	Al Ahli (KSA)	DEF	0	0	9	3%	0	0	0	0
18	Nawaf AL TEMYAT	28/06/1976	Al Hilal (KSA)	MID	56	2	144	53%	0	0	1	0
19	Mohammed MASSAD	17/02/1983	Al Ahli (KSA)	MID	5	1	10	4%	0	0	0	0
20	Yasser AL KAHTANI	10/10/1982	Al Hilal (KSA)	FOR	45	2	171	63%	1	0	0	0
21	Mabrouk ZAID	11/02/1979	Al Ittihad (KSA)	GK	33	3	270	100%	0	0	0	0
22	Mohammad KHOJAH	15/03/1982	Al Shabab (KSA)	GK	8	0	0	0%	0	0	0	0
23	Malek AL HAWSAWI	10/08/1981	Al Ahli (KSA)	FOR	5	3	83	31%	0	1	0	0
						Team Totals			2	2	5	0

SERBIA & MONTENEGRO

Coach: Ilija Petkovic

In World Cup 2006

No.	Player	Date of Birth	Club	Position	Caps	Games	Minutes played	%age	Goals	Assists	Yellow cards	Red cards
1	Dragoslav JEVRIC	08/07/1974	Ankaraspor (TUR)	GK	40	3	270	100%	0	0	0	0
2	Ivan ERGIC	21/01/1981	Basel (SUI)	MID	1	2	135	50%	0	0	0	0
3	Ivica DRAGUTINOVIC	13/11/1975	Sevilla FC (SPA)	DEF	26	1	90	33%	0	0	1	0
4	Igor DULJAJ	29/10/1979	Shakhtar Donetsk (UKR)	MID	37	3	270	100%	0	0	1	0
5	Nemanja VIDIC	21/10/1981	Manchester United (ENG)	DEF	20	0	0	0%	0	0	0	0
6	Goran GAVRANCIC	02/08/1978	Dynamo Kiev (UKR)	DEF	25	3	270	100%	0	0	2	0
7	Ognjen KOROMAN	19/09/1978	Portsmouth (ENG)	MID	25	2	97	36%	0	0	2	0
8	Mateja KEZMAN	12/04/1979	Atletico Madrid (SPA)	FOR	47	2	130	48%	0	0	0	0
9	Savo MILOSEVIC	02/09/1973	Osasuna (SPA)	FOR	98	3	138	51%	0	0	0	0
10	Dejan STANKOVIC	11/09/1978	Internazionale (ITA)	MID	58	3	270	100%	0	1	1	0
11	Predrag DJORDJEVIC	04/08/1972	Olympiakos (GRE)	MID	34	3	270	100%	0	0	0	0
12	Oliver KOVACEVIC	29/10/1974	CSKA Sofia (BUL)	GK	3	0	0	0%	0	0	0	0
13	Dusan BASTA	18/08/1984	Crvena Zvezda (SCG)	DEF	2	0	0	0%	0	0	0	0
14	Nenad DJORDJEVIC	07/08/1979	Partizan Belgrade (SCG)	DEF	15	2	132	49%	0	0	0	0
15	Milan DUDIC	01/11/1979	Crvena Zvezda (SCG)	DEF	11	2	180	67%	0	0	1	0
16	Dusan PETKOVIC	13/06/1974	OFK Beograd (SCG)	DEF	12	0	0	0%	0	0	0	0
17	Albert NADJ	29/10/1974	Partizan Belgrade (SCG)	MID	42	3	165	61%	0	0	3	1
18	Zvonimir VUKIC	19/07/1979	Partizan Belgrade (SCG)	MID	25	1	21	8%	0	0	0	0
19	Nikola ZIGIC	25/09/1980	Crvena Zvezda (SCG)	FOR	11	2	111	41%	1	0	0	0
20	Mladen KRSTAJIC	04/03/1974	Schalke 04 (GER)	DEF	45	3	195	72%	0	0	1	0
21	Danijel LJUBOJA	04/09/1978	VfB Stuttgart (GER)	FOR	15	2	65	24%	0	0	0	0
22	Sasa ILIC	30/12/1977	Galatasaray (TUR)	MID	32	1	90	33%	1	0	0	0
23	Vladimir STOJKOVIC	28/07/1983	Crvena Zvezda (SCG)	GK	0	0	0	0%	0	0	0	0
							Team Totals		2	1	12	1

SOUTH KOREA

Coach: Dick Advocaat

In World Cup 2006

No.	Player	Date of Birth	Club	Position	Caps	Games	Minutes played	%age	Goals	Assists	Yellow cards	Red cards
1	LEE Woon Jae	26/4/1973	Suwon Bluewings (KOR)	GK	97	3	270	100%	0	0	0	0
2	KIM Young Chul	30/06/1976	Seongnam Ilhwa Chunma (KOR)	DEF	12	2	180	67%	0	0	1	0
3	KIM Dong Jin	29/01/1982	FC Seoul (KOR)	DEF	34	2	180	67%	0	0	1	0
4	CHOI Jin Cheul	26/03/1971	Chonbuk Hyundai Motors (KOR)	DEF	62	3	270	100%	0	0	1	0
5	KIM Nam Il	14/03/1977	Suwon Bluewings (KOR)	MID	66	3	203	75%	0	0	0	0
6	KIM Jin Kyu	16/02/1985	Jubilo Iwata (JPN)	DEF	23	2	135	50%	0	0	1	0
7	PARK Ji Sung	25/02/1981	Manchester United (ENG)	MID	60	3	270	100%	1	0	0	0
8	KIM Do Heon	14/7/1982	Seongnam Ilhwa Chunma (KOR)	MID	32	0	0	0%	0	0	0	0
9	AHN Jung Hwan	27/01/1976	MSV Duisburg (GER)	FOR	61	3	92	34%	1	0	1	0
10	PARK Chu Young	10/07/1985	FC Seoul (KOR)	FOR	18	1	65	24%	0	0	1	0
11	SEOL Ki Hyeon	08/01/1979	Wolverhampton Wanderers (ENG)	FOR	67	2	70	26%	0	0	0	0
12	LEE Young Pyo	23/4/1977	Tottenham Hotspur (ENG)	DEF	85	3	242	90%	0	0	0	0
13	LEE Eul Yong	08/09/1975	Trabzonspor (TUR)	MID	47	2	112	41%	0	0	0	0
14	LEE Chun Soo	09/07/1981	Ulsan Hyundai (KOR)	FOR	62	3	251	93%	1	0	2	0
15	BAEK Ji Hoon	28/02/1985	FC Seoul (KOR)	MID	12	0	0	0%	0	0	0	0
16	CHUNG Kyung Ho	22/05/1980	Gwangju Sangmu (KOR)	FOR	40	0	0	0%	0	0	0	0
17	LEE Ho	22/10/1984	Ulsan Hyundai (KOR)	MID	11	3	248	92%	0	0	1	0
18	KIM Sang Sik	17/12/1976	Seongnam Ilhwa Chunma (KOR)	DEF	42	2	30	11%	0	0	0	0
19	CHO Jae Jin	9/7/1981	Shimizu S-Pulse (JPN)	FOR	21	3	262	97%	0	1	0	0
20	KIM Yong Dae	11/10/1979	Seongnam Ilhwa Chunma (KOR)	GK	15	0	0	0%	0	0	0	0
21	KIM Young Kwang	28/06/1983	Chunnam Dragons (KOR)	GK	6	0	0	0%	0	0	0	0
22	SONG Chong Gug	20/02/1979	Suwon Bluewings (KOR)	DEF	51	1	90	33%	0	1	0	0
23	CHO Won Hee	17/04/1983	Suwon Bluewings (KOR)	DEF	13	0	0	0%	0	0	0	0
							Team Totals		3	2	9	0

SPAIN

Coach: Luis Aragones

In World Cup 2006

No.	Player	Date of Birth	Club	Position	Caps	Games	Minutes played	%age	Goals	Assists	Yellow cards	Red cards
1	Iker CASILLAS	20/05/1981	Real Madrid (SPA)	GK	58	3	270	75%	0	0	0	0
2	Michel SALGADO	22/10/1975	Real Madrid (SPA)	DEF	50	1	90	25%	0	0	0	0
3	Mariano PERNIA	04/05/1977	Getafe (SPA)	DEF	1	3	270	75%	0	0	0	0
4	Carlos MARCHENA	31/07/1979	Valencia (SPA)	DEF	27	1	90	25%	0	0	1	0
5	Carlos PUYOL	13/04/1978	Barcelona (SPA)	DEF	47	3	270	75%	0	1	2	0
6	David ALBELDA	01/09/1977	Valencia (SPA)	MID	33	2	126	35%	0	0	1	0
7	Gonzalez RAUL	27/06/1977	Real Madrid (SPA)	FOR	95	4	179	50%	1	0	0	0
8	Hernandez XAVI	25/01/1980	Barcelona (SPA)	MID	36	4	276	77%	0	1	0	0
9	Fernando TORRES	20/03/1984	Atletico Madrid (SPA)	FOR	30	4	291	81%	3	0	0	0
10	Jose Antonio REYES	01/09/1983	Arsenal (ENG)	MID	19	1	69	19%	0	1	1	0
11	Sanz LUIS GARCIA	24/06/1978	Liverpool (ENG)	FOR	10	3	158	44%	0	0	0	0
12	Guerrero Antonio LOPEZ	13/09/1981	Atletico Madrid (SPA)	DEF	10	1	90	25%	0	0	0	0
13	Andreas INIESTA	11/05/1984	Barcelona (SPA)	MID	3	1	90	25%	0	0	0	0
14	Xabi ALONSO	25/11/1981	Liverpool (ENG)	MID	26	3	234	65%	1	0	0	0
15	Garcia SERGIO RAMOS	30/03/1986	Real Madrid (SPA)	DEF	11	3	270	75%	0	0	0	0
16	Marcos SENNA	17/07/1976	Villarreal (SPA)	MID	3	3	154	43%	0	0	0	0
17	Sanchez JOAQUIN	21/07/1981	Real Betis (SPA)	MID	38	3	161	45%	0	0	0	0
18	Cesc FABREGAS	04/05/2019	Arsenal (ENG)	MID	4	4	214	59%	0	1	1	0
19	Santiago CANIZARES	18/12/1969	Valencia (SPA)	GK	45	1	90	25%	0	0	0	0
20	Gutierez JUANITO	23/07/1976	Real Betis (SPA)	DEF	15	1	90	25%	1	0	0	0
21	David VILLA	03/12/1981	Valencia (SPA)	FOR	8	4	208	58%	3	0	0	0
22	Ibanez PABLO	03/08/1981	Atletico Madrid (SPA)	DEF	14	3	270	75%	0	0	0	0
23	Jose Manuel REINA	31/08/1982	Liverpool (ENG)	GK	3	0	0	0%	0	0	0	0
								Team Totals	9	4	6	0

SWEDEN

Coach: Lars Lagerback

In World Cup 2006

No.	Player	Date of Birth	Club	Position	Caps	Games	Minutes played	%age	Goals	Assists	Yellow cards	Red cards
1	Andreas ISAKSSON	03/10/1981	Rennes (FRA)	GK	39	3	270	75%	0	0	0	0
2	Mikael NILSSON	24/06/1978	Panathinaikos (GRE)	DEF	27	0	0	0%	0	0	0	0
3	Olof MELLBERG	03/09/1977	Aston Villa (ENG)	DEF	64	4	360	100%	0	0	0	0
4	Teddy LUCIC	15/04/1973	Haecken (SWE)	DEF	81	4	304	84%	0	0	3	1
5	Erik EDMAN	11/11/1978	Rennes (FRA)	DEF	37	4	360	100%	0	1	0	0
6	Tobias LINDEROTH	21/4/1979	Copenhagen (DEN)	MID	58	4	346	96%	0	1	1	0
7	Niclas ALEXANDERSSON	29/12/1971	Gothenburg (SWE)	MID	87	4	360	100%	0	0	1	0
8	Anders SVENSSON	17/07/1976	Elfsborg (SWE)	MID	66	1	61	17%	0	0	0	0
9	Fredrik LJUNGBERG	16/04/1977	Arsenal (ENG)	MID	57	4	360	100%	1	0	1	0
10	Zlatan IBRAHIMOVIC	03/10/1981	Juventus (ITA)	FOR	38	3	206	57%	0	0	0	0
11	Henrik LARSSON	20/09/1971	Barcelona (SPA)	FOR	89	4	360	100%	1	0	1	0
12	John ALVBAGE	10/08/1982	Viborg (DEN)	GK	2	0	0	0%	0	0	0	0
13	Petter HANSSON	14/12/1976	Heerenveen (NED)	DEF	13	1	52	14%	0	0	0	0
14	Fredrik STENMAN	02/06/1983	Bayer Leverkusen (GER)	DEF	1	0	0	0%	0	0	0	0
15	Karl SVENSSON	21/03/1984	Gothenburg (SWE)	DEF	1	0	0	0%	0	0	0	0
16	Kim KALLSTROM	24/08/1982	Rennes (FRA)	MID	34	4	226	63%	0	0	0	0
17	Johan ELMANDER	27/05/1981	Brondby (DEN)	FOR	18	2	21	6%	0	0	0	0
18	Mattias JONSON	16/1/1974	Djurgarden (SWE)	FOR	53	4	140	39%	0	0	1	0
19	Daniel ANDERSSON	28/08/1977	Malmo (SWE)	MID	47	1	1	0%	0	0	0	0
20	Marcus ALLBACK	05/07/1973	Copenhagen (DEN)	FOR	56	4	167	46%	1	1	2	0
21	Christian WILHELMSSON	08/12/1979	Anderlecht (BEL)	MID	29	4	220	61%	0	0	0	0
22	Markus ROSENBERG	27/09/1982	Ajax (HOL)	FOR	8	0	0	0%	0	0	0	0
23	Rami SHAABAN	30/06/1975	Fredrikstad (NOR)	GK	1	1	90	25%	0	0	0	0
								Team Totals	3	3	10	1

SWITZERLAND

Coach: Kobi Kuhn — In World Cup 2006

No.	Player	Date of Birth	Club	Position	Caps	Games	Minutes played	%age	Goals	Assists	Yellow cards	Red cards
1	Pascal Zuberbühler	08/01/1971	FC Basel (SUI)	GK	40	4	390	100%	0	0	0	0
2	Johan DJOUROU	18/01/1987	Arsenal (ENG)	DEF	2	3	87	22%	0	0	1	0
3	Ludovic MAGNIN	20/04/1979	VfB Stuttgart (GER)	DEF	30	3	300	77%	0	0	1	0
4	Philippe SENDEROS	14/02/1985	Arsenal (ENG)	DEF	12	3	232	59%	1	0	1	0
5	Xavier MARGAIRAZ	07/01/1984	FC Zurich (SUI)	MID	3	2	29	7%	0	0	0	0
6	Johann VOGEL	08/03/1977	AC Milan (ITA)	MID	85	4	390	100%	0	0	1	0
7	Ricardo CABANAS	17/01/1979	FC Cologne (GER)	MID	37	4	376	96%	0	0	1	0
8	Raphael WICKY	26/04/1977	Hamburger SV (GER)	MID	67	4	378	97%	0	0	1	0
9	Alexander FREI	15/7/1979	Rennes (FRA)	FOR	45	4	382	98%	2	0	1	0
10	Daniel GYGAX	28/08/1981	Lille (FRA)	FOR	22	2	80	21%	0	0	0	0
11	Marco STRELLER	18/06/1981	FC Cologne (GER)	FOR	10	3	126	32%	0	0	1	0
12	Diego BENAGLIO	08/09/1983	Nacional Funchal (POR)	GK	1	0	0	0%	0	0	0	0
13	Stephane GRICHTING	30/03/1979	Auxerre (FRA)	DEF	6	1	87	22%	0	0	0	0
14	David DEGEN	15/2/1983	FC Basel (SUI)	FOR	3	0	0	0%	0	0	0	0
15	Blerim DZEMAILI	12/04/1986	FC Zurich (SUI)	MID	3	0	0	0%	0	0	0	0
16	Tranquillo BARNETTA	22/05/1985	Bayer Leverkusen (GER)	MID	13	4	390	100%	1	1	1	0
17	Christoph SPYCHER	30/03/1978	Eintracht Frankfurt (GER)	DEF	21	1	90	23%	0	0	1	0
18	Mauro LUSTRINELLI	26/02/1976	Sparta Prague (CZE)	FOR	5	2	8	2%	0	1	0	0
19	Valon BEHRAMI	19/04/1985	Lazio (ITA)	MID	6	1	3	1%	0	0	0	0
20	Patrick MULLER	17/12/1976	Lyon (FRA)	DEF	64	4	374	96%	0	0	0	0
21	Fabio COLTORTI	03/12/1980	Grasshopper Zurich (SUI)	GK	2	0	0	0%	0	0	0	0
22	Hakan YAKIN	22/02/1977	Young Boys Berne (SUI)	MID	46	3	178	46%	0	1	1	0
23	Philipp DEGEN	15/02/1983	Borussia Dortmund (GER)	DEF	15	3	390	100%	0	0	1	0
							Team Totals		4	3	12	0

TOGO

Coach: Otto Pfister — In World Cup 2006

No.	Player	Date of Birth	Club	Position	Caps	Games	Minutes played	%age	Goals	Assists	Yellow cards	Red cards
1	Ouro-Nimini TCHAGNIROU	31/12/1977	Djoliba (MLI)	GK	9	0	0	0%	0	0	0	0
2	Dare NIBOMBE	16/06/1980	Mons (BEL)	DEF	16	3	270	100%	0	0	0	0
3	Jean-Paul ABALO	26/06/1975	Apoel Nicosia (CYP)	DEF	65	2	142	53%	0	0	2	1
4	Emmanuel ADEBAYOR	26/02/1984	Arsenal (ENG)	FOR	29	3	254	94%	0	0	1	0
5	Massamasso TCHANGAI	08/08/1978	Benevento (ITA)	DEF	34	3	270	100%	0	0	1	0
6	Yao AZIAWONOU	30/11/1979	Young Boys Berne (SUI)	MID	32	2	95	35%	0	0	1	0
7	Moustapha SAIFOU	01/06/1983	Stade Brest (FRA)	FOR	34	3	241	89%	0	0	2	0
8	Kuami AGBOH	28/12/1977	Beveren (BEL)	MID	4	1	24	9%	0	0	0	0
9	Thomas DOSSEVI	06/03/1979	Valenciennes (FRA)	MID	10	2	84	31%	0	0	0	0
10	CHERIF-TOURE Mamam	13/01/1983	Metz (FRA)	MID	39	3	234	87%	0	0	1	0
11	Robert MALM	21/08/1973	Stade Brest (FRA)	FOR	1	1	4	1%	0	0	0	0
12	Eric AKOTO	20/07/1980	Admira Wacker (AUT)	DEF	32	0	0	0%	0	0	0	0
13	Ridhmond FORSON	23/05/1980	JA Poire sur Vie (FRA)	FOR	8	3	209	77%	0	0	0	0
14	Adekanmi OLUFADE	07/01/1980	Al Sailiya (QAT)	FOR	24	1	32	12%	0	0	0	0
15	Alaixys ROMAO	18/01/1984	Louhans-Cuiseaux (FRA)	MID	13	2	180	67%	0	1	2	0
16	Kossi AGASSA	02/07/1978	Metz (FRA)	GK	49	3	270	100%	0	0	0	0
17	MOHAMED Kader	08/04/1979	Guingamp (FRA)	FOR	46	3	270	100%	1	0	0	0
18	Yao Junior SENAYA	19/04/1984	YF Juventus (SUI)	FOR	16	3	166	61%	0	0	0	0
19	Ludovic ASSEMOASSA	18/9/1980	Ciudad Murcia (ESP)	DEF	5	1	61	23%	0	0	0	0
20	Affo ERASSA	19/02/1983	Moulins (FRA)	MID	6	0	0	0%	0	0	0	0
21	Franck ATSOU	01/08/1978	Al Hilal (KSA)	MID	13	0	0	0%	0	0	0	0
22	Kodjovi OBILALE	08/10/1984	Etoile Filante (TOG)	GK	0	0	0	0%	0	0	0	0
23	Assimiou TOURE	01/01/1988	Bayer Leverkusen (GER)	DEF	1	2	126	47%	0	0	0	0
							Team Totals		1	1	10	1

TRINIDAD & TOBAGO

	Coach: Leo Beenhakker					In World Cup 2006						
No.	Player	Date of Birth	Club	Position	Caps	Games	Minutes played	%age	Goals	Assists	Yellow cards	Red cards
1	Shaka HISLOP	22/02/1969	West Ham (ENG)	GK	24	2	180	67%	0	0	1	0
2	Ian COX	25/03/1971	Gillingham (ENG)	DEF	16	0	0	0%	0	0	0	0
3	Avery JOHN	18/06/1975	New England Revolution (USA)	DEF	57	2	75	28%	0	0	2	1
4	Marvin ANDREWS	22/12/1975	Rangers (SCO)	DEF	98	0	0	0%	0	0	0	0
5	Brent SANCHO	13/03/1977	Gillingham (ENG)	DEF	40	3	270	100%	0	0	1	0
6	Dennis LAWRENCE	01/08/1974	Wrexham (WAL)	DEF	63	3	270	100%	0	0	0	0
7	Chris BIRCHALL	05/05/1984	Port Vale (ENG)	MID	19	3	270	100%	0	0	0	0
8	Cyd GRAY	21/11/1976	San Juan Jabloteh (TRI)	DEF	39	2	180	67%	0	0	1	0
9	Aurtis WHITLEY	01/05/1977	San Juan Jabloteh (TRI)	MID	24	3	181	67%	0	0	2	0
10	Russell LATAPY	02/08/1968	Falkirk (SCO)	FOR	66	1	24	9%	0	0	0	0
11	Carlos EDWARDS	24/10/1978	Luton Town (ENG)	MID	51	3	270	100%	0	0	0	0
12	Collin SAMUEL	27/08/2019	Dundee United (SCO)	FOR	18	1	51	19%	0	0	0	0
13	Cornell GLEN	21/10/1980	Los Angeles Galaxy (USA)	FOR	35	3	100	37%	0	0	0	0
14	Stern JOHN	30/10/1976	Coventry City (ENG)	FOR	95	3	270	100%	0	0	0	0
15	Kenwyne JONES	05/10/1984	Southampton (ENG)	FOR	29	2	129	48%	0	0	1	0
16	Evans WISE	23/11/1973	Waldhof Mannheim (GER)	FOR	16	2	56	21%	0	0	0	0
17	Atiba CHARLES	29/09/1977	W Connection (TRI)	DEF	19	0	0	0%	0	0	0	0
18	Densill THEOBALD	27/06/1982	Falkirk (SCO)	MID	38	3	239	89%	0	0	1	0
19	Dwight YORKE	03/11/1971	Unaffiliated	FOR	54	3	270	100%	0	0	1	0
20	Jason SCOTLAND	18/02/1979	St. Johnstone (SCO)	FOR	25	0	0	0%	0	0	0	0
21	Kelvin JACK	29/04/1976	Dundee (SCO)	GK	32	1	90	33%	0	0	0	0
22	Clayton INCE	13/07/1972	Coventry City (ENG)	GK	63	0	0	0%	0	0	0	0
23	Anthony WOLFE	23/12/1983	San Juan Jabloteh (TRI)	MID	4	0	0	0%	0	0	0	0
								Team Totals	0	0	10	1

TUNISIA

	Coach: Roger Lemerre					In World Cup 2006						
No.	Player	Date of Birth	Club	Position	Caps	Games	Minutes played	%age	Goals	Assists	Yellow cards	Red cards
1	Ali BOUMNIJEL	13/04/1966	Club Africain (TUN)	GK	48	3	270	100%	0	0	0	0
2	Kari ESSEDIRI	29/07/1979	Rosenborg (NOR)	FOR	7	1	9	3%	0	0	0	0
3	Karim HAGGUI	20/01/1984	Strasbourg (FRA)	DEF	26	3	270	100%	0	0	1	0
4	Alaeddine YAHIA	26/09/1981	Saint-Etienne (FRA)	DEF	13	1	34	13%	0	0	0	0
5	Zied JAZIRI	12/07/1978	Troyes (FRA)	FOR	61	3	225	83%	1	1	3	1
6	Hatem TRABELSI	25/01/1977	Ajax (HOL)	DEF	56	3	270	100%	0	0	1	0
7	Haykel GUEMAMDIA	22/12/1981	Strasbourg (FRA)	FOR	13	1	11	4%	0	0	1	0
8	Mehdi NEFTI	28/11/2019	Birmingham City (ENG)	MID	29	3	215	80%	0	0	0	0
9	Yassine CHIKHAOUI	22/09/1986	ES du Sahel (TUN)	FOR	1	1	81	30%	0	0	0	0
10	Kaies GHODBANE	07/01/1976	Konyaspor (TUR)	MID	89	3	57	21%	0	0	0	0
11	SANTOS	20/03/1979	Toulouse (FRA)	FOR	28	1	12	4%	0	0	0	0
12	Jaouhar MNARI	08/11/1976	Nuremberg (GER)	MID	37	3	270	100%	1	0	1	0
13	Riadh BOUAZIZI	08/04/1973	Erciyesspor (TUR)	MID	85	3	188	70%	0	0	2	0
14	Adel CHEDLI	16/10/1976	Nuremberg (GER)	MID	38	3	225	83%	0	0	1	0
15	Radhi JAIDI	30/08/1975	Bolton Wanderers (ENG)	DEF	89	3	270	100%	1	0	2	0
16	Adel NEFZI	16/03/1974	US Monastir (TUN)	GK	0	0	0	0%	0	0	0	0
17	Chaouki BEN SAADA	01/07/1984	Bastia (FRA)	FOR	11	1	12	4%	0	0	0	0
18	David JEMMALI	13/12/1974	Bordeaux (FRA)	DEF	2	1	90	33%	0	0	0	0
19	Anis AYARI	16/02/1982	Samsunspor (TUR)	DEF	24	2	146	54%	0	0	1	0
20	Hamed NAMOUCHI	14/02/1984	Rangers (SCO)	MID	14	3	270	100%	0	0	0	0
21	Karim SAIDI	24/03/1983	Lecce (ITA)	DEF	15	0	0	0%	0	0	0	0
22	Hamdi KASRAOUI	18/01/1983	Esperance (TUN)	GK	6	0	0	0%	0	0	0	0
23	Sofiane MELLITI	18/08/1978	Gaziantepspor (TUR)	MID	14	0	0	0%	0	0	0	0
								Team Totals	3	1	14	1

UKRAINE

							In World Cup 2006					
	Coach: Oleg Blokhin											
No.	Player	Date of Birth	Club	Position	Caps	Games	Minutes played	%age	Goals	Assists	Yellow cards	Red cards
1	Oleksandr SHOVKOVSKYI	02/01/1975	Dynamo Kiev (UKR)	GK	68	5	480	100%	0	0	0	0
2	Andriy NESMACHNYI	28/02/1979	Dynamo Kiev (UKR)	GK	49	5	480	100%	0	0	1	0
3	Oleksandr IATSENKO	24/02/1985	FC Kharkiv (UKR)	DEF	1	0	0	0%	0	0	0	0
4	Anatoliy TYMOSCHUK	30/03/1979	Shakhtar Donetsk (UKR)	MID	55	5	480	100%	0	0	1	0
5	Vladimir YEZERSKYI	15/11/1976	Dnipro Dnipropetrovsk (UKR)	DEF	24	1	90	19%	0	0	1	0
6	Andriy RUSOL	16/01/1983	Dnipro Dnipropetrovsk (UKR)	DEF	23	4	314	65%	1	0	2	0
7	Andriy SHEVCHENKO	29/09/1976	AC Milan (ITA)	FOR	64	5	472	98%	2	1	0	0
8	Oleg SHELAYEV	05/11/1976	Dnipro Dnipropetrovsk (UKR)	MID	9	5	435	91%	0	0	1	0
9	Oleg GUSEV	25/04/1983	Dynamo Kiev (UKR)	MID	25	5	435	91%	0	0	0	0
10	Andriy VORONIN	21/07/1979	Bayer Leverkusen (GER)	FOR	32	4	368	77%	0	0	0	0
11	Serhiy REBROV	03/06/1974	Dynamo Kiev (UKR)	MID	70	4	178	37%	1	0	0	0
12	Andriy PYATOV	28/06/1984	Vorskla Poltava (UKR)	GK	1	0	0	0%	0	0	0	0
13	Dmytro CHIGRYNSKYI	07/11/1986	Shakhtar Donetsk (UKR)	DEF	0	0	0	0%	0	0	0	0
14	Andriy GUSIN	11/12/1972	CSK VVS Samara (RUS)	MID	64	5	283	59%	0	0	0	0
15	Artem MILEVSKIY	12/01/1985	Dynamo Kiev (UKR)	FOR	0	4	89	19%	0	0	1	0
16	Andriy VOROBEY	29/11/1978	Shakhtar Donetsk (UKR)	FOR	53	4	245	51%	0	0	0	0
17	Vladislav VASHCHUK	02/01/1975	Dynamo Kiev (UKR)	DEF	58	3	212	44%	0	0	0	1
18	Serhiy NAZARENKO	16/02/1980	Dnipro Dnipropetrovsk (UKR)	MID	15	0	0	0%	0	0	0	0
19	Maksym KALINICHENKO	26/01/1979	Spartak Moscow (RUS)	MID	21	4	328	68%	1	2	2	0
20	Oleksiy BELIK	15/02/1981	Shakhtar Donetsk (UKR)	FOR	15	1	19	4%	0	0	0	0
21	Ruslan ROTAN	29/10/1981	Dynamo Kiev (UKR)	MID	19	3	129	27%	0	0	0	0
22	Vyacheslav SVIDERSKYI	01/01/1979	Arsenal Kiev (UKR)	DEF	6	3	129	27%	0	0	0	0
23	Bohdan SHUST	04/03/1986	Shakhtar Donetsk (UKR)	GK	2	0	0	0%	0	0	3	0
								Team Totals	5	3	12	1

USA

							In World Cup 2006					
	Coach: Bruce Arena											
No.	Player	Date of Birth	Club	Position	Caps	Games	Minutes played	%age	Goals	Assists	Yellow cards	Red cards
1	Tim HOWARD	06/03/1979	Manchester United (ENG)	GK	16	0	0	0%	0	0	0	0
2	Chris ALBRIGHT	14/01/1979	Los Angeles Galaxy (USA)	DEF	20	0	0	0%	0	0	0	0
3	Carlos BOCANEGRA	25/05/1979	Fulham (ENG)	DEF	40	2	180	67%	0	0	0	1
4	Pablo MASTROENI	29/08/1976	Colorado Rapids (USA)	DEF	48	2	89	33%	0	0	0	0
5	John O'BRIEN	29/08/1977	Chivas (USA)	MID	31	1	45	17%	0	0	0	0
6	Steve CHERUNDOLO	19/02/1979	Hanover 96 (GER)	DEF	35	3	195	72%	0	0	0	0
7	Eddie LEWIS	17/05/1974	Leeds United (ENG)	MID	69	2	163	60%	0	0	1	0
8	Clint DEMPSEY	09/03/1983	New England Revolution (USA)	MID	21	2	151	56%	1	0	0	0
9	Eddie JOHNSON	31/03/1984	Kansas City Wizards (USA)	FOR	18	2	75	28%	0	0	0	0
10	Claudio REYNA	20/07/1973	Manchester City (ENG)	MID	112	3	219	81%	0	0	1	0
11	Brian CHING	24/05/1978	Houston Dynamo (USA)	FOR	20	0	0	0%	0	0	0	0
12	Gregg BERHALTER	01/08/2019	Energie Cottbus (GER)	DEF	44	0	0	0%	0	0	0	0
13	Jimmy CONRAD	12/02/1977	Kansas City Wizards (USA)	DEF	15	2	129	48%	0	0	0	0
14	Ben OLSEN	03/05/1977	Washington DC United (USA)	MID	34	1	51	19%	0	0	0	0
15	Bobby CONVEY	27/05/1983	Reading (ENG)	MID	39	3	158	59%	0	0	0	0
16	Josh WOLFF	25/02/1977	Kansas City Wizards (USA)	FOR	47	1	14	5%	0	0	0	0
17	DaMarcus BEASLEY	24/05/1982	PSV Eindhoven (HOL)	MID	58	3	209	77%	0	1	0	0
18	Kasey KELLER	29/11/1969	Borussia Moenchengladbach (GER)	GK	93	3	270	100%	0	0	0	0
19	Marcus HAHNEMANN	15/06/1972	Reading (ENG)	GK	6	0	0	0%	0	0	0	0
20	Brian McBRIDE	19/06/1972	Fulham (ENG)	FOR	92	3	256	95%	0	0	0	0
21	Landon DONOVAN	04/03/1982	Los Angeles Galaxy (USA)	MID	81	3	270	100%	0	0	0	0
22	Oguchi ONYEWU	13/05/1982	Standard Liege (BEL)	DEF	14	3	270	100%	0	0	1	0
23	Eddie POPE	24/12/1973	Real Salt Lake (USA)	DEF	80	2	136	50%	0	0	2	1
								Team Totals	1	1	5	2